JEWS
GENTILES
AND THE CHURCH

Discovery
House
PUBLISHERS
BOX 3566 · GRAND RAPIDS, MI 49501

*PUBLISHING BOOKS THAT FEED
THE SOUL WITH THE WORD OF GOD.*

JEWS
GENTILES
AND THE CHURCH

A New Perspective
on History and Prophecy

David L. Larsen

Unless otherwise indicated, Scripture is taken from the Holy Bible: New International Version (North American Edition). Copyright © 1973, 1978, 1984 by the International Bible Society.

Library of Congress Cataloging-in-Publication Data
Larsen, David L.
Jews, gentiles, and the church: a new perspective on history and prophecy / David L. Larsen.
    p. cm.
  Includes bibliographical references and index.
  ISBN 0-929239-42-3
  1. Bible—Prophecies—Jews. 2. Judaism (Christian theology)
3. Palestine in Christianity. 4. Israel (Christian theology)
I. Title
BS649.J5L346 1995   94-43624
231.7'6—do20   CIP

Discovery House Publishers is affiliated with Radio Bible Class, Grand Rapids, Michigan.

Discovery House books are distributed to the trade by Thomas Nelson Publishers, Nashville, Tennessee 37214.

Printed in the United States of America

95 96 97 98 99 / RRD / 10 9 8 7 6 5 4 3 2 1

To
Paul and Elizabeth
Mary and David

My brothers and sisters
Heirs of the promises
Companions on the outer and inner journey.

CONTENTS

INTRODUCTION

WRITING ABOUT THE HOPE OF ISRAEL has been delightful but arduous —with much reading and research. I have had a life-long interest in and love for the Jewish people. For reasons I have not always understood I have increasingly been fascinated with the course of Jewish history and with the explosive developments in the establishment of the Jewish State in Israel. This volume is a modest contribution to the contemporary debate and discussion among evangelical Christians on many issues related to Israel and the Jews.

The great bulk of material in our Bibles relating to the Jews demands our attention. Garry Wills, distinguished professor of history at Northwestern University has convincingly argued that "The Bible is not going to stop being the central book in our intellectual heritage."[1] If he is right, and I believe he is, the focus of our questions here is not extraneous.

Christians today often differ on the meaning of Israel in relation to God's purpose. A recent *Christianity Today* cover story on this topic quoted Marvin Wilson from Gordon College about how "Christians are looking for a way of sorting out the issues ."[2] Hopefully, this book will probe and clarify some of the issues concerning God's plan for Israel.

While of special interest to serious Bible students, this work is also for the general reader who may have only a casual curiosity about these questions. New interest seems to be growing for Jewish and Holocaust studies and a handbook of evangelical articulation would seem helpful.[3] I have annotated references not only to show support for my data but to provide a working bibliography for further reading on specific issues and points. Frequently I have dipped into poetry and literature to show the pervasiveness of these Jewish themes in western thought.

One major section of the work addresses the future of the Jews in biblical prophecy. Professor Wills has spoken to this complex and controversial area in words we would do well to ponder:

> An understanding of Christian prophecy will be more needed, not less, in the next few years, as 'signs of the times' are read by everyone under the impending deadline of a millennium.[4]

Clearly the position we take with regard to God's ancient covenant people has ramifications for the church of Christ. I argue here that even though Israel failed God in many ways, yet God is set on restoring her. Canvassing the history of the Jews in this book will remind us again and again of how the Church has also failed. On what basis can we expect mercy and deliverance? The very character and faithfulness of God are in play in the drama of the action we chronicle in these pages.

In what emerges on these pages, the debits are all my own. On the credit side is my continuing tenure at Trinity Evangelical Divinity School where colleagues and students are helpful catalysts, stimulating inquiry and application. My family, particularly my wife Jean, is always an encouragement to me. Hans and Kristine Zimmerman have been very dear friends and the gift of God to me in this project beyond anything they can understand. My praise is to God.

> For great is His love toward us, and the faithfulness of the Lord endures forever (Psalm 117:2).

> Let Israel say: His love endures forever. Let the house of Aaron say: His love endures forever. Let those who fear the Lord say: His love endures forever (Psalm 118:2–4).

AD GLORIAM DEI.

PART

I

THE
SCRIPTURAL
FOOTINGS

The LORD has sworn and will not change his mind.

Psalm 110:4

CHAPTER

THE COMMONWEALTH OF ISRAEL AND THE COVENANTS

The history of the Jew is a dark, troublesome enigma to me.
I am not able to understand it. It does not fit into any of our categories.
It
is a
riddle.

W. F. Hegel

How odd of God
To choose the Jews.

Ogden Nash

In a desert land he found him,
in a barren and howling waste.
He shielded him and cared for him;
He guarded him as the apple of his eye.[1]

Deuteronomy 32:10

THE HISTORY OF THE JEWISH PEOPLE is of relentless fascination. Many book titles underscore the uniqueness and mysteriousness of this ancient people—*The Amazing Jew, The Wandering Jew, Israel the Miracle, The Anguish of the Jews, Stranger than Fiction: A History of the Jews, The Remarkable Jew.*[2]

The remarkable story of the Jews began almost 4000 years ago.[*] Distinguished secular historians like Barbara Tuchman see the establishment of the state of Israel in 1948 after 1900 years of exile as "a unique historical event. . . . Viewing this strange and singular history one cannot escape the impression that it must contain some special significance for the history of mankind, that in some way, whether one believes in divine purpose or inscrutable circumstance, the Jews have been singled out to carry the tale of human fate."[3]

Paul Johnson in *A History of the Jews* asserted that "the Jews are the most tenacious people in history" and that "no people has ever insisted more firmly than the Jews that history has a purpose and humanity a destiny."[4] To understand Israel's destiny necessitates going back to the beginning of the 4000-year history of this miracle people.

GOD CHOOSES

The Old Testament doctrine of a chosen people, one selected by God "for his own possession above all the people that are on the face of earth" (Deuteronomy 7:6),

◊ ◊ ◊

[*] "So through a holy event there comes into existence this category decisive from the point of view of the history of faith, of the "holy people," the hallowed body of people, as image and claim."—Martin Buber concerning the Exodus [5]

"History is not always made by men alone. . . Israel is a personal challenge, a personal religious issue. We are God's stake in human history. We are the dawn and the dusk, the challenge and the test. The presence of Israel is the repudiation of despair. Israel calls for a renewal of trust in the Lord of history."—Abraham Joshua Heschel [6]

is the chief clue for the understanding of the meaning and significance of Israel.[7]—George Ernest Wright

The Jews are essentially special in the plan and purpose of God.* The Jew is God's timepiece. The Jew is the key to history and prophecy. As D. M. Panton put it, "The Jew is God's dial." And all of this is to be explained in terms of an elective decree of God's sovereign grace.

God did not choose the Swedes, the Germans, the Indians, the Egyptians or any other racial or ethnic group in the same way in which He selected the Jews.

Few notions have been so obnoxious to moderns as the biblical teaching on election and predestination. But the decrees of a holy and loving God, far from negating authentic human response and responsibility, lift human life and experience out of anything that is arbitrary and simply random, into the bright sunlight of a gracious and transcendent God whose control is total and whose ways are just.

When God Chose the Jews

As Stephen so movingly put it in his address to the Sanhedrin, "The God of glory appeared to our father Abraham while he was still in Mesopotamia, before he lived in Haran. 'Leave your country and your people,' God said, 'and go to the land I will show you'" (Acts 7:2–3). The reference is to the summons of God to Abraham when he was in Ur of the Chaldeans (as described in Genesis 12:1–3).[8] In a much more sophisticated setting than some have imagined, God called Abram the descendant of Shem out of the Hamitic civilization in which he seemed to be flourishing. Abraham's name occurs seventy-four times in the New Testament. He is the key figure for both Jews and Christians. He became the father of the Jewish people, and God always remembered Abraham.

In his great valedictory, Moses explained to Israel her heritage:

> The LORD did not set his affection on you and choose you because you were more numerous than other peoples, for you were the fewest of all peoples. But it was because the LORD . . . kept the oath he swore to your forefathers that he brought you out with a mighty hand and redeemed you from the land of slavery (Deuteronomy 7:7–8).

◊ ◊ ◊

* The "election of Abraham and his descendants for a specific role in divine providence, and the donation of the land, are inseparable in the Biblical presentation of history."—Paul Johnson [9]

Though the Jews have populated the earth for centuries, they are relatively few (less than 1/2 of 1 percent of the world's population—yet they receive 12 percent of the Nobel Prizes). Designated and identified in Abraham's time, but developed and made into a nation in the Exodus from Egypt, this people has been set apart from all other nations—God said: "For the LORD's portion is his people, Jacob his allotted inheritance" (Deuteronomy 32:9). Balaam said in his oracle: "I see a people who live apart and do not consider themselves one of the nations" (Numbers 23:9b).

How God Chose the Jews

How do we deal with the scandal of particularity? God chose Israel "out of all the peoples on the face of the earth to be his people, his treasured possession"(Deuteronomy 7:6).[10] Is this a matter of national pride or arrogance? As H. H. Rowley pointed out, "Sometimes God chooses those who are not quite so choice."[11] As the Lord said: "It is not because of your righteousness that the LORD your God is giving you this good land to possess, for you are a stiff-necked people" (Deuteronomy 9:6). Or as Paul put it, it is "not by works but by him who calls" (Romans 9:11–12).*

Why God Chose the Jews

From the Bible, the fact of when and how God chose Israel seems clear. It all began with Abraham and the choice was God's alone. But why did He do it? Why did He make Israel His "firstborn son" (Exodus 4:22)? Moses put it rather simply to Israel: "It was because the LORD loved you" (Deuteronomy 7:8). But did that love have a purpose? The purpose of God's election was not salvation (as if the Lord gave some preferential claim to the Jews), but His purpose was service. As Rowley emphasized, the divine potter is not an aimless dilettante. "The uniqueness of His choice of Israel was the uniqueness of the degree in which He purposed to reveal His character and His will through her, and for this she was supremely suited"[12] (cf. Exodus 19:3–6; Deuteronomy 5:2ff.). The discipline of service is the corollary of election as the history of Israel discloses most impressively.

God had a missionary purpose in electing Israel. "And all peoples on earth will be blessed through you" (Genesis 12:3c), the Lord said to Abraham. What David L. Cooper called "the romance of Jewish history" is evident at this point[13]—all nations are seen in relation to the testimony and witness of Israel (cf. Deuteronomy 32:8—"When the Most High

◇ ◇ ◇

* The principle of selection is also seen in Christ's setting apart of the twelve apostles and concentrating His efforts in their training in order that He might reach multiplied others through them.

gave the nations their inheritance, when he divided all mankind, he set up boundaries for the peoples according to the number of the sons of Israel.")

Through His sovereignly chosen vessel, the Lord purposed to give us His written Word, to send His beloved Son for alienated and estranged humanity, and to promulgate a witness for monotheism in a polytheistic and idolatrous world (cf. Isaiah 43:10–13).

The children of Israel were to be "the people of the ear, who heard God's Word . . . the receiving station for the waves out of eternity."[14]

Jonah's resistance to God's all-encompassing love becomes a picture of the history of Israel—a nation running away from God's purpose for them.*

Sholom Aleichem, often called "the Jewish Mark Twain ," gives us the unforgettable portrait of Tevye, the dairyman, and his seven daughters, as immortalized in *Fiddler on the Roof*.[15] Especially memorable is Tevye's running dialogue with God. He wrestles with being part of the chosen people—it is a burden sometimes almost unbearable. In extremity he seems to say, "I am tired of being one of the chosen. Could you choose someone else for a while?" But the fact of being chosen is a given.

As Paul said, "But as far as election is concerned, they are loved on account of the patriarchs, for God's gifts and his call are irrevocable"(Romans 11:28b–29). And in God's call and promise is where the case for the hope of Israel begins.

GOD PROMISES

Blessed is the nation whose God is the LORD, the people he chose for his inheritance (Psalm 33:12).

But now listen, O Jacob, my servant, Israel, whom I have chosen. This is what the LORD says—he who made you, who formed you in the womb, and who will help you: Do not be afraid, O Jacob, my servant, Jeshurun, whom I have chosen (Isaiah 44:1–2).

◊ ◊ ◊

* But God's choice of Israel must not be seen as a mistaken choice. In Matthew 23:1–3 our Lord excoriates the hypocritical Pharisees but recognizes they sit in Moses' seat and urges, "So you must obey them and do everything they tell you." They were essentially sound in their teaching although unbalanced in their application. (Note also Romans 3:1–2, and bear in mind that Israel's checkered history was the preparation for the coming of the Messiah, the Lord Jesus Christ, Galatians 4:4–5.)

You only have I chosen of all the families of the earth; therefore I will punish you for all your sins (Amos 3:2).

What God Promised

There was no period when Israel did not believe she was the chosen people, "and that choosing took place in history," John Bright insisted. And at certain points in that history God made promises to Israel. The promise narratives in the Old Testament are pivotal.[*]

God's promises to Abram at his call are foundational (cf. Genesis 12:1–3). The promises are essentially three:

GOD'S THREE PROMISES TO ISRAEL		
1	**2**	**3**
The promise of the land Leviticus 26 and Deuteronomy 27–28	The promise of the seed 2 Samuel 7	The promise of the blessing Jeremiah 31

Abraham is seen as the mediator of God's blessing (Galatians 3:6–9); it descended from him to all the nations (Zechariah 8:13),[16] and was ultimately made manifest through his greatest and most glorious progeny, the Lord Jesus Christ (John 8:53–58).

If the overarching purpose of God is the blessing of humankind, then the promises of land and seed (property and posterity) are the divine appointed means to that end. Thus God's faithful fulfillment of His promises as given to Abram is properly a most central concern for all those who believe and are the descendants of Abraham in the broadest sense.[†]

Indeed, God has given His oath and pledge in relation to His promises. The writer to the Hebrews in speaking of God's promise to Abraham indicated that "because God wanted to make the unchanging nature of His purpose very clear to the heirs of what was promised, He confirmed it with an oath" (cf. Hebrews 6:13–18). God has kept His promises and He will keep His promises because "it is impossible for God to lie."[‡]

◊ ◊ ◊

* Claus Westermann and Walter Kaiser both see the divine promise as the controlling motif of the Old Testament. [17]

† "The 'fulfillments' are taken as expositions, confirmations and expansions of the promise."—Jurgen Moltmann [18]

‡ "The promises of posterity and of the land are clear from the outset."—Martin Noth. In Genesis 15 "the promise of the land predominates decisively."—Von Rad and Zimmerli

---

The promise of the land is key to God's plan and purpose.

"Israel's mission to the world is inseparably linked with her posses-sion of and her presence in the land of Israel."[19] In any reasonable his-torical-grammatical approach to God's promises about the land and to the author's intention (both the divine and the human author must be in our purview), it would seem that Israel and her land are going to be unique in perpetuity.The one cannot be without the other. As Erich Sauer asked: "Who gives us the right to take Jews to mean Christians, Jerusalem to mean now only the church, and Canaan heaven?"[20]

How God Promised

But are not the promises conditional?* A covenant is a bond. The cov-enantal bond is a further reinforcement of the promise and a means of administering the promise.[21]

The covenant is not earned (although Abraham needs to make a response to God as in Genesis 15:9–12,17–18, just as sinners must make a response to the gracious offer of unmerited salvation). The covenants with Abraham, David, and Levi are not reciprocal.

Thus the existence of the posterity and the ownership of the property from the standpoint of the Old Testament "covenants of promise" can never be in doubt. The Mosaic and Sinaitic Covenants, however, link possession of the land and prosperity in the land to obedience. Here is where the conditions come into the picture.†

Abraham and his immediate descendants did not in God's purpose possess the promised land (but Abraham indeed purchased the burial-place for Sarah as described in Genesis 23). Later the chosen people were dispersed in captivity because of their disobedience. "Any member of the line of David may by sin forfeit his own share in the promise, but he may not forfeit that which belongs to his successors to eternity."[22] The promissory covenants of the Old Testament guarantee both the physical posterity and property of God's ancient people in perpetuity.‡ Temporary dispossession does not mean loss of the inheritance. The ful-fillment of the land-promise becomes critical for anyone contemplating the fidelity of God to any or all of His promises.[23] The character of God

◊ ◊ ◊

* See the Appendix for a chart of statements about the covenant.
† The "conditionality attaches not to the promise, but to the participants who would benefit."—Walter Kaiser [24]
"Possession and plenty are conditional then and now."—J. Barton Payne
‡ "The promise undergoes expansion, but it never suffers observable abroga-tion." "The presence of the Jewish state of Israel today may be regarded as an ear-nest of the future conquest of the world by Christ."—Thomas McComiskey [25]

is on the line here. J. H. Kurtz understood the importance of the land when he wrote:

> As the body is adapted and destined for the soul and the soul for the body, so Israel for that country and that country for Israel. Without Israel the land is like a body from which the soul has fled; banished from its country, Israel is like a ghost which cannot find rest.[26]

As the people, so the land and all of this for a blessing upon "all peoples on earth" (Genesis 12:3).

GOD DISCLOSES

It seems to me that most disastrous consequences must follow upon our believing that anything false is found in the sacred books; that is to say, that the men by whom the Scriptures have been given to us, and committed to writing, did put down in these books anything false.—St. Augustine to Jerome, xxviii, 3

The veracity and trustworthiness of the Bible can be undercut by a tendency to spiritualize or overdo typology in such a way that all control of interpretation is lost and meaning becomes subjective. Like much literature, the Bible has both literal and symbolic passages. It is generally prudent to heed A. B. Davidson's rule with respect to interpreting biblical prophecy: "Read it literally—assume the literal meaning is his meaning." However, wooden literality that fails to see the figurative is as unsound as excessive spiritualizing that avoids the historical. The most advisable approach to interpretation is to seek the plain, natural and normal meaning of a text in its content. Let us be like Luther who said, "I have based my preaching on the literal Word."[27]

The last seven chapters of Deuteronomy (28–34) are really the matrix out of which the great prophecies of the Old Testament regarding Israel emerge.[28]

26:3–13; 28:1–14	The conditions of blessing to follow obedience
31:16–21	The coming apostasy
28:15–60	The affliction that God would bring upon Israel, while still in the land, because of her apostasy
28:32–39, 48–57	Israel will be taken captive
27; 32	The enemies of Israel will possess her land for a time
28:38–42; 29:23	The land itself will remain desolate

28:63–67; 32:26	Israel will be scattered among the nations
28:62	The time will come when Israel will be "few in number"
28:44–45	Though punished, Israel will not be destroyed if she repents
28:40–41; 30:1–2	Israel will repent in her tribulation
30:3–10	Israel will be gathered from the nations and brought back to her divinely given land

The prophecy in Deuteronomy goes beyond anything that Israel historically experienced in the return from Babylonian and Persian exile. Prophecy in Deuteronomy displays the phenomenon of "prophetic telescoping," or what Geerhardus Vos calls "foreshortening of the beyond-prospect." To use J. Barton Payne's words, "Biblical prophecy may leap from one prominent peak in predictive topography to another, without notice of the valley between, which may involve no inconsiderable lapse in chronology."[29]

The curses and judgment as pronounced by God were historically and literally fulfilled.* Should not then the blessing and promises of restoration be similarly fulfilled historically and literally? Jeremiah spoke of the shattered covenant. God desired to "fulfill the oath" sworn to the fathers about "a land flowing with milk and honey" (Jeremiah 11:5) and called on the people to hear and obey, but "the house of Israel and the house of Judah [broke] the covenant which [God] made with their forefathers" (11:10). The result was calamity and judgment. Should not the promises of restoration be understood in their natural and plain sense?† (Note Jeremiah 31:10—must not the scattering and the gathering, both

◊ ◊ ◊

* "How can we possibly determine how God may be expected to fulfill predictions in the future, except by observing how in point of fact He fulfilled them in the past? If this is not a safe principle, where can we find one?"—Patrick Fairbairn[30]

† "The promises of the first coming of Christ were fulfilled literally. . . . Combined with these prophecies of the first coming, there often stand in the very same sentence prophecies of the second coming, and by the plain meaning of the words, and by their later fulfillment in the life of Jesus of Nazareth, it is evident that the first part of such sentences is to be taken literally. Who therefore can justify the taking merely 'spiritually' of one and the same sentence? . . . No, the 'spiritualizing' of these promises of the Messianic kingdom . . . and a transference of them to some other corporate system, were nothing else than a veiled breach of covenant by God as regards Israel. But this is impossible."—Eric Sauer[31]

immediate and ultimate, be understood in this context as comparable in genre?)

The inability of some to take God's promises literally continues. Understandably, the Jewish scholar Michael Wyschogrod of Baruch College faulted the Vatican and the U.S. Bishop's Statement on the Middle East for noting that Jewish ties to the land "have deep biblical roots,"but then not taking that seriously, "not only as something the Jews have but as something the church must struggle with. That decision was made when the church decided to make the Hebrew Bible its own. And this is so even if the church chooses to persist in spiritualizing the promises of the land, an ancient strategy not easy to defend in the new theological climate of Jewish-Christian dialogue."[32]

Certainly the plain sense of language in the Old Testament should compel Bible students to believe in an ultimate and permanent restoration of the Jews to their ancient homeland at the end of this age, and the New Testament has many additional reasons for believing in a future for the Jews.

It is impossible to escape the conclusion that God has something for literal Israel. [*]

Amos sounded Israel's hope:

And I will bring back my exiled people Israel. . . . I will plant Israel in their own land, never again to be uprooted from the land I have given them (Amos 9:14–15).

There is to be a third commonwealth for Israel. After a long time without king, prince, or sacrifice 28(Hosea 3:4), Israel will be restored to her land, the land of promise. There is much biblical support for the expectation of the new Davidic kingdom in the context of a restored and reunited Israel in her land,[†] as the following chart indicates.

◊ ◊ ◊

[*] Donald Gowan pointed out that A. B. Davidson devoted the last chapter of his *Old Testament Prophecy*, to "The Restoration of the Jews," and he himself goes beyond Davidson to hold "That Jerusalem will be in the future the source of full knowledge of the one true God remains without question in these sources (cf. Isaiah 66:20), and since Israel will be found in its completeness dwelling in and around the holy city there is no compromise with the continuing conviction of election to a special place in the saving work of God.[33]

KEY OLD TESTAMENT PASSAGES ABOUT THE LAND			
Genesis	12:7; 13:14–17; 15:7–21; 17:1–8; 24:7; 28:13–15	**Jeremiah**	12:14–17; 16:14–15; 18; 23:5–8; 30:18–21; 31:10–14, 23, 25, 22–40; 32:37–41; 33:10–13
Exodus	12:25; 13:5, 11; 32:13; 33:1	**Ezekiel**	11:17–21; 17:22–24; 34:11–31; 37:1–14
Numbers	11:12; 14:15–16, 23; 32:8	**Hosea**	13:9–14:9
Deuteronomy	1:8; 6:10; 9:28; 12:20; 19:8; 27:3	**Micah**	2:12
Joshua	23:5	**Zephaniah**	2:19–20
Isaiah[33]	5:25–26; 11:11–12; 66:19–20	**Zechariah**	12:10–11

Such was and has been the understanding of the Jews and many Christians also. In testimony given to the United Nations Special Committee on Palestine by Rabbi Fischman, Chief Rabbi of Jerusalem (1947, Part III, 104) the rabbi responded to Sir Abdur Rahman, Judge at that time of the Lahore High Court in India (the initials Q and A will indicate the question and the response respectively):

Q: When was the promise made by God?
A: The promise was given to Abraham, Isaac, and Jacob about 4000 years ago.

Q: When was it confirmed by God?
A: It was reaffirmed to Moses.

Q: According to the Jews, was their return to this country not to take place with the appearance of the Messiah?
A: No. In accordance with Jewish tradition, the Jews should return to Palestine before the Messiah comes, and Jerusalem should be a part of Palestine, in accordance with the tradition, the Messiah will arrive.

◊ ◊ ◊

† (previous page) Isaiah excelled both in his use of the antecedent theology of the Abrahamic-Mosaic-Davidic promise and in his new contribution and development of that doctrine—Walter Kaiser [34]

GOD DISCLOSES

Q: How long after the return of the Jews to Palestine will the Messiah arrive, according to you?

A: This is a thing nobody can tell.[35]

> The Lord will have mercy on Jacob yet,
> and again in His border see Israel set.
> When Judah beholds Jerusalem,
> The stranger seed shall be joined to them:
> To Jacob's House shall the Gentiles cleave,
> So the prophet saith and his sons believe.
>
> —Robert Browning

CHAPTER

THE CHRIST OF ISRAEL
AND THE KINGDOM

Then Simeon blessed them and said to Mary, his mother: "This child is
destined to cause the falling and rising of many in Israel,
and to be a sign that will be spoken against,
so that the thoughts of many hearts
will be revealed."

Luke 2:34–35

Salvation is from the Jews.

John 4:22c

For I tell you that Christ has become a servant of the Jews on behalf of
God's truth, to confirm the promises made to the patriarchs
so that the Gentiles may glorify God for His mercy.

Romans 15:8–9

The doctrine of the Old Testament is the foundation and norm
of the doctrine of the New Testament.
Both Testaments together
constitute the canon.

Johannes Cocceius

AFTER FOUR HUNDRED YEARS OF PROPHETIC SILENCE, John the Baptist came "in the spirit and power of Elijah" heralding the long-awaited Messiah. While there are many striking contrasts between the Testaments, more than ever the essential continuity between them is being stressed by seeing Jesus Christ as the focus of prophetic fulfillment.[1] Jesus Christ is the connection, the fulfiller, the climax of revelatory history (Hebrews 1:1–3).

When we appreciate the remarkable scope of Old Testament prophecy,[*] we recognize the deep and broad stream of Old Testament promise.[2] Jesus understood that the Old Testament promise culminated in His own person and work (cf. Matthew 5:17–18; Luke 24:44; John 5:39), as did the apostles and prophets of the New Testament (cf. Acts 8:30–35; 2 Corinthians 1:20).[†]

As Charles Ryrie observed, "If the hundreds of prophecies concerning Christ's first coming were fulfilled literally, how can anyone reject the literal fulfillment of the numerous prophecies concerning His second coming and reign on earth?"[3]

While how the New Testament writers understood and used the Old Testament may be debated, the messianic expectation in it seems widely affirmed.[4] John Bright stated that "the Old Testament is normative

◊ ◊ ◊

* Speaking in *The Centrality of the Messianic Idea for the Old Testament*, H. L. Ellison accurately reflected: "Jesus Christ virtually claimed that such a unifying principle exists, viz. the witness of all parts of Scripture to Him." He quoted Rabbi Ochanan (possibly back to A.D. 70): "All the prophets prophesied only with reference to the days of the Messiah."[5]

† No one has written more thoroughly of this magnificent body of prophecy beginning with the first messianic prophecy in Genesis 3:15 than has E. W. Hengstenberg in his four classic volumes, *The Christology of the Old Testament*. [6] A very conservative cataloguing of the personal references to Christ in the Old Testament is amassed by J. Barton Payne in his *Encyclopedia of Biblical Prophecy*. [7]

Scripture . . . it was for Jesus . . . so for us also." He argued that on one point the New Testament is unanimous: Jesus lived, died, and rose again "according to the Scriptures." "And Christ is indeed the crown of revelation through whom the true significance of the Old Testament becomes finally apparent."[8]

The New Testament writers approached the Old Testament from an eschatological perspective. They delighted in the fulfillment of Old Testament prophecy in Christ.[*] And indeed "He came to that which was his own, but his own did not receive Him" (John 1:11). Why so?[†]

The Jewish people as a whole refused the claims of Christ because of a selective preference among the several prophetic portraits of the Messiah. The Old Testament pictures Messiah as Divine Warrior and King, Suffering Servant, the Son of Man coming with the clouds of heaven. One of the very latest of the newly released Dead Sea Scrolls speaks of the "piercing" of a Messiah.[9] This is what was finally objectionable to Judaism as it has been to us. "Yet to all who received him, to those who believed in his name, he gave the right to become the children of God" (John 1:12).

THE PRESENTATION OF JESUS THE MESSIAH

Jesus Christ is the same yesterday and today and forever. Do not be carried away by all kinds of strange teachings (Hebrews 13:8–9).

I praise you, Father, Lord of heaven and earth, because you have hidden these things from the wise and learned, and revealed them to little children (Luke 10:21).

Christ is the image of the unchangeable God and therefore likewise unchangeable.—Athanasius

The person and work of Jesus the Messiah are at the epicenter of "[God's] eternal purposes which he accomplished in Christ Jesus our Lord" (Ephesians 3:11). Coherence is found in Christ (Colossians 1:17).[‡]

◊ ◊ ◊

[*] "Excitement for the new era lies in the coming of Christ, the center of redemptive history. Saints from the old era join with saints of the new era in the worship of Christ. Attention shifts from hope in comfort, reconciliation, consolation, redemption and kingdom, to Jesus. He is the focus of the fulfillment of the prophetic word, and in this way the glorious future is present in Jesus."—Willem Van Gemeren[10]

[†] The Messiah was not rejected by the Jews because of the literalistic hermeneutic they used, as Oswald T. Allis argued in *Prophecy and the Church*.

New Covenant

The failure under the old covenant and the deep-seated spiritual deficiency it revealed are addressed under the terms of a new covenant (cf. Jeremiah 31:31–34 and the argument of the entire epistle to the Hebrews).

From the beginning God's purpose has involved Israel for the sake of "all peoples" (Genesis 12:3). The angelic birth announcement of the Savior was proclaimed "for all the people" (Luke 2:10). Jesus burst through the ethnic envelope with His announced agenda, "I have other sheep that are not of this sheep pen. I must bring them also. They too will listen to my voice, and there shall be one flock and one shepherd" (John 10:16). The Great Commission of our Lord overrides any Jewish exclusivity. The church of which Jesus spoke and of which the apostolate was the embryonic form would be a spiritual organism in which ethnic identity would yield to oneness in Christ (cf. Ephesians 2:11–22; Galatians 3:14, 26–29). All who believe become the spiritual progeny of Abraham (Galatians 3:8–9) and are "grafted in among the others and now share the nourishing sap from the olive root" (Romans 11:17).

Thus Israel's rejection has meant "riches for the world" (Romans 11:12) and "because of their transgression, salvation has come to the Gentiles" (Romans 11:11), but not simply as retributive justice but with a redemptive purpose, "to make Israel envious." The taking away of the kingdom of God from Israel and the giving of it "to a people who will produce its fruit" (Matthew 21:33–44) does not nullify the unconditional promises given to Abraham and David. The pattern of prophetic fulfillment is invariably enlargement and expansion of the promises, not constriction or limitation.*

The promise of the New Covenant through Jeremiah has two aspects: "One applies to Israel and the other applies to the church. It is the death of Christ that provides the basis for both aspects."[11] "The New Covenant is the continuation and glorious perfection of the covenant with Abra-

◊ ◊ ◊

‡ (previous page) "The Old Testament dispensation is a forward-stretching and forward-looking dispensation," Geerhardus Vos insisted. "The Old Testament, through its prophetic attitude postulates the New Testament."[12]

* This is what Willis Beecher called the "cumulative" fulfillment of prophecy and what Van Gemeren masterfully called the "process of unfolding progressive fulfillment of Bible prophecy." As Van Gemeren so aptly put it, "The hermeneutics of progressive fulfillment looks at God's promises as a vine that grows, extends its branches in various directions, bears fruit and keeps developing. Applying this to redemptive history, I believe that we are still at the stage of branching and budding and that the stage of the mature, productive vine takes us to the second coming of our Lord."[13]

ham (Galatians 3:9,14; Romans 4)."[14] The New Covenant is everlasting in relation to Israel and her seed (Isaiah 61:8–9) and everlasting for the church (Hebrews 13:20–21), and so God repeated it three times to Abraham (Genesis 17:7,13,19).

Multiple Fulfillments

An understanding of multiple fulfillments of biblical prophecies is crucial in explaining the relationship of Israel and the church. The determinate sense of an Old Testament prophecy as intended by the inspired prophet can be understood through historical-grammatical exegesis. To surrender this basic meaning is to lose control of language and to surrender abjectly to the autonomy of the interpreter. But there may be an expansion or enlargement of the scope and application of the promise.[*]

This is not to be read back into the Old Testament text as such, but

---

a Biblical text may encompass more than is immediately evident.

Such would seem to be the case with the promise of the New Covenant in Jeremiah 31. The extension of the New Covenant beyond "the house of Israel and . . . the house of Judah" does not negate the basic terms of Jeremiah 31 and stands in perfect consistency with what the Old Testament as a whole teaches about God's purpose for the Gentiles as well as for the Jews.

Numerous passages in the New Testament exhibit the same phenomenon of multiple fulfillments. The angel Gabriel announces to Mary:

> You will be with child and give birth to a son, and you are to give him the name Jesus. He will be great and will be called the Son of the Most High. The Lord God will give him the throne of his father David, and he will reign over the house of Jacob forever; his kingdom will never end (Luke 1:31–32).

Verse 31 is obviously to be understood in its natural and plain sense. On what basis shall we "spiritualize" verse 31?[15] Surely Messiah's kingdom involves expanded and enlarged significance in the teachings of Jesus (as the next section shows), but this does not remove the literal reign of Jesus Christ "over the house of Jacob forever." Consistency in interpretation requires our coming to terms with figurative and symbolic language where it occurs but it does preclude our excising the plain

◊ ◊ ◊

[*] "An Old Testament prediction may have a single, determinative meaning with multiple fulfillments."—Paul Feinberg [16]

meaning of a text in favor of a spiritualized meaning, as in this case the spiritual exaltation of the church.

Christ is called the Son of David in the New Testament and is said to carry the key of David (Revelation 3:7). He is of "the Root and Offspring of David (Revelation 22:16). Not only is Jesus the genealogical descendant of David (Acts 2:30; 13:23,33; Romans 1:3; Hebrews 7:14; Revelation 5:5) but He is heir to "the sure blessings promised to David" (Isaiah 55:3–4 compared with Acts 13:34). We do not possess a manual of Old Testament interpretation written by the apostles;[17] yet Paul's use of the Isaiah passage (harking back to 2 Samuel 7) is eminently plausible. A prophecy of resurrection is not on the face of the text; but if David's greater Son is to rule forever (2 Samuel 7:16), then it follows that this greater Son cannot be allowed to molder in the dust of death. The resurrection of Christ is a necessity. None of this does away with the promise to David but demonstrates that "forever" must be taken seriously.

The words of Jesus to His disciples in sending them out ("You will not finish going through the cities of Israel before the Son of Man comes," Matthew 10:23b) would seem to be addressed also to the emissaries of Jesus who will perform a similar mission just prior to the Lord's return in glory. Jesus spoke about the messianic banquet in terms that do not seem to indicate any cancellation of the prophesied feast. In Matthew 8:11, Jesus said, "Many will come from the east and the west, and will take their places at the feast with Abraham, Isaac and Jacob in the kingdom of heaven." Our Lord spoke of "the renewal of all things, when the Son of Man sits on his glorious throne" (Matthew 19:28). There certainly is significant expansion and enlargement of the Old Testament promise, and there may be implied a suspension of privilege or interruption, but no nullification of the promise. Jesus intimated that there was a day coming when the Jews will receive Him and see Him (Matthew 23:37–39). He seemed to speak of Israel's receptivity to the Antichrist in the time of the end (John 5:43). All these passages in Matthew are compelling evidence for "the hope of Israel."

Indeed the well-tutored followers of Jesus after the resurrection put the question to our Lord: "Lord, are you at this time going to restore the kingdom to Israel?" (Acts 1:6). Jesus corrected their desire to know the time, but He did not seek to change their notion that indeed there would be a restoration of the kingdom to Israel. The prophecies about Israel and the kingdom still stand. And Peter in Acts 3:21 spoke of this: "He must remain in heaven until the time comes for God to restore everything, as he promised long ago through his holy prophets."[18*]

On what grounds would the distinguished writer, Samuel J. Andrews, author of a notable work on the life of Christ, writing in 1898, boldly claimed that "He [Christ] confirmed God's promise that after these judgments . . . the Jews would be gathered to their own land and acknowledge Him as their King?" Andrews saw the immutable nature of the Old Testament promise (cf. 1 Chronicles 16:15–18) only confirmed and corroborated by Jesus. And so may we.

THE PROCLAMATION THROUGH JESUS THE MESSIAH

Your throne, O God, will last for ever and ever; a scepter of justice will be the scepter of your kingdom (Psalm 45:6).

These are the words of the Amen, the faithful and true witness, the ruler of God's creation (Revelation 3:14b).

They will make war against the Lamb, but the Lamb will overcome them because he is Lord of lords and King of kings (Revelation 17:14a).

Hallelujah! For our Lord God Almighty reigns (Revelation 19:6b).

Kingdom Promised

When John the Baptist and Jesus began their public ministries, they both preached "Repent, for the kingdom of heaven is near" (Matthew 3:2; 4:17).[*]

The kingdom of God was the commanding theme of our Lord's teaching.

There are 55 references to the *kingdom* in Matthew alone (where the phrase *kingdom of heaven* is used rather than *kingdom of God* as in Mark and Luke). The Bible has over 200 references to an eschatological kingdom. It is, in the words of John Bright, "The Book of the Coming Kingdom of God."

The purpose of God's working is essentially doxological, i.e. "to the praise of his glory" (Ephesians 1:6, 12, 14), "that God may be all in all" (1 Corinthians 15:28).

◊ ◊ ◊

[*] (previous page) R. B. Girdlestone analyzed the "restitution passages" of the Old Testament (based on Leviticus 25:10; Daniel 9:25) and concluded that "their fulfillment is not yet complete."[19] "That Israel has a great future is clear from Scripture as a whole. There is a large, unfulfilled element in the Old Testament which demands it, unless we spiritualize it away or relinquish it as Oriental hyperbole."

[*] "The apocalyptic element is not merely accidental to our Lord's teaching, but it is all-pervading and determinative."—E. F. Scott [20]

The work of God in Christ by the Spirit may be viewed in three ways:

THE WORK OF CHRIST		
Prophet	**Priest**	**Potentate**
Revelation: the divine disclosure	Redemption: the divine deliverance from sin	Regulation: the divine dominion

Kingdom Explained

The kingdom of God is the rule and reign of God, i.e. the governmental aspect of the counsels of His will.[*] It is more than kingly power and authority and George Ladd has rightly claimed that "the kingdom of God is the effectual restoration of God's reign in a world which has rebelled against Him."[21]

In placing the first couple in the Garden of Eden, God gave them dominion over the earth (Genesis 1:26, 28).[22] Satan, the fallen vice-regent, usurped this dominion by deceiving them and now "the whole world is under the control of the evil one" (1 John 5:19b). God's purpose in history involves, in His sovereign strategy, the effective re-establishment of divine rule upon this earth.[23] In Old Testament times God established beachheads in subjection to Him, enclaves surrendered to His will. Israel was at the apex of His program. Gideon voiced this affiliation: "The LORD will rule over you" (Judges 8:23). The theocracy in Israel was a critical development (2 Samuel 7), but the hope was always focused in the messianic King (cf. Psalm 2:6, "I have installed my King on Zion, my holy hill").

This kingdom was to be an earthly kingdom; Hebrew prophets spoke of a very earthly, this-worldly venue for the expression and experience of the divine program. Paralleling biblical teaching about the resurrection of the body is the biblical idea of a transformed space-time order, in which Israel remains a geopolitical entity. The advent of the messianic King brought the imminence of the kingdom because of the imminence of the King. So Jesus said, "The kingdom of God is within you" (Luke 17:21). "But if I drive out demons by the Spirit of God, then the kingdom of God has come upon you" (Matthew 12:28).

With the rejection of the messianic King ("We will not have the man to rule over us") and the repudiation of the righteous standards of the

◊ ◊ ◊

[*] A. B. Bruce in his standard treatment saw the kingdom of God as the highest good in the church.[24] George Ladd's helpful survey showed the deficiency of this typical non-eschatological approach. Rather, as Ladd has shown, the kingdom of God is the sovereign rule of God. [25]

kingdom (as set forth in the constitution of the kingdom, Matthew 5–7), the earthly kingdom is deferred. The landowner's son is slain (Matthew 21:33 ff.) but this will not thwart the accomplishment of God's purposes. Thus in setting out "the mysteries of the kingdom" in the parables of Matthew 13, our Lord described the interim kingdom that will span the church age until "the kingdom of the world has become the kingdom of our Lord." (Revelation 11:15b). So the kingdom of God is preached in the book of Acts (Acts 28:31) and hailed as a crucial part of the Christian's experience (Colossians 1:13).

Scripture uses the idea of the kingdom in at least five ways, as the following chart indicates.

THE KINGDOM CONCEPT	
Universal Kingdom	Our sovereign and transcendent God reigns always. "His kingdom rules over all!" (Psalm 97:1; 99:1; 103:19).
Mediatorial Kingdom	Outcroppings of the control of God are seen in the history of Israel and promises are made of an earthly kingdom "that will never be destroyed" (Daniel 7:14).
Transitional Kingdom	The kingdom of our age is not linked to any nationalistic identity. The equation of the kingdom with the church after the fashion of the Augustinian error fails to see God's kingdom rule as operative in the church but not coextensive with the church.
Eschatological Kingdom	The rule of God is set up on earth when Christ returns in power and glory, a further transitional phase in which the glory of God is expressed in the time-space order. All the promises of the theocratic kingdom will be fulfilled to Israel.
Eternal Kingdom	The everlasting kingdom cannot commence until the "last enemy"—death—is destroyed. "Then the end will come, when he hands over the kingdom of God the Father after he has destroyed all dominion, authority, and power. For he must reign until he has put all his enemies under his feet" (1 Corinthians 15:24–25).

The expansion and elaboration of the kingdom promises proceed magnificently, and the promises made to Israel of an earthly kingdom continue. If language means anything at all and if historical-grammatical exegesis has any validity whatever and if biblical authors were to have any understanding of their writings, there will be a literal messianic kingdom on the earth with Jesus Christ on the throne.[26] This kingdom will be universal and its blessings will be spiritual, ethical, social, economic, political, physical, and ecclesiastical.[27]*

Kingdom Understood

God's ancient people understood something of the kingdom. They spoke of *malekut schamayim* (kingdom of the heavens). In the Talmud and the Targums they reflect their expectation.[28] When Jesus and John the Baptist begin speaking of the kingdom they obviously assumed the validity of the general understanding among the Jews.[*]

They gave no clarifying redefinitions to set the record straight. Jesus in his early comments to Nicodemus, "Israel's teacher," spoke of the kingdom of God on the premise of a shared understanding of what that term represented (John 3:3, 5).[†] "The things concerning the kingdom of God" (Acts 1:3) are glorious, both in their present implication and their future import.[29] In the light of the discussion, the question of the apostles just before Jesus' Ascension is a reasonable and a rational inquiry: "Lord, are you at this time going to restore the kingdom to Israel?" (Acts 1:6). The problem was on the timing not on the underlying truth of it.

THE PREDICTIONS BY JESUS THE MESSIAH

Heaven and earth will pass away, but my words will never pass away (Matthew 24:35).

In these last days he [God] has spoken to us by His Son (Hebrews 1:2).

For the testimony of Jesus is the spirit of prophecy (Revelation 19:10b).

At the heart of our discussion is the nature and interpretation of biblical prophecy and apocalyptic writings. In the Old Testament, for example, we find in Jeremiah 25 both a more contemporary chronological prophecy of the seventy-year captivity of the Jews (Jeremiah 25:11ff., with which Daniel wrestled; see Daniel 9:2), and a more

◊ ◊ ◊

* (previous page) "The idea of a kingdom of God on earth was the expectation of every Old Testament sage and prophet."—A. C. Conrad [30]

* "A literal interpretation of the Old Testament prophecies gives us just such a picture of the earthly reign of the Messiah as the premillennialist pictures. That was the kind of a Messianic kingdom that the Jews of the time of Christ were looking for, on the basis of a literal interpretation of the Old Testament."—Floyd Hamilton [31]

† "The Old Testament prophecies if literally interpreted cannot be regarded as having been fulfilled or as being capable of fulfillment in this present age."—Oswald T. Allis [32]

long-range prophecy bearing upon Israel's ultimate possession of the land in perpetuity (Jeremiah 25:5). In view of the historical fulfillment of the short-range prophecy, should we not reasonably expect that the long-range prophecy will have as literal an historical fulfillment?

The Destruction of the Temple and the Advent of the Lord

The Olivet discourse (Matthew 24–25; Mark 13; Luke 21) reveals a short-range and a long-range prophecy and their relationship. The prophecies of our Lord concerning the destruction of Jerusalem[*] and the temple and then the Parousia[†] (Advent) are the climax of His teaching.[‡]

There is the telescoping or foreshortening of prophecy in the Olivet discourse with the two foci being the destruction of Jerusalem in A.D. 70 and the eschatological event known as the Parousia. Matthew's account surely is but an extrapolation on the earlier statement in the mission discourse (Matthew 10:17–22). (The close relationship to the book of Daniel and Daniel 9:24-27 especially is often remarked and the ties with the prophecies of Jeremiah and Ezekiel[**] are noticeable.[33]

The transcendently beautiful second temple was slated for destruction with the city of Jerusalem according to Jesus' prediction. In Matthew 24–25 and in Luke 19:41–44 there are no vague or general statements but the minute particulars of time, place, persons, marked circumstances. Pierson identified twenty-five distinct predictions—and on the law of compound probability, the chance of all meeting in one fulfilling event is 1 in 20,000,000.[34] Comparing the predictions with the historical fulfillment (as described in Josephus, an eyewitness, and Tacitus), we cannot but agree with Eusebius:

◊ ◊ ◊

[*] "It is probably, that looking upon the future in terms of prophetic symbolism, His [Jesus'] mind passed beyond the immediate to the ultimate future, in such fashion that the coming doom of Jerusalem was thrown upon the background of the final and universal judgment."—Bishop Gore [35]

[†] "The whole history of Christianity, down to the present day, that is to say, the real inner history of it, is based on the delay of the Parousia."—Albert Schweitzer [36]

[‡] "The place which these utterances occupy in the gospel narrative, the sanctity that surrounds the occasions on which they were made, the sense of solemnity which enshrouds them, all go to prove that Jesus Himself regarded them as amongst His most important deliverances. We cannot set them aside without setting on one side what Jesus Himself regarded as being of primary importance."—H. T. Andrews [37]

[**] "His [Jesus'] words are in the tradition of Israel's prophecy (cf. Jeremiah 7:1–15; Ezekiel 24:15–23) and have not been simply made up by Christian writers in the light of later events."—B. Vawter [38]

If anyone compares the words of our Savior with the accounts of the historian, how can anyone fail to wonder and to admit the foreknowledge and prophecy of our Savior were truly divine and marvelously strange.

The words of Jesus spoken in another context come to mind: "I have told you now before it happens, so that when it does happen you will believe" (John 14:29).

The Interval and the Tribulation

The bulk of the Olivet discourse speaks of the messianic woes or the Tribulation just prior to the Parousia. Jesus described what precedes the Tribulation, the Tribulation itself, and the deliverance of His own in the Tribulation. Of whom was He speaking when He used the second person plural throughout?

Jesus intimated there would be an interval between the destruction of Jerusalem and the Parousia (hints of a delayed Parousia—Luke 18:1ff.; Mark 13:35; Luke 19:12; Matthew 25:5; 24:14; Luke 21:24). Jesus here, as in Matthew 10:23 and 26:64, spoke to His disciples as representatives of Jewish believers in the Tribulation of the end time. The Parousia has a focus on the land (Zechariah 14:3–9) and the Olivet discourse has a distinctly Palestinian emphasis. The church, "which is Christ's body," has yet to be established on the Day of Pentecost, so the successors to the apostles would logically seem in this frame of reference to be Jewish believers at the end of the age.

Careful verse by verse exegesis of the Olivet discourse is vital for any system that seeks to understand the sequence of end-time events.[39] The reference to "the abomination that causes desolation" in Matthew 24:15 and Mark 13:14 shows Jesus' belief in a final national restoration of Israel at the end of human history.* This ghastly representation of the Beast (cf. Revelation 13:14–17) presupposes a restored temple in Jerusalem for its display. This formidable eschatological adversary is described in 2 Thessalonians 2:3–4. Prophecies of a new temple to be erected in the Messianic Age were given long before A.D. 70 (cf. 1 Enoch 53:6; 90:28, 29; Jubilees 1:17, 27; 4:26) and Mark 13:2 ff. reflects the Old Testament Jewish hope of a new temple in messianic time and so must be interpreted eschatologically and not historically.[40]

Flight from Jerusalem

Jesus spoke of flight from the Holy City when the Abomination of Desolation stands in the temple (Matthew 24:16 ff.; Mark 13:14 ff.; Luke 21:20 ff.). Christians fled Jerusalem before Titus came from Britain in the

◊ ◊ ◊

* "The promise of the restoration of the sanctuary was a promise of the Messianic kingdom."—Desmond Ford [41]

spring of A.D. 70 with 80,000 men and sealed off the city. They took refuge in Pella across the Jordan, and not one Christian was killed! However, Jesus was not speaking to Christians who fled in spring but to Jews of another time. He's concerned lest their flight be in winter (more than in just cold weather).* Moreover, may their flight not be on that sacred day "the Sabbath."

Survival of People

Jesus spoke of "great distress in the land and wrath against this people" and of Jerusalem being "trampled on by the Gentiles until the times of the Gentiles are fulfilled" (Luke 21:23b–24). But in all of this mayhem, God's ancient covenant people survive as the prophets in the Old Testament foretold (cf. Jeremiah 31:35–37). Indeed, when the fig tree blossoms and sprouts, the summer will be near (Matthew 24:32ff.; Mark 13:28ff.; Luke 21:29ff.). The meaning of *genea* has a long history of interpretation and like the whole passage it bristles with difficulties, but I understand the word to mean "race, kind or species."[†42]

Hence the case would seem to build that not only does the Old Testament repeatedly express the "the hope of Israel," but that Jesus is in every respect consistent with that expectation—and not only Jesus but also, as we will see, the apostles and the apostolic church.

◊ ◊ ◊

* As Bengel insisted, "not in cold or tempestuous weather, or as Schlatter, in the rainy season when the wadis swirl with a torrent of water making flight most difficulty.

† Henry Alford sees *genea* here to mean "a race or family of people," a national restoration after winter dryness, "the future reviviscence" of that race. [43]

CHAPTER

THE COURSE OF
THIS AGE AND
THE CONSUMMATION

Of the increase of his government and peace there will be no end.
He will reign on David's throne and over his kingdom,
establishing and upholding it with
justice and righteousness
from that time on
and forever.
The zeal
of the
LORD
Almighty
will accomplish this.

Isaiah 9:7

For as lightning that comes from the east is visible even in the west,
so will be the coming of the Son of Man . . . At that time
the sign of the Son of Man will appear in the sky,
and all the nations of the earth will mourn.

Matthew 24:27, 30

It may be said with truth,
that the Hebrews
were the first
to discover
history
as the epiphany (i.e. the unveiling, the revelation) of God.

Mircea Eliade

WHAT THE OLDER TESTAMENT says about the coming Messianic Age is obviously very closely linked to the coming of the Messiah. The prophecies relating to the first advent of the Messiah were fulfilled, and Bible students should expect the prophecies related to the second advent of the Messiah to be literally fulfilled. Christ's own predictions of His passion were exactly fulfilled (cf. Matthew 12:40; 16:21; 17:22–23; 20:17–19), and the general pattern of fulfillment of Bible prophecy is quite striking.[1]

The Lord Jesus enlarged and expanded our understanding of the Messianic Kingdom but did not cancel Israel's hope. A meticulous investigation of Jeremiah's and Ezekiel's promises of Israel's restoration to the land (thirteen direct promises in Jeremiah and eight in Ezekiel) shows how these were fulfilled in the sixth century before Christ.[2] As W. H. Brownlee concluded,

---

"The theological significance of the land of Israel is in fact the key to biblical theology."[3]

It is hard to see how some[4] can argue that Jesus universalized the territorial promises or that Jesus incorporated into Himself Israel as a whole in order to fulfill her history and prophecy.* How possibly can we hold as some[5] have that the resurrection of Jesus was the resurrection of Israel? Or that the Jewish remnant was in reality to be a Gentile remnant? Or that the church was the new Israel of God? Are we wrong in retaining ethnic and geographic points of reference in speaking of the fulfillment of Isaiah 11:11–15?[6]

◊ ◊ ◊

* This in contrast to Qumran literalism which argued that a purified Israel would lead to a purified land.[7]

In maintaining a distinction between Israel and the church we are not imposing a Jewish application on Scriptures such as Matthew but seeking to be sensitive to the fact that both doom and restoration are in the prophets and that the prophecies of restoration were read and given equal weight with the passages of doom in the first century.[8] Indeed, the Pharisees who sat in Moses' seat believed there was an unseverable link between Israel, Yahweh, and the land.

As Jurgen Moltmann wrote, "theology is eschatology" and as George Ladd declared, "eschatology is really the anchor of the Christian Gospel."[9] The concept of "already but not yet" is seen throughout the New Testament.* This is altogether consistent with what Jesus taught and with what the apostles and the early church believed.†

And this has been the general understanding of the Jews to this day— "We are convinced that there is a divine plan and purpose to the history of the Jewish people," states a thoughtful contemporary Jewish analyst. Though living for so long "in a land not their own," they have looked forward to "the end of days" (Genesis 49:1) and to the complete redemption (*Ge'ulah Shelemah*). Indeed Elijah would come before Messiah (Malachi 4:5–6), but the sure sign of redemption would be "the ingathering of the exiles." This glorious redemption would not be, however, without the "pangs of the Messiah," (*havlei Mashiah*).[10] How the apostles and the early church viewed this Messiah and His kingdom reinforces the ancient longings for redemption.

THE STORY OF
THE MERCY OF GOD

I am not ashamed of the gospel, because it is the power of God for the salvation of everyone who believes: first for the Jew, then for the Gentile (Romans 1:16).

But concerning Israel, he says, "All day long I have held out my hands to a disobedient and obstinate people" (Romans 10:21).

For God has bound all men over to disobedience so that He may have mercy on them all (Romans 11:32).

◇ ◇ ◇

* "To the eschatology of the Exile, the Messianic kingdom was placed in the forefront of both prophetic and popular expectation. This kingdom was to be introduced by the day of Yahweh . . . as the result of this judgment a new and regenerate Israel emerges—the Messianic kingdom."—R. H. Charles [11]
† "The Jews are God's Special People, whose leader (King-Messiah) will overturn the misfortunes of their history and restore their preeminence."—William Barclay

The earliest Christians were Jewish and the early Christian church was Jewish. Jesus made it abundantly clear that the church that He was to build (cf. Matthew 16:17–18) would not in fact be new wine in the old wine skins or new patches on the old garment. Jewish Christians had a deep struggle with the inclusion of Gentiles in the church (cf. Acts 10–11 and Galatians 2:11ff.). The fundamental insight that "there is neither Jew nor Greek . . . for you are all one in Christ Jesus" (Galatians 3:28) did not come easily for those steeped in their Judiastic exclusivism. Jesus' bold intimations of racial and ethnic inclusivism were not easy to accept.

But is it only Paul's loyalty to his race and past that motivates the inspired apostle to insist that the gospel be proclaimed "first for the Jew?" Are these merely the clinging remnants of an outmoded world view or does Paul's passionate argument in Romans 9–11 that God has not rejected His people (Romans 11:1–2) reflect a sensitivity to Israel's special place and purpose in the plan of God? God's honor (Jeremiah 30:17) and God's fidelity to His promises, both then and now, are on the line in the resolution of this issue.

Writings of Luke

Why does the New Testament refer to "the land" so seldom?[*] Few of the exiles chose to return to the land as early as the days of Ezra and Nehemiah, and the Jewish Diaspora became quite detached from the land.

Dr. Luke's record has a geographical emphasis which centers on the land.[12] Luke recognized the old hope for survival and restoration (cf. Luke 24:18–24). Even in the end of the book of Acts, Luke shared Paul's testimony before Agrippa:

> And now it is because of my hope in what God has promised our fathers that I am on trial today. This is the promise our twelve tribes are hoping to see fulfilled as they earnestly serve God day and night" (Acts 26:6–7a).

Paul must have been referring to the golden age of the prophets, the Messianic Kingdom, the salvation of Israel (Luke 2:29–33) in magnificent harmony with that of which aged Zechariah sang in which he exulted in "the horn of salvation for us in the house of his servant David . . . to show mercy to our fathers and to remember His holy covenant, the oath which he swore to our father Abraham"(Luke 1:69–73).

◊ ◊ ◊

* W. D. Davies observed the general neglect of "the land" in the New Testament documents, and this for a people who saw themselves "living at the center [the navel] of the land" (Ezekiel 38:12). But Davies correctly does not see the metamorphosis of the promises such as to deprive Israel ultimately of her land. [13]

Luke shared Paul's emphasis on continuity in the promises* (Acts 13:17, 26, 32–33) and Stephen's five references to the land in Acts 7:2–7 which underscored Luke's "continuous emphasis on Jerusalem."[14] Luke's emphasis buttresses the territorial imperative for a people who are increasingly deterritorialized.†

Book of Hebrews and Writings of Peter

The book of Hebrews reflects something of the deep inner struggle of Hebrew Christians in the first century (a struggle which ameliorated somewhat after the destruction of the temple in A.D. 70) and the central place of eschatology‡ in the Christian scheme of things (see 10:25).[15] The one reference in the New Testament to "the promised land" is in Hebrews 11:9 (although the use of Deuteronomy 5:16 in Ephesians 6:3 implies it). Peter said nothing about the land, although end-time reality had his attention(1 Peter 4:5, 7).

Writings of Paul

While we do not have express reference to the land in Paul, he did refer to Israel as the repository of the covenants and the promises (Romans 9:4) and avoided the word *Israel* as a synonym for the church (we should understand Galatians 6:16 as a reference to ethnic Israel, not to the church).[16]

The apostle Paul's continuous ministry and preaching to both Jew and Gentile must be seen in the light of his conviction of the end coming soon and his understanding of the Messianic Kingdom as preceding "the age to come." In this as well as in his tremendous yearning for the conversion of the Jews, Paul echoed his rabbinic Judaism. Ideas out of the prophets embedded in late Old Testament, apocryphal, and pseudipigraphal writings can be traced in Paul's great desire** for the ingathering of the dispersed and his confident belief in the eternal relationship between God and Israel and the fervent expectation of a golden age.[17]

◊ ◊ ◊

* The New Testament, of course, transcends the land, Jerusalem, and the temple "but its history and theology demand a concern with these realities," indeed requiring us to recognize "the historic centrality of our doctrine of the land, mutatis mutandis."—W. D. Davies[18]

† Even Henry J. Cadbury pointed out that there is an apocalyptic sense in the Acts similar to that in the synoptics. All of this he saw as based on the Jewish apocalyptic hope, of which he said, "The Book of Acts does not spiritualize away the concrete eschatological hopes of Christianity,"[19] since Christ will restore everything promised (3:21).[20]

‡ C. K. Barrett saw the influence of rabbinic literature that looks forward to a restored Jerusalem under earthly conditions.[21]

What then has happened to Israel? Romans 9–11[*] was not a parenthesis in Paul's argument but indeed the rationale of his whole ministry. He began by maintaining that the whole purpose of God's election of Israel is that He might show mercy (Romans 9:15). Paul insisted, "It does not, therefore, depend on man's desire or effort, but on God's mercy" (Romans 9:16). This emphasis on the oceanic mercy of God threads throughout—"Therefore God has mercy on whom he wants to have mercy." (9:18). Both Jews and Gentiles are described as "the objects of his mercy" (9:22).

Paul cited Hosea's family life as showing the mercy of God. Because of idolatry and spiritual adultery, God's ancient people were called "Lo-Ammi," or "not my people" (Hosea 1:9). But this is not the end of the story. There is great hope for this ancient people and thus the mercy of God is brought into the boldest possible relief. Israel shall once again be called "ammi," or "my people" (Hosea 1:10–11; 2:19–23).

Charles Lee Feinberg has shown that blessings are promised in Hosea to Israel nationally:

PROMISES TO ISRAEL IN HOSEA				
National Increases 1:10a	National Conversion 1:10b	National Reunion 1:11a	National Leadership 1:11b	National Restoration 2:1

This is not only Israel's story—but also the story of every Gentile who comes to Christ, as Paul indicated in Romans 9:24–26 and Peter in 1 Peter 2:10.[22] "We no more deserve such privilege than did those to whom Hosea first addressed these words. Yet we have failed to grasp the fullness of the faith unless we perceive that it has made us "Sons of the living God."[23]

Historical Israel is this model, and it is a model of mercy.

◊ ◊ ◊

** (previous page) W. D. Davies remarked about the "tenacity with which Paul clung to his father's ways and the emotional intensity of his concern for the salvation of Jewry."[24]

* It is significant that Rudolf Bultmann paid no attention to Romans 9–11 and that Gunther Bornkamm seemed embarrassed by the apocalyptic and futuristic aspects of the Christian faith. These prominent scholars in our century are indeed "interpreters with dark glasses."

The promise is not recast or revised nor does God renege on Israel—but, according to His intentions from the beginning, He enlarges and expands and extends the promise to include and involve the Gentile world.

God's Word has not failed, "but Israel, who pursued a law of righteousness, has not attained it. Why not? Because they pursued it not by faith but as if it were by works. They stumbled over the 'stumbling stone' (Romans 9:31–32). Israel would not receive the lowly, suffering Messiah even though a number of the ancient rabbis understood the idea of a suffering Messiah from the Old Testament. Paul described the Israelites for whose salvation he prayed:

> They are zealous for God, but their zeal is not based on knowledge. Since they did not know the righteousness that comes from God and sought to establish their own, they did not submit to God's righteousness. Christ is the end of the law so that there may be righteousness for everyone who believes (Romans 10:2–4).

Israel did not obey the laws, and most seriously, "Paul thought Israel was responsible and guilty for failing to believe."[25] There has always been one way of salvation in both Old Testament and New Testament times: "by grace through faith" (cf. Acts 17:30–31; Romans 3:25–26; 4:1–8; Galatians 3:6–9; Ephesians 2:8–9). As George Ladd insisted, "Israel must be saved in the same way as the church—by turning in faith to Jesus as their Messiah (Romans 11:23), and the blessings which Israel will experience are blessings in Christ.[26]

But is the mercy of God really seen in its regal resplendence if God backs off from His promises? God will not back off from His promises, and Israel's failure was not final according to Scripture. Is there not immeasurable comfort for believers today that notwithstanding our failures, God's mercy endures to all generations?

THE MYSTERY OF THE IDENTITY OF ISRAEL

God did not reject his people, whom he foreknew (Romans 11:2).

Did they stumble so as to fall beyond recovery? Not at all! (Romans 11:11).

For if their rejection is the reconciliation of the world, what will their acceptance be but life from the dead?(Romans 11:15).

And if they do not persist in unbelief, they will be grafted in, for God is able to graft them in again (Romans 11:23).

Who is a Jew? In the church which is Christ's body ethnicity is submerged and there is "neither Jew nor Greek" (1 Corinthians 12:13; Galatians 3:23). Paul steadfastly maintained that the Old Testament unequivocally foresaw the inclusion of the Gentiles in God's plan of salvation (cf. Romans 15:8–12 with Genesis 12:3). The mystery not made known until New Testament times was not that the Gentiles could be saved but that converted Jews and Gentiles would blend and bond in a new spiritual organism—the church (Ephesians 3:2–6, 8–9; Romans 16:25–27).

View of James

A key contribution for the delineation of these issues is the speech of James, the half-brother of our Lord, at the Jerusalem Council in Acts 15:13–18. Peter had spoken directly to the point and concluded by offering, "We believe it is through the grace of our Lord Jesus that we are saved, just as they are" (referring in the last instance to the Gentiles). James confirmed that the Gentiles were included in the words of the prophets, and this shows how the early church understood Old Testament prophecy (indeed, James no less).[27] "The law of double reference" operates here as in Hosea 1–2, which refers to Israel's historical experience but also applies to Gentile conversions. In Peter's great sermon on Pentecost he used Joel 2:28–32 as partially fulfilled in the effusion of the Holy Spirit on Pentecost (Acts 2:16–21) but clearly fulfilled in terms of celestial phenomena reserved for the Day of the Lord.

Analogously, Amos 9 has an essentially eschatological and apocalyptic setting. In Amos 9:13–15 the prophet spoke about the Messianic Kingdom and the permanent restoration of God's ancient people to the land.[28] Following the Septuagintal text, James (eight centuries after the writing of Amos) showed that it was God's purpose to include Gentiles in salvation. However, it is a mistake to spiritualize this passage so as to argue that only the church is the recipient of all the Messianic Kingdom blessings.[29]

The rebuilding of "David's fallen tent" (Acts 15:16) is not here the resurrection of Christ[30] nor is it the building of the Christian church* (ala Matthew 16:18), but in its context the "earthly, territorial and national" blessings of a restored Israel in its land and the consequent blessing of Gentile conversions.[31] Instructively James added "I will return" in the place of "in that day," making it very clear that this will take place in

◊ ◊ ◊

* The widespread notion that the church has simply replaced Israel as the beneficiary of the promises of the Old Testament has serious and dangerous ramifications. Some have argued that "the displacement theory" inevitably leads to anti-Semitism and that "the myth of supersession" implies "that the Jews are superfluous, that they belong to no divine scheme of things."[32]

connection with the second advent of our Lord. The point of the citation is what James saw as the essential harmony of God's purpose in saving Gentiles, whether in the first century or during the messianic reign.

View of Scholars

No one in this century has been a more vigorous opponent of the "displacement theory" (the church replacing Israel) than the Danish scholar, Johannes Munck, in his classic *Christ and Israel.** Munck held that in both early Christianity generally and in St. Paul more particularly, Israel holds a special place in God's plan in perpetuity. He believed that the promise of the second coming presupposes the conversion of Israel and that "God is storing up eschatological wrath but plans in the meanwhile to save all Israel in the last days." [33, 34]

George Ladd helpfully diagramed the balance achieved in Romans 11:

ROMANS 11	
Israel	**Gentiles**
Present Rejection of Israel	Reconciliation of the World
Future Restoration of Israel	Life from the Dead

"Life from the dead" means the blessing for the Gentiles as the result of the restoration of Israel just as in Acts 15:16ff.).[35]

In a yet unpublished series of lectures on "Israel's Covenant and History," S. Lewis Johnson outlined Romans 11 and showed that Israel has a future:

1. 11:1–10: Israel's failure not total;

2. 11:11–27: Israel's failure not final.[36]

The discussion throughout Romans 11 is of the nation of Israel as a whole, not individuals of the nation. Those who have not seen the nation of Israel in Romans 11 have given numerous explanations. Many have followed Calvin and Luther in displacing Israel totally with the church.† In recent years some have moved away from spiritualizing Israel toward a semi-spiritualization of Israel (which does not necessar-

◊ ◊ ◊

* Munck pointed out that Paul's addition of *"ekei"* in quoting from Hosea 1:10 in Romans 9:26 underscored the natural designation of Palestine here, in which "Gentiles nations will gather in Jerusalem and the Messianic kingdom will be established there." [37]

ily see the land or the Messianic Kingdom as part of the plan).* Many of the old postmillennialists saw national conversion for Israel at the end of the age.†

Israel will have its turn again, for the pattern is as Johannes Munck has shown:

the "no" of the Jews;
the "yes" of some Gentiles;

the "yes" of the Jews;
and then the "yes" of many more Gentiles.‡

Israel still has "most-favored nation" status with God.

Israel's repentance will also be a sign.** The implications of a recognition of "the hope of Israel" have yet to be fully and satisfactorily explored on the part of some, but the doxological outburst of the apostle

◇ ◇ ◇

† (previous page) Luther wavered on this but finally denied the final conversion of Israel. Anders Nygren is typical: "The Christian Church is the true Israel."

* Van Gemeren spoke of "Israel as the Hermeneutical Crux in the Interpretation of Prophecy" and showed that Henricus Groeneweger, a follower of Cocceius, expressed hope for the Jews and the land. [38]

† This was true of Charles Hodge and many of the Puritans before him. [39] Professor K. H. Rengstorf of Munster illustrated the renewed interest in Paul's teaching in Romans 9-11 by admitting, "During the years of its sufferings the Confessing Church (of Germany) learnt that Romans 9–11 held the key to the understanding of the New Testament." [40]

‡ G. C. Berkouwer saw Israel as a sign before the Parousia. The election of Israel for Paul was "completely and unassailably irrevocable." [41] Karl Barth spoke of "the history of the Jews [as] the most astonishing and provocative of these constants" and Zechariah 2:8 as still applicable. [42]

** D. Martyn Lloyd-Jones, who although never terribly fond of eschatological themes, stood with his Puritan forebears and on the basis of Romans 11:28–32 boldly asserted: "A day is coming when the bulk of the nation of Israel is going to believe the gospel." [43] This will not be simply a remnant, but the Jews as a nation. As over against Hoekema, Hendricksen, and Ridderbos, he foresaw a national conversion with a great impact on the Gentile world. Indeed, "The Jews are going to come in after "'the fullness of the Gentiles.'" [44] Even John Murray admitted to the evidence of "large-scale reclamation of the Jews." [45] Noteworthy commentators in our time like C. E. B. Cranfield and C. K. Barrett have taken a strong position exegetically for the conversion of unbelieving Israel (although the latter is caught in the trap of an unbiblical universalism). [46] The British in recent years have somewhat discounted eschatology, but men such as Errol Hulse, Michael Griffiths, Geoffrey Grogan, J. I. Packer, and William Still are part of "a re-emphasized theology of Israel's hope."

Paul at the end of Romans 11 can hardly be understood apart from seeing "the deliverer [coming] from Zion [and turning] godlessness away from Jacob [and taking] away their sins" (Romans 11:26–27). This demonstrates the mercy of God as directed "on them all" (11:32).

Does a separate plan for Israel lead to a twofold people of God?* Will not a perennial Israel require a permanent land? Does not the land as an everlasting possession require an everlasting Israel? Elliott Johnson expressed well the relationship between Israel and the church as spiritually related but theologically distinct: "In this view, the church is not the antitype of Israel but a people formed of Jew and Gentile while Israel was set aside."[47]

If Israel has a future, what role does the Kingdom play it it? And how did the early church understand the Kingdom?

THE CERTAINTY OF THE GLORY AND VICTORY OF THE KINGDOM

For he must reign until he has put all his enemies under his feet (1 Corinthians 15:25).

On his robe and on his thigh he has this name written: KING OF KINGS AND LORD OF LORDS (Revelation 19:16).

He seized the dragon, that ancient serpent, who is the devil, or Satan, and bound him a thousand years. He threw him into the Abyss, and locked and sealed it over him, to keep him from deceiving the nations anymore until the thousand years were ended. After that, he must be set free for a short time (Revelation 20:2–3).

Up to this juncture we have seen that there is a present and a future aspect of the Kingdom of God and that the Messianic Kingdom of Old Testament promise will find its fulfillment in the eschatological kingdom. We have also assayed the strong biblical evidence for believing that Israel has a unique and continuing place in the wrap-up of human history in the epoch of the end time. But how do these realities meld and fit together?

Israel and Kingdom in New Testament Writings

We are not surprised that the New Testament does not focus substantively on Israel and the Messianic Kingdom because its theme is primarily Christ and His church. After all, the Messianic Kingdom (which

◊ ◊ ◊

* "Ecclesiology has never reckoned with the polar relationship of the church and Israel."—Hendrickus Berkhof[48]

the New Testament calls the millennial reign of Christ) is an intermediate phase. The sequence of resurrections and judgments before and
after the Millennium prepares us to recognize that "the final Consummation does not arrive with the coming of Christ to the Millennial Kingdom but lies beyond the thousand years."[49]

The multiple sequence characterizes prophetic unfolding. After all,
there are "coming ages" (Ephesians 2:7), not simply "the age to come."
A great day is coming when the veil will be taken away for Israel (2 Corinthians 3:14–16) and this people will be converted, of which Paul's own
sudden and dramatic meeting with the risen Christ is a pattern for those
who should subsequently put their trust in Christ (1 Timothy 1:16).

The existence of an intermediate phase of further overlap ("the powers of the coming age" having broken into this present evil age; cf.
Hebrews 6:5) is intimated in 1 Corinthians 15:24–28. The first resurrection (to life) occurs in connection with the Second Coming of Jesus
Christ. The second resurrection (to damnation) follows the establishment of Christ's actual reign on earth. Not until after the Great White
Throne Judgment following the Millennium is death destroyed (Revelation 20:14). The victory of the kingdom is in phases: to use Oscar Cull-
man's analogy, the first advent of Christ is D-Day, and the Second
Advent is V-Day, and the latter is phased likewise, in three:

(1) the resurrection of Christ;

(2) the resurrection of believers at Christ's coming;

(3) the resurrection of the "rest of the dead" after the Millennium.[50]

The Millennium, according to *The Interpreter's Bible*, will be

a period of the rule of Christ during which He will complete the subjugation
of all the opposing forces which had been defeated on the cross. [After] the
Parousia, then the visible rule of Christ and the saints would come. The
length of this rule of Christ is not specified but it corresponds to the thousand
years in Revelation (cf. the Jewish apocalypses from the period between Paul
and Revelation: II Baruch 30:1; II Esdras 7:26-29). . . . An intermediate kingdom cannot be explained away here.[51]

The idea of an intermediate or interim phase of the kingdom was pervasive in apocalyptic Judaism.* The millennial kingdom is the initial
stage of the everlasting kingdom.

There may be chiliastic (pertaining to millellnnium) implications in
1 Thessalonians 2:12 and 2 Thessalonians 1:5–12.[52] Surely Paul's classic
description of the deliverance of the creation in Romans 8:18–25 and

◊ ◊ ◊

* Rabbi Eliezer spoke of the days of the Messiah as 1000 years (similarly in *Sybylline Oracles*, Book II and the *Twelve Patriarchs*).

Peter's treatment of a new heaven and a new earth in 2 Peter 3 need to be included in any survey of relevant passages. The theme of kingdom rule is not limited to a single passage as some allege. The writer to the Hebrews spoke of the conquest of our enemies and Christ's rule in 2:5–8, and this is manifestly not the eternal state in view (cf. the original Psalm quoted, 8:4–8 and Revelation 21:1). The Hebrews passage speaks of earthly dominion and must be considered in the light of Psalm 110 as quoted in the New Testament. So Daniel T. Taylor was correct in his insistence 150 years ago:

"The doctrine of the personal reign of Christ in the new earth is of the Bible."[53]

Chapter 7 of this book will demonstrate that this understanding of the intermediate Messianic Kingdom has been persistent and at times dominant in the history of the Christian church.[54]

Israel and the Kingdom in Revelation

The kingdom hope for Israel and the church is predictably in the Apocalypse of John.* The language and style of this book† seem quite different from the Gospels and the Epistles written by the "beloved disciple," but the genre of the material being treated and the advanced age of John at the time of writing (phenomena with many counterparts in writers in all fields) help us to understand these aspects of the book. We are dealing with visions, after all. The close affinity between the Old Testament and the book of Revelation is at once evident. Westcott and Hort calculated that in the 404 verses of Revelation, 265 contain Old Testament language and at least 550 references are made to the Old Testament.[55]

Whether we consider the unveiling of the Son of Man (Revelation 1:9–20; cf. Daniel 7:13) or the beast out of the sea and the beast out of the earth (13:1–18, cf. Daniel 7:8), the familiar Jewish apocalyptic milieu is there. The 144,000 of Revelation 7 are clearly Jewish, coming from every tribe except Dan[56] and stand in stark contrast with the great Gentile multitude. The woman who gives birth to the man-child in Revelation 12 cannot be the church nor Mary Baker Glover Patterson Eddy. The woman is Israel (Isaiah 9:6), and she is persecuted and pursued by the dragon. The restored temple is in view as well as the two witnesses whose

◊ ◊ ◊

* "It is only through this doctrine of the Kingdom that the Apocalypse can or will be understood and consistently interpreted."—George Peters[57]

† The "Jewishness" of the Apocalypse is undeniable.[58] The linkage of the Revelation to the Olivet discourse is also quite striking.[59]

bodies are exposed on the streets of the city of Jerusalem (Revelation 11). Then after the coming of the King in power and great glory (19:11–21), the kingdom is set up on earth and Christ rules for 1000 years (20:1–10).

The Cambridge Bible closes the argument about the Millennium when it says of Revelation 20:4:

> This passage is quite sufficient foundation for the doctrine (of the millennial rule of Christ) even if it stood alone, and there are many other prophecies which, if not teaching it plainly, may fairly be understood to refer to it.

The 1000-year period is referred to six times in Revelation 20. Satan is bound during this period with conspicuous attendant blessing but then released at the end of the 1000 years to demonstrate conclusively that even after 1000 years of the perfect society under the direct rule of Christ with His saints, those who are not regenerate will rebel and follow the Master of Deception to disaster and despair.[*]

The Lord Jesus Christ will return with all His saints and angels (cf. Zechariah 14:3–8 in whose context is the connection of Israel's repentance and restoration along with Messiah's reign):

> The LORD will be king over the whole earth. On that day there will be one LORD, and his name the only name (Zechariah 14:9).

This will be the consummation of history as we have known it, the omega point toward which all events are moving. Thus God will ring down the curtain on space-time history and "the knowledge of the glory of the Lord shall cover the earth as the waters cover the sea" (Habakkuk 2:14). Then after the judgment of the wicked dead (Revelation 20:11–15) and the destruction of the last enemy, death itself, believers move on to the endless aeons of eternity and the infinite challenge and opportunity of service and ministry forever and ever

◊ ◊ ◊

[*] Those of amillennial (or realized millennial, to use Jay Adams' phrase) or post-millennial persuasion dismiss the idea of a literal reign of Christ after the Parousia. J. Marcellus Kik referred to this as a "carnal conception of such a reign."[60] Such interpreters have seen the first resurrection as the new birth and the thousand years as the gospel dispensation.[61] G. Vos in the *International Standard Bible Encyclopedia* understood the first resurrection in this context to be "a state of glorified life enjoyed with Christ in heaven by martyrs during the intermediate period preceding the parousia." Philip Hughes argued that the first resurrection is the resurrection of Christ.[62] In this view, what possibly can the loosing of Satan represent? Satan is relentlessly deceiving the nations now. He is not bound nor does he have a long chain. But that day is coming.

PART

II

THE
HISTORICAL
FLOW

I the LORD do not change.
So you, O descendants of Jacob, are not destroyed.

Malachi 3:6

CHAPTER

THE UNSPEAKABLE ANGUISH OF WORLD-WIDE DISPERSION

*The world has by now discovered
that it is impossible to destroy the Jews.*

Lord Beaconsfield (Disraeli)

*All things are mortal but the Jew:
all other forces pass, but he remains.
What is the secret of his immortality?*

Mark Twain

*The Jews are divinely preserved
for a purpose worthy of God.*

St. Jerome

FREDERICK THE GREAT REPUTEDLY ASKED his chaplain to give him one commanding evidence for the existence of God. The chaplain replied: "The amazing Jew, your Majesty."

For 4000 years this people has had a sense of identity. Paul Johnson called the Jews "the most tenacious people in history." Abraham purchased burial property in Hebron 4000 years ago, and the Jews are still there![1] John Bright has observed that there has been no period when Israel did not believe she was the chosen people, "and that choosing took place in history."

As Gerhart Riegner, the redoubtable champion of European Jewry, earlier in this century held: "There's simply no logic in Jewish history. If there were, we would have disappeared a hundred times over by now. We surely would never had had a state of our own.[2]

How have the Jews virtually alone avoided genetic regression of IQ and achievement and been successful for 4000 years?

The Hittites and the Kenites and the Canaanites are gone. But the Jews are like Jonah, the stubborn prophet—tossed out into the swirling and stormy seas, ostensibly consumed by the great fish but indigested, then vomited up on the land once again.[*]

Their Name

The Jews have carried several names. Their progenitor was called "Abram the Hebrew" (Genesis 14:13). Early Mesopotamian tablets and Bronze Age Egyptian sources speak of the *habiru*—evidently "a term of abuse used of difficult and destructive non-city-dwellers who moved from place to place."[3] Others have understood the term to mean "caravaner." They were like poor Joe in Dickens's *Bleak House* who testified: "I'm always a-moving on, sir." Some have emphasized the sense of "one

◊ ◊ ◊

[*] Other peoples have experienced diaspora. Koreans speak of the 2,500,000 Koreans in the diaspora, but this is relatively recent and far more limited.

has crossed over" in the word, referring to Abram crossing over the Euphrates when he came out of Ur, and thus one "across the river" has been suggested as the meaning.

The appelation of Israel traces back to Jacob, grandson of Abraham, who was given this name, which means "having power with God or God's fighter" (cf. Genesis 28:13; 32:28). Jacob's twelve sons constituted the nation. When the nation sundered in the days of King Rehoboam, the ten northern tribes were called Israel. They were conquered by Assyria in 722 B.C. and taken into captivity. The southern kingdom, which lasted until 586 B.C., was comprised of the tribe of Judah and the small tribe of Benjamin; it was called Judah. During the captivity in Babylon and Persia, the title "Jew" was used of persons from both northern and southern Israel. Some from the northern kingdom fled south to escape the Assyrians, but later the Babylonians took them captive. (cf. Esther 3:6–9; 8:9; Daniel 3:8–12). "The loose application of 'Jew' to the entire race was preserved after the restoration to Palestine."[4] The word *Israelite* then today is a synonym for Jew.[*]

Three Periods of Stress

Erich Sauer described the historical background of the worldwide Jewish dispersion as "three principle periods of distress:"[5]

(1) The oppression in Egypt and absence from the land of promise for 400 years as foretold when God made a covenant with Abram (Genesis 15:12–21). The Jews were exiles but brought back (Deuteronomy 4:20; Exodus 6:6).

◊ ◊ ◊

* There is the massive and bizarre argument of the British-Israelites that the ten lost tribes are to be indentified with the Anglo-Saxons (Britain and the United States). Although this strange glitch in supposed fact and sound judgment has waned in the wake of the decline of Britain among the nations and the increasing diversification of her polyglot population, there are still those who believe that the stone Jacob slept on at Bethel is now the Stone of Scone, that Britain is the crushing stone of Daniel 2 (which had some appeal in the zenith of the British Empire in Victorian times), and that the smoke of London is the Shekinah.[6] The fact is that the then northern tribes were never lost. Some of the residuum left in the land after the captivity of the north are mentioned as being involved in Josiah's revival (cf. 2 Chronicles 34:6–7, 9, 33). Fully one quarter of those who comprised the remnant that returned to the land after the Decree of Cyrus were from the north, and Girdlestone is absolutely correct in asserting: "From the time of the Restoration until the final fall of Jerusalem, at the hand of the Romans, all the tribes were regarded as represented in the land of Israel, though many families of all the tribes were also to be found in the neighboring countries" (Acts 2:7–11).[7] The fact is that Israel was restored as a twelve-tribed nation (cf. Acts 2:23; 3:12; 9:15; 26:6–7; James 1:1; 60: 1 Peter 1:1).[8]

(2) The captivity or banishment of Israel and Judah (in its several aspects, the invasions of Nebuchadnezzar coming in 606, 597, and 587–86 B.C.), the latter lasting exactly seventy years as prophesied (2 Chronicles 36:20–21), with Israel returning quite cleansed and renewed of her grievous and gross idolatries, as described in Ezra, Nehemiah, and the post-exilic prophets.

(3) The subjugation under the Romans, Pompey's first invasion in 63 B.C. (the fourth beast of Daniel 7 on a rampage); the destruction of Jerusalem and the temple under Titus in A.D. 70; and the bloody and violent suppression of the Bar-Cochba rebellion by Hadrian in A.D. 135.

Even in biblical times oppression and suffering followed this ancient people.

THE AGONY OF EXPULSION

I will scatter you among the nations and will draw out my sword and pursue you. Your land will be laid waste, and your cities will lie in ruins (Leviticus 26:33).

Then the LORD will scatter you among all nations, from one end of the earth to the other (Deuteronomy 28:64a).

There will be great distress in the land and wrath against this people. They will fall by the sword and will be taken as prisoners to all the nations. Jerusalem will be trampled on by the Gentiles until the times of the Gentiles are fulfilled (Luke 21:23b–24).

What the biblical writer called the "dark days" came to Israel and Judah as a consequence of their heinous idolatry (cf. Jeremiah 44:16–18). A relatively modest remnant returned to the land as described in Ezra and Nehemiah. Substantial colonies of Jews continued to live in Assyria, Babylon, and Egypt. Jeremiah was forcibly taken to Jewish colonies in Lower Egypt to Tahpanhes, a center on a branch of the Nile in the Delta. There were other colonies in Migdol, Memphis, and in Upper Egypt. (Jeremiah 44:1ff.). At times the exiles were nostalgic for home (Psalm 137) and the sojourn in exile had its times of severe stress, but on the whole they became prosperous enough and well-settled so as not to find a return to land of Israel and its more constrictive environment altogether pleasing. Poignant vignettes of the life in exile are seen in the books of Esther, Ezekiel, and Daniel in the Old Testament. By the time of Christ there were as many Jews living outside of Palestine as lived in the land.

Life under the Roman eagle and her surrogates, the Herods, was a mixed bag.[9] While there were interludes of tolerance and a semblance of tranquility, there came a series of Jewish wars against the Romans and a great devastation as Jesus had predicted. Israel's unwillingness to "recognize the time of God's coming" (Luke 19:44b) exposed her to a great national catastrophe. Increasingly violent tensions in Palestine and the futility of the efforts of Agrippa II to control the situation created the justified apprehensions of Josephus that a crisis was at hand.

Titus's Destruction of Jerusalem

The checkered history of the second temple period climaxes when 50,000 elite Roman troops under Titus finally reduced Jerusalem, a crowded city of 2.7 million persons (according to Josephus). The temple was destroyed on the very anniversary of the destruction of the first temple in 586 B.C. Immediately 500 Jewish leaders were crucified, and then a mass slaughter commenced that made the nightmare under Antiochus Epiphanes in 170 B.C. pale in insignificance.[10]

An estimated 100,000 captives were sent to Egypt where there was a great glut on the slave markets (a most remarkable fulfillment of the prophecy found in Deuteronomy 28:68). Josephus gave the number of those Jews who perished as 1,100,000 (this includes many Jews and proselytes who entered Jerusalem prior to the siege to observe Passover and witness a deliverance such as the Maccabees experienced). Josephus described the Roman action:

> Now, as soon as the army had no more people to slay or to plunder, because there remained none of the objects of their fury, Caesar gave orders that they should now demolish the entire city and temple . . . there was left nothing to make those that came thither believe it has ever been inhabited.[11]

H. Graetz lamented, "Who can picture the sufferings and the humiliation of the Judaean capitol.[12]

Titus went on to Rome for his triumphal procession, having saved out of the carnage 700 of the handsomest captives and the two leaders of the Zealots. The nation was effectively no longer in existence. The holy city was a heap or rubble (Daniel 9:26). The final action involved the suicide of 960 Jews who chose death in the fortress Masada west of Jerusalem toward the Dead Sea, rather than Roman captivity or torture, and thus Masada became synonymous with the Jewish determination—"No more Masada."

What remained of the population in Israel was greatly impoverished and numerically small. Although under the oppressive shadow of Rome, the remnant now without a temple rallied to the law—"the one gathering point."[13]

Bar-Cochba Rebellion

While the Sadducees and priesthood sank with the cessation of animal sacrifice and the abolition of the traditional Sanhedrin, the Pharisees and the rabbis came into their own, particularly as Jamnia (or

Jabne) came into prominence over on the seacoast as a center of literary and religious activity. Some restoration of the Sanhedrin took place at Jamnia, and resistance to Rome continued after A.D. 70. A flare-up against Trojan took place among the Jews in Mesopotamia in A.D. 116. The resistance culminated in the Bar-Cochba Rebellion of A.D. 135.

Again the first waves of revolutionary impulse originated in Galilee. Bar-Cochba was an impressive physical specimen. He presented himself as a liberator. The whole episode had a messianic tinge. Rabbi Akiba piped: "This is the Messianic King." Dio Cassius estimated his followers at 580,000. He fled to Betar*where there was a frightful massacre by the Romans. At this time there were 285 villages and 50 castles in the land, but these suffered greatly and once again the plow passed over Jerusalem. Jerusalem was made into a Roman colony, Aelia Capitolina. Jewish slaves sold for no more than a horse. Some hegemony remained for Jews in Palestine (more as an implication of the Parthian wars) and "Babylon became second mother to the Jewish nation"[14]; that is, the community in exile in Babylon assumed greater leadership, and the tension between Jews of the *yishuv* (in Israel) and the Jews of the *galut* (in the Diaspora) began to be painfully apparent.

Importance of Land

During the next three centuries when there was a steadily growing conflict with burgeoning Christianity (and mutual persecution and aversion mounting), the Jews still looked to *eretz*-Israel.†

The Jerusalem Talmud in A.D. 190 listed 400 villages and small towns as having Jewish residents. Up until the sixth century an independent Jewish tribe lived on Tiran, at the southern end of the Gulf of Akabah. But the sacred soil of Palestine continued to have appeal and attraction to Jews abroad because those who died there "expected a surer and easier resurrection."[15] The Jews through all of these tremendous tragedies, maintained an unbroken connection with their homeland. The land itself was described in the mid-second century by Julian the Apologist as "devastated, consumed by fire and uncultivated." But the Jews loved the land and longed for it.

In A.D. 362 Julian (called the apostate), who had relaxed certain laws for the Jews, attempted to reconstruct Jerusalem and the temple to the great encouragement of the Jewish elements still in the vicinity.[16] But

◊ ◊ ◊

* The name taken much later in Poland by the young Zionist organization out of which Menachem Begin came.

† "The Jews became more and more what they properly and essentially were: strangers in the pagan world. The restoration in the Holy Land continued to be a subject of religious hope which they held with unconquerable tenacity."—Emil Schurer[17]

Julian died in battle with the Persians. Theodosius dissolved the Patriarchate in Palestine in A.D. 425, but even in this time there was immigration in and out of the land.[18]

In all of this the autonomous center of Jewish life in Babylon assumed increasing importance. Knowledgeable scholars agree that "Babylonian Jews lost to some extent the moral simplicity and integrity of former times and were given to luxury, vanity and ambition."[19] So exile from the land was not altogether the answer. Nor were Babylon and environs always safe. Yazdegerd II, King of Persia (A. D. 440–457), suppressed the Jews and forbade the Sabbath. His successor slaughtered half of the Ispaham community and produced a great flight of Jews from Mesopotamia from whom the Jews of Malabar on the coast of Madras in India may be the descendants. As far as enemies, the Jews constantly lived on the slopes of a volcano.[20]

Importance of Torah and Talmud

Even as the importance of the Judean center dwindled, Judaism turned in upon itself and dedicated immense energy to building a fence around the Torah, the law.* The process of elaborating the collective memory of the Jewish people began with the Torah, the first five books of the Old Testament as augmented by oral tradition. (See John Phillips's helpful chart on the following page.)

The Palestinian Talmud closed about the time Jewish life in Palestine became virtually negligible. Paralleling the Palestinian Talmud was the Babylonian Talmud, the product of the Babylonian academies that flourished from A.D. 300–600. The completed work bristles with hostility toward Jesus Christ and is pervaded with endless hair-splitting, but it became "the educator of the Jewish nation," and as Ellisen observed, "not only did it provide a universal education for Jewish youths of 10 to 15 years duration, it also 'made them physicians, mathematicians, astronomers, grammarians, philosophers, poets and businessmen.'"[21]

Of course there were protests against the rigidities of Talmudic Judaism such as was led by Anan ben David in Mesopotamia, the Jewish Luther (A.D. 740–800) who founded the Karaites (champions of the Scripture). They would not accept the Talmud but clung to the Torah and the prophets. The Karaites knelt in prayer. Karaism created a deep

◊ ◊ ◊

* "They did not lose their identity in the emergent Dark Ages communities. Judaism and the Jewish remant were preserved in the amber of the Torah . . . the Jews survived because the period of intense introspection enabled their intellectual leaders to enlarge the Torah into a system of moral theology and community law of extraordinary coherence, logical consistency and social strength. Having lost the Kingdom of Israel, the Jews turned the Torah into a fortress of the mind and spirit, in which they could dwell in safety and even in content."—Paul Johnson[22]

schism in the Diaspora and survives in small groups in the Middle East and the Crimea. Another alternative to Talmudic Judaism was Kabbalism or Jewish mysticism, which came to climactic expression in Spanish Judaism with the *Book of Zohar* and was transplanted back to Safed in Northern Galilee when the Jews were expelled from the Iberian Peninsula in the fifteenth century. More traditional centers of Jewish Law and learning were maintained in Tiberias and Lydda.

DEVELOPMENT OF THE PALESTINIAN TALMUD	
Date	**Portions**
c. 400 B.C.	Midrash "Exposition" of the Torah
A.D. 69–220	Mishna "Teachings" Under Hillel
C. A.D. 227	Gemara "Learning"
A.D. 371–500	Talmud 2,500,000 Words 613 Commandments Finished by Mar Jose[23]

Scattered Abroad

With conditions worsening in the aftermath of the collapse of the Roman Empire, there followed a period of colonization in Europe, preceding the conquest of Spain by the Arabs in A.D. 711. In many situations unbelievable pressure was put upon Jews to convert to Christianity, but generally they refused. The increasing intolerance of the Byzantine Court, which excluded Jews from office and proscribed the building of synagogues, influenced the Jews to go farther and farther away from Palestine and the Middle East. Yet always some Jews would return as in A.D. 1211 when 300 Jews returned from France and England. The first crusade in A.D. 1096 had attempted the mass extermination of the Jews.

Some Jews went into Arab lands. Indeed there was a Golden Age for the Jews in Moslem lands, especially Spain where the great Maimonides blazed new trails of remarkable cultural achievement. The Jews were traders and merchants establishing significant centers in places like Iraq and points east, and while Mohammed himself disliked the Jews, the Koran regards them as "people of the Book" and prescribes tolerance. Joseph Wolff, born in Bavaria in 1796, the son of a rabbi, studied at the University of Halle, was much influenced by Henry Drummond, and made many missionary journeys, including a long trip through Arab lands where he saw Jews living in eager expectation of their Messiah. He even visited what is today Saudi Arabia.[24]

Clearly by the eighth century most Jews were living in the East with "a not unimportant nucleus surviving precariously in Palestine."[25] Italy was the oldest center of organized Jewish life from the west (as we remember even from Acts 2). New communities were taking shape in Russia, Poland, France, and Germany. In A. D. 700 the Khazar King Bulan and many of his retinue chose Judaism as their faith after a debate among spokesmen for Christianity, Judaism, and Islam. This Jewish state existed between the Volga and the Don Rivers in the Caucasus Mountains. Subsequently, after about two centuries this extensive geographical area was invaded by the Russians and did convert to Islam.

A powerful centrifugal force dispersed the Jews in all directions from Palestine. Yet their continued observance of the Passover year by year testified to their expectation—*L'shanah hablaah bi Yerushalayim!* "Next year in Jerusalem!"

THE DILEMMA OF GHETTOIZATION

Among those nations you will find no repose, no resting place for the sole of your foot. There the LORD will give you an anxious mind, eyes weary with longing, and a despairing heart. You will live in constant suspense, filled with dread both night and day, never sure of your life. In the morning you will say, "If only it were evening!" and in the evening, "If only it were morning!"—because of the terror that will fill your hearts and the sights that your eyes will see (Deuteronomy 28:65–67).

Israel is a scattered flock that lions have chased away. The first to devour him was the king of Assyria; the last to crush his bones was Nebuchadnezzar king of Babylon (Jeremiah 50:17).

Moses in his valedictory that we call "Deuteronomy" described the disgrace that will attach to the Jews disseminated through the whole world. He says, "You will become a thing of horror and an object of scorn and ridicule to all the nations where the LORD will drive you" (Deuteronomy 28:37). The word *ridicule* or *byword* (AV) is the Hebrew word *sheninah* and comes very close to the extremely negative epithet *sheeny*, which is a totally offensive name used in many settings to demean the Jew.[26] Deuteronomy foretells the beginning of the saga of *The Wandering Jew*, cast out among the nations and told "Thou shalt go on till the end of time."[27]

Jews in Northern Europe

During the period of the organizing of European Jewry (from A. D. 711 to 1096 and the beginning of the Crusades), the main immigrations from the Mediterranean basin were over the Pyrenees into France and the Low Countries; over the Apennines into Germany, and through the Balkans to Poland and Russia. The immigrations were the foundations of Ashkenazic or Northern European Jewry as over against Sephardic Jewry coming from Southern Europe and Muslim lands.[*]

The degradation heaped upon the Jews by the medieval church is one of the most tragic chapters in human history. Of course there were those who spoke up against such persecution, as Pope Gregory I who insisted: "We forbid the burdening and the oppressing of the Jews," and as did the Emperor Charlemagne who took the Jews under patronage. Others like St. Bernard spoke against anti-Semitism as well as Raymond Lull, one of the pioneers of Jewish missions. The Jews, notwithstanding strictures against usury, were increasingly willing to lend money to Gentiles and thus de facto became the banking system of medieval times. As the merchants, doctors, and lawyers the Jews were virtually the only urban people in Europe.

Jews in England

The Jews were relatively late in coming to England, arriving with William the Conqueror in the eleventh century. Here the likes of Richard the Lion-Hearted ruthlessly persecuted them.[†]

The Magna Carta of 1215 itself legalized injustice against the Jews. Not until Oliver Cromwell opened England to the Jews in the seventeenth century did they return, and not until 1858 was a Jew admitted to Parliament. The first was Baron Lionel de Rothschild. The House of Rothschild , which rose out of the Nathan Meyer family in Frankfurt, came into its own in the financing of the Napoleonic Wars out of its German, French, and British branches.

Jews in Spain

The Andulusian Epoch was one of the most brilliant in Jewish history with the great Maimonides (born in Cordoba, Spain) epitomizing both the stellar strengths of the age and its sad underside. A gifted thinker, Maimonides sought to fuse Judaism with Aristotelianism, but in 1148 was forced to flee Spain, going to Egypt where he was responsible for a stupendous renaissance of learning. He was buried in Tiberias where his tomb was appallingly desecrated. The public burnings of the Jews in Spain was called the *auto-da-fe*. Even prior to their expulsion by Ferdi-

◊ ◊ ◊

* Gibbon, in speaking of the inevitable recourse of persecuting the Jews, reminds his readers that the "exiled nation had founded some synagogues in the cities of Gaul; but Spain since the time of Hadrian was filled with their numerous colonies."[28]

† This was forever memorialized in Sir Walter Scott's *Ivanhoe*.

nand and Isabella (patrons of Columbus) many Jews had to flee; thousands of refugees went to Portugal, Greece and Turkey, and the Netherlands, where a vigorous culture took root, out of which emerged Spinoza and the like. Forced conversions and baptisms gave rise to the Marranos (meaning the "damned" or some have argued "swine") the secret Jews, some of whom though outwardly Catholic still to this day practice certain of the ancient rites of Judaism.[29] Such lived in constant terror of the Inquisition fires.

Jews in France

In France Rousseau spoke of the Jews as "an astonishing spectacle. But Zion destroyed has not lost her children . . . they mingle with all the people yet are not confused with them," and Voltaire lamented "Madrid's and Lisbon's horrid fires, the yearly portion of unhappy Jews,"[30] but Voltaire became viciously anti-Semitic.

The earliest legislation of record in France was an ordinance directed against the Jews.

Under the inspiration of the Inquisition, the entire Jewish community in Strasbourg was burned in 1349.

Jews in Germany and Poland

The more lethargic German Jews saw the birth of a Jewish cultural center in the Rhineland and cruel burnings and forced baptisms in Mainz. Natural catastrophes and health scourges were frequently blamed on the Jews. In the Pale of Settlement (Polish regions seized by Russia), the Jews lived in constant fear of massacre. Government-sponsored and instigated pogroms (meaning "devastation") would sweep through an area without warning taking many lives. The Fourth Lateran Council introduced the mandatory wearing of a badge or yellow emblem for the Jews, sometimes a yellow or red hat. These were but further instances in Israel's long night of weeping.

The Jewish response to increasing geographic proscription reflected a deep and difficult dilemma. Should such pressure be passively accepted even though the ghettoization made the persecuted populace even more vulnerable? Apparently the word *ghetto* was first used in Venice and comes from the word *gheta*, which is associated with the cannon factory in the vicinity where the Jews were consigned in the sixteenth century as far away from St. Mark's Cathedral and square as possible. Heavy additional taxes were paid by the Jews to make possible the *modus vivendi*, although they were not allowed citizenship.[31] Thus arose the shtetls of eastern Europe, but here life was hazardous and uncertain as it was even for the Court Jews who obtained special favor. The bottom line was ever: "The Jew at court, however wealthy or powerful, knew he was never really safe and he did not have to look far to find Jews who were in desperate trouble."[32] The great Chmielnicki massacres in Poland and Lithuania (1648-56) beggar description.[33]

Jewish Movements

Periodic spurts of desperation gave rise to several alternative movements. Joseph Nasi led a group of pious Jews in an abortive effort to establish a Jewish Palestine in the second half of the sixteenth century. A highly emotional and very personal kind of Judaism called Hassidism (comparable to Pentecostal or charismatic tendencies in some Protestantism and Catholicism, or the Sufis or dervishes in Islam). The founder was Israel ben Eliezer (1770–1776) or Baal Shem Tov as he is referred to today. Some Jews turned to kabbalistic mysticism as already noted, and others sought hope in Messianism of various kinds. A rash of false messiahs had obvious appeal to the frightened and desperate. Among these were Moses of Crete in the fifth century who captivated the entire Jewish community on the island of Crete, Abu Issa of Isfahan who raised an army of 10,000, Abraham Abulfia of Spain, and Shabbathai Zevi who led a great movement in the seventeenth century but then stunned his followers by converting to Islam.[34] Amazingly some remnants of this movement still exist and maintain a Donme synagogue in Istanbul, Turkey.[35] The shock of Islam, the nightmare of the Crusades, and the ceaseless pressures of persecution all raised the question of the survival of dispersed Israel, and not for the last time.

The day by day life of many Jews through the centuries is illustrated by Pierre VanPassen's sketch of Jews living in a North African setting as found in his Days of Our Years. As soon as the Jews closed up their shops in the Jewish quarter for the Sabbath, rowdy elements would begin to sweep refuse and offal from the city into the Jewish quarter and up against the doors of Jewish homes. Of course Jews would not lift a hand to rid themselves of the stench of the sweepings on the Sabbath but would have to endure this olfactory assault until the end of the day.

Some Jews went as far away as China, where a substantial colony flourished at Kaifeng;[36] others to Mexico and Southern America; some to Ethiopia, Singapore, and Gibralter; others to Egypt, Syria, Yemen; and some to India.[37] How the Jews survived in these countries and many others is an amazing chronicle.

THE MIRACLE OF PRESERVATION

Indeed, he who watches over Israel will neither slumber nor sleep (Psalm 121:4).

"Only if these decrees vanish from my sight," declares the LORD, "will the descendants of Israel ever cease to be a nation before me." This is what the LORD says: "Only if the heavens above can be measured and the foundations of the earth below be searched out will I reject all the descendants of Israel because of all they have done," declares the LORD (Jeremiah 31:36–37).

Though scattered everywhere, surviving! A man who lived in Paris through the violence and vicissitudes of the French Revolution was asked how he fared in it all. His reply was concise: "I survived." This has been a national experience for God's ancient covenant people, and the providential hand of God protected them.

In one of the Jewish prayer books is the following petition used by countless Jews across many centuries: "Blessed art Thou, O Lord our God, King of the Universe, for keeping us alive, preserving us and permitting us to attain this day."

At the dawn of their history, the children of Israel languishing in Egyptian bondage cried to the Lord. The first final solution was proposed (Exodus 1–2), but God was faithful to His covenant with Abraham, Isaac, and Jacob (Exodus 2:23–25). The long period of duress was answered by God's power in the Exodus. Not even the onslaughts of the mighty empires of antiquity could erase this small and resented people. As the prophet Isaiah observed:

> Unless the LORD Almighty had left us some survivors, we would have become like Sodom, we would have been like Gomorrah (Isaiah 1:9).

Many an ancient people has passed into oblivion and been absorbed and assimilated in the ebb and flow of the historical process. Esther and her cousin, Mordecai, faced the fiendish plot to annihilate and exterminate the Jews in that time. But wicked Haman was up against the purposes of God, who in His providence foiled all of the devious designs against His vulnerable people.

In Max Dimont's masterful *The Indestructible Jew*, the case is solidly made for a kind of manifest destiny for the Jews in which their experience trains them for survival in order to accomplish their mission (although he concurs with Abraham Heschel that the Jew is a messenger who every now and then forgets his message). He quoted Isaac Luria who was born in Jerusalem in 1534 and who had propounded the thesis that Israel's history divides into three parts: (1)contraction: gathered together in the first 2000 years; (2)breaking of the vessels: exile for the next 2000 years; (3) restoration: at last. Luria saw the progression as essentially, a day of wrath, a day of judgment, and an age of salvation.[38]

Dimont himself saw six tangential circles representing the six societies in terms of which Jewish history unfolds:[39]

DIMONT'S VIEW OF ISRAEL'S HISTORY

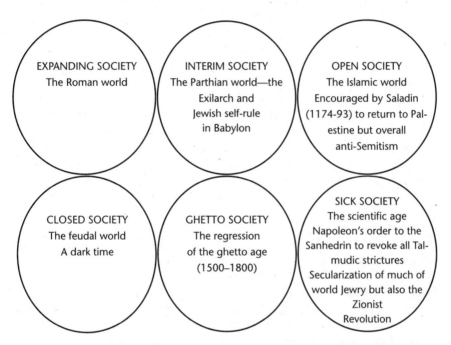

EXPANDING SOCIETY
The Roman world

INTERIM SOCIETY
The Parthian world—the
Exilarch and
Jewish self-rule
in Babylon

OPEN SOCIETY
The Islamic world
Encouraged by Saladin
(1174-93) to return to Palestine but overall
anti-Semitism

CLOSED SOCIETY
The feudal world
A dark time

GHETTO SOCIETY
The regression
of the ghetto age
(1500–1800)

SICK SOCIETY
The scientific age
Napoleon's order to the
Sanhedrin to revoke all Tal-
mudic strictures
Secularization of much of
world Jewry but also the
Zionist
Revolution

Yet in all of this kaleidoscopic change, the Jews have remained an identifiable ethnic and religious entity. Is this just happenstance? Is this just an accident? The phenomenon is no more an accident or a fluke of chance than is the existence of our remarkable planet in an infinitely expanding universe.

The eye of faith sees God at work in His sovereign wisdom.

We cannot succumb to deism in which God essentially disengages or unplugs from time-space history, nor can we in the face of such staggering injustice and horrendous suffering give way to belief in a finite or limited God.[*]

◇ ◇ ◇

* This is the view of Rabbi Harold Kusher, who wrote the popular *Why Bad Things Happen to Good People,* and the late eminent personalist Edgar Sheffield Brightman of Boston University.

God has preserved His ancient covenant people as He has indeed preserved His new covenant people—we are always just a generation away from extinction, but God has kept us and this is of immense and awesome encouragement and consolation.

So to this present time approximately 200,000 Jews live in Argentina, where they have had times of great suffering and persecution and seasons of greater toleration and peace.[40] Only about 600 Jews live in Portugal but there remain many secret Jews who are baptized Catholics in name but who observe Sabbath. Four hundred Jews live in Christchurch, New Zealand. Alexandria in Egypt once boasted 40,000 Jews but has now shriveled to 150 elderly and invalids. Approximately 1800 Jews remain in Zimbabwe, with three synagogues in the capital. Some 300 Jews live in Thailand, 70 families in the Philippines, 1200 in Hong Kong, 600 in Japan, 500 in Singapore. 7500 Jews live in Denmark, a country which has always been hospitable to the Jews with Copenhagen known as "the Jerusalem of Scandinavia." A close-knit community of 350,000 Jews live in Mexico. Most families send their young people to spend a year in Israel. For some 4000 years God has miraculously preserved this people.

Whenever it looks like the end is at hand, unforeseen horizons appear. When low population trends among Israelis portended numerical inferiority to the high population of Palestinians in Israel and the occupied territories by 2010,[41] a tidal wave of immigrants came from what was the Soviet Union. American Jews in their prosperity and religious laxity have a 50 percent intermarriage rate and have represented a very serious threat to the integrity of Jewish identity in the United States. But then come emigres from abroad and a revival of religious orthodoxy and some very virile trends are in evidence.

Who can deny the very impressive historical evidence with regard to this people? Israel has been like the burning bush which Moses confronted in the desert (Exodus 3:2), "Though the bush was on fire, it did not burn up."

CHAPTER

THE INCREDIBLE HISTORY OF WORLD-WIDE ANTI-SEMITISM

*For, alone among all nations, this one
refused to have any intercourse
with the other peoples. . . .*

The Stoic Posidonius of Apamea

*Those whose lot it was that their fathers worshipped the Sabbath,
Pray to nothing now but the clouds and a spirit in heaven;
Since their fathers abstained from pork,
they'd be cannibals sooner
than violate that taboo.
Circumcised, not as the Gentiles,
They despise Roman law, but learn and observe
the reverse Israel's code, and all from the sacred volume of Moses
Where the way is not shown to any but true believers,
Where the uncircumcised are never led to the fountains.*

The Roman author, Juvenal the Satirist[1]

ACCOMPANYING AND UNDERLYING JEWRY'S worldwide dispersion has always been the frightful virus of anti-Semitism.* The term *anti-Semitism* was first used in 1879 by a rabid racist named Wilhelm Marr who employed it strictly with reference to the Jews.[2] Anti-Semitism is religious and racial prejudice and hatred directed against the Jewish people. It is to be distinguished from anti-Judaism, which is opposition to the religion of the Jews (like anti-Mormon means disagreement with Mormonism but not antagonism toward Mormon people as such) or anti-Zionism, which is opposition to aspects of or the very existence of the state of Israel. We see anti-Judaism in the New Testament on the part of early Christians just as we see anti-Christianity on the part of many Jews. This face-off was inevitable given the competing concepts under debate. The early Christians were hardly anti-Semitic since they were in fact also Jews.[†] The unfortunate and tragic reality is, however, that anti-Judaism and anti-Zionism may easily and unconsciously become anti-Semitism.

On the surface anti-Semitism displays common psychological and sociological aberrations—prejudice, stereotyping, and scapegoating. Stereotypes are sets of characteristics allegedly possessed by a population or institution or class and assumed to be present in all members of the class. Consider American stereotypes of the Japanese, the blacks, and

◊ ◊ ◊

* The Semitic peoples are, of course, broader than simply the Jews (Shem, the oldest son of Noah, being the progenitor) and include the Arab people, the Maltese (their language is the only Semitic language spoken by a European Christian population), the Syrians, etc.[3] The Canaanites who possessed Palestine before and during the time of the patriarchs were Hamites not Semites.

† This does not rule out the possibility that a Jew can be anti-Semitic, as was Karl Marx, but is only to say that the New Testament documents provide no basis for imputing ethno-centric prejudice or racist theories to the apostle Paul and company.

the Jews. Unquestionably there are ethnic, religious, and generational tensions across the entire spectrum of human experience. AntiSemitism is similar to hatred for Gypsies, Croats, or Serbs, Mexicans or Puerto Ricans, Swedes or Norwegians. Venomous rivalry exists within Israeli society between European Jews (the whites) and Oriental Jews (the blacks). Intermarriage in Israel is marriage that breaks down the walls between these two groups which are so antithetic and competitive in Israeli society.

Christians have persecuted Jews and Jews have persecuted Christians, and this must be seen in the first instance to be a manifestation of the essential sinfulness and depravity of all human beings. Cain slew Abel and "man's inhumanity to man" becomes endemic. "Nature red with tooth and claw" parallels the human story of violence and conflict. Whoever is on the top of the heap tends to "lord" it over the minorities. "The will to power" fuels the engines of the human enterprise. The Jews have been a conspicuous minority from the beginning (Deuteronomy 7:7).[*]

Although anti-Semitism shares the characteristics of all racial prejudice, it is unique. Only as we understand the singularity of anti-Semitism will we begin to comprehend the Jewish destiny.[†]

THE CAUSES OF ANTI-SEMITISM

I see a people who live apart and do not consider themselves one of the nations (Numbers 23:9b).

There is a certain people dispersed and scattered among the peoples in all the provinces of your kingdom whose customs are different from those of all other people and who do not obey the king's laws; it is not in the king's best interest to tolerate them (Haman to Xerxes, Esther 3:8).

◊ ◊ ◊

[*] I cannot agree with the weighty scholarship of Professor Langmuir of Stanford who has argued that anti-Semitism as such is not found until the eleventh century. It is true, as Langmuir argues, that many of the "irrational fantasies about Jews" seem to take more specific and concrete shape about this time,[4] but we see in Bible times real hatred for the Jews (as in wicked Haman or Antiochus Epiphanes). Some of the anti-Jewish texts cited by Josephus in Against Apion or Justin Martyr's *Dialogue with Trypho* (c. A.D. 140) are more than religious polemic. We sense here image and fantasy as baggage of culture.

[†] I believe with Francois Mauriac that "Anti-Semitism requires an accounting of Christianity." Professor Valentin who taught at Uppsala in Sweden is also correct in asserting that "Anti-Semitism is no longer a problem which concerns only the Jews and their enemies. It concerns everyone."[5]

The Jews are a race apart. They have made laws according to their own fashion, and keep them.—Celsus

If the four wild beasts prophesied by Daniel in Daniel 7 project the four great Gentile world powers (Babylon, Medo-Persia, Greece, and Rome) which would dominate history during "the times of the Gentiles," then Daniel 8 revisits the scene of ferocity and viciousness to indicate that both Medo-Persia and Greece to the Jews would be like domestic animals. This more humane treatment is seen in the Edict of Cyrus in 539 B.C. permitting the return and the surprising benevolence of Alexander the Great to the inhabitants of Jerusalem.[6]

Unfortunately, kind and compassionate treatment of this remarkable people has been the exception rather than the rule. Why anti-Semitism? The roots of resentment and hatred for the Jews are complex and much discussed. Roman poets and philosophers mocked and scorned the Jewish way of life as in the cases of Chaeremon (Nero's tutor), Lysimachus (librarian in Alexandria), Apion, Tacitus, Horace, Martial, Cicero, and Juvenal the satirist.[7] The Jews marched to a different drumbeat, and those who resist conformity are always resented. Christians were in time persecuted for the same reason. Persecution and pressure tended to come in waves—there were periods of great intensity. What caused such outbursts?

Jewish "otherness" was part of their divine appointment. Observing the Sabbath or the food laws or the rite of circumcision[*] set them apart and made them scape-goats whenever some disaster happened. But anti-Semitism goes beyond typical racism and religious bigotry—it is a response to Judaism itself.[†]

A body of data supports the contention that Jews do have a different sociological pattern from their non-Jewish neighbors by virtue of Jewish law—even if Halachaic law is not observed formally by the majority of the Jews in the world. Jews are twice as likely to go to college than Gentiles (reflecting the religious obligation of study) and are five times more likely than Gentiles to be admitted to an Ivy League School. Jews are over represented in the field of science by 231 percent, in psychiatry by 47 percent, in law by 265 percent, in dentistry by 299 percent, and in mathematics by 283 percent. The very terms of their apartness have fostered scholarship and achievement in order to survive, but these have made

◇ ◇ ◇

* This is shared, of course, by Muslims, but resented by the uncircumcised, e.g. Voltaire who was obsessed on the point, thus giving rise to the bizarre notion that anti-Semitism has an erotic component.

† Prager and Telushkin properly argue that the causes of anti-Semitism are the principle elements of Judaism, namely the Jewish conception of God, law, and peoplehood.[8]

them susceptible to jealousy, resentment, and the other prices of "otherness." Thus some people have spoken of the Jews as "the pariahs of privilege."

Not all Jews are the same or think the same in some simplistic sense (for where there are two Jews there are three arguments, as the old saw has it), but the Jews are a strikingly cohesive and resilient people as history everywhere attests. While there is some evidence of an erratic missionary impulse from time to time[*] and while there have always been those who converted to Judaism, proselytizing has never been strong, and to this day seekers are generally turned down three times before any further discussion about conversion to Judaism.

The problem for the Jews has not generally been their aggressiveness in promoting their own religion, but their essential indigestibility among the nations among whom they have been disseminated. The powerful novels of the American Jewish writer, Chaim Potok, wrestle with the tension between identity and assimilation for Jews on the American scene.[†]

In Potok's *The Chosen*, Danny Sanders, son of a Hassidic rabbi, wrestles with maintaining cultural and religious forms so at odds with the times, such as long earlocks and tassels as badges of righteousness. His friend Reuven Malter, who is raised in a more traditional Orthodox Jewish home, grapples with the issues in a slightly different form, but the issue is there. Some, of course, like Moses Mendelssohn in eighteenth-century Germany (grandfather of the composer of Christian music, Felix Mendelssohn), sought integration. Heinrich Heine lamented that "My Jewishness is my misfortune" and felt that his baptism was "the entrance ticket to European culture."

But increasingly overt anti-Semitism made assimilation problematic. Further, the unyielding "closed hermeneutics" of rabbinic teaching set Judaism farther apart in the face of the vigorous growth and pressure of a conversionary religion like Christianity.[‡]

◊ ◊ ◊

[*] Compare Matthew 23:15 and the rabbinic literature that speaks of Abraham and Sarah as master missionaries.[9]

[†] Note especially *The Chosen, The Promise, My Name Is Asher Lev*, and *In the Beginning*.

[‡] The brilliant Jewish scholar of our time, Jacob Neusner, has effectively argued that the Talmudic texts are to be interpreted "by their own intrinsic logic," i.e. the Jews have stood apart not only in life-style but in the very way they reasoned and thought about reality.[10] The resolution to all quandaries and incongruities would come in a future messianic age. In the face of the challenge of fourth-century monk, Aphrahat, who wrote against the Jewish claim for continued divine election, Neusner pointed out "the coded polemic" used by the rabbis who responded and therefore sealed themselves off.

Living out the rabbinic teachings only accentuates and exacerbates "otherness."

What sets anti-Semitism drastically apart from the genocidal victims of history like the Gypsies, Native Americans, Druse, Kurds, Armenians, Bahais, all of whom have suffered beyond description, is the proximity of the Jews to God's redemptive plan for humanity.

Expulsion of Jews from Spain

The expulsion of the Jews from Spain in the fifteenth century under Ferdinand and Isabella demonstrated demonic and evil supernaturalism appealing to the very worst in humankind. The edict of expulsion, effective in March of 1492, shortly before the voyage of Columbus, called for Jews to repent and convert or to leave without their money or to face death. Not since the first and second centuries had Jews faced such a blanket terror, although episodically and in fewer numbers they were sent shipping elsewhere, as from England in 1290. What happened in Spain was a blatant affront to God's purpose.

Christian, Muslim, and Jewish cultures experienced an extraordinary renaissance on the Iberian Peninsula. Isabella of Castile, probably in her time the most powerful ruler in western Europe, joined her kingdom with that of Ferdinand of Aragon and together they took on all comers. They had an exemplary marriage on the whole, were religiously devout, and had significant friendships and relationships with many observant Jews and many conversos (the Jews who had converted). Many Jews lived and prospered in Spain. About 200,000 Jews lived in their domain (2 percent of the population). The king and queen sought to protect the Jews in the 1470s.[11] Jewish physicians and bankers and pawnbrokers were active in the royal court.

There were harsh rivalries among peoples in the fifteenth century, but endemic anti-Semitism stood out and pervaded the culture. Perpetuating the spirit of the great massacres of 1096 in connection with the Crusades, many pillaged the Jews and others called for forced baptisms.

The converso Fernando Rojas wrote La Celestina in 1499 and satirically shared his view that "Isabella's policies . . . [had] destroyed Spain's old social order of Christians, Gentiles and Jews and, with it, all human values for the sake of a superficial national unity."[12]

When the Black Death came, the Jews were blamed. They purportedly poisoned wells, profaned the host, committed ritual murders, and kidnapped children. Any kind of military setback was attributed to the Jews (as when the Jews were blamed for the French defeat in 1870–71). In this irrational climate, many thousands of Jews converted in the fourteenth century, but they were always suspect. Money and power were usually at the bottom of the tension. Limits on interest were set in 1476 and Jews were proscribed in terms of what they could wear. Certain passionate preachers accused the conversos of secretly practicing their former religion. Isabella chose Tomas de Torquemada, an austere Dominican friar, to investigate the situation. An all-out attack on the conversos were launched in 1481, and many were executed.

In implementing her reconquista (the driving out of the Moors from southern Spain), Isabella used fear of Islam and of the outsider Jews to galvanize and unify her forces. Notwithstanding the reluctance of many (including her confessor), Isabella reinstituted the medival inquisition with all of its horrors and abuses under Torquemada. Eradication of the Jewish presence began in certain provinces—not a Jew was left in Andalusia by mid-1484.[13] The total expulsion of all Jews was ordered in 1492 on the pretext of "an international conspiracy among Jews" and up to 200,000 Jews fled to Portugal (from which they soon had to leave), Italy, Greece, Turkey (the sultan of Turkey opened his gates to them), and to North Africa, taking with them their customs and their Ladino dialect (Hispanicized Hebrew, cf. Yiddish or Germanicized Hebrew). What a tragedy. What a collective trauma.[14]

The New Testament and Anti-Semitism

The sad history just chronicled raises the question: Is Christianity by nature anti-Semitic? Some allege that the New Testament documents are anti-Semitic, and sorrowfully some Christians have been prone to anti-Semitism,[*] often mild but nonetheless malevolent. This is our sinfulness and it is altogether inconsistent with the New Testament spirit toward all peoples. Judaeophobia is a very antithesis of Christian faith.[†]

To be sure, Origen articulated the divine punishment theory to explain Jewish suffering, but the clear teaching of the New Testament is that all sinners are equally guilty of deicide, since our sins were laid on Jesus. We were all there when "they crucified our Lord."[‡]

The "displacement theory" by which Israel is totally and finally replaced by the church in the plan and purpose of God (as against the

◊ ◊ ◊

* Some like Rosemary Ruether have argued that anti-Semitism is deeply rooted in Christianity itself.[15]

† As Leon Poliakov, author of the masterful and classic multivolume history of anti-Semitism, paid tribute to Jacob Boehme's benevolent view of the Jews and his confidence in the imminent restoration of the chosen people, he remarked insightfully: "[Boehme's positive view] is typical of Christians at any period (but particularly today) who have studied and thought about the Epistle to the Romans."[16]

‡ F. F. Bruce clearly demonstrated both the Synoptic and Johannine emphasis on the Roman part in Christ's crucifixion and that John's reference to the "Jews" is particularly to the religious establishment of that time.[17]

bipolar view developed in chapter three) may lurch dangerously toward anti-Semitism. Any careless implication that the Jews are superfluous or unrelated to the divine scheme of things is dangerous.[*]

No Christian can be in any sense anti-Semitic and in harmony with what Christianity truly is. Popular anti-Semitism tinges most of us more significantly than we probably realize. We need to analyze our language, our stereotypes, and our attitudes. Anti-Semitism is a sin and has led to suffering beyond what words can tell.

THE CANCER OF ANTI-SEMITISM

And beside that I am a mortal enemy of the Jews.—Sancho Panza in *Don Quixote*

If it be the part of a good Christian to detest the Jews, then we are all good Christians.—Erasmus

It was Jews. It was an insolent race. Spread over the world, they cover its face.—Racine, seventeenth century, in *Esther*, II, 2

I regard the Jewish race as the born enemy of pure humanity and everything that is noble in it.—Richard Wagner

Malignant anti-Semitism has spread uncontrollably through humanity. While not altogether a different disease from earth's perennial tribalisms, anti-Semitism is unique, given the worldwide dispersion of the Jews and their special abiding place in the plan and purpose of God. Leon Poliakov in his *History of Anti-Semitism* delineated three stages in hatred for the Jews:

THREE STAGES OF JEWISH HATRED		
1	**2**	**3**
Anti-Semitism justified theologically—up to the French Revolution	Anti-Semitism justified racially—up to the Holocaust	Anti-Semitism in a new anti-Zionist guise—up to the present.[18]

◊ ◊ ◊

[*] To say that "Luke has written the Jews off" is a serious mistake. Tiede's position that the "many in Israel who will rise and fall" are at the center of the Luke-Acts narrative and that "God is never done with Israel" are more the fact than Haenchen's position that Luke gives us "a final rejection of Israel and its being replaced with the Gentiles.[19]

Hatred of the Jews has ravaged the body of Christ from very early in her existence. The deicide lie made a vicious anti-Semite out of John Chrysostom, probably the finest preacher among the Fathers of the church. Ambrose of Milan steadily lambasted "the perifidious Jew."*

What convenient scapegoats the Jews were as the empire crumbled. That John the Baptist, our Lord, and the apostles did not state or imply at any time the end of the Jews, leaves Christianity with a credibility gap of immense proportions when now the baptized seed of Abraham, Isaac, and Jacob loose themselves from their spiritual forebears. The Qur'an holds that the Jews are cast aside (2:88; 4:46, 52; 5:13, 60, 64, 78), but how can Christians do so?

The denigration of the Old Testament Scriptures has always been part of anti-Semitism. Some of the rabbis have spoken of Higher Criticism with its misrepresentations of the Old Testament as "a higher anti-Semitism."[20] Marcion in the early centuries was not the last who attempted to de-Judaize Christ and Christianity. The neglect of the Old Testament in the pulpit and the dropping of Hebrew as a requirement in seminary preparation for ministry are more subtle symptoms of spiritualizing and docetism. In Islam there is a denial that Jesus really died ("They did not kill him"), and consistently Muslims tend to deny the Holocaust. This is a fast and dangerous track on which one thing leads quickly to another. So when I read Boettner's assertion, "Judaism is a thing of the past—He is through with them as a national group," I wince. This is code language that can open a wrong door. We must come back again and again to the Scriptures and ask: What do they teach?

Anti-Semitism has darkened the minds of many stellar Christian lights, and this should caution us about our views. Savonarola drove the Jews out of Florence. Of course there were always voices that protested such crass violence, such as Richard Simon, the eminent Hebraist, and Blaise Pascal, the philosopher. The most effective preacher of his time in Spain, St. Vincent Ferrer (c. 1400), pled against any use of force in seeking the conversion of the Jews (and was blessed by a supernatural gift of tongues as he spoke to people who did not understand his native Catalan).[21]

Luther

Luther's scatological diatribes against the Jews are all too familiar. The early Luther favored tolerance (note his pamphlet of 1523, "The Jesus was Born a Jew"). But Luther became disillusioned when the Jews did

◊ ◊ ◊

* It becomes clearer as we listen to the strident and shrilll rhetoric of the anti-Semites that Frank Littell's basic thesis is sound: "The cornerstone of Christian anti-Semitism is the superseding or displacement myth that old Israel is written off in favor of New Israel."[22]

not convert, and he turned on them, accusing them of ritual murder and the poisoning of wells. Even the most sympathetic Luther scholars quail at the Reformer's intemperate argumentation. To be sure Luther used inordinately rough language and invective on all whom he opposed, be they peasants, Roman Catholics, or Jews. But his students Jonas and Osiander held out hope for "a common liberated future for Jews and Christians."[23] Contrariwise, in his hateful attitude toward the Jews, Luther became increasingly a child of his times rather than a follower of Jesus the Nazarene, and the architects of the Holocaust would later use Luther's words to support their cause.[*]

Voltaire

France[†] has seen a particularly strong demonization of the Jews across the centuries. A populist anti-Semitism generally prevailed throughout France. Voltaire's cruel sentiments qualify him to be "The High Priest of modern anti-Semitism." Arthur Hertzberg in his brilliant *The French Enlightenment and the Jew* shows Voltaire (for a complexity of reasons) to be angry at both Christians and Jews but particularly mean-spirited toward the Jews, to whom he said:

> You have surpassed all nations in impertinent fables, in bad conduct and barbarism. You deserve to be punished, for this is your destiny.

This is racial anti-Semitism that attributes innate qualities of an unchanging character to the Jews. On the other hand, his sometime secretary, Lessing, argued on behalf of the Jews and doubtless Rousseau's Calvinistic background restrained him to some degree. He spoke of the possibility of "a free state, schools and university where they can speak and argue without danger."

Napoleon

Napoleon exhibits a rather typical ambivalence toward the Jews. In Franz Kobler's splendid study of Napoleon and the Jews, he has shown how in setting out on his Middle-Eastern campaign in 1798, Napoleon saved the Jews of Malta. In Cairo he issued the first statute ever made for the Jews outside of Europe. He referred to the "Jewish nation" and indicated he favored a restitution of the high priesthood. Scriptures were read in the tent of the commander-in-chief, and although unable to capture Acre, he fought for and won Esdraelon, making proclamation: "The prophets foresaw the restoration of the rightful heirs of Pal-

◊ ◊ ◊

* Happily, John Calvin's discourse is quite devoid of such scurrilous and vile "blood libel."
† Italy has been relatively free from anti-Semitism, perhaps because of her anti-clericalism.

estine." He summoned an "Assembly of Jewish Notables" to Paris in 1806 and set up the "Sanhedrin," which he then ordered to revoke all Talmudic strictures. Clearly Napoleon had his own idiosyncratic agenda, political and economic more than religious, but even more significantly, as Emil B. Cohn has pointed out, "The Napoleonic wars and the Congress of Vienna which closed them created a Europe supercharged with unrest." This is the soil in which the Dreyfus Affair would take place.

Anti-Semitism in Poland and Russia

Winds of change were blowing adversely for the Jews in Poland, which had half of the two million Jews in Europe. Tsar Alexander I of Russia was at first quite sympathetic to the Jews in his country, and his advisors, Lewis Way, a British missionary who was burdened for the Jews, and Johann Jung-Stilling, who spoke about the restoration of the Jews in Palestine and the rebuilding of the temple, exerted a very positive influence.[24] In the quagmire of the Napoleonic era, however, the tsar turned against the Jews. The nineteenth century saw many *pogroms* (a Russian word meaning massacre or devastation) in Russia, and in 1881 the May Laws of General Ignatiev drove the Jews into a geographically circumscribed area called "the pale of settlement." The tsar also used the infamous *Protocols of the Elders of Zion*, a notorious anti-Semitic counterfeit, to distract the Russian people from what was going on in Russia. This alleged revelation of a worldwide Jewish conspiracy to seize control of the world has been the centerpiece in the foreign policies not only of Russian and Soviet, but also German and Arab peoples. The *Protocols* are quoted as authority next to the Qur'an at scholarly meetings of Muslims. Dismissed at a famous trial in Switzerland in the 1930s by the presiding judge as "nothing but ridiculous nonsense," their substance has continuing currency. As late as 1979 in the novel *The Raised Curtain* by Yuri Kolesnikov, published by the official Military Publishing House in Moscow, a rabbi allied with Hitler and Mussolini deliberately provoked pogroms so as to compel Jews to go back to Palestine. The *Protocols*, a forgery, was historically, to use Norman Cohn's phrase, a "warrant for genocide." Tragically it still is.

Anti-Semitism in Germany

Germany is a special case, as we shall insist in the next chapter, but inflammatory writing and discourse throughout the nineteenth century and earlier, prepared the way for the tragedies in our century. Writing in 1788, Goethe recognized economic interdependence with the Jews. His character Wilhelm Meister says: "We will tolerate no Jews among us." Kant advocated the euthanasia of the Jew and his disciple Fichte has been called "the first prophet of the Aryan faith."[25] Hegel thought of the Jews as an enslaved people forever; Schopenhauer felt they were an irrelevancy and Schleiermacher opined: "Judaism is long since dead." From Schleiermacher's viewpoint, Christianity relates to Judaism as it does to paganism. This is the rank subsoil of anti-Semitism in which disaster is born. In some cases Jews were protected even though hated, and some philo-Semitism could be found among monied classes.

Anti-Semitism Worldwide

Surely opposing voices were raised. Spener spoke in defense of the Jews; John Wesley started to learn Spanish in order to reach the Jews in Georgia of whom he said: "Some of them seem nearer the mind of Christ than many of those who call Him Lord."[26] John Locke predictably argued for tolerance and Pastor Jurieu (adversary of Bossuet in the eighteenth century) affirmed vigorously: "Jerusalem must be rebuilt for them and that they will be regathered in their land."[27] But the German obsession with purity of blood (as seen in Feuerbach and Richard Wagner),[28] the furies of the French Socialist, Pierre Proudhon, who said that "Jew is the evil element," and the literary anti-Semitism found in English writers like Defoe, Pope, Swift, Fielding, Richardson all reveal a fundamental pathology in human culture. Shakespeare's Shylock is the stereotype although he does speak some good sense. Dickens's Fagin in *Oliver Twist* catered to the stereotype, so Dickens countered with lovely Mr. Riah in *Our Mutual Friend.* Ultimately there come the consequences—as in Stalin who cut down 66 million people, including many Jews through his state-sponsored anti-Semitism.[29]

Anti-Semitic literature sells well in Japan, as shown by Masami Uno's *If You Can Understand Judea, You Can Understand the World,* in which the author finds the Jews responsible for the Great Depression of the 1930s and David Rockefeller a closet Jew. The 1975 United Nations' declaration that Zionism is racism (finally rescinded in December of 1991 with twenty-five Arab nations opposing the measure), the upsurge of the *Pamyat* in the former Soviet Confederacy (with reports of Kiev synagogue attacks and "Hanukka at Kremlin ... [drawing] anti-Semitic taunts"), the controversy over the just disclosed existence of Jewish census records shared with the Nazis in 1940 in France, all reveal a generally high level of anti-Semitic activity both past and present. Academia is still in shock in the wake of the disclosure that now deceased Yale professor and leader in the Deconstructionist Movement, Paul de Man, hid his Nazi past and tried to bury his publication, *The Jews and Contemporary Literature,* in which he argued that Jewish writers are second-rate. But in this as a victim of Waldheimer's disease he only followed Heidegger, Paul Althaus, Kittel, Emanuel Hirsch, and others who walked the Nazi line.

The tragic clashes between blacks and Jews in Brooklyn in the summer of 1991;[30] the position of actress Vanessa Redgrave that "the state of Israel must be overthrown ... there can be no room for such a state";

and Professor Leonard Jeffries of the City College of New York spewing forth his venom against "whites, Jews and the Mafia," along with minister Farrakan of Chicago, are genuine reasons for considerable uneasiness. The persistence of the Ku Klux Klan[31] and its fearmongering along with the story of David Duke and the whole Gerald Winrod-Identity Movement-Aryan Nation syndrome must give pause to all of us. The more sophisticated anti-Semitism of Patrick Buchanan as analyzed by William F. Buckley, Jr. is most disquieting.[32] There are disconcerting developments in the 1990s that make this discussion of anti-Semitism very contemporary.

It is possible to raise the cry "anti-Semitic" precipitously and inaccurately; some construe any reservation concerning the policies of the State of Israel as anti-Semitic. Jews and Gentiles alike may take serious and deeply felt exception to a policy of settlement or a position on land for peace without anti-Semitism. An American can be adamantly opposed to United States's policy on any issue and not be disloyal or unpatriotic. It is important that we distinguish the things which differ here. If opposing some Israeli policy is anti-Semitic, then many Israelis are anti-Semitic.

Nevertheless, the findings of fact are clear and compelling. An ancient animosity and prejudice still is found and is flourishing in our world. Its name is anti-Semitism.

THE CURSE OF ANTI-SEMITISM

I will make you into a great nation and I will bless you: I will make your name great, and you will be a blessing. I will bless those who bless you, and whoever curses you I will curse; and all peoples on earth will be blessed through you (Genesis 12:2–3).

I have lived, Sir, a long time, and the longer I live the more convincing proof I see of this truth; that God governs in the affairs of men.—Benjamin Franklin at the Constitutional Convention of 1787

Our cursory tracing of anti-Semitism barely touches the problem. This scourge is hydra-headed; there is theological anti-Semitism, cultural anti-Semitism, and political anti-Semitism.[33] There is what has been called country-club anti-Semitism. Although arguably there may be some group characteristics (such as the penurious Scot or the emotionally stolid Swede), applying alleged group behavior to individuals is unfair and unjust and is indeed the essence of prejudice (judging beforehand). We all deserve a hearing on the merits of the case (see "For God does not show favoritism" [Acts 10:34ff.; Romans 2:11]). Everyone's ideas should be evaluated one at a time.

When school bus service was dropped in a community in which we lived and a projected carpool excluded a Jewish child, my wife protested and was told by other parents that she and the Jewish family could make their own plans.

We may not be shocked by anti-Semitism but nonetheless keenly disappointed when we see the sickening anti-Semitism of Henry Ford or Charles Lindbergh; or the raucus anti-Semitism of Father Coughlin just prior to the Second World War or Gore Vidal; or the parochial anti-Semitism of Henry Adams; or the barmy anti-Semitism of an Ezra Pound or H. L. Mencken (who as evidence now shows was not only anti-Christian but anti-black and anti-Semitic); or the sly anti-Semitism of a T. S. Eliot or G. K. Chesterton or Hilarie Belloc. Arnold Toynbee's attitude toward the Jews and his reference to "Semitic fossils" troubles us. This is the hard data, and a just and fair God will not allow those who hate His people to escape.

Given the uniqueness of Israel's election and call and the "otherness" that is both the cause and effect of anti-Semitism, we can see that treatment of the Jews is one of many touchstones of divine blessing or cursing. It is not the sole factor in determining blessing or cursing, but our philosophy of history must factor in what Scripture clearly says.

Those who are kind to the Jews and bless them, receive special blessing from God. Contrariwise, those who mistreat and malign God's ancient people will experience a curse from God.

This principle must never be used to justify unfairness to the Palestinians or any other people and justice for all must be our objective.

The Jewish apologist, Manasseh ben Israel, put the matter quite overtly in the mid-seventeenth century: "And do we not see that those Republiques do flourish and much increase in trade who admit the Israelites?"[34] To expunge Jewry from the citizenry is to experience a serious depletion and deprivation.

Curses on Spain

In expelling the Jews from Spain in 1492 (which was not reversed until this century), Ferdinand and Isabella immediately gained booty but in the long-range impoverished Spain intellectually. A case in point is the remarkably productive scholar and statesman, Don Isaac ben Judah Abrabanel, who, forced out of Spain, went on to a brilliant career in Naples and Venice.[35] Spain lost a critical component in her civilization that more tolerant lands were to gain. In her study of this period, Rubin has spoken of the Turkish Sultan Bayezid II, who "marveled greatly at the expelling of the Jews from Spain, since this was to expel its wealth," and she observed that "many Castilians themselves subsequently argued that the sovereigns' expulsion of the Jews and Spain's concomitant loss of skilled fiduciary and business leaders, was responsible for that kingdom's eventual economic decline."[36]

Spain through the risk-taking and wisdom of Ferdinand and Isabella was unquestionably "Europe's premier nation" in the fifteenth and sixteenth centuries. But the cruelties of the Inquisition and of her mistreatment of the Jews weighed on Isabella's mind. In her last years she saw one tragedy after another in her family and nation and "by the late sixteenth century Spain's proudest moments were behind it . . . its Armada was destroyed by the English in 1588."[37] And Spain, which staked out such vast holdings and wealth in the New World, was prostrated for centuries in weakness and turmoil. Was she not under a curse?

Curses on Germany

A similar analysis of Germany's great loss in her reducing the Jewish population to .06 percent shows that major cities lost up to 80 percent of their qualified physicians and that the worlds of music and science were irreversibly reduced by the German defeat in World War II.[38] Racism of any kind undermines and undercuts the vitality of any culture, but anti-Semitism is a particularly vicious and fiendish blow to the well-being of any society.

Blessings and Curses on Great Britain

Benjamin Disraeli's father had his children baptized, but Disraeli was always proud of his Jewishness. This future Prime Minister of Great Britain believed that Christianity made a completed Jew, but this diminished in no sense his pride in being Jewish.

In the often chronicled incident in Parliament, a certain member rose and cast aspersion on the Jewishness of Disraeli, to which Disraeli drawing himself up to his full height and with considerable indignation made reply: "Sir, you accuse me of being a Jew and I am proud to answer to the name, and I would remind you that half of Christendom worships a Jew and the other half a Jewess. And I would also remind you that my forefathers were worshipping the one true and living God while yours were naked savages eating acorns in the woods of Britain."

The four-thousand-year civilization of this people and their undeniable genius have made them an incalculable asset in any national life.

Great Britain, a friend to the Jews since Cromwell opened the door to the Jews betrayed them in the White Paper of 1939, the first of an unfortunate series of such acts. What has been the experience of the British since the World War II? Is not the pattern of blessing and cursing clear? Do not the Lord's "brothers" become a crucial point of reference and the basis for judgment? (Matthew 25:31–46).

Blessings on the United States

The United States has often been guilty of jingoistic diplomacy and many sins, but from the arrival in this country of twenty Sephardic Jews fleeing persecution in Brazil in the seventeenth century, this country has been overall a haven for the Jews and a place where they have enjoyed security and safety. I believe God has blessed the United States for blessing the Jews. I reiterate, this is only one factor in the welter of factors that must be taken into account, but it is a factor of importance and is consistent with the revealed principles in terms of which a sovereign God deals with the nations ("Righteousness exalts a nation, but sin is a disgrace to any people" [Proverbs 14:34]).

What becomes so incongruous and unacceptable is any form of anti-Semitism among those who profess adherence and loyalty to the Christian gospel. How can any Christian be other than loving and grateful for the Jewish people who have given us our Bible and our Savior, and who have such a special and abiding place in the unfolding plan and purpose of God? Ogden Nash thought it was "odd of God to choose the Jews," but it has been further said by another:

> But not so odd
> As those who choose
> The Jewish God
> And spurn the Jews.[39]

Yet the darkest chapters in the history of this suffering people must still be examined.

CHAPTER

THE UNIMAGINABLE
ATROCITY OF
THE HOLOCAUST

Land where shall Israel leave her bleeding feet?
And when shall Zion's songs again seem sweet,
And Judah's melody once more rejoice.
The hearts that leaped before its heavenly voice?
Tribes of the wandering foot and weary heart.
How shall ye flee away and be at rest?
The wild dove hath her nest—the fox his cave—
Mankind their country—Israel but the grace.

Lord Byron

I looked at the earth, and it was formless and empty;
and at the heavens, and their light was gone.
I looked, and there were no more people.

Jeremiah 4:23, 25a

The suicidal self-destructiveness of the European state system in two
world wars gave lie to the notion of superior Western rationality,
while the distinction between civilized and barbarian
that was instinctive to Europeans in the 14th century
was much harder to make after
the Nazi death camps.

Frances Fukuyama in *The End of History and the Last Man*

T HERE IS AN INDISPENSABLE AXIOM of journalism—"Jews are news"—according to Charles Krauthammer, a senior editor at *Time* magazine.[1] Although comparatively infinitesimal numerically (one-tenth of 1 percent of the world's population yet holders of sixteen Nobel Prizes), the Jewish people and their history are focal for many reasons, several of which we have already explored. The scope and sweep of her history (as most creatively and magnificently portrayed in James Michener's *The Source*, as an example) both thrill and appall us.

Two epochal events, and it would not be hyperbole to say earth-shaking events, have been at the center of the global village in this century and seriously affected the Jews and their destiny. They both stand in symbiotic relationship to worldwide dispersion and anti-Semitism. They are the Holocaust under Nazi Germany and the establishment of the State of Israel in 1948.[2]

Anyone writing or speaking of the Holocaust must feel what the Jews themselves have described as "the dialectical tension between speech and silence." There is a danger in vulgarization and trivialization or what Yehuda Bauer was concerned to call "the popularization of the Holocaust."[3] The conspiracy of silence about the Holocaust (or the *Shoah*, to use the Hebrew word) did not end with the closing of the death camps. The unbelievability of the horrors of the Holocaust and the indescribable nightmare of its victims and survivors made comment almost seem irreverent.

The Holocaust has indeed been exploited by politicians and others and even denied by "revisionists." This last development is particularly galling and inexplicable. No event in Jewish history and few events in human history as a whole have been more massively researched than the Holocaust, and yet its reality continues to be denied in some circles. That approximately 50,000,000 persons died in World War II; that 12,000,000 (Jews, Gypsies, Poles, and others) died in Hitler's death camps; that 6,000,000 Jews were murdered in the years of the Nazi Empire (1933–45)—these are undeniable and clearly substantiated facts. The Holocaust must be seen as a central event in human history. And indeed long-hidden Soviet documents are suggesting that the Holocaust death toll may be even higher.[4]

Some believe the Holocaust never happened. A character in Garry Trudeau's popular *Doonesbury* comic strip argued that the Holocaust was "a hoax . . . pure fiction . . . a Zionist sob story."[5]

Arthur R. Butz, professor of electrical engineering and computer science at Northwestern University, has gained a following by maintaining that the Holocaust is "a monstrous lie" in his 1977 volume, *The Hoax of the Twentieth Century*. French author Robert Faurisson and British historian David Irving (author of *Churchill's War*) are of the same ilk. In what can aptly be termed a "macabre battle," the Nazis have denied that the extermination camps ever existed and groups like the Liberty Lobby and the Carto network obstinately deny that these atrocities ever took place.*

The Institute for Historical Review (which belongs to the Liberty Lobby) offered $50,000 to anyone who could prove Jews were gassed in Auschwitz death camp. A Holocaust survivor waged a five-year battle in the courts and received $90,000 in damages from the Institute.[6] Controversies continue over Holocaust Studies Programs in schools and the rights of those who claim genocide never happened.[7] We are dealing here with the most vicious anti-Semitism, with those of whom Elie Wiesel has correctly said, "They are normally deranged . . . they have no basis except viciousness and hatred of everything Jewish."

Genocide (a term invented by Raphael Lemkin in this century) is a proper description of what the Turks did to the Armenians, or the Japanese in the Rape of Nanking, or Stalin, Mao Tse-tung, and Pol Pot in their countries, or the Serbs in Bosnia. History is replete with testimonies to ghoulish human depravity as seen in the fate of people of color on several continents, or Native Americans in North and South America, or the Aborigines in Australia.

The word *Holocaust* was first used in the late 1950s to refer to the experience of European Jewry. Their experience is "uniquely unique," and Hitler's "final solution" was of such a magnitude of evil in its aim to destroy all Jews and Jewish civilization in Europe as to make comparison of the Holocaust with anything else obscene.[8]

◊ ◊ ◊

* The American evangelical historian David A. Rausch has rendered truth an invaluable service by his scholarly exposure of these hate groups who argue that the whole notion of the Holocaust is trumped up to give Jewry reparations for sufferings that never occurred.[9]

The Jews of Europe were peculiarly vulnerable— helpless in the sense that they were not a nation, had no military. The world was not prepared for what happened—there was no precedent. In what comes closest, the Turks massacred many Armenians (half of the Armenians in Anatolia) but did not touch the Armenians in Istanbul and other places. When Konski reported to Supreme Court Justice Felix Frankfurter what was happening to the Jews in Poland, he responded. "I am unable to believe you." The Holocaust is more than "another human-rights violation."

The depth and duration of the hatred, the diabolic plan ("We ask nothing of the Jews except that they disappear") and the irreversible result of this Jewish Gehenna have made Auschwitz the metaphor and paradigm of evil.

There really is no analogy in abortuaries, Hiroshima, Dresden, or My Lai. The Holocaust is without parallel.

THE SUPREME POGROM

How long, O LORD? Will you forget me forever? How long will you hide your face from me? How long must I wrestle with my thoughts and every day have sorrow in my heart? How long will my enemy triumph over me? (Psalm 13:1–2).

My eyes fail from weeping, I am in torment, my heart is poured out on the ground because my people are destroyed, because children and infants faint in the streets of the city. All your enemies open their mouths wide against you; they scoff and gnash their teeth and say, "We have swallowed her up. This is the day we have waited for; we have lived to see it" (Lamentations 2:11, 16).

To forget the Holocaust is as serious a problem as denying its reality. For this reason "thou shalt tell" has become imperative for the survivors. A massive literature has been built, and efforts like the video project of the Yale Archive for Holocaust Testimonies with its preservation of actual oral witnesses are critical.[10]

I shall never personally escape the emotional and spiritual experience of Yad Vashem in Jerusalem, the center of Holocaust studies in Israel. The experience was all the more shaking because it began with the inspection of the exhibits with a survivor of Treblinka who recognized familiar faces and was unable to complete the examination.

The survivors, now becoming aged, have had to cope with physical, psychological, emotional, and spiritual devastation impossible to relate. At first many of them were unable to tell or hear of it. Memories of such degradation, starvation, torture, and even cannibalism have painful repercussions. Reading of such material can assist us in a resensitization of our own spirits. The United States Holocaust Memorial Museum on Raoul Wallenberg Place in Washington, D.C., has three floors of permanent exhibits telling the entire story of the Holocaust and its unspeakable evil, "to ensure that Americans in every generation will come to remember the Holocaust as a catastrophic failure of humanity and a dire warning about the fragility of freedom."

Generally the causes of the Holocaust have been of limited and parochial interest to British and American historians, and have been repressed and revised by German, Polish, and Russian writers.[11] But there have recently come some encouragements not the least of which is the opening of the first permanent Holocaust memorial in Germany— the villa where the Wannsee Conference was held on January 20, 1942, and where such fateful decisions were made about the future of the Jews. The Red Cross has just offered tracing services for families of victims out of the National Archives, most of which are new names.[12]

Books and films like *The Diary of Anne Frank*, Claude Lanzman's *Shoah*, NBC's *Holocaust* series broadcast in Germany in 1979, powerful novels like David Grossman's *See Under Love,* and regrettably the resurgence of neo-Nazism are all part of kindling *Yom Ha Shoah*, "Days of Remembrance." The movie *Triumph of the Spirit* tells the true story of the survival of the Greek Jew, Shlomol Arouch, who literally punched his way through Auschwitz. The deeply moving film *Europa, Europa* is the factual narrative of a Polish boy of Jewish descent who survived.

A new semi-documentary film by the Polish director Andrzej Wajda tells the story of the Jewish pediatrician Dr. Janusz Korczak who stayed with his orphans in the Warsaw Ghetto and perished with them at Treblinka.[13] Movie director Steven Spielberg's Academy Award-winning film *Schindler's List*, the true story of an Austrian businessman who saved 1500 Krakow Jews from extermination in Nazi death camps, has stirred the emotions of many Americans and Europeans.

Elie Wiesel, almost peerless as a chronicler of the Holocaust, laments the danger of forgetting and cites the passage in the Colombian Nobel Prize-winning novelist Gabriel Garcia Marquez's classic, *One Hundred Years of Solitude*, in which a whole village was under a curse, and the curse was that they forgot.[14] We must not forget the Holocaust because the Holocaust was not a chance mishap that the Germans didn't really mean. Anti-Semitism is endemic. Jews always sit on the brink of the volcano, and it erupted in Europe in the twentieth century with a brutality and violence that must leave the world shaken and forever unnerved.

Adolph Hitler

Adolph Hitler, who came to power in 1933, became a vicious anti-

Semite in Vienna, which had always been a hotbed of anti-Semitism of a particularly virulent strain. His pathological hatred of the Jews was the engine that gave thrust to his Nietzschian "will to power." In the political vacuum and economic nightmare that beset the Weimar Republic in postwar Germany, Hitler took advantage of deadlock; and after becoming Chancellor on January 30, 1933, it took him only eight weeks to consolidate his power and begin his attack on the Jews.

Paul Johnson shared some of Hitler's diatribes that reflected the Nazi and new German state policy: "I shall have gallows erected, in Munich for example in the Marienplatz, as many as traffic permits. Then the Jews will be hanged, one after another, and they will stay hanging until they stink. As soon as one is untied, the next will take is place, and that will go on until the last Jew in Munich is obliterated. Exactly the same thing will happen in the other cities until Germany is cleansed of its last Jew."[15]

Hitler's *Mein Kampf* ("My Struggle") itself reflects the implacable Jew-hatred that issued in "the final solution."

The World Turns Its Back

The Nuremberg Laws of 1935 stripped Jews of their basic rights. Hitler had opened Dachau seven weeks after he took power. More than 200,000 Jews had already fled. The thousand-year Reich was flying high. The murder of a Nazi diplomat in Paris by a young Jew gave ostensible pretext for Kristal Nacht in November of 1938. With the burning of synagogues, destruction of Jewish property (for which Jews were blamed and heavily fined), 20,000 more Jews were sent to the concentration camps. Hitler's efforts at Aryanization were known to all—his constant references to the Jews as no better than vermin were not hidden.

In the late 1930s medieval bigotry returned in the new context of modern militaristic dictatorship. The Fourth Lateran Council had ordered Jews 700 years earlier to wear a yellow Star of David as a badge of shame, and Pope Eugenius IV in 1442 issued a decree that "From now on, and for all time, Christians shall not eat or drink with the Jews, nor admit them to feasts, nor cohabit with them, nor bathe with them." Did the general population know what was happening as the noose tightened around the Jewish populace? Gordon J. Horwitz has documented what life was like around the concentration camps. Other than for a tiny minority, the masses chose to turn their backs on what was taking place. "They failed to see that in turning their backs on the events occurring in their midst they quietly acquiesced in the killing."[16] Many worked in the camps themselves. The facts indicate that the "myth of the innocent" was indeed a fabrication.

The convening of the international conference on the refugee problem at Evian, France, in July of 1938, was a cruel hoax. The nations of the world (with the exception of Australia and the Dominican Republic) would not relax immigration quotas. Nobody wanted the Jews. As Hitler expanded his frontiers and furthered his diabolical designs, the world avoided the Jews and in fact abandoned European Jewry to their fate at the hands of a lunatic.

The Final Solution

At the Wannsee Conference in January of 1942, Reinhard Heydrich, chief of the security police, led in the completion of plans for the "final solution" to the Jewish problem—the liquidation of all Jews in German-held territory. The *Einsatzgruppen,* or mobile killing units, were not working efficiently enough so that now the entire German state apparatus and the SS were mobilized in the most savage butchery ever witnessed—the total liquidation of European Jewry. When Heydrich was assassinated in Czechoslovakia, the community of Lidice near Prague was completely destroyed with all of its inhabitants.

The nineteen major camps and killing centers became the milieu for those who had been uprooted, transported, tormented, and were now to be exterminated.[*] It is with respect to these approximately 6,000,000 victims that we are saying we must not forget them. No wonder Israel has a "Masada Complex." Itzhak Katznelson's elegy *The Song of the Slaughtered Jewish People* is an appropriate jeremiad. There were less than twenty years between *Mein Kampf* and the final solution. Elie Wiesel lamented that only the killers were interested in Jewish children, not the friends. The SS killers would go out after dinner to kill children sneaking out of the ghettos to find bread.[17] Neville Chamberlain's Munich led to the invasion of Czechoslovakia and Franklin Delano Roosevelt's Evian made possible the Crystal Night.

And the legacy continues in the lives of the children of the survivors. Said one: "I am a prize exhibit of the everlasting impact of the Holocaust. Everything my parents experienced and failed to come to terms with has been handed down to me and via me to my children (nightmares, overprotectiveness, fearfulness, endless commemoration)."[18]

How can we be indifferent to the final plea of Mordechai Anielewicz, twenty-one-year-old leader of the Warsaw ghetto uprising: "Aware that

◊ ◊ ◊

[*] The destruction process has been detailed by Professor Raul Hilberg in his monumental *The Destruction of the European Jews.*[19,20,21,22]

our days are numbered we urge you: remember how we have been betrayed."[23]

THE INSIDIOUS PATHWAY

Will evildoers never learn—those who devour my people as men eat bread and who do not call on the LORD? . . . Oh, that salvation for Israel would come out of Zion! When the Lord restores the fortunes of his people, let Jacob rejoice and Israel be glad! (Psalm 14:4, 7).

Is it nothing to you, all you who pass by? Look around and see. Is any suffering like my suffering that was inflicted on me, that the LORD brought on me in the day of his fierce anger?. . . Moreover, our eyes failed, looking in vain for help; from our towers we watched for a nation that could not save us (Lamentations 1:12; 4:17).

How could the Holocaust happen? How could the brilliant culture of enlightened Germany that has given us Kant, Beethoven, Goethe, and Thomas Mann also spawn a Hitler, a Himmler, and a Heydrich? How could even the most depraved human beings perpetrate such monstrous barbarities as are voluminously documented in the fast-growing and irrefutable evidence accumulating as the indictment of the centuries?[24]

Why did so few in Germany protest? Where was the Christian church in all of this? How could cruel criminals like Adolf Eichmann, Josef Mengele, and Klaus Barbie, "the butcher of Lyon," continue unabated? Why did the world do virtually nothing when it knew what was happening? Why did the United States freeze its European immigration quotas at this time? Why did Britain sharply decrease certificates for British-occupied Palestine? Why was the exit door barred from without?

Some have alleged that the Jews themselves were unbelievably passive and nonresistant. One son of a survivor complained, "I can't understand their sheeplike acquiescence.[25] Is this a factual representation? In a searing piece of Israeli self-criticism, historian Tom Segev argued that Zionist leadership was not all that concerned about the fate of the Jews in Europe and that David Ben-Gurion used the "black hole" of the Holocaust more for partisan political advantage than anything else.[26] The Kastner Affair in the early fifties exposed a raw nerve in Israel as it grappled with the issues as to whether bargaining with the Nazis for escape was tantamount to betrayal.

Emil Fackenheim, a leading Jewish philosopher of our time, in his epochal *To Mend the World*, argued that the moral debasement of the Nazi nightmares defies all known categories and is beyond the scope of reason and language and but underscores the moral ruin of Western culture. The root problem is the spiritual problem of the human race.[27] David Rausch most helpfully quoted Otto Friedrich:

> The evidence of Auschwitz has demonstrated many things about humanity. It has demonstrated that men (and women) are capable of committing every evil the mind can conceive, that there is no natural or unwritten law that says of any atrocity whatever: "This shall not be done."[28]

So much for any lurking vestiges of belief in the inherent goodness of human nature and the inevitability of human progress.

The Roots of Hate

But we need to be more case-specific. The Holocaust was conceived and carried out in the heart of Christendom. Germany since the Reformation had been at the very center of professing Christianity. German universities had set the pace and tone for biblical scholarship (sometimes positively and sometimes negatively). German technology reigned supreme for decades. J. Willard O'Brien was right when he asserted that the Holocaust was planned, supervised, and executed by university men and women who were trained before Hitler came to power (described by Franklin Littell as "technically competent barbarians").[29] But how could this people come to see Adolph Hitler as savior and lord and the Jew as the devil?

The anti-Semitic atmosphere pervasive in central Europe in the early days of the twentieth century and before was the subsoil out of which emerged this grotesque anomaly. The slave-labor utilization, the gas chambers, the euthanasia, and the experimental programs all found root in long-standing anti-Semitism. Germany, as the previous chapter demonstrated, was not unique in harboring deep and destructive resentment of the Jews. Anti-Semitism* was a popular aspiration—a demonic hatred rising spontaneously in any environment.[30]

Many years before Hitler, Martin Luther had castigated the Jews, advocating that Germany be rid of them by sending them all back to Palestine! Hitler quoted often from Luther's vicious tirade of 1543, entitled *The Jews and Their Lies*. Luther called for the burning of synagogues and the prohibition of rabbinic activity. The pathological anti-Semitism of Nazi Germany drank deeply at these springs.[†]

The early, ugly nationalism in Germany is vividly described by Paul Johnson in his new and powerful *The Birth of the Modern*, "They formed

◊ ◊ ◊

* Sholom Aleichem's dark novel, *The Bloody Hoax*, draws on a real case, the Beiliss blood libel trial in which an innocent Jewish man was accused of murdering a gentile boy. The novel was made into a Yiddish play well entitled "Hard to Be a Jew."[31]

the world's first youth movement, wore their hair long, grew beards—for them a symbol of their Teutonic race—and at their first mass rally in Wartburg in 1817, they reintroduced medieval book burning."[32] The authoritarian nature of Bismarckian society had an overlay of Jew-hatred,[33] and thus when Bismarck, the kaiser, and von Hindenburg were gone, "most Germans fell in with the youth gang mode of authority represented by Hitler."[34] Hitler's obsession with the Jewish problem (*Judenfrage*) tapped into the continuing "syphilis of anti-Semitism."[*]

We must not pass over the deep internal struggle of many German Jews with respect to their own identity. Many sought assimilation. Both Reformed Judaism and the Reconstructionism of Mordecai Kaplan were efforts to find some quasi-religious footing for the Jews in German society. Karl Marx is an example of the kind of Jewish self-hatred that arose in this soil. Baptized in the State Church for pragmatic reasons only, Marx ultimately moved to a smoldering and bitter anti-Semitism. Heinrich Heine, the noted poet and writer, went through a Judaizing period after "a painful reading of Basnage's *History of the Religion of the Jews*." He came to loathe the patience of the Jews under suffering and started to write a novel in this period, *Rabbi*, in which a character speaks: "Comrades in exile, nomads, my unhappy friends."[35] But his search for viable Jewish identity was futile. German Jewry lived uneasily but was not prepared for the avalanche of violence that ensued.

Certainly there was religious protest from Protestants and Catholics as the sick scenario unfolded. The Barmen Declaration of 1934 represented opposition in Germany, and the Fano Conference in Denmark the same year brought several ecumenical groups together to join in a "church struggle" against Hitler and his treatment of the Jews. The fact is that both inside and outside Germany, particularly in the United States, and Britain, Arthur Morse's accusation in *While Six Million Died* must be seen as essentially accurate: there was "complicity in the murder by inaction, based on ill-will and stupidity."[36]

◊ ◊ ◊

† (previous page) Luther's view of the relationship of the church and state led him to support the nobility in the Peasant's Revolt and to move against the Jews, because as Littell has well argued, what was heresy was also treason against the state and therefore to be forcefully put down. This must be seen in stark contrast with Roger Williams and the Providence Agreement in which full freedom of conscience was to be allowed all people, and no one was to violate "the consciences of the Jews."[37] Martin Luther's trusted colleague, Martin Bucer, shared the same fomenting sentiments, but his antagonist, Philip of Landgrav, evidences a more moderate position with respect to the Jews.

* The mean-spirited caricatures of Jews in *Grimm's Fairy Tales* are part of the picture (e.g. *The Jew in the Thistles*).

Of course there were voices of warning raised in and outside of Germany as Hitler's hoards gained momentum, but they were not many. Martin Heidegger, once again rising in popularity in this country, is not apparently penalized for his Nazi past. He joined the Nazi Party in Germany in the early 1930s, made speeches praising Hitler and was rewarded with high academic position at Freiburg University.[38] The Arabs had their own version of the final solution as Haj Amin al-Husseini, Grand Mufti of Jerusalem, fled to Germany in 1941 to get Hitler's help "to do to the Jews in the Middle East what Hitler was doing to the Jews in Europe."

Indifference of the World

Thus with the British betrayal in the White Paper of 1939 backing away from the Balfour Declaration, and the deeply entrenched anti-Semitism in the U. S. State Department,[39] we have a shameful chronicle. President Roosevelt was coldly indifferent to put the best face on it[40] (and mildly anti-Semitic and ill-informed, according to Paul Johnson's evaluation)[41] and the American people were, according to four polls taken when Hitler stepped up his persecution of the Jews, 71 to 85 percent opposed to increasing immigration quotas to help the refugees. Where was Christian concern?

The 20,000 Jews left in the Warsaw ghetto were led by adolescents. That battle lasted longer than the Battle of France. Yet from the beginning the American press gave minimal coverage to what Hitler was doing to the Jews. It was never front page. Although the exact data have been debated, it seems clear that by the summer of 1942 the nature of what Hitler was doing was made known to the West. H. G. Wells the historian asked: "What is the reason that in every country where Jews reside, sooner or later, anti-Semitism arises?"[42] President Roosevelt seemingly responded to the Holocaust by saying: "Tell your leaders (the Polish underground) that we shall win the war." (The Bermuda Conferences of April were intended only to relieve pressure for nonaction.)

The Vatican and Pope Pius XII did virtually nothing,[*] although Pope John Paul II, the first Pope to speak of Israel by name, uses the Hebrew word *Shoah* for the Holocaust, and did visit Auschwitz. Just recently the Roman Catholic Church has abolished a Bavarian pilgrimage closely linked to the murder of the Jews in the Middle Ages.[43] In this lack of protest the Roman Catholic Church must hang its head in shame with the others.

◊ ◊ ◊

* Rolf Hochmuth's famous *The Deputy* demonstrates this.[44] For the longest time the Vatican refused to recognize the state of Israel; only in 1994 did the Vatican and Israel begin diplomatic relations.

The lack of a unified resistance movement among the Jews is an undeniable fact and bears analysis. Yet Bruno Bettelheim's "death instinct" thesis that the Jews should have fought back harder is difficult to accept. Although he himself spent a year in Dachau and Buchenwald, his is an egregious oversimplification.[45] Viktor E. Frankl, another distinguished psychiatrist and a prisoner at Auschwitz for three years, sees it differently,[46] as did Jean Amery who took his own life finally but not before giving us a powerful and profound testimony.[47] Read about the last voyage of the *Struma* in which 769 refugees drowned at sea after being refused entry into Palestine. Read until you weep about the 900 refugees on the *St. Louis* who stopped off at Miami and were refused entrance and then were refused entry into Cuba in 1939. Read John Bierman's *Odyssey*, the last great escape from Nazi-dominated Europe, 500 Jews crowded on the decrepit paddle steamer, the *Pentcho*, desperately seeking to find their way down the Danube from Bratislava, capital of the Nazi puppet state of Slovakia. They suffered shipwreck, starvation, and internment. "Yet they survived!"[48] Read *Hasidic Tales of the Holocaust* to realize what these people did when the only way out seemed to be up the chimneys of the camps.[49] In the midst of such cataclysmic despair and desperation, they cherished a hope.

"In the Nuremburg War-Crime Trials a witness appeared who had lived for a time in a grave in a Jewish grave-yard, in Wilna, Poland. It was the only place he—and many others—could live, when in hiding after they had escaped the gas chamber. In a grave nearby a young woman gave birth to a baby-boy. The eighty-year-old gravedigger, wrapped in a linen shroud, assisted. When the new-born child uttered his first cry, the old man prayed: 'Great God, hast Thou finally sent the Messiah to us? For who else than the Messiah Himself can be born in a grave?' But after three days the man saw the child sucking his mother's tears because she had no milk for him."[50]

This book is a study of the hope of Israel. Never since biblical times have Israel's hopes been more unlikely of fulfillment than in the *Shoah* (Holocaust). I agree here with Paul Johnson: "The first World War made the Zionist state possible. The Second World War made it essential."[51]

THE SEARCH FOR PREVENTION

My soul is in anguish. How long, O Lord, how long? (Psalm 6:2).

Remember, O LORD, what has happened to us; look, and see our disgrace . . . Why do you always forget us? Why do you forsake us so long? (Lamentations 5:1, 20).

I know you will not believe me. I know, but you must.—Zalman Gradowsi in Auschwitz[52]

Against the Jews

The ceaselessly simmering cauldrons of anti-Semitic hatred inevitably boil over. Our century has witnessed a climactic eruption. The British man of letters Hilaire Belloc (1870–1953), a notorious anti-Semite, predicted the Holocaust in his book *The Jews* (1922) in which he also characterizes the Balfour Declaration as "a crime for which the British government would pay dearly." The story of the Lodz ghetto in Poland is typical in showing that Polish anti-Semitism prepared the way for and continued to follow in the fate of the 200,000 Jews crowded into the squalid two-square-mile area allotted to them.[53] We have already spoken of the Jihad Moquades of the Grand Mufti of Jerusalem, a co-conspirator with Hitler in the destruction of the Jews.

The Jews as sinners like us all have themselves been outrageously intolerant and highly bigoted in some contexts. We have only to consider the Jewish Defense League led by the late Rabbi Meir Kahane and aspects of the intifada to realize that. Israeli laws and policies have not always been fair to minority segments of population. Israeli complicity in Lebanese camp massacres at Sabra and Shatila was recognized even by the Israeli Supreme Court. A prominent Israeli religious leader, Rabbi Israel Hess, writing in the official magazine of Bar-Ilan University students, used the title "Genocide: A Commandment of the Torah." He advocated the extermination of the Arabs in Israel as the descendants of the Amalekites.[54] Rabbi Ginsburg justified terrorism for his students on the basis that "Jewish blood is not the same as Arab blood."[55] Rabbi Israel Ariel has argued that only the killing of a Jew is murder and that killing of a non-Jew is not punishable by society.[56] There are factions in Israel that argue against the idea that Jews and Gentiles are equal and who hold that Gentiles are more beast than human.[57] The sobering fact is that the persecuted so quickly become the persecutors. Hatred is a damnable cancer virtually endemic in the human spirit, and this is what makes fighting continuing anti-Semitism so difficult.

The kind of Jew-hatred that crystallized in the Holocaust may be on occasion more subtle, then more surly, and then again more sinister. It has many faces. We see it in the prominent French politician Le Pen who rode a crest of anti-foreigner bigotry and in prominent writers like Henry Miller and Ernest Hemingway, who exert great influence long after their deaths through plays and prose. Kurt Vonnegut accomplished his own ends by arguing that the firebombing of Dresden is "the greatest massacre in European history" (extensive damage and the loss of 35,000 lives).[58] Joseph Campbell, mogul of myth and darling of Public Television, was a bantering anti-Semite and a disappointing racist.[59] The anti-Semitic attitudes of the British Prime Minister before and early on in World War I, Herbert H. Asquith, are well-known, and the tapes of former President Nixon are appalling. And what shall we say about the anti-Semitic cabals of black leaders like Minister Farrakan, Malcolm X, or Jesse Jackson? How distressing to learn that the little French priest who wrote the classic *Diary of a Country Priest* was in point of fact a proto-Fascist who followed Edouard Drumont (1844–1917), "the acknowledged father of modern French anti-Semitism."[60]

Even more difficult to identify and analyze is the dispute between Meyer Levin and Lillian Hellman over the forms in which *The Diary of Anne Frank* should be presented. Both Levin and Hellman were Jews, but Hellman argued that *The Diary* was "too Jewish" and should be expurgated.[*]

With the Jews

Yet there have been through history bold and courageous individuals, both Jews and Gentiles, who have protested the anti-Semitic scourge. Corrie ten Boom, memorialized through *The Hiding Place* and now through a museum in Haarlem in the Netherlands, bears gracious testimony to Christian principle. Maximilian Kolbe, the heroic priest, spent his last hours in Block 18 in Auschwitz. The Avenue of the Righteous at Yad Vashem bears eloquent testimony to many who were dedicated to the preservation of the Jews when their friends were negligible. Dietrich Bonhoeffer's solidarity with the Jews is well-known. He rightly maintained: "Christianity must not only defend Judaism, but the fate of Christianity is linked to the fate of Judaism."[61] This honor roll must include names like the evangelical scholars G. Douglas Young, David A. Rausch, and many others.

Franklin Littell quoted Joep Westerweel, a Dutch Plymouth Brother, and a martyr:

> Anybody who takes part in the persecution of the Jews, whether voluntarily or against his will, is looking for an excuse for himself. Some cannot give up a business deal, others are doing it for the sake of their families; and the Jewish professors must disappear without protest, for the sake of the university. . . . I have to go through these difficult days without breaking, but in the end my fate will be decided and I shall go like a man.[62]

Philip Hallie's book *Lest Innocent Blood Be Shed* tells the story of the little commune of Le Chambon-sur-Ligon in France and of the efforts of Andre and Magda Trocme and other citizens who saved 5,000 Jews

◊ ◊ ◊

[*] William Styron's *Sophie's Choice* has shown the grave dangers of an "anti-historical approach to the Holocaust and revisionist denials of Nazi evil."[63] These are difficult misrepresentations to combat and are very widespread in their influence and impact.

The Unimaginable Atrocity of the Holocaust

from death during World War II (portrayed also in the film *Weapons of the Spirit*). Douglas Huneke's *The Moses of Rovno* narrates the gripping story of Fritz Graebe, the German Christian, who risked his life to lead hundreds of Jews to safety. Because he testified at the Nuremberg Trials, he was hounded out of postwar Germany and lives today in the Bay Area of California. In *The Doctor and the Damned*, Dr. Albert Haas told of his experience both as French Resistence spy and as a doctor in several concentration camps. Known as Hungarians, both he and his wife were in fact Jews.

It would be easy to oversimplify highly complex situations in which both individuals and nations are caught in immensely difficult circumstances. Since 1987, 187,000 Kurds have died tragically. What shall we say about the killing fields of the Khmer Rouge regime in southeast Asia? We only think of the drug traffic, abortion, pornography and the misery of America's permanent underclass to realize that it is not easy or really possible for individuals to do much. Even government seems hamstrung by an inability or an unwillingness to act. But thinking realistically and honestly is the first step. This is why German historian Ernst Nolte's historical revisionism and his "Genghis Khan-was-not-a-gentleman-either syndrome"[64] must be challenged. We must accept history and seek to learn from it.

We must stand on the ramparts of current events and be watchmen on the wall, ready and willing to warn and act. An enraged Henry K. Morganthau finally got to Franklin D. Roosevelt. A Raoul Wallenberg was used to spare 100,000 Jews in Hungary.

The General Assembly of the Free Church of Scotland expressed alarm in November of 1938 in the following words:

> The Free Church, mindful of what the world owes to the race divinely chosen to be vehicles of revelation of God's moral law, and the immeasurably higher destiny awaiting Israel when the veil shall be lifted, compassionates, with special poignancy the lot of so many innocent sufferers. The church calls on her faithful people to be diligent in prayer for the redemption of Israel, and to join with prompt generosity in all practical forms of aid.

In 1942, the Church of Scotland passed the following resolution:

> This Conference . . . deplores any denial to persons of Jewish descent the right of equal treatment before the law and of other rights due to their status as ordinary citizens and urges that all governments shall take immediate steps to restore to the full status of human dignity such Jewish people as have been deprived of it, and, in particular, that all legislation unjustly diminishing the rights of the Jews, as such, shall be repealed at an early date. . . . The Conference urges His Majesty's Government in conjunction with other

Allied and friendly nations to provide for some scheme of emigation for Jews who cannot find a home in Europe.

The German Protestant Peter von der Osten-Sacken was getting it right when he affirmed: "The Word of God to the Jews is as reliable as God's Word to the Gentiles. We Christians can only rely upon the loyalty of God to the extent that we confess and testify to this same loyalty extended to Israel."[65] On the fiftieth anniversary of the Barmen Declaration (1984), the Reformed Alliance stated: "The return of the Jews to the homeland is a confirmation of God's loyalty."[66] Wolfgang Gerlach in describing the 1980 Synod of the Church of the Rhineland, observed that they were "turning away from the doctrine which enabled the church to disinherit Israel, and turning toward a common theology of promise and hope."[67] Thus a major counteractant to continuing anti-Semitism must be the ringing conviction that God's last word to Israel is not that of alienation and estrangement, that "God makes even the wrath of men to praise Him," and that even in our age of unspeakable violence, there is something more to be said and there is another factor to be processed.

So Bodenheim says to the banker who was savagely beaten for protesting "They did not mean me" (in Franz Werfel's *Cella, or the Survivors,* Werfel being a distinguished Jewish writer, 1890–1945): "They did not mean you—they do not mean me. Whom do they mean? Israel is not a nation, Israel is an order of the blood, which one enters by birth, involuntarily." But to this must be added revelatory words from the prophet Isaiah:

> See, darkness covers the earth and thick darkness is over the peoples, but the LORD rises upon you and his glory appears over you. Nations will come to your light, and kings to the brightness of your dawn. Lift up your eyes and look about you: all assemble and come to you; your sons come from afar, and your daughters are carried on the arm . . . Who are these that fly along like clouds, like doves to their nests? For the nation or kingdom that will not serve you will perish; it will be utterly ruined. Although you have been forsaken and hated, with no one traveling through, I will make you the everlasting pride and the joy of all generations. No longer will violence be heard in your land, nor ruin or destruction within your borders, but you will call your walls Salvation and your gates Praise. Then will all your people be righteous and they will possess the land forever. They are the shoot I have planted, the work of my hands, for the display of my splendor. The least of you will become a thousand, the smallest a mighty nation. I am the LORD; in its time I will do this swiftly" (Isaiah 60:2–4, 8, 12, 15, 18, 21–22).

CHAPTER

THE INEXTINGUISHABLE LIGHT OF CHRISTIAN EXPECTATION

The people of all other nations but the Jewish
seem to look backwards and also to live for the present;
but in the Jewish scheme everything is prospective and preparatory;
nothing, however trifling, is done for itself alone,
but all is typical of something yet to come.

Samuel Taylor Coleridge

Only he who cries out for the Jews may sing Gregorian chants.

Dietrich Bonhoeffer

Praise be to the LORD, the God of Israel,
from everlasting to everlasting.
Amen and Amen.

Psalm 41:13

THE MANY ERUPTIONS OF HATRED over the millennia underscore the argument for the essential uniqueness of Jewish duress and buttress our contention that the Holocaust is not different in degree but in kind.

Anti-Semitism continues even today. Recently the press has reported that in Russia about 1,000 people, many chanting anti-Semitic slogans, gathered at Moscow's television center demanding the immediate establishment of all-Russian television programming. "Take the Jews from television and return it to the Russians" said one banner.[1] Such pernicious anti-Semitism is always simmering beneath the surface, and it occasionally bubbles up into plain sight.

All too frequently Christians and Christian theologians have gone right along with the prevailing currents of prejudice even in the most extreme situations.[2] Well-intentioned advocates of the doctrine that the church displaces Israel have unfortunately played right into the hands of those consumed with hatred of the Jews. Typical of such comments is the statement of a widely known Dutch theologian: "The fleshly seed of Abraham will have lost its right to a place in the world" (speaking in the context of the trial of Jesus Christ). He consigned the Jews in perpetuity to the status "wandering Jew." Jewry is dismissed. "The outcast Jew is driven from his unwhitened grave."[3] Such language only exacerbates the already bad situation and throws gasoline on the flames of shameful anti-Semitism.

Yet many in the history of the Christian church have understood the Old and New Testaments to teach that God's ancient covenant people, the Jews, though temporarily laid aside as the focal vehicle of the redemption mission, have yet ahead a special future. Indeed the taproots of Western civilization reach back into Jewish and Christian prophecy and end-time literature. Christians are also people of the future— the sons and daughters of the resurrection, "people before the time." God has yet to speak a glorious "yes" to Israel. This is an authentic and appropriate component of Christian eschatology—the hope of Israel.

Two particular views of the future have persisted through two millennia of Christian expectation. By no means all followed Augustine and his forerunners in a facile equation of the church and the Kingdom. Others saw the church and the Kingdom as significantly related. They saw room for the temporal and historical fulfillment of promises made in Scripture concerning a Theocratic Kingdom in time-space reality, and there have been those through the history of doctrine who have not hesitated to describe the particularly Jewish complexion of that earthly kingdom. One of the key issues under discussion is the relationship between Israel and the church. This chapter continues to build the case, not for the displacement and exclusion of Israel, but for an enlargement and expansion of the promises and Israel's ultimate redemption.*

THE FOREGLEAMS OF LIGHT

In your unfailing love you will lead the people you have redeemed. In your strength you will guide them to your holy dwelling (Exodus 15:13).

Jesus came proclaiming the Kingdom—but the Church appeared. The Church is a witness to the Kingdom; the Church points to the Kingdom.—Alfred Loisy

The Millennial Kingdom is the time of blessedness on earth for Israel restored to God, for Israel reclaimed to Christ, and lies beyond His Second Coming, beyond the resurrection from the dead.—Nathaniel West[4]

As over against the classical world of antiquity that generally held to a cyclical view of history, Christianity stood with Judaism in an insistence upon a linear view of history, the conviction that history is moving toward a divinely appointed climax and crescendo, the omega

◊ ◊ ◊

* In what will doubtless be seen as a classical treatment, the Korean theologian Seock-Tae Sohn has shown that both Israel and the church are seen in Scriptures as "the people of inheritance," and that the idea of the election of both is pervasive.[5] Sohn has brilliantly analyzed metaphors which are used of both Israel and the church in relation to God: husband and wife; father and son; farmer and vineyard; shepherd and sheep; potter and clay; master and servant; Yahweh's holy people. He has accurately shown how explicit Scripture is as to how restoration will follow rejection. He is correct in his insistence that the very attributes of God are at stake in the outcome of the covenant.[6] He has admitted rejection cannot be seen as final or complete. Too much Scripture shows that God will not abandon His people (1 Samuel 12:22), that Israel is forever (2 Samuel 7:24), that Yahweh's engagement with Israel is forever (Hosea 2:19-20). But then suddenly Sohn has jumped to the conclusion without demonstration that in the New Testament "Jesus is substituted for Yahweh and Christians replace Israel."[7]

point, in the period known among the Jews as *aharit hayamim,* or "the End of Days" (Genesis 49:1). The goal is *Ge'ulah Shelemah* or the Complete Redemption.*

Early Christianity not surprisingly shared significant common ground with Jewish views of the *eschata* (the last things). In his classic study, Schurer characterized Jewish eschatology as consisting of the following elements:

JEWISH ESCHATOLOGY
The coming of tribulation and confusion (the Messianic woes)
Elijah before Messiah
The appearance of Messiah
The final attack on Messiah
Destruction of these powers
Restoration of the Jews according to Ezekiel 40–48
Return of dispersed Israel
Kingdom glory with Jerusalem at the center
Renewal of the world
General resurrection and final judgment.[8]

Students of the Old and New Testament prophecy will immediately identify themes and motifs common to both. Jewish thinkers building on the Old Testament had a rather fully developed doctrine of the Anti-Messiah out of which grew the New Testament depiction of the Antichrist or the Man of Sin.[9]

But Christianity and Judaism were in serious confrontation in the early centuries. Although born and nurtured in the bosom of Judaism, it was soon apparent that Christianity was not new wine in the old wineskins nor a new patch on the old cloth. Tension with mutual persecution and recrimination was inevitable. By the second and third centuries this tension began to relax because it was clear that the electrifying expansion of Christianity would only marginally envelop the Jews.[10] Growth in the main was in the Gentile world. Both Christianity and Judaism were sometimes seen as *religio illicita,* and both enjoyed periods of relative peace with Rome and with each other.

◊ ◊ ◊

* J. J. Van Oosterzee did not overstate the matter when he said that all true theology is teleology that will lead to eschatology.

The *adversus Judaeos* (against the Jews) preaching in early Christianity as found in *The Epistle of Barnabas*, Justin Martyr's *Dialogue with Trypho*, Melito's *Paschal Homily*, and Tertullian's *Answer to the Jews* are not to be seen as anti-Semitic invective. R. S. MacLennan has helpfully pointed out that Jewish culture was well-entrenched at the time Christianity came upon the scene. "Jews were at home in the Roman world of late antiquity," and Christian apologists had to "find ways to tell their new converts who they were and how they were to relate to the Judaism of their Jewish neighbors.[11]

What is most striking about the dialectic between Jews and Christians is that the church never embraced the Marcionite heresy of dispensing with the Old Testament, nor do we accept the replacement theory which would call the church "the new Israel." The redundancy of Israel is never used as an argument in even the sharpest and most vitriolic clashes, as in the fulminations found in *The Epistle of Barnabas* (c. A.D. 132) which are largely directed to the point of the fulfillment of Old Testament prophecy in Christ.[12]

Throughout the Patristics the hope of the Second Advent of Christ is central and imminent.[13] The essential continuity is with the New Testament documents themselves.

Ignatius warned: "The last times are coming upon us."

Premillennialism[*] finds it roots in the apostolic period, but it extends, with a few notable exceptions, through the Patristic period, virtually without serious challenge until the Augustinian debacle.

Virtually all premillennarians hold to a literal view of the fulfillment of prophecy relating to the Messianic Kingdom and therefore in most cases seem to be more hospitable to an expectation for the Jewish people. Many premillennialists are dispensational, but some have only a tinge of dispensationalism. There are also premillennialists who might be called "covenantal millennialists" such as D. H. Kromminga or George Ladd. Some postmillennialists like Jonathan Edwards or Charles Hodge discount the Messianic Kingdom as such but do see something unique and special for the Jews at the end of history. Even some amillennialists who would totally discount the Messianic Kingdom see something special for the Jews, like D. M. Lloyd-Jones, J. H. Bavinck, and Richard De Ridder.

◊ ◊ ◊

[*] Millennium comes from the Latin meaning "1000 years" and picks up the view that the promised Messianic Kingdom will in fact be established upon earth. The Greek equivalent to the word is *chiliad,* and the early Christians were sometimes called "chiliasts." [14]

What is incontrovertible in all of this, as long-time Wheaton Professor Henry C. Thiessen said, is that "the Fathers held not only the premillennial view of Christ's coming but also regarded that coming as imminent. The Lord had taught them to expect His return at any moment, and so they looked for Him to come in their day."[15]

Even some Rabbis spoke of the 1000 years of the Messiah and of a prior resurrection according to Daniel 12:3.[16] The *Sybylline Oracles* (200–100 B.C.) give a most vivid account of the Messianic Kingdom (especially in Book II), and the *Testaments of the XII*, Patriarchs from roughly the same time period speaks at length about the messianic woes and the coming Messianic Kingdom. *II Enoch* (A.D. 1–50) speaks of the millennium or temporary Messianic Kingdom and uses the figure 1000 years. This is the subsoil out of which New Testament and Patristic thinkers* emerged in their expression.

Papias

Papias, an auditor of the apostle John, in the fragments from his *Exposition of Oracles of the Lord* (A.D. 130–140) made his belief in the Millennium clear.[17] Even the author of *The Epistle of Barnabas* spoke of the seventh age of rest (corresponding to the seven days of creation) as coming before the onset of eternity itself.

Justin Martyr

Justin Martyr (c. A.D. 100–165) was explicit in his conviction of a millennial kingdom bounded by two literal resurrections. He believed in the restoration of Jerusalem. His famous *Dialogue with Trypho* is an effort to convert a Jewish seeker to Christ. He cherished the hope of Christ's return. Skevington Wood summarized the argument:

> Justin informs Trypho that he himself, along with other orthodox Christians, looks forward to the establishment of the earthly Kingdom, with its centre at Jerusalem, which will last for a thousand literal years. The city will be "built, adorned, and enlarged" as the prophets Ezekiel and Isaiah declare.[18]

Irenaeus

Irenaeus, also in the second century and certainly orthodox, has been called the first great systematic theologian of the church (A.D. 130–200). He vigorously argued that allegorization of the Bible plays into the hands of the gnostics. An avid student of Daniel the prophet, Irenaeus understood Daniel 9:24–27 to project a time period of 490 years for prophetic fulfillment. Some have suggested he had a doctrine of the rapture. He does hold to a literal, earthly kingdom with the rebuilding of

◇ ◇ ◇

* Thinkers as diverse as Gibbon, Harnack, Mosheim, Neander, and Schaff agree that premillennialism was the dominant view in the Patristic period.

Jerusalem. After three and a half years of the tyranny of the Antichrist at the end of time, the Lord will return to establish His kingdom and restore to Abraham his promised inheritance in accordance with Matthew 8:11. In sharp contrast are the allegorists like Clement of Alexandria who believed all of Daniel's numbers were fulfilled at Christ's first advent and then Origen, who repudiated the millennium and blew hot and cold on the bodily resurrection of the believer. Spiritualizing tendencies have always wreaked havoc in the church. Irenaeus warned against spiritualizing the promises to the Jews.[19]

Tertullian

Montanist chiliasm is seen in Tertullian (A.D. 155–222), who believed[*] in the primacy of the literal sense and that a literal millennium would follow the resurrection of the dead. Like Irenaeus, Tertullian went deeply into the book of Daniel and taught that Daniel 9:24–27 predicted both the time of Christ's birth and death. He saw the millennium as an interim kingdom before the final translation of the saints into heaven. Tertullian fascinatingly observed, "At His last coming He will favor with His acceptance and blessing the circumcision also, even the race of Abraham, which by and by is to acknowledge Him."[20]

Hippolytus

Hippolytus[†] (A. D. 170–235) was a prolific writer and wrote among his many books a valuable work entitled *A Treatise on Christ and the Antichrist*. Hippolytus[‡] believed that the Antichrist would be a Jew from the tribe of Dan. He taught that the seventieth week of Daniel is separate from the previous sixty-nine. He believed that the Antichrist would raise up a temple in Jerusalem.

Stalwarts of Millennialism

A nagging Greek influence continued to undermine the received view, but as Daley observed, "Despite Origen's criticism, the millennial hope remained strong in the 3rd and 4th centuries."[21] Of course Eusebius had doubts about the book of Revelation itself, and Jerome in confronting the millennarian Ebionites (a Jewish-Christian sect with severe

◊ ◊ ◊

[*] Crutchfield pointed out that Cyprian (A.D. 200-258), similarly a strong premillennarian, did not believe the church included all saints of all ages. [22]

[†] Skevington Wood quoted Professor Hans Lietzmann to the effect that "the question of prophecy and fulfillment dominates the thought of Hippolytus." [23]

[‡] Leroy Froom, the noted Adventist historian of prophecy, paid this tribute to Hippolytus: "His was the peak of prophetic witness before the attacks on the Christian hope set in and the reversal of premillennial interpretation which occurred after the Council of Nicaea in 325." [24]

doctrinal deviation)[25] railed at what he termed "the Jewish error—the materialistic expectation of a coming kingdom which would last 1000 years .[26] Jerome was born in what we now call Yugoslavia and was much influenced by Origen (he translated his *Homilies on Jeremiah*). As an extreme ascetic, he was swept along in a Platonic revulsion against all things material, although some have seen an argument for the conversion of the Jews in his commentary on Daniel 9:24.[27]

Nonetheless, the line holds on classical millennarianism with stalwarts like Methodius, the Slavonic Enoch; Lactantius in a fully argued eschatology; Appolinarius (A. D. 310–390); Firmicus and most of Latin eschatology in the fourth century; Ephrem, the most noted Syrian poet and exegete, and many others.

Under the relentless inroads of Greek thought a chiliastic conviction gradually subsides and then comes a watershed in eschatology—"the Augustinian revolution."[28]

THE FLICKERING LIGHT

You are to be holy to me because I, the LORD, am holy, and I have set you apart from the nations to be my own . . . when they are in the land of their enemies, I will not reject them or abhor them so as to destroy them completely, breaking my covenant with them. I am the LORD their God. But for their sake I will remember the covenant with their ancestors whom I brought out of Egypt in the sight of the nations to be their God. I am the LORD (Leviticus 20:26; 26:44–45).

Israel, the created people of God, abides Israel, and the history of Israel is not a mere frame in which to hang pictures of the New Testament Gentile church.—Nathaniel West [29]

The ligatures and sinews that bind biblical teaching about the future Messianic Kingdom and hope for the Jews with the views of many of the early church fathers are in plain evidence.[*]

Although it was not universally held or a controlling motif, the concept of a future Messianic Kingdom was far from absent in the early church fathers. Prominent representatives of various wings and branches in early Christian thought attest to it.

The millennial concept of the Bible and the early church is basic in understanding what has happened to modern Israel.[†]

◇ ◇ ◇

[*] I. A. Dorner has observed, "A point undoubtedly common to both Jewish and Christian apocalyptics, is the period of blessedness on earth, called the 1000 years."

Some serious cracks begin to appear in the generally held view of the earthly reign and the Jewish hope under the aegis of Clement of Alexandria and Origen (A.D. 185–254). We have already referred to Origen's rather harsh view of the Jews. Apparently born in Alexandria of Greek parents, Origen was Neo-Platonic in his views and shrank back even from the idea of a bodily resurrection. He was the champion of spiritualizing and allegorizing the Scriptural text and his influential views began to weaken apocalyptic expectation. Jerome followed in a similar vein.

Augustine

Systematized spiritualization is seen in Jerome's distinguished and brilliant contemporary, Augustine, the North African (A.D. 354–430). The prevalence of Augustine's ideas causes the light of apocalyptic expectation to flicker very low through medieval times. The legacy of his earlier Manichaean dualism coupled with his Neoplatonic thinking along with his strong guilt over early sensuality move him to a rejection of the millennial kingdom altogether. In his Philonic approach to the text of Scripture, he denies any unique future for Israel.* Rome itself become the New Jerusalem.

All of this finds expression in his famous *The City of God*. After all the empire is in serious decline, the barbarians are at the door, and the church of the Constantinian era is spiritually adrift. His solution does not focus on God's plan and the Christian hope so much as on a radical realized eschatology that sees the church as the Messianic Kingdom and Satan now bound. With the eclipse of civil authority in the growing chaos, the religious hierarchy is left to take power for itself, which eventually leads to the medieval papacy. The insecurity of the times was counterbalanced by this kind of kingdom triumphalism, unscriptural and unrealistic as it was.

Origen and Augustine's city of God is clearly not the Messianic Kingdom of Jewish and Christian prophecy.† Because Augustine's ideas were so pervasive through the Middle Ages and because modern amillennialism essentially follows his view, an understanding of Augustine is cru-

◊ ◊ ◊

† (previous page) The third commonwealth (the State of Israel) is the fulfillment of a millennial hope, the rebirth of the nation on its ancestral soil."—Salo Wittmayer Baron[30]

* "St. Augustine definitely abandoned the millenniarist tradition and adopted a thoroughly spiritual eschatology. But he preserved the traditional social realism in his attitude to the Church: indeed, he reinforced it by his identification of the Church with the millennial kingdom of the Apocalypse."—Christopher Dawson[31]

† Augustine is "entirely alienated from the realistic literalism of the old apocalyptic tradition."[32]

cial. Augustine adopted the hermeneutic of Tychonius who followed Origen, spiritualizing the first resurrection and secularizing the millennium.Yet even Augustine cannot totally escape Zechariah 12–14; he does see the repentance of some Jews when Christ returns.[33]

Gregory I

Gregory I (A. D. 540–604) followed Augustine's lead and argued that the loosing of Satan at the end of the 1000 years (Revelation 20:7 ff.) is the rise of the Antichrist at the end of the church age. Of Gregory, Farrar said, "With him theological originality ceased for 500 years."[34]

Millennialists after Augustine

Only a few names after Augustine can be cited as exceptions to his dominant views, among whom are Gaudentius of Brescia, Hilarianus, Evodius (c. A.D. 412), and Commodian the Syrian. Some of the more curious sects that arose in protest of the increasing corruption of Christendom during this long period, e.g. the Albigenses or Cathari in the twelfth century, the Humiliati, the Paulicians, the Bogomilo of Bulgaria and the Waldensians, all of whom exhibit millennial conviction.[35]

Richard of St. Victor and Bruno of Segni sounded the trumpet for a return to what the Bible taught. Anselm of Havelberg (d. 1158) began the demolition of Tychonianism and lay the foundation for Joachim of Fiore. Of course there was a great flurry around A.D. 1000, and Cistercian eschatology (Bernard of Clairvaux) moved strongly back toward an emphasis on the Second Advent.

Joachim (1130–1202) made a pilgrimage to the Holy Land. This deeply moved him, and he began to expound more millennial views. Out of an inductive study of the book of Revelation he concluded that the chiliasts were right. In this he was supported by Haimo of Auxerre and the Venerable Bede who insisted that Revelation 20 required a "future earthly Sabbath."[36]

Joachim influenced many in the Roman church (such as Savonarola, the Franciscan Visionaries, and the Jesuit Manual e Lacunza de Diaz), as well as Protestants (Bishop Jewel, Thomas Muntzer, Melchior Hofmann, and others). Dante had Joachim safely in Paradiso.[37]

John Wycliffe and John Hus, morning stars of the Reformation, were confirmed millennarians. Interestingly, Christopher Columbus quoted Joachim, and himself wrote *Book of the Prophecies*. Still, biblical Christianity had languished for 1000 years and so generally had the Christian hope.

THE FUELING OF THE FLAME

For you singled them out from all the nations of the world to be your own inheritance, just as you declared through your servant Moses when you, O Sovereign LORD, brought our fathers out of Egypt (1 Kings 8:53).

They will be called the Holy People, the Redeemed of the LORD; and you will be called Sought After, the City No Longer Deserted (Isaiah 62:12).

In days to come Jacob will take root, Israel will bud and blossom and fill all the world with fruit (Isaiah 27:6).

Luther's Contribution

The Augustinian misinterpretation nearly blotted out the idea of a Messianic Kingdom and the restoration of the Jews. Although there were contrarians, it was not until the Reformation that any significant alteration took place. Although the whole medieval synthesis was crumbling, ironically it was the anti-Semitic Martin Luther who gave the body blow, albeit largely unawares. Three factors can be isolated:

1) Luther's characteristically strong conviction that the Lord's return was very near reopened the whole area of eschatology.

2) Luther was an historicist in understanding prophecy, i.e. that the Pope was the Antichrist and that Islam was a specific matter of prophetic disclosure. Thus there were 1000 years of history beyond Augustine's life time for divine providence to unfold.

3) Luther's notion of the two kingdoms blasted loose Augustine's facile identification of the church with the kingdom.

Continental Support

Froom (himself an historicist and not a futurist) identified others in this time frame who were awakening from eschatological slumbers, such as François Lambert of Avignon (1487–1530) who revived hope in the future millennium very much after Joachim, the Trinitarian chiliast of whom we have already spoken; Alfonsus Conradus of Mantua; Bibliander of Zurich as well as William Tyndale (1494–1536); Ridley and Latimer, who were all very literal in their understanding of the future earthly reign, i.e. a future millennium supplants the idea of a past millennium. Francisco Ribeira of Salamanca (1537–1591) wrote a great commentary on Revelation. "Jewish national restoration was an organic part of Christian doctrinal system"[38] in the Reformation period. The Jews and their future are alluded to in 108 Reformation writers up to the Peace of Westphalia.

Indeed Osiander of Nuremberg preached the coming Messianic Kingdom, and Dürer drew after and quoted Joachim. Calvin had no eschatological interest (although Servetus was a millennarian). The likes of Martin Bucer, successor to Zwingli, and Theodore Beza, Calvin's successor (who broke with Calvin on Romans 11:15–26 and argued that "the whole Jewish nation shall be joined to the Church of Christ" as did Voetius) along with Peter Martyr and others were moving back into the chiliastic orbit. Additionally there was Anabaptistic chiliasm and theosophical chiliasm.

Pietistic chiliasm is seen in Philip Spener, who as early as 1676 talks about the coming of "a final, splendid phase of the Kingdom of Christ on earth and the conversion of the Jews" in his *Chiliasmus*.[39] While Daniel Cramer of Stettin (1568–1637) may be one of the trailblazers in German premillennialism, Spener shares a notable niche along with Johannes Cocceius (1603–1669) and J. A. Bengel (1687–1752). Schrenk says of the latter two: "Both are missionary theologians who await the conversion of the Jews.[40]

In his study of Cocceius, McCoy quoted Bernard Weiss's comments on Jeremiah 31:33–34 as reflecting the influence of Cocceius and his belief in the conversion of the Jews and their possession of the Holy Land:

> When He (God) spoke thus, no Israelite could think of anything else than the new covenant of grace and forgiveness which God was to enter into with His people in the Messianic time.[41]

In his *Panegyricus De Regno Dei*, Cocceius celebrated the coming restoration and conversion of the Jews. Cocceius greatly influenced Witsius, Vitringa, and Lampe, and of course, John Wesley followed Bengel. As diverse a sample as E. W. Hengstenberg who argued that chiliasm is necessary, Pierre Jurieu (1637–1713) who pastored the Walloon Church at Rotterdam, Arminians like Grotius and Professor Van Limborch, the former Jesuit DeLabadie all held to something very special for the Jewish people.

Much of the development of burning interest and concern about the fate and future of the Jews on the continent must be traced to the one Franz Delitzsch of Leipzig hailed:

> To whom do we owe it that the Evangelical Church of today, no longer brands as heterodoxy the chiliastic view of the End-Time, but has taken it up into her deepest and innermost life, so that today, a believing Christian can scarcely be found who does not enjoy it? To whom do we owe it that the Church of today believes in a glorious future for Israel and sees in Old Testament prophecy not merely the glory of the Gentile Church but of Israel in a literal sense? We owe it to none other than Bengel.[42]

Liberals never cared for this idea and for the most part stood with Schleiermacher in the belief that Christianity is related to Judaism and paganism in exactly the same way.

English Support

But it is especially in England that we see the evolution and development of what some have called "premature Zionism." This is the thesis of the noted historian Barbara Tuchman in her *Bible and Sword:*

England and Palestine from the Bronze Age to Balfour.[43] Douglas Culver documented the growing interest and conviction in Elizabethan and Stuart England.[44] One has only to think of the martyred Francis Kett (d.1589), whose *The Glorious and Beautiful Garland* trumpeted the national return of the Jews, or Thomas Draxe (d.1618) who spoke of "their future calling and conversion," or Thomas Brightman (1552–1607), one of the fathers of English Presbyterianism, who like John Bale before him (1494–1563) saw Revelation 2–3 setting forth seven periods of church history and who wrote many commentaries, tilting toward a unique future for the Jews. We must recall that the Jews had been expelled from England in 1290 by Edward I, and we can then understand why advocates for the Jews courted the belligerence of James I (who himself was quite a student of the book of Revelation) and Archbishop Laud.

Francis Bacon in *The New Atlantis* spoke glowingly of the Jewish future. Giles Fletcher, Elizabeth's ambassador to the Russian court of Ivan the Terrible, and Sir Henry Finch (1558–1625), the noted jurist, both spoke of Jewish restoration and the Jewish kingdom and paid a great personal price for so doing. Joseph Mede (1586–1638), professor of Greek at Cambridge wrote an influential volume, *The Key to Revelation* along these lines and greatly moved John Milton. This was a time of much prophetic discourse and serious exposition.

The Puritans were very interested in eschatology, and most of them held to the restoration of Israel, including John Cotton, Thomas Shepherd, John Eliot, William Perkins, John Owen, the Mather dynasty, and others. John Owen wrote:

> The Jews shall be gathered from all parts of the earth where they are now scattered, and brought home into their homeland" before the "end of all things" prophesied by St. Peter can occur.[45]

In his massive work of 1669, *The Mystery of Israel's Salvation Explained and Applied*, Increase Mather wrote:

> When once God begins this work of Israel's salvation, it shall be carried on with speed and irresistible might—at their return they shall even fly (Isaiah 11:14). Some have doubted whether they should ever possess the land of their Fathers—but the Scripture is very clear and full on this.[46]

We have already spoken of Roger Williams' millennarianism. With the Fifth Monarchy Men and the Cromwellian readmission of the Jews to England in 1656,[47] the future seemed promising.

THE FULL LIGHT OF DAY

> *But Zion said, "The LORD has forsaken me, the Lord has forgotten me." Can a mother forget the baby at her breast and have no compassion on the child she has borne? Though she may forget, I will not forget you! See, I have engraved you on the palms of my hands; your walls are ever before me (Isaiah 49:14–16).*

The moon will be abashed, the sun ashamed; for the LORD Almighty will reign on Mount Zion and in Jerusalem, and before its elders, gloriously (Isaiah 24:23).

It would be incorrect to overdraw the belief in the earthly reign of Christ and the restoration of the Jews, but it would not be overstatement to say that such belief existed and was not extreme or marginal. Confidence in this belief surely ebbed and flowed, but the idea of a future for Israel has been strangely persistent through all of the passing years and the variegated experience of the Jewish people scattered abroad.

Some in Christendom have always been ready to endorse Gibbon's jaundiced view that "the Jews, their nation and their worship" have been "forever banished" from Jerusalem and its environs.[48] Others have felt that Jerusalem will again be *umbilicus urbis* (center of the earth). Believers from diverse backgrounds have championed the return of the Jew to the land. Holger Paulli (1644–1714), the Dane, taught that the Jews must return to Palestine as a prerequisite of the Second Advent; the Huguenot leader Isaac de Peyrere wrote *Concerning the Return Home of the Jews*, and the Camisards shared the same essential insight. Such English worthies as William Carey, missionary to India; Henry Martyn who was martyred in Persia, Andrew Fuller (1745–1815), the Baptist, and Charles Simeon the powerfully influential evangelical Anglican of Cambridge were all devotees of Christian Zionism. According to Simeon's biographer, his "warmest interest" was the restoration and conversion of the Jews.

Peter Toon quoted Robert Baillie who in 1645 claimed that most divines in London at that time were chiliasts. Grotius found that eighty books expounding the millennium had been published in England by 1649.[49]

Jewish Interest in Great Britain

Post-Reformation English civilization, saturated as it was by the Bible and touched as it was episodically by spiritual revival and renewal, must be seen as the staging ground for the emergence of the World Zionist Movement that led ultimately to the birth of the State of Israel in 1948. Correspondingly millennialist enthusiasm was strong at the time of America's founding, and this "heightened eschatological consciousness" provided immense motivation for the subsequent explosion of the Protestant missionary expansion.

With the assertion of British gunships under Sir Sidney Smith off Palestine and Napoleon's inability to take Acre in 1799, Palestine became a renewed object of English interest and affection. The Palestine Association was founded in 1804 for the purpose of fostering biblical research and geographic exploration, which in time became the Palestine Exploration Fund.[50] Tuchman sketched the crucial contribution that this organization made just in terms of the maps and surveys drawn by Colonel Condor and his colleagues, maps vital to General Allenby's campaign in 1917–18.[51] The most interesting account of the English involvement and background is to be found in former Prime Minister Harold Wilson's volume entitled *The Chariot of Israel.*

Also founded at the turn of the century was the London Society Promoting Christianity among the Jews. Early impetus for this effort came from a wealthy barrister, Lewis Way, who had been converted. He was informed that a magnificent stand of oaks on his property by the last will and testament of a former owner was not to be cut down until the restoration of the Jews. This notion intrigued him, and he set himself to the study of the Bible "and came so under the thrall of the study of prophecy that he gave up the law, studied divinity, took orders, donated thirteen thousand pounds to bring the Jews' Society out of debt, and thereafter remained for twenty years its principal financial backer."[52]

Associated closely with Way in this impressively effective enterprise, was the Irish Hebraist Alexander MacCaul who, as missionary to Poland and then publisher and teacher for the Society, guided it into expansive impact. MacCaul's daughter, whom he taught Hebrew at three, became the wife of James Finn, British consul at Jerusalem from 1845 to 1862, who played such a pivotal role in the survey of Jerusalem undertaken by H. H. Kitchener and Charles Wilson (of "Wilson's Arch" fame).

Mrs. Finn, who worked tirelessly with her husband "to reopen the Holy Land to 'its rightful owners, the Hebrew nation,' was to be a living link between Shaftesbury and Balfour."[53] Anthony Ashley Cooper, or Lord Shaftesbury (1801–1885) was of course an outstanding Christian humanitarian and social reformer. Shaftesbury was influenced by his close friend, Bishop Edward Bickersteth, in his study of biblical prophecy and the conviction that "Christ would come again suddenly and soon.[54] He studied Hebrew under MacCaul and advocated in correspondence with the British Foreign Secretary, Lord Palmerston, British support for a Jewish national homeland in Palestine.

Evidence of the significant effect of this correspondence can be seen in a letter Lord Palmerston wrote to his ambassador to Contantinople about the Jews:

> There exists at the present time among the Jews dispersed over Europe, a strong notion that the time is approaching when their nation is to return to Palestine . . . I have to instruct Your Excellency strongly to recommend (the Turkish government) to hold out every just encouragement to the Jews of Europe to return to Palestine.[55]

Another British diplomat, Laurence Oliphant (1829–1888), actually persuaded the Turkish government to charter Jewish settlement in

Gilead. He wrote of his dream in a book entitled *Land of Gilead*. He ultimately settled in Haifa where his secretary was the Hebrew poet Imber, author of *"Hatikvah"* which became the national anthem of the State of Israel.[56]

The historian Ernest Sandeen spoke of the nineteenth century as "drunk with millennialism." With John Nelson Darby (1800–1882) and the rise of the Plymouth Brethren we have a very vital group whose outreach far exceeded their own numbers. Darby himself made seven visits to the United States. Edward Irving (d.1834), originally of the Church of Scotland and assistant to the eminent Thomas Chalmers, was strongly drawn to the restoration of the Jews and with Henry Drummond, popular financier and member of Parliament, sponsored the important Albury Conferences, the first of which was in 1829. The platform of Albury included commitment to the restoration of Israel to Palestine, the Second Coming of Christ before the Millennium and the judgment after the Millennium.[*]

Alarmed by Walter Scott's portrayal of the persecution of the Jews (as in *Ivanhoe*), Scottish Christians were exercised about the Jews. With the backing of Scriptural analysis of such respected leaders as Robert Haldane and Thomas Chalmers, four Church of Scotland ministers were sent on a Mission of Inquiry to Palestine, including Dr. Robert Candlish and Robert Murray M'Cheyne. M'Cheyne and the Bonar brothers (Andrew and Horatius) had become strong millenarians largely under the influence of Irving. Out of the visit to Palestine came a mission to the Jews in Budapest led by John Duncan, later known as Rabbi Duncan and slated to become the first professor of Hebrew at New College, Edinburgh. Fruit of the Budapest mission included Alfred Edersheim, David Baron, and Adolph Saphir, noted Hebrew Christians.[57]

Popular writing like Benjamin Disraeli's romantic novel *David Alroy* (1853) reflects the yearning and longing for a Jewish homeland which was under such widespread discussion. George Eliot's *Daniel Deronda* (1876), her last novel, is clearly a passionate plea for the building of a Jewish state in Palestine. In 1862 the Prince of Wales, the future Edward VII, visited Palestime, the very same year in which Moses Hess announced that "the hour had struck" for the revival of the Jewish nation.[58] Earlier Colonel George Gawler had traveled to Palestine with the Jewish philanthropist Sir Moses Montefiore and saw orange groves purchased and planted for Jewish immigrants.

◊ ◊ ◊

* This is a stream of thought so significant for the understanding of contemporary evangelicalism and its impact on the political and social life of our times that Garry Wills, the recondite historian from Northwestern University, retells and meticulously traces the history of the Albury Conferences in his pivotal *Under God: Religion and American Politics* (New York: Simon & Schuster, 1990).

Jewish Interest in America

Across the Atlantic there were similar stirrings. In 1814, John McDonald, Presbyterian pastor in Albany, New York, issued a book entitled, *A New Translation of Isaiah Chapter Eighteen: A Remarkable Prophecy Respecting the Restoration of the Jews, Aided by the American Nation.*[59] Likewise, M. M. Noah, an American Jewish lawyer and American Consul in Tunis, became burdened for the Jews and shared his views with James Madison, Thomas Jefferson, and John Quincy Adams, who wrote in 1825, "I really wish the Jews again in Judea, an independent nation."[60] The Chicago businessman, William E. Blackstone, wrote a widely read volume entitled *Jesus is Coming* (1878). This book called for the restoration of the Jews to their old homeland. He wrote:

> Other nations come and go, but Israel remains. She passes not away. God says of her: "For a small moment have I forsaken thee; but with great mercies will I gather thee" (Isaiah 54:7–8).[61]

He gathered over four hundred signatures from leading Christians and Jews and presented *A Memorial to President Harrison* (1891) in the interest of Palestine for the Jews.[62] The Methodist evangelist, Phoebe Palmer, wrote a best-selling book entitled *Israel's Speedy Restoration and Conversion Contemplated, or Signs of the Times.* J. A. Seiss, a popular exponent of these views, wrote widely, became president of the Lutheran Seminary in Philadelphia, and served the largest Lutheran congregation in North America.

The full transference of the British zeal is clearly in evidence in the series of prophetic conferences beginning at Holy Trinity Church in New York City in 1878, featuring Lord Shaftesbury and the Episcopal Bishop William Nicholson. These conferences (called the Niagara Conferences) along with the Northfield Conferences (especially 1880–1899) were reproduced widely in all parts of the country.[63] Advocates of the Jewish hope included J. Hudson Taylor, D. L. Moody, Robert Speer, the great missionary statesman who became a premillennialist, A. B. Simpson, and many more.

But while all of this was transpiring, another whole chain of events in Judaism itself was forging a convergence of interest and intent which will substantively answer to the cry in Thomas Moore's *Sacred Songs of 1816:*

> Then Judah, thou no more shalt mourn
> Beneath the heathen's chain;
> Thy days of splendor shall return
> And all be new again.

THE
SEQUENTIAL
FACTS

He is the LORD our God;
his judgments are in all the earth.
He remembers his covenant forever,
the word he commanded, for a thousand generations,
the covenant he made with Abraham, the oath he swore to Isaac.
He confirmed it to Jacob as a decree,
to Israel as an everlasting covenant:
To you I will give the land of Canaan
as the portion you will inherit.
Psalm 105:7–11

CHAPTER

8

THE STIRRINGS OF THE DREAM OF ZION

To Edom!
For millennia, now as brothers,
We've borne with each other an age;
You bear the fact I'm still breathing,
And I—I bear your rage.

But often you got in strange tempers
In dark times since the Flood,
And your meekly loving talons
You dyed in my red blood.

And now our friendship grows firmer
And daily increases anew,
For I too have started raging—
I'm becoming much like you!

Heinrich Heine

Then the LORD said to Abram after Lot had departed from him,
"Lift up your eyes from where you are and look
north and south, east and west.
All the land that you see
I will give to you and
your offspring
forever."

Genesis 13:14–15

In your good pleasure
make Zion prosper;
build up the walls
of Jerusalem.

Psalm 51:18

HEINRICH HEINE'S TORMENTED POEM (facing page) reflects the tensions of his dual heritage. He was going through a Judaizing phase after reading a history of the persecution of the Jewish people. Although baptized into the German State Church, he felt his ties with Judaism, in 1827 he spoke of as "the great Jewish sorrow . . . the abyss of Jewish destiny."

In Heine's poem "Edom" is a symbol of Jew hatred (*Judenhass*), and Heine identified with the plaint of the exiles:

> By the rivers of Babylon we sat and wept when we remembered Zion. There on the poplars we hung our harps, for there our captors asked us for songs of Zion! (Psalm 137:1–2).

Rooted and nurtured in the soil of Scripture itself,* the concept of Zionism, or Jewish nationalism, has lived in Jewish hearts if only sentimentally over the centuries wherever they have been and whatever may have been their circumstances.†

At the conclusion of the Passover observance after the eldest child rises and opens the door, the head of the household then recites:

> Thou God of Abraham, Isaac, and Jacob, long have we waited for Thy promise. We beseech Thee now to send Thine anointed whom Thou hast promised, the Son of David. Have mercy upon Thy people Israel. Gather us according to Thy Word and we shall be Thy people and Thou wilt delight us as of old . . . Behold all things are ready and we wait."[1]

◊ ◊ ◊

* Although the Roman Catholic Church has been very ambivalent about Zionism, there is a bona fide Catholic Zionism.[2]

† Arthur Hertzberg, a distinguished Jewish-American scholar, who in his continuing torment over the Holocaust wrote movingly of his "lifelong quarrel with God,"[3] argued in his *The Zionist Idea* that Zionism was "always enshrined in Jewish hearts."

Then the door is closed and again the head of the household recites:

How long, O Lord, how long? Behold our suffering. We are scattered among the heathen. We grow faint, yet we hope. Lord our God, may it please Thee to gather Thy people speedily. Restore us Thy favor, at least next year may we celebrate this feast with Thee in Jerusalem, Thine own habitation.[4]

The paradox has been pointed out that while Orthodox Jews prayed three times a day for deliverance and mourned the destruction of the temple and left a brick bare over the door as a symbol of the desolation of Zion, very few had returned except a small number to die and be buried in *eretz* (land) Israel.[5] Links with the land were not established until the last half of the nineteenth century with the rise of Zionism.

In other words, the beautiful lines of the eleventh-century Hebrew poet, Judah Halevi, went from being pious desire to a practical dynamism in modern times.

O city of the world with sacred splendor blest,
My spirit yearns to thee from the far-off West,
A stream of love wells forth when I recall thy day,
Now is thy temple waste, they glory passed away.
Had I an eagle's wings, straight would I fly to thee,
Oh, how I long for thee! Albeit thy King has gone.
Could I but kiss thy dust, so would I fain expire,
As sweet as honey then, my passion, my desire.[6]

The fact is that in 1844 there were only 7,120 Jews in Jerusalem. Granted that from 63 B.C. there was no semblance of Jewish sovereignty in the land. Of the 3,000,000 Jews who emigrated from Russia between 1882–1914, only 1 percent went to Palestine. But what so changed this situation?

PRECURSORS OF ZIONISM

In that day the Lord will reach out his hand a second time to reclaim the remnant that is left of his people from Assyria, from Lower Egypt, from Upper Egypt, from Cush, from Elam, from Babylonia, from Hamath and from the islands of the sea (Isaiah 11:11).

The land is Israel's everlasting possession, which only they shall inherit and in which only they shall settle, and if perchance they are exiled from it, they will return to it again, for, it is theirs in perpetuity and no other nation's.—Rabbi Bahai's commentary on the Torah[7]

All the weaning of the centuries, all the enlightenment of modern times, have been unable to banish a longing for that land from their hearts.—David Kaughman in 1877[8]

Western European Jews

With the enlightenment and the French Revolution, western European Jews tasted of and aspired to "equality before the law."[*] Yet Jews still remained on the margins just as surely as the millions of Jews on a much lower socio-economic platform in the Pale of Settlement in Eastern Europe. The tension and the polemic in the nineteenth century were sharp, and the struggle for Jewish identity is seen in Heine, and Karl Marx, whose "On the Jewish Question" reflects bitterness and confusion. Sigmund Freud later on wrestled with the same issues and found them irresolvable.[9]

Jews in England

In England the only way for a rising Jew to get into Parliament was by being baptized, and this was the road taken by Benjamin Disraeli, David Ricardo, and Manasseh Lopez. Sir Moses Montefiore made seven trips to Palestine in the interest of land acquisition for settlement (and the old windmill outside the wall of the Old City of Jerusalem is a vestige of his time and interest). Baron Rothschild is called by some "the father of the *yishuv*" because of his sponsorship of the early colony at Rishon-le-Zion.

The establishment of a British consulate in Jerusalem by Lord Palmerston, largely under the influence of his step-son-in-law, Lord Shaftesbury, made a more humanitarian and philanthropic approach possible. As M. E. Young, first to hold this post, recorded in his minutes from the Foreign Office:

> I am directed by Vicount Palmerston, to state to you that it will be a part of your duty as British Vice-Consul at Jerusalem, to afford protection to the Jews generally: and you will take an early opportunity of reporting to his Lordship upon the present state of the Jewish population in Palestine.

The Land Option

The land loomed larger as a possible option when social and cultural assimilation proved elusive. Despite improving fortunes the Jews of England and the continent were outsiders. A few weeks after his baptism Heine wrote to a friend: "I am now hated by Christian and Jew alike; I

◇ ◇ ◇

* Reformed Judaism stemming from Germany in the 1840s and later Mordecai Kaplan's Reconstructionist Judaism are both efforts to integrate Judaism as painlessly as possible. Growing liberalism and nationalism led thinkers like Moses Mendelssohn (1729–1786) to chart out a Jewish enlightenment called the "Haskalah." Nachman Krochmal (1785–1840) tried an Hegelian framework for emancipated Jews in which he argued that Judaism was not a revealed religion but revealed legislation. Herman Cohen and Franz Rosenweig both emphasized Jewish ethicality.

very much regret my baptism, nothing but misfortune has occurred to me since."

Judaeophobia erupted with regularity even in the more suave salons of the West.[10] But with the assassination of Alexander II in Russia in 1881 and the revival of indescribable pogroms in Odessa and many parts of Russia led by Alexander III, and along with the Dreyfus Affair in France, the possibility of the establishment of a Jewish homeland in Palestine becomes an increasingly well-focused objective.

Napoleon

When Napoleon conquered the Holy Land in 1798, he issued a decree declaring Palestine, the home of its "rightful heirs." He advocated the restoration of the Jews. This may have been "an meaningless gesture," more reflective of French dreams of domination in the Levant (eastern Mediterranean area) than anything religious or even compassionate.[11] Nevertheless, Napoleon stands as the first head of state to call for a Jewish state in Palestine.

Foreign Interest

Helmut Von Moltke was the first German to recognize the importance of Palestine and this he did in the 1840s. Four German religious colonies were established in the 1860s and 1870s. Palmerston's political angle cannot be disentangled from his expression of British interest.The eccentric Illinois banker, Horatio B. Spafford, planted an American colony in Jerusalem. Something was happening, as the rise in Jewish population indicates:

Growth of Jewish Population in Palestine	
1844	7,120
1922	33, 971
1948	100,000

Ottoman Empire

Against the backdrop of "the drowsy and negligent sway of the Ottoman Empire," tottering toward its demise in World War I,[12] were rising Jewish aspirations. The inefficiency, graft, bribery, and corruption of the Ottoman administration of Palestine were beyond belief. All of the major European powers had their lines in the Palestinian sea—Britain, France, Germany, and Russia. Britain tried to prop up Turkey as a bulwark against Russia through most of the nineteenth century, but in 1880 Gladstone pushed Turkey over toward Bismarck and the Germans, and this had immense long-term consequences.

Jewish Voices

Jewish voices were increasingly heard. The German Rabbi Zevi Hirsch Kalischer (1795–1874) sought to enlist funds from the Frankfurt Rothschilds to purchase *eretz* Israel or at least Jerusalem from the Turks. Rabbi Judah Alkalai (1798–1878) from Semlin near Belgrade thought the kingdom should be immediately established in Palestine for the soon-coming Messiah. He was the first to advocate that spoken Hebrew be used in the new state. He himself made *aliyah* (ascent, immigration to Israel).[13] His appeal was:

> Let us take to heart the examples of Italians, Poles and Hungarians, who laid down their lives and possessions in the struggle for national independence, while we, the children of Israel, who have the most glorious and holiest of lands as our inheritance are spiritless and silent. We should be ashamed of ourselves! All the other people have striven only for the sake of their own national honor; how much more should we exert ourselves, for our duty is to labor not only for the glory of our ancestors but for the glory of God who chose Zion!

Secular Jewish voices were also heard such as Moses Hess, called the founder of German Social Democracy (1812–1875). His book *Rome and Jerusalem: The Last National Problem* (1862) argued for a national Jewish society. The Damascus Affair (1840) in which the Jewish Community in Damascus was accused of ritual murder shook Hess greatly. He became increasingly pessimistic about Jewish prospects in Europe.[14] He wrote:

> It is only with the national rebirth that the religious genius of the Jews will be endowed with new strength and again be reinspired with the prophetic spirit. Therefore as soon as the political situation in the East takes a favorable turn, the establishment of Jewish colonies in Palestine must at once be begun, as a first step towards the resettlement of Jews as a nation in their historic home.

In his thought Hess wrestled about the place of the Arabs in a Jewish Palestine. He was way ahead of his times, but his socialism did indeed become part of the new order in the *yishuv* (the settlement, the Jewish community in Israel), and the Labor Government reburied him in Tiberias with the establishment of the State of Israel.*

Leon Pinsker

A more direct call for a resurgent Jewish nationalism came out of the Odessa pogroms from Dr. Leon Pinsker whose pamphlet, *"Self-emanci-*

◊ ◊ ◊

* Of course anti-Semites like Fichte, Bruno Bauer, and Paulus were delighted to hear of the possibility of the Jews going back to the land of their fathers because they considered the Jews unassimilable.

pation" (1882) built on the premise that Jew-hatred "was a phenomenon lying deep in human psychology." Speaking of the Jews, he maintained:

> This people is not counted among the nations, because since it was exiled from its land it has lacked the essential attributes of nationality, by which one nation is distinguished from another. True we have not ceased even in the lands of our exile to be spiritually a distinct nation; but this spiritual nationality, so far from giving us the status of a nation in the eyes of the other nation, is the very cause of their hatred for us as a people. Men are always terrified by a disembodied spirit, a soul wandering about with no physical covering; and terror breeds hatred.

The Franco-Russian forgery *Protocols of the Elders of Zion* was in wide circulation throughout this whole period.[15] An illegal organization in Russia, the Hovevei Zion (Lovers of Zion), mobilized to encourage immigration, 7,000 left in 1882. Dr. Pinsker was the first head of Lovers of Zion. Odessa was a Russian city open to the Jews, and it became a remarkable center of Jewish economic, religious, and educational progress.

Peretz Smolenskin

Peretz Smolenskin (1842–1885) called on all Jews, emancipated and Orthodox, to consider emigration. "But why should we not emigrate and thus reduce the number of Jews in the countries where they are hated?"[16] But of course the Ottoman Turks were opposed to such immigration into Palestine. They welcomed immigrants to settle anywhere in their vast holdings with the exception of Palestine. The only stipulation was that they had to become citizens of Ottoman Turkey. Underlying the policy was of course the desire not to have any further "national problems" in Turkey; after all, most of these Jews were Russians, and Russians were enemies of the Turks. While some concessions were obtained in 1888, these were to be granted to individuals not any en masse. The Ottomans opposed land sales to the Jews and became increasingly angry over the influx taking place. Many altercations and incidents are part of the record.[17]

Maxim Gorky

Not all Russians in the late nineteenth century were anti-Semitic. The eminent Russian writer, Maxim Gorky (d.1936 at age 68) passionately condemned anti-Semitism. He encouraged the growth of Jewish culture in Russia and favored political Zionism. He was a close friend of such Jews as Chaim Bialik, Sholom Aleichem, Shalom Asch,[18] Jabotinsky (Menachem Begin's mentor), and Berl Katzenelson, another early leader in Israel. His stories often used Jewish themes, and his play *Zhid* touched seriously on Zionistic concerns. His interest all traces to an experience he had early in his life working for a traditional Jewish family near Dobraya, close to the home of David Bronstein (Leon Trotsky).

Eliezer Ben Yehuda

Another very crucial precursor of Zionism, Eliezer Ben Yehuda (1858–1922), was born in Lithuania, studied medicine in Paris, and immigrated to Palestine in 1881. His name was actually Perlman but he took the pen name Ben Yehuda (Son of Judah) in his early writing for the Zionist cause. His burden was that Hebrew become the spoken language for the *yishuv*. He immigrated because of this conviction, and even though he faced tremendous opposition (and great physical illness), he succeeded. He argued: "Let the remnants of our people return to the land of their fathers; let us revive the nation and its tongue will be revived, too!"[19] But the critical breakthrough had not come yet.

PIONEERS OF ZIONISM

For the living, the Jew is a dead man; for the natives an alien and a vagrant; for property holders a beggar; for the poor an exploiter and a millionaire; for patriots a man without a country; for all classes, a hated rival.—Leon Pinsker

Describing the mourning for the destruction of the temple by exiled Jews on the ninth of Ab: "I have sat on the floor in stocking feet among fellow-mourners, listened to the sobbing recital of the Lamentations of Jeremiah and, by the light of the commemorative candles, seen the tears run down the cheeks of grown men. This was no mechanical ritual. It came from the heart of a frustrated people. It was real, poignant and terrifying, a Fourth of July in reverse.—Maurice Samuels[20]

Oh, that salvation for Israel would come out of Zion! When the LORD restores the fortunes of His people, let Jacob rejoice and Israel be glad! (Psalm 14:7).

Zionism

Although the word *Zionism* itself was not used publicly until Nathan Birnbaum employed it in discussion in Vienna on the evening of January 23, 1892,[21] the notion of the national restoration of the Jews in Palestine was increasingly in the air. As the winds of nationalism became cyclonic in Europe, little wonder that the Jews in their conspicuous marginality began to think of a national homeland. The Odessa pogroms of 1881–82, the Kishinev Massacre in Russia, and the Dreyfus Affair in France all blew the Jews toward Palestine. Jews were not really secure anywhere.

Theodor Herzl

The breakthrough in establishing a Jewish homeland came under the unlikely aegis of a pompous, brilliant, but spiritually shallow assimilated Jew, Theodor Herzl, the father of modern Zionism.* Born to assimilated, German-speaking Jews in Budapest on May 2, 1860, Herzl was raised in an affluent and very literate but totally irreligious environment. As a young man Herzl was fascinated with Savonarola of Florence. He received an excellent legal education but was interested in and clearly gifted in writing. After his first eighteen years he moved with his family to Vienna, which now had a population of 118,000 Jews. One of his best friends at the University of Vienna was Oswald Boxer who was sent by the Jewish community to Brazil to explore the possibility of resettling Eastern European Jews there, but who came down with yellow fever and died at age thirty-two.[22] Even Herzl's legal background was part of his preparation for his very special life's work.

Although apparently wrestling with a congenital heart defect, Herzl protested anti-Semitic diatribes at the League of German Students on the occasion of Wagner's death. Herzl gradually came to see assimilation as a failure. He became a Doctor of Jurisprudence in 1884 and gave himself to writing plays such as the satirical *The New Ghetto*, which disclosed a thinly veneered Jewish self-hatred.

Herzl struggled with his identity. Pathetically tied to his mother, his domestic life was always strained. One prominent psychoanalyst argued strenuously that the Jewish people owe a great debt of gratitude to Herzl's unhappy marriage.[23] His son Hans was neither circumcised nor given a Jewish name.

Going to work for the staunchly pro-German *Neue Freie Press*, he was assigned to Paris. "Paris changed Herzl. French anti-Semitism undermined the ironic complacency of the Jewish would-be non-Jew."[24] It would also appear that from this time Herzl struggled with systemic lupus.

Herzl's coverage of the Dreyfus trial was the turning point. Alfred Dreyfus, an Alsatian Jew, was a French army officer accused of selling French military secrets to the Germans.

Dreyfus claimed, "I am being persecuted because I am a Jew."[25]

Dreyfus in a farce of a trial was found guilty (in late December, 1894) and sent to the infamous Devil's Island, where he was effectively destroyed. Led by literati such as Bernard Lazare,[26] the Catholic poet Charles Peguy, Victor Hugo, Emile Zola, and others, Dreyfus finally was

◇ ◇ ◇

* (previous page) In his recent, definitive biography of Herzl entitled, *The Labyrinth of Exile: A Life of Theodor Herzl*,[27] Ernst Pawel meticulously has shown the greatness and the limitations of the man who saw that the Jews had no future in Europe and who proposed to do something about it.

brought back to France and exonerated, but it was clear to all what deep rivers of anti-Semitism ran even in enlightened and refined France. The Dreyfusards, as they were called, were not popular as anti-Semitic riots tore through the country and Zola had to flee France.

Herzl now saw clearly that a sovereign Jewish state was essential. Because the Ottoman Empire was in rigor mortis and might be chewed up by Russia, Herzl entertained the possibility that the Jewish state should be located somewhere in Canada or Argentina. In May of 1895 Herzl called on the immensely wealthy Jewish philanthropist, Baron Maurice de Hirsch, who was pushing for Russian Jews to relocate in Argentina and by this time had finally moved 3000 to Argentina in what became a dismal failure. When asked by Hirsch for his alternative, Herzl responded: "My alternative is to call a congress of Jewish notables to discuss migration to a sovereign Jewish state."[28] This really marked the end of deliverance through the philanthropy of wealthy Jews. Something more substantive and significant had to be done, and Herzl saw what it was.

In his search for backing Herzl transcribed his thinking in a small volume entitled *Der Judenstaat (The Jewish State)*, published in 1896. Although flamboyant in style, Herzl had limited originality. What he did, though, that no one else had done before him was to paint "the Zionist solution on the canvas of world politics and it has never left it since."[29] The basic thesis of the book is that the Jews have only one way to go and that is out! Herzl, as a true son of the enlightenment, foresaw no private property in the Jewish state, and apparently the issue of Arab nationalism never crossed his mind. Yet the eighty-six-page tractate was dynamite.

Chaim Weizmann, who played such a major role in the Jewish story, was a student at the University of Berlin and described the impact of Herzl's tract:

> I was in my second year in Berlin when, in 1896, Theodor Herzl published his tract, now a classic of Zionism, *Der Judenstaat* . . . It was an utterance which came like a bolt from the blue. Fundamentally, the Jewish State contained not a single new idea for us; that which so startled the Jewish bourgeoisie, and called down the resentment and derision of the Western Rabbis, had long been the substance of our Zionist tradition . . . Not the ideas, but the personality which stood behind them appealed to us. Here was daring, clarity and energy. The very fact that the Westerner came to us unencumbered by our own preconceptions had its appeal. . . . We were right in our instinctive appreciation that what had emerged from the *Judenstaat* was less a concept than a historic personality.[30]

Herzl envisioned the robes of the high priests in the Jewish state and the cavalry with yellow trousers and white tunics and the officers with silver breastplates. Quite a vision!

How "God makes even the wrath of men to praise Him!" It was vicious and brutal Jew-baiting that made Theodor Herzl and his friend, Max Nordau (1849–1923, also born in Budapest) consciously Jewish. While Nordau came from an observant home and assimilated too (took a non-Jewish name, married a Danish Protestant), he shared much with Herzl and gave a great opening address at the Basel Congress in 1897 in which he spoke of modern Jews as the "New Marranos." He also led the opposition to the Uganda option which became such a bone of contention as Herzl struggled valiantly to achieve some opening in Palestine itself.

Support for the implementation of *Der Judenstaat* did not come from the Western-establishment Jews.

The Rothschilds and the bankers basically said no.

What are called "the huddled masses of the Ostjuden" from eastern Europe were the ones who responded. David Ben-Gurion, then a ten-year-old boy in Russian Poland, heard that "The Messiah had arrived, a tall, handsome man, a learned man from Vienna, a doctor no less."[31] The Chief Rabbi of Sophia proclaimed Herzl the Messiah. But now what became known as "Frock-coat Zionism" led Herzl on a frenetic search for diplomatic backing. This phase of the quest took him to see the Pope, the Tsar, the Sultan, the Kaiser. His message was ever: "We are a people, one people." The going was tough. Against doctor's orders, he kept on.

Some adulated him; many hated him. One delegate at the first Zionist Congress testified:

> This is no longer the elegant Dr. Herzl of Vienna; it is a royal descendant of David arisen from the grave who appears before us in the grandeur and beauty with which legend has surrounded him. Everyone is gripped as if a historical miracle had occurred . . . it was as if the Messiah, son of David, stood before us. A powerful desire seized me to shout through this tempestuous sea of joy: "Jechi Hamelech, *Long Live the King*."[32]

Herzl became the first President of the World Zionist Organization, and at the first meeting the Jewish flag (of blue and white colors, the same colors as the prayer shawls) was adopted, as was the national anthem, "*Hatikvah*." We can understand Herzl's diary entry: "In Basel, I created the Jewish state."[33]

A Protestant clergyman, William Hechler, chaplain at the British embassy in Vienna, was an avid student of Bible prophecy. He connected the return of the Jews to Palestine with the fulfillment of prophecy. He started the search for the lost Ark of the Covenant. More importantly, he won over Kaiser Wilhelm II to support Zionism. He traveled extensively with Herzl. A destitute Polish diplomat named Philip Nevlinsky also worked on the Ottoman connection but died in 1899.

The significance of the Kaiser's tie with Turkey (even though it yielded nothing to Herzl) was that it aligned Turkey, "the old man of Europe," with the Axis powers in World War I and ultimately thrust Palestine into the British Mandate of 1922. In discussions with the Sultan, Herzl met with an adamant refusal to part with Jerusalem or anything in Palestine.

"Come anywhere but Palestine."

Gladstone of England, son of a Scot evangelical mother, was favorable to the Jewish State, but he lost power in the backwash of General Gordon's death at Khartoum.[34] Russia favored immigration but distrusted Zionism. Victor Emmanuel of Italy opined that "Palestine must and will get into your hands" and encouraged him morally as did Austro-Hungary. But no opening came.

Joseph Chamberlain, colonial secretary in the Balfour government which came to power in 1902, was Herzl's next best chance after five futile visits into the Turkish scene. Chamberlain offered a Cyprus option (which was not practical) and then proposed part of Sinai or an area around El Arish (which the Sultan and Egypt rejected). Then came the East African option—a plateau in Kenya or Uganda.

This was a demoralizing and exhausting time for Herzl, and in persisting he literally died for the cause. He had come to believe that anti-Semitism was incurable. Herzl tirelessly trumpeted the cause in the Zionist organ *Die Welt* and wrote a utopian novel called *Altneuland* (*Old-New Land*). Herzl has been called "the first Jewish statesman since the destruction of Jerusalem." He had no real spiritual vision in his drive. In fact he wrote:

I meant to go to the Pope . . . if you do as I say, I shall make myself the leader of a huge movement aiming at voluntary and honest conversion to Christianity."[35] In his diary after the Basel congress, he wrote of his vision of the Jewish State: "In five years, perhaps, but certainly in fifty, everyone will agree.

Only six months longer—1948.[36] Herzl had said the Jewish state would be certainly established in fifty years; it only took forty-six.

PROFILES OF ZIONISM

Hear my prayer, O LORD, listen to my cry for help; be not deaf to my weeping. For I dwell with you as an alien, a stranger, as all my fathers were (Psalm 39:12).

"Return, faithless people," declares the LORD, "for I am your husband. I will choose you—one from a town and two from a clan—and bring you to Zion" (Jeremiah 3:14).

O LORD, the hope of Israel, all who forsake you will be put to shame (Jeremiah 17:13).

Though I completely destroy all the nations among which I scatter you, I will not completely destroy you. I will discipline you but only with justice; I will not let you go entirely unpunished (Jeremiah 46:28b).

All of the longings of proto-Zionism come into new focus with the all too brief but brilliant career of Theodor Herzl. In despair because of the truculent Turks, Herzl now suffered under the infamous Kishinev pogrom of 1903 in which scores of Russian Jews were slaughtered. He immediately determined to take "the Uganda option" from the Balfour government, but the Zionist organization threatened to come apart at the seams. Herzl presented Uganda as a temporary measure (a *nachtasyl*, a mere haven for the night); and although Nordau was the chief spokesman, the Russian Jews walked out of the Congress. Herzl gasped, "These people have a rope around their necks, and still they refuse."[37]

Interestingly, the young English lawyer Herzl hired to draw up the charter for colonization was David Lloyd George, the future prime minister who plays such a large subsequent role in this story.

The Russian Jews insisted that Palestine could be the only option and returned to Russia for a rump congress at which they fiercely denounced Herzl. One rabid Russian Jew sought to assassinate Max Nordau shouting, "Death to the East African!"[38]

The whole titanic struggle was too much for Herzl, and he died July 3, 1904, at the age of forty-four. His death sent shock waves throughout the Jewish world. Ten thousand mourners followed the funeral cortege. Bankrupt at his death, Herzl was buried simply and placed next to his father until the Jewish people could transfer his "remains to Palestine" and the "coffins" of his immediate family."[39] On August 17, 1949, Herzl's casket, along with those of his parents and family, was brought to Israel and reburied on Mount Herzl in Jerusalem.

Herzl was succeeded in leadership by the Lithuanian Jew David Wolffsohn who was able to bring the movement together, and official unity was restored by the Congress of 1907.

Considering how disparate Judaism was in its far-flung Diaspora, the very existence of Zionism must be seen as a miracle and something of the measure of its leader, Theodor Herzl.

Some students of Bible prophecy to this day understand "the noise" referred to in Ezekiel's great prophecy of national resurrection in Ezekiel 37 as Herzl's call for nationhood in 1895 which was subsequently followed by a shaking and a coming together of the dry bones.[40]

What became undeniably clear to all including Herzl was the fact that Ottoman Turkey stood in the way of Zionist aspirations. World War I removed that problem. The Kaiser had abandoned his earlier Zionism in order to lure Turkey to his side in a Holy War against Britain. This was, as history shows, a most critical mistake. As it was expressed on November 9, 1914, by British Prime Minister Herbert Asquith: "The Turkish Empire has committed suicide."[41]

Asher Ginsberg

By no means were all Jews enamored of the Zionist cause. Some found themselves deeply troubled over the lack of spiritual direction in the movement. When Herzl and Nordau went to the synagogue at the first Zionist Congress in 1897, it was the first time either had been in a synagogue since childhood. One of the prime spokesmen for spiritual values in the early days of Zionism was the Russian writer Asher Ginsberg (1856–1927), who wrote under the pen name Ahad Ha'am ("One of the People").

Although Ginsberg sharply inveighed against the spiritual bankruptcy of political Zionism, He praised Herzl:

Herzl gave us the Congress, the Organization, the Bank, the National Fund. Whether these are to be reckoned great achievements we cannot yet know. All depends on whether they endure and in what form they continue to exist. But one thing Herzl gave us involuntarily, which is perhaps greater than all he did on purpose. He gave us himself, to be the theme of our Hymn of Revival, a theme which imagination can take and adorn with all the attributes needed to make of him a Hebrew national hero, embodying our national aspirations in their true form.[42]

Anti-Zionists

The radical socialist and even Marxist ideas of some of the early theoreticians of Zionism have persisted in Israeli politics to this day. Early on ultraorthodox Jewry as a whole was early on opposed to Zionism. Since it was their view that only the Messiah could establish the Messianic Kingdom, the secular state would then have to be seen as impious and opposed or ignored. The anti-Zionist Neturei Karta in Jerusalem to this day calls for Arab rule in Palestine. The Satmar Hasids are anti-Zionist but the Lubavitchers are in a sense pro-Zion, although Rabbi Schneerson, who lived in Crown Heights in Brooklyn before his death, refused to set foot in Israel until the Messiah came and legitimized the state.

Rabbi Abraham Kook

Most Orthodox have come over to the Zionistic perspective, largely through the influence of the first Chief Rabbi of Palestine under the British Mandate, Rabbi Abraham Isaac Kook (1865–1935). Rabbi Kook bridged Orthodoxy and Zionism by arguing that the people of Israel, the

Torah, and the land of Israel are one. He argued that even Jews in the galut (exile of Jews from Palestine) must be nurtured by the miracle of what transpires in the redemption taking place in eretz Israel. While the Messiah has not come, Messianic days have come.

Vladimir Jabotinsky

The more right-wing, ultra-nationalistic Zionist thinker has been Vladimir Jabotinsky (1880–1940), mentor of Menachem Begin. A man of striking intellectual acumen, Jabotinsky argued for racial determinism and a militant nationalism. He followed Carlyle's "great men of history" idea.

American Jews

Understandably many North American Jews have been troubled by aspects of the Zionist argument.* Aliyah from America has been limited, as we can well understand. American Jews have been most generous in their support of the Jewish State but more reluctant to become part of the action. Only one in ten American Jews thinks Jews should live in Israel. The American olim (immigrants to Israel) are the least integrated in modern Israel. About 600,000 Israeli citizens live in North America.[43] Typical is the prolific output of the widely influential Jewish scholar, Jacob Neusner, who winces at holocaust theology and argues strenuously that a Jewish American's first loyalty must be to the United States. He speaks of Zionism as "reversion to an invented past." While wishing the State of Israel well, Neusner really wants no part of it.[44] A far more radical dissociation is to be seen in the extremely rabid thinking of M. I. T. linguist, Noam Chomsky, who saw the State of Israel as the chief destabilizer of world peace.[45] Considering the opposition to Zionism, its survival as a relatively cohesive force can only be understood over against the biblical and historical background.

The prophetic ideas constitute "the hope of Israel" and which Zionism, political (as in Herzl and Nordau), cultural (as in Martin Buber) and spiritual (as in Ahad Ha'am) coalesced to further.

Erosion of Ottoman Turkey

The years leading up to World War I brought the discouragement of delay and great difficulty to Zionism, but there were encouragements also. The decline of Ottoman Turkey stimulated spasms of hopefulness.

◊ ◊ ◊

* The fact is, as the renown British Jewish scholar, Dr. Isidore Epstein has argued in his very influential book on Judaism: "Interlocked with these Messianic prophecies is the doctrine of the remnant of Israel which, rehabilitated in Zion, will form the nucleus of the universal kingdom of righteousness, around which all the nations of the world would be gathered."[46]

The Young Turk Revolution of 1908 brought a new regime which, however, maintained the same attitude toward the Jewish aspiration for nationhood—"Autonomy is treason." The brief war between Turkey and Italy in 1911 "gave a fresh impetus to Zionist activities. The Turkish government emerged weakened from this conflict and the Balkan Wars."[47] Another seismic shuffle of the Young Turks took place in 1912.

Immigration to Israel

New waves of emigration (largely from Russia and in response to the continuing pogroms) came in 1904. By 1907 there were 70,000 Jews in Palestine and about 500,000 Arabs. Most Jews lived in the cities, but more of the new immigrants were people of the soil.[*] Tension between Jewish settlers, those Jews who had always maintained a presence at the sacred sites, and the Arabs in the land were constant and immediate. Granted, an occasional and exceptional welcome was extended. After all, the Arabs were very poor on the whole and some were receptive to economic bolstering.

Yusaf Deya Pasa al-Khalidi, leader of an old Jerusalem family, remarked to Chief Rabbi Kah very early on,

---

"Who can challenge the rights of the Jews on Palestine? Good Lord, historically, it is your country."[48]

Attacks, however, began on Jewish settlements, and the role of Arabs and Islam loomed large in the Jews' search for a homeland.

While many Jews twisted and writhed in identity crisis (Mahler had to become a Catholic in order to become top musician in Vienna, and Arnold Schönberg became a Catholic, then a Protestant, and finally reverted again to Judaism), the Vatican viewed Zionist aspiration with dismay.[49] The liberal and neoorthodox Protestant establishment quite consistently opposed Zionism (Reinhold Niebuhr would be an exception). The conciliar movement and such influential publications as *The Christian Century* scarcely deviated from a strong "displacement theory," arguing that "the old Israel has ceased to exist," and dismissing Dr. Stephen Wise's concerns about reports of the Holocaust as "exaggerated."[50]

◊ ◊ ◊

* Few have depicted the early settlement of Yishuv any better than Meyer Levin, who was born in Chicago in 1905 and who died in Israel in 1981. His two novels, *The Settlers* and *The Harvest,* dramatize what it meant for the immigrants to settle in malarial swamps and to turn the desert into a blossoming rose. The experience of one Russian Jewish family is traced from generation to generation. His film, *The Illegals*, treats the illegal prestate immigration to Mandatory Palestine.

The most evident exception was Bible-believing Christians.[*] So pervasive was this evangelical identification with the Jews that even Charles Haddon Spurgeon, prince among Victorian preachers, believed in the national conversion of the Jews and testified that "our hope is the personal, premillennial return of the Lord Jesus Christ in glory."[51]

◊ ◊ ◊

[*] Timothy Weber has demonstrated that "the conservative evangelical movement at the end of the nineteenth century . . . recognized in premillennialism a way to remain both Biblical and evangelical under difficult circumstances."[52]

CHAPTER

THE COUNTERPOINT OF THE MOVE OF MILITANT ISLAM

The Syrian Minister of Defense, General Mustafa T'Las,
euologizing a war hero who had killed twenty-eight Israelis:

"He butchered three of them with an ax and decapitated them.
In other words, instead of using a gun to kill them
he took a hatchet to chop their heads off.
He struggled face-to-face with one of them,
and throwing down his ax managed to break his neck
and devour his flesh in front of his comrades.
This is a special case.
Need I single it out to award him the Medal of the Republic?
I will grant this medal to any soldier
who succeeds in killing twenty-eight Jews,
and I will cover him with
appreciation
and honor
for his
bravery."

Quoted by Pulitzer Prize Winner Saul Bellow[1]

THE BRAVADO OF A SWAGGERING Syrian warrior (facing page) might be ignored as a deranged tirade, but the implacable alienation between the Arabs and Jews, accentuated by the rise of radical Islam, cannot.

The land of Palestine has been inhabited since paleolithic times. Early in the second millennium before Christ when Abraham came from Ur of the Chaldeans there were Canaanites in the land (Genesis 13:7). Other nomadic peoples came into the land such as the Hittites from the north and later the Philistines, a sea people who probably emigrated from Crete. Genesis 16 and 21 tell us about the conception of Ishmael by Hagar when Abraham's wife, Sarah, could not bear children and of the rivalry when at last in fulfillment of the promise Sarah did give birth to a son, Isaac. Abraham pleaded for Ishmael, and while God gave him no promise like Isaac received, God did warn:

> He will be a wild donkey of a man; his hand will be against everyone and everyone's hand against him, and he will live in hostility toward all his brothers (Genesis 16:12).

The conflict between Ishmael and Isaac has lived on through their descendants, the Arabs and the Jews. God promised to make Ishmael into a great nation with many progeny and the father of twelve rulers (cf. Genesis 17:20; 25:12–18). Interestingly, in 1905, the year that David Ben-Gurion arrived in Jaffa, the early Arab nationalist, Negib Azoury wrote:

> Two important phenomena manifest themselves at this time: they are the awakening of the Arab nation and the latent efforts of the Jews to reconstitute the ancient monarchy of Israel on a very large scale. These two movements are destined to fight each other continually, until one of them prevails over the other. Upon the final outcome of the battle between these two peoples, representing two opposed principles, the fate of the entire world will depend.[2]

Little Palestine, standing at the crossroads of three continents has never been shielded from turmoil. Jerusalem, "city of Peace," has known siege and attack and bloodshed beyond description.[3] Since Joshua's time the Jews have always had a presence in the land, and as we have seen, the idea of return has never been far from their minds. Settled communities of Nabatean Arabs have existed since the days of Alexander the Great. The Muslim caliphs quickly asserted dominance and were interrupted only by the Christian Crusaders who forbid Jews and Muslims to enter Jerusalem.[4] From the defeat of the Crusaders by the Saracens up to World War I and the collapse of the Ottoman Turks, the tensions were largely of a tribal nature. Intermittent outbreaks shattered the peace. A more moderate Ottoman officer like Ismail Kemal Bey actually welcomed Zionists "who were contributing to the development of the wealth of the country and giving the population an example and a stimulus by the establishment of wine and perfumery industries."[5]

The story of who has inhabited the land is complex and often confusing.[6] Most Arab people became Muslim, although some Arabs remained Christian, as part of the Roman Catholic, Greek Orthodox, or Middle Eastern religious communities. Well-known moderates like long-time Bethlehem Mayor Elias Freij and even radical extremist guerilla leaders like George Habash and Nayif Hawatmeh are so-called Christian Arabs. Yasser Arafat married a "Christian" Arab woman. Christian Arab villages especially cluster around Nazareth. But with the rise of Arab nationalism early in this century, and then the increasing radicalization of Islam, "Christian" Arabs have tended more and more to emigrate from Palestine and all Arab countries.

The surge toward an Islamic revolution since the 1970s and the master plan for a single unified Muslim state to rule the world have infinitely complicated the situation in the Middle East. There are one billion Muslims in the world—one in five persons is a Muslim. Islam has 150 sects, so it is not monolithic; yet it is rare for Muslims to support Israel. To understand why is important to any comprehension of Israel's quest for a homeland.

THE ORIGINS OF ISLAM

O God, do not keep silent; be not quiet, O God, be not still. See how your enemies are astir, how your foes rear their heads. With cunning they conspire against your people; they plot against those you cherish. "Come," they say, "let us destroy them as a nation, that the name of Israel be remembered no more" (Psalm 83:1–4).

The Birth of Islam

Islam, which mean "submission or surrender to God," rose in the deserts of what we call Saudi Arabia in the sixth century after Christ. The rabid religious monism of Mohammed germinated in the polytheism and animism of Mecca. Mohammed was born into a prominent family in Mecca about A.D. 570. Upon the death of his parents and grandfather, he was raised by an uncle, whose son Ali was to become very central in Shi'ite Islam. Marrying a wealthy widow and achieving economic success as a merchant, Mohammed was deeply troubled spiritually and sought after God in the desert. Here in a dream, the angel Gabriel allegedly came to him and commenced the revelations that were to constitute the 114 suras or chapters (78,000 words) of the Holy Qur'an. Some measure of the intense dedication of Muslims in the propagation of their faith is to be seen in the requirement that applicants for admission to al-Azhar University in Cairo, the center of world Islamic culture and the home to in excess of 30,000 students at last report, must know the Qur'an by heart.

Christian, Judaic, and Zoroastrian influences can be traced in the shaping and formulation of Islam. Mohammed borrowed from all of these traditions and synthesized a new religion that was fanatically monotheistic. "There is one God and Mohammed is his prophet" asserts the Muslim creed. Theology pushed the system, but history, that is, the vacuum left in the wake of the collapsed Roman Empire, pulled it. Mohammed proclaimed his ideas so fiercely that opposition in Mecca forced him to flee to Medina. This flight has become known as the *Hejira,* or emigration of A. D. 622, and the Muslim calendar counts time from this date. Consolidating his power, Mohammed was able to come back to Mecca and take it by force, destroying heathen worship in the idol temple known as the Ka'aba and turning the area around the Ka'aba into a mosque. He died two years later. He himself did not write a single word of the Qur'an, but one year after his death, his successor, Abu Bakr, compiled the prophet's teaching. A dozen years later the third caliph, Othman, ordered the destruction of this first edition and the writing of a revision.

The Doctrine of Islam

At the heart of Islam is a doctrine of the one true God called Allah. Though the plural of majesty is consistently used, Allah is one. "Thus Islam appeared, not as a new religion, but as a revival of pure Abrahamic monotheism, purified at once of the accretions of Judaism and Christianity and superseding them as the final revelation."[7] Muslims use a rosary with "the ninety-nine most beautiful names of Allah." "Worry beads" are in evidence in Arab and Muslim countries.

Judaic monotheism beyond question influenced Mohammed. He had contacts with Jews in several cities, and they were not very receptive to many of his ideas. His very elaborate angelology and demonology show some reliance on Zoroastrian thinking, especially in his notions of *jinn* or *geni,* a group of spirits midway between human beings and angels. Christian influence was unfortunately mediated through the heretical Nestorian church that rejected Chalcedonian Christology. While Zechariah, John the Baptist, and Jesus are considered prophets along with twenty-two named from the Old Testament, Mohammed is the last and the greatest of the prophets.

Chief Christian concerns with Islamic doctrinal formulation are in the areas of the doctrine of God, the Trinity, the person and work of Christ, and salvation. Islam is a highly deterministic and indeed fatalistic religion (the operation of the principle of *kismet*). Zwemer alleged that "Islam is not original, not a ripe fruit, but rather a wild offshoot of foreign soil grafted on Judaism,"[8] and indeed many allusions from the Old Testament are found in the Qur'an. There is no reference to God as love in Islam. Sin is seen as violation of law without a more profound analysis. Moral purity or sanctification are not seen in the Qur'an, nor is the word *holiness* used. There is no incarnation of Deity, no redemption, no word for conscience, no Fatherhood of God.[*]

Mohammed spoke of the commonality of Christianity and Judaism with Islam in his characterization of Jews and Christians as "people of the Book." His attitudinal change toward Christians,[†] however, is perhaps reflective "of his growing hostility to the Greeks and their Christian Arab allies, Orthodox or Monophysite."[9]

In his first year at Medina, Mohammed adopted a number of Jewish customs, but his clashes with the Jewish community and their unwillingness to accept him as "the prophet" led to a growing rift, echoed in the Qur'an by increasingly strident and denunciatory language.

Early on the "people of the Book" were not pressured to convert to Islam. The Qur'an itself says "Let there be no compulsion in religion" (2.256) and "You have your religion and I have mine" (109.6). Special taxes and terms were levied, but increasingly the option became the Qur'an, the sword, or slavery![10]

Jews were more and more subject to hardship at the hands of the Muslims, as a famous passage from the Qur'an shows:

> You will surely find that the most hostile to the Believers are the Jews and the idolaters, while those who have the greatest affection to them are the ones who say "We are Christians" (5:86).[11]

◊ ◊ ◊

[*] "Every wise man must acknowledge that the true religion ascribes the greatest perfection to the Supreme Being, and not only conveys the worthiest conception of all His attributes, but demonstrates the harmony and equality existing between them. Now their religion was defective in acknowledging only two active principles in the Deity. His will and His wisdom, while it left His goodness and greatness inoperative."—Raymond Lull, the first missionary to the Muslims (A. D. 1315)[12]
[†] "It is evident, throughout the Quran that Mohammed had no direct knowledge of Christian doctrine."—H. A. R. Gibb[13]

The problem in part stemmed from the fact that Jewish centers were right in the middle of expanding Muslim and Christian growth.

The Spread of Islam

After the death of Mohammed (who supposedly ascended to heaven on his horse from what is now the site of the Dome of the Rock in Jerusalem), his successors encouraged a series of holy wars (*jihad*). Within a century, they had created a Muslim empire that spread from northern Spain to India. The increasingly inward, bickering, and corrupt churches of the Middle East and North Africa collapsed.[*] The subjugation of women (the Qur'an approves four wives but Mohammed himself had eleven), the practice of slavery, and the continual use of shame-words for the Jews made life vexatious and well-nigh intolerable for Christians and Jews.

The watchwords from the Qur'an were:

> Fight against those who do not believe in God or in the Last Day, who do not forbid what God and His prophet have forbidden or practice the true religion, among those who have been given the Book, until they pay the poll-tax from their hand, they being humbled (9:29).

While anti-Semitism is not inherent in Islam as a religious system, given the historical background between Jews and Arabs, the seeds of resentment and rivalry embodied in the Qur'an, and the cruel treatment of the Jews by the founder, Mohammed himself, the growing animosity between these two segments of the human family is not surprising. Given the move of Jews toward the Holy Land, irresistible force would meet immovable object. The result could only be catastrophic.

THE MODUS OPERANDI OF ISLAM

> *With one mind they plot together; they form an alliance against you—the tents of Edom and the Ishmaelites, of Moab and the Hagrites, Gebal, Ammon and Amalek, Philistia, with the people of Tyre. Even Assyria has joined them to lend strength to the descendants of Lot* (Psalm 83:5–8).

◇ ◇ ◇

[*] The candlestick was removed from these once thriving centers of Christian influence. Some splendid bursts of light brought sparkling civilizations in some areas (under prodigies such as Avicenna and Averroës, although it must be admitted that they were in large part the products of Greek, especially Aristotelian influence), but on the whole there was a cruelty and violence in the conflicts.

Beliefs and Sects

Islam is a total way of life, whatever its schisms and sects, as seen in the following tables:

FIVE PILLARS OF ISLAM				
Repetition of the Creed	Five Daily Prayers Facing Mecca to Be Repeated in Arabic	Observance of Ramadan or the Full Month of Fasting	The Practice of Almsgiving	The Pilgrimage to Mecca (the *hajj*)

MAJOR ISLAMIC GROUPS
Sunni The majority wing in Islam, Sunni is generally moderate. After the death of Mohammed, a consensus prevailed that his successor should be chosen by the community from his tribe, who were called "people of the Sunna and the Community." Those who advocated the choice of Mohammed's cousin, and son-in-law, had to wait until he was selected as the fourth caliph, but by this time he was sixty years of age.
Shi'ite Ali was mortally wounded by a sword thrust. His followers are called Shi'ites (meaning follower). Distinctive in many ways from the Sunni, the Shi'ites consider Ali the first Imam. They recognize twelve imams, the last of whom is in "concealment." He will return as the Mahdi or Messiah to set up the perfect reign of righteousness on earth. Students of the life of Gordon of Khartoum will recall that what he faced in the Sudan was the fanaticism of Muslims who believed that in fact Mohammed Ahmad ibn Abdullah was the Muslim Messiah, the long-waited Mahdi.[14]
Druse and Alawite Splinters from Shi'ites. President Asad of Syria is an Alawite.

Isma'iliya

While Islam is essentially a lay movement and any male Muslim may function as an imam (spiritual leader) to lead prayers and give brief sermonic comments in the mosque on Friday, there has developed a caste of professional scholars and teachers (the *ulama*, "those who have knowledge"). The Isma'iliya sect recognizes only seven imams, the seventh of whom is to return as the Mahdi. This is the group of which the Agha Khan is the titular head.

Wahhabis

The Wahhabis are a purist strain of the Sunni and advocate going back to the Qur'an. They do not use rosaries and are very superstitious. The House of Ibn Saud in Saudia Arabia, custodians of the most holy sites of Islam are Wahhabis.[15]

Sufis

The Sufis or mystics in Islam are the rough equivalent of the Hassids in Judaism or the Pentecostals/Charismatics in Christianity.[16] Among its many orders are the whirling dervishes and other eccentrics called fakirs by Westerners.

Abmadiyya

A more modern and exceedingly missionary-minded sect in India and Pakistan are the Abmadiyya, who claim that Jesus did not die on the cross but escaped only to die later in Kashmir where his tomb is displayed.

Baha'i

Later monotheistic sects like the Baha'i (whose founder Bab was slain by the Persians in 1850) have had a very hard going and have been much persecuted in modern Iran.[17]

History has shown Islam to be aggressive and missionary-minded. Thus pan-Islam has always seemed threatening to the West.

The reason the Jews and the Muslims through much of history have been point and counterpoint is their shared historical and geographical heritage. Muslims argue vigorously that God's covenant was between Abraham and Ishmael, not Abraham and Isaac. Pondering Genesis 22, we are told, will lead us to see that it was really Ishmael who was to be offered on Mount Moriah even though it says Isaac. In the House of Islam therefore, Eid al-Adha is the feast of sacrifice commemorating Abraham's offering of Ishmael. Not all Palestinian Arabs are ethnic Arabs, that is, many are descended from previous inhabitants such as Jubusites, Ammonites, Canaanites, and other peoples Israel was ordered to displace in Bible times. The Arabs swept up all of the remnants of these people when they filled the vacuum left by Jewish dispersion. "The people themselves used the name the ancient Israelites gave their ancestors—Falistini in Arabic, Palestinian in English."[18] Most of these Palestinians are Muslim, and the adversarial relationship is clearly from time immemorial.

The Counterpoint of the Move of Militant Islam

Tribalism

Notwithstanding the inevitable tendency to fragmentation, Islam whether in Africa, Asia, Europe, or America, retains an essential unity.[*] There is impressive evidence of a rebirth, a resurrection, a renewal of Islam in our time.[19] A new zealotry and militancy have arisen. Long repressed by a hated colonialism (which finally ended with the Suez Crisis in 1956) and bolstered by unbelievable petroleum resources, some 200 million Arabs have exerted their power. This century started with the Turkish massacre of Christian Armenians; much later came the demolition of the only Arab democracy, Lebanon; now there are five Muslim states in the new Commonwealth of Independent States (formerly the Soviet Union). How will little Israel fare?

How do we understand the Arab mind, the Islamic mentality?

Charles Glass, quoting an Egyptian diplomat, explained the Arab mind:[†]

> Egypt is the only nation-state in the Middle-East. The rest are tribes with flags . . . the great majority of the Levant's people still look to traditional community and sectarian leaders for protection, favors, money and jobs. Loyalty to families, village, tribe and sect has always been stronger than ideology.[20]

Mercilessness to external foes; mercilessness to internal foes; President Asad's massacre of tens of thousands in his own town of Hama in 1982; the fact that most of the casualties in the intifada in Israel (from 1987 on) were Palestinian on Palestinian; a Syrian spy's impregnation of an Irish girl and then use of her to carry a bomb on board a doomed aircraft; public amputations in Saudi Arabia and the film *Death of a Princess*; the atrocities of Saddam Hussein; the whole Salman Rushdie affair—all display a total lack of civility.

Why with all of the petro-dollars and education and wealth are these able and brilliant people making "no inventions or discoveries in the sciences or the arts, no contribution to medicine or philosophy?"[21] Glutted with Western goods (50 percent of Arab food is imported), yet sending 8,000,000 immigrants to Europe and many to America. There is no move to democracy in any quarter, not even in Kuwait after all the West did to preserve her independence. Blaming this stall on "imperialism" will not suffice.

◊ ◊ ◊

[*] "The history of Islam in the 19th and 20th centuries is a history of revival and efforts at readjustment under the double stimulus of challenge from within and pressing dangers from without."—Sir Hamilton Gibb[22]

[†] No one has written more provocatively and thoughtfully about the Arab mind and Arab culture today than David Pryce-Jones in his brilliant *The Closed Circle: An Interpretation of the Arabs*.

Tribal society is a closed circle. About all that these Arab tribes hold in common is their hatred for the Jews. Shame and honor totally dominate. "Dropouts, eccentrics, the inspired inventor, the truly modest, or genuine non-conformist have no place here."[23] "Techniques of fear" breed a culture of dissembling. Modernization is widely seen as primary degradation. Technology is used and prized if it stabilizes the traditional. Complete male domination and "the cult of virility" along with "the cult of virginity" (the continuing and inhumane practice of female circumcision) are just plain scary.

Toadying up to the Nazis in World War II, continuing publication and governmental distribution of the mendacious *Protocols of the Elders of Zion,* unwillingness to consider any partition of Palestine, absolute irresolution in the matter of Palestinian refugees to this day, endless bombing and assassinations, and the near collapse of the work ethic in much of the Arab world have left them in virtual paralysis. This kind of tribalism is by no means limited to the Middle East (cf. Northern Ireland and other dreary wastelands on our planet), but is in any place a mindless masochism. The need to assert honor becomes the perennial escape route from honest facing of the real issues.[24] Self-hatred and chronic feelings of inferiority are traps and pits. In all of this, sadly and tragically, Arabs are the losers.

THE ONSLAUGHT OF ISLAM

Do to them as you did to Midian, as you did to Sisera and Jabin at the river Kishon, who perished at Endor and became like refuse on the ground. Make their nobles like Oreb and Zeeb, all their princes like Zebah and Zalmunna, who said, "Let us take possession of the pasturelands of God" (Psalm 83:9–12).

Because of the violence against your brother, Jacob, you will be covered with shame; you will be destroyed forever. On the day you stood aloof while strangers carried off his wealth and foreigners entered his gates and cast lots for Jerusalem, you were like one of them. You should not look down on your brother in the day of his misfortune, nor rejoice over the people of Judah in the day of their destruction, nor boast so much in the day of their trouble (Obadiah 10–12).

Conquering the World

The desert is hard and the wild storms in the desert are harsh. Islam seems to have taken on something of the texture of the desert out of which she has arisen. Out of the waste-howling wilderness came Islam to conquer. Of the conviction that Mohammed the prophet was the prophet of whom Moses prophesied in Deuteronomy 18:15 and the strengthening *parakletos* (comforter) of whom the Lord Jesus gave promise, Islam went forth to seize the earth. Outside of the unassimilable Jews and small groups of Christians, all peoples were quickly enveloped in their lightning-like advance. In his awesome *jihad,* or holy war, the Arab commander-in-chief El Okbar conquered all of North Africa. When he reached the Atlantic Ocean he rode his horse out into the water, drew his sword, and cried "Bismellahi! If the ocean were not in my way, I would carry the prophet's message even farther west."[25]

Only Charles Martel's brave stand halted the progress of the Muslim invaders at the Battle of Tours in A.D. 732, holding them back to the Gates of the Pyrenees. Moorish domination of Spain was not finally ended until 1492 during the reign of Ferdinand and Isabella. In the East the Ottoman Turks captured Constantinople in 1453 and stripped the once proud city of its wealth and libraries, turning lovely St. Sophia Cathedral into a mosque. In the years just prior to the Reformation, the Muslims were pounding on the gates of the city of Vienna, and all of Europe was afraid.

The stretch of Muslim expansion reached all the way across India to Malaysia and the Philippines (in which almost 3,000,000 Moros or Moors live). In England, France, and Sweden, Islam is already the second largest religious body. In France there are two Muslims for every Protestant. Hundreds of mosques are being built in Western countries. Mosques and Muslim Study Centers are springing up everywhere in the United States. The reach of Islam to African-Americans is seen in the stridently militaristic Black Muslim group. The appeal of Islam to blacks must be seen as affording an opportunity to strike out at the white religious establishment.[*]

Islamic eschatology (with an obvious Jewish and Christian influence) centers events of the last days in Jerusalem. A great seducer (very similar to the Anti-Christ or Anti-Messiah of Christian and Jewish apocalyptic) will seek to disrail Muslim progress, but Jesus Christ will come down to destroy him. Everyone will be integrated into Islam, and two final trumpets will sound, one for the living and one for the dead. The final judgment is based entirely on works, and really the only provision for taking away sin is by kissing "the black stone" in the Ka'aba in Mecca.[26]

Most alarming at the present time is not the kind of aggressiveness in outreach with which Islam has been associated from the beginning of its march in power, nor the higher birthrate among Muslims,[†] but the

◊ ◊ ◊

* American Muslims are generally affected by Western culture, but curiously *The Invitation*, published by the Islamic Information Center of America, features articles by a Ph.D. that attempt to make a serious argument for Koranic polygamy as superior to monogamy inasmuch as polygamy solves the problem of "surplus women." Thus, it is argued, Islam is "the best system in the world."[27]

† Christian Arabs have a lower birthrate than do the Muslim Arabs, and this is really what did in the Christians in Lebanon.

resurgence of an extremely fundamentalistic Islam. Its most dramatic exhibit is with the Islamic Republic founded by the Ayatollah Khomeini in Iran in 1979. With the imposition of Islamic penal law[*] in Iran and partial adoption of the same in the Sudan and in Pakistan, the question as to just how far this will all go is quite real.

In an engaging article entitled "The Muslims Are Coming! The Muslims are Coming," Daniel Pipes quoted Leon Uris's warning in his 1984 novel, *The Haj*: "We have an enraged bull of a billion people on our planet, and tilted the wrong way they could open the second road to Armageddon."[28]Another victim of Muslimphobia advised: "The implication of the Soviet collapse . . . might be that Muslim armies would again be besieging the gates of Vienna." The alarming vote in Algeria in early 1992 gave the Islamic Salvation Front 188 of 206 seats in the parliament and left the ruling National Liberation Front with only fifteen seats. This Islamic tide led to the denial of the vote and the establishment of military rule. Militant Islamic students herald their objectives: "Victory to the Just Struggle of the Wretched of the Earth Against Imperialism, Zionism and Reaction in the Way of Constructing a Free, Monotheistic and Classless Society."[29] Even though Muslim seers are trained in isolation from contemporary life, Iran's rapid development of nuclear technology and the embrace of technology by "the electronic" imams of Egypt for the circulation of their message,[30] put us on notice that Muslim strategies are current.

Controlling the Jews

While all of Western civilization is the broad target of the contemporary Islamic resurgence, the narrower and sharper focus as always is the Jews and the Jewish state.

When in 1838 Sir Moses Montefiore visited Palestine, he found 3000 Jews in Jerusalem and about the same number in Hebron, Tiberias, and Safed in the north. These Jews were living in abject poverty, "treated like dogs by the Turks,"[†] allowed to possess only two synagogues and their graves on the Eastern slope of Olivet, "but were not permitted to own an inch of land" in Palestine.[31]

Some one hundred years later, the Grand Mufti of Jerusalem sought Hitler's help in implementing the Arab version of the final solution.

◊ ◊ ◊

* Called the Shari'a, involving flagellations, stonings, limb amputations, segregation of the sexes, women not allowed to drive a car, no usury, etc.
† While the Israelis have not always treated the Arabs fairly, they have guaranteed the Muslim holy places of their control.

Unquestionably a *jihad*, or holy war, was declared against the Zionist Jews before the modern State of Israel came into being. "Jewish sovereignty in the Middle East seems to contradict the teachings of the Koran, and thus calls into question the validity of Islam itself."[32] The influence of the P. L. O. among Arabs living in Israel and the occupied territory seems to be receding, and the influence of the Islamic Movement or Hamas seems to be growing. The radicalization of Islam in Israel bodes no good. A recent "International Conference to Support the Islamic Revolution in Palestine" held in Teheran included 400 delegates from sixty Islamic countries. The conference called for "the elimination of the Zionist existence" and total opposition to any peace process involving Israel. Escalation of the activities of Hizbullah, the Shi'ite extremist organization, demonstrates the implacable and irrational nature of this hatred for everything Jewish.

The history of Islamic terrorism has involved the use of every vicious means and tactic conceivable.[33]

The war against the Jewish state is really a war against the Jewish presence in Palestine.*

Syrian Minister of Defense, Moustafa Tlass's best-selling book, *Matzoh of Zion,* is just the retelling of the old anti-Semitic bloodlibel about the murder of a Gentile in Damascus in the 1840s and the making of bread out of his blood for Passover.[34] This is insane rage. What can be done?

THE OUTCOME FOR ISLAM

The word of the LORD came to me: "Son of man, set your face against Mount Seir; prophesy against it and say: This is what the Sovereign LORD says: 'I am against you, Mount Seir, and I will stretch out my hand against you and make a desolate waste. I will turn your towns into ruins and you will be desolate. Then you will know that I am the LORD. Because you harbored an ancient hostility and delivered the Israelites over to the sword at the time of their calamity, the time their punishment reached its climax, therefore as surely as I live, declares the Sovereign Lord, I will give you over to bloodshed and it will pursue you. Since you did not hate bloodshed, bloodshed will pursue you'" (Ezekiel 35:1–6).

Former President Chaim Herzog of Israel, in addressing the European Council in Strasbourg, told the parliamentary assembly that Western leaders do not understand the Middle East and that Islamic fundamen-

◊ ◊ ◊

* Early Jewish efforts by such leaders as Martin Buber, Hugo Bergman, and Ernst Simon for a binational community were totally rebuffed.

talism is the main danger facing the world. "The Western powers have literally fallen flat on their faces time after time . . . when it comes to understanding and appreciating the world-shattering events in our area," he was quoted as saying. Israel is in a unique position as she bears the brunt of Islamic assault. Her very existence as a nation is regarded as an obscenity by her foes, and the United Nations for many years (until 1991) termed Zionism as racism.

Hitler's old axiom from *Mein Kampf* concerning the effectiveness of lying propaganda is once again verified in human experience. Hitler argued that "the skillful and unremitting use of propaganda can persuade people that Heaven is hell, for the broad mass of the people in the primitive simplicity of its heart more readily falls victim to a big lie than a small one." The frightening deceptions concerning Jews and the Jewish state peddled through the world and inculcated into hundreds of thousands of young Arab minds create the most ominous prospect of future carnage and catastrophe.

Arabs and the Present

Yet in the interest of fairness it must be said that there has been manifest unfairness and injustice on the side of the Jews and Israel as well.

Support for basic Zionist aspiration does not and should not require the friends of Israel to believe that her birth was an immaculate conception.

Americans do not argue for the actions of their own government under any circumstances, and Israeli actions and policies show them to be sinners like us all.

The Arab people and Muslims everywhere are human beings who must be respected and regarded as being created in God's image and having the same rights as anyone else. Early travelers into the Levant moved into the realm of "The Arabian Nights" and found a fascinating albeit a fierce people.[35] It is well to read the impressions of more recent travelers who give a more personal dimension to the nameless and faceless struggles of a people struggling to come out of medievalism into modernity.[36]

Although bearing the Christian witness to Islam has been difficult, and in cases seemingly impossible, Christian compassion and concern must be stoked by the recognition of the fact that these one billion persons are also those for whom Jesus Christ died. Their austere religion seems to know nothing of the warm rays of God's love.[*] Because conversion strikes at the heart of a Muslim's sense of identity, there are few individual conversions. Word of a true people movement to Christ among Muslims in Indonesia is one of the first such in history. Such is the power of the gospel of Christ and such is our great God of the impossible. Christians should be emboldened to pray and encourage witness for Christ among our Muslim friends everywhere. What God is doing in an "underground church" in the most inaccessible Muslim countries can hearten us. That water baptisms were held in Saudi Arabia during "Operation Desert Storm" is in itself most extraordinary. Saudi Arabia will never be the same.

Arabs and the Future

In the long-term God has special blessing for the offspring of Ishmael. God will keep His promise as made to Abraham:

> And as for Ishmael, I have heard you: I will surely bless him; I will make him fruitful and will greatly increase his numbers. He will be the father of twelve rulers, and I will make him into a great nation" (Genesis 17:20).

Some of the ultimate blessing for these peoples will come during the messianic or millennial kingdom.

If, as amillennialists argue, that the kingdom blessings for Israel are all fulfilled in the church during this age, upon whom are the promises of blessing for all the other nations being fulfilled in this age? Who is Egypt? Assyria? Jordan? How do these "spiritualize" out?

Isaiah 2:1–5 speaks of the Lord's temple in Jerusalem "in the last days." This is the time when "the law will go out from Zion, the word of the LORD from Jerusalem" (2:3b). Then "all nations will stream to it," and "many peoples will come and say, 'Come let us go up to the mountain of the LORD, to the house of the God of Jacob. He will teach us his ways, so that we may walk in his paths'" (2:2b–3a). Thus the priestly and mediatorial function for which Israel was chosen will be fulfilled (cf. Exodus 19:5–6). The millennial picture encompasses the Arabs and Muslim nations as well.

Psalm 67 speaks of a future for the nations that will never be obtained during time-space history. This is not universalism in the sense that all will be saved, which is clearly not taught in Scripture. The passage does

◊ ◊ ◊

* (previous page) Christian missionaries to Muslims like Henry Martyn, Samuel Zwemer,[37] and J. Christy Wilson have rendered exemplary service. Christian scholars like Dr. J. N. D. Anderson and Dr. J. Dudley Woodberry have made an immense contribution to the cause of Christ through their faithful labors. Christians from Arab and Muslim lands have been most helpful in explaining Islam in the world.[38] The Fellowship of Isa led by Dr. Edward Joseph has pioneered in creative ways of bearing witness to Muslims.

portray a time when divine rule elicits the praises of all nations and "all the ends of the earth will fear him" (67:7).[*]

In a more direct way, the late Wilbur M. Smith's *Egypt in Bible Prophecy* treated the import of the 250 verses about Egypt in the Old Testament that were prophetic and future at the time of their utterance. Egypt is a major Arab and Islamic nation. Smith pointed out that Isaiah 19:17–25 clearly speaks of a great and ultimate healing for Egypt.[39] Where is this in history? It must be millennial. Egypt will radically shift spiritually. Egypt will come to recognize and worship Israel's God (19:19). Indeed the trio of leading nations in the Millennium is here indicated to be Israel, Assyria, and Egypt (19:24). While there will come humiliating disaster "at the gulf of the Egyptian sea" (11:15), Assyria and Egypt as well as Israel will be "a blessing on the earth" (19:24).[†]

The inclusion of Arab/Muslim countries in prophecies of future blessing needs to be much underscored, for the purpose of the election of Israel is for blessing to the nations. Some promises have been for the Hashemite Kingdom of Jordan. God promised: "Yet afterward, I will restore the fortunes of the Ammonites" (Jeremiah 49:6).[40] Indeed in the great psalm of messianic rule (Psalm 72) in which the benefits of the Lord's reign are magnificently represented, it is indicated that "the desert tribes will bow before him" (72:9) and "the kings of Sheba and Seba will present him gifts" (72:10), perhaps referring to the gifts of South Arabian monarchs.[‡]

Scripture is a motherlode for those who would prospect for what God has promised to Arab and Muslim people in the future golden age of messianic rule. The final word is an upbeat word.

The modern face-off between Israel and her Arab/Islamic neighbors pivots on the age-old issues of biblical and prophetic significance. The late Charles Malik, Lebanese statesman and former president of the United Nations General Assembly, observed correctly:

> To dismiss the present conflict between the children of Isaac and Ishmael (the Israelis and the Arabs) as just an ordinary politico-economic struggle is to have no sense whatsoever of the holy and ultimate in history.[41]

◊ ◊ ◊

[*] Andrew Bonar was correct in seeing this psalm as dealing with circumstances at Christ's return in glory and the establishment of temporal blessings for Israel with a striking spiritual overtone for all the peoples of the earth, including Arab and Muslim peoples.

[†] Note Daniel 11:40–43 as it touches another significant role for Egypt in the wrap-up of human history.

[‡] Both Delitzsch and Kidner see these names in this way.

And Henry Grunwald in a widely circulated speech on A.D. 2000 and what is coming, commented concerning the ancestral rage[*] in the Middle East:

> For a long time, nationalism and tribalism will remain intractable forces, especially in the Middle East, where they are mixed with deep religious passions, hatreds and dreams of revenge.[42]

The recent accords between Israel, the P. L. O., and Jordan face substantive obstacles and must yet be tested by time. What can change the cycle of hate in the Middle East? Scripture has some answers.

◊ ◊ ◊

[*] As the West faces the mounting tide of militant Muslim advance, every effort should be made to secure basic human rights for all peoples. The distinguished evangelical theologian Carl F. H. Henry has recently expressed concern that "religious rights of some minorities are non-existent in some countries." He cited "harassment, persecution and punishment" of foreign workers in Saudi Arabia.[43] Such practices as beheading and crucifixion of citizens or foreigners should not be allowed.

THE QUICKENING OF THE PULSE—WORLD WAR I AND THE BALFOUR DECLARATION

Do not be afraid,
for I am with you;
I will bring your children
from the east
and gather you
from the west.
I will say to the north,
"Give them up!"
and to the south,
"Do not hold them back."
Bring my sons
from afar
and my daughters
from the ends of the earth.

Isaiah 43:5–6

But you, O mountains of Israel, will produce branches and fruit for my people Israel, for they will soon come home. I am concerned for you and will look on you with favor; you will be plowed and sown, and I will multiply the number of people upon you, even the whole house of Israel. The towns will be inhabited and the ruins rebuilt. I will increase the number of men and animals upon you, and they will be fruitful and become numerous. I will settle people on you as in the past and will make you prosper more than before. Then you will know that I am the LORD. I will cause people, my people Israel, to walk upon you. They will possess you, and you will be their inheritance; you will never again deprive them of their children.

Ezekiel 36:8–12

SHAKESPEARE WROTE THAT "there's a divinity that shapes our ends, rough-hew them as we will." Again and again we have seen God's providence in relation to His ancient covenant people Israel. God has preserved this people across the centuries in the face of the most diabolical onslaughts.

The land itself since the collapse of Jewish autonomy after the brief interlude under the Maccabees has been successively governed and plundered by one marauding power after another. Since then there has never been an independent Palestinian state. Through all of the centuries of this era there have been small contingents of Bedouin in the land, essentially nomadic. Small colonies of Jews have even in the most bitter times maintained a precarious existence around the sacred sites. Small clusters of Christians have also eked out a marginal survival in the increasingly harsh environment that became characteristic of what God Himself called "the glory of all lands" (Ezekiel 6:15 ASV).[1] What has been an historic and fabled beauty deteriorated through violence and neglect. The magnificent water conservation system of the ancients fell into wrack and ruin. The land reverted to dreary desert with little appeal.

During the days of the notoriously corrupt Ottoman Turks, Palestine became a source of revenue for the greedy. Mark Twain, believing Jerusalem to be "the knobbiest of cities," lamented in his *Innocents Abroad:*

> Palestine sits in sackcloth and ashes. Over it broods the spell of a curse that has withered its fields and fettered its energies. . . . Nazareth is forlorn; about that ford of Jordan where the host of Israel entered the Promised Land with songs of rejoicing, one finds only a squalid camp of fantastic Bedouins . . . Palestine is desolate and unlovely. And why should it be otherwise? Can the curse of the Deity beautify a land? Palestine is no more of this work-day world. It is sacred to poetry and tradition—it is dream-land.

The well-known and prolific English novelist Anthony Trollope visited Palestine in 1853 in the course of his extensive travels and wove *unimpressive* details of the Holy Land into various of his fictional pieces.

In her engaging collection of observations by "famous travelers," Linda Osband gave the British traveler Robert Curzon's description of the asphyxiation of 500 worshipers at the Ceremony of the Holy Fire in the Church of the Holy Sepulchre.[2] Later in the 1850s the American missionary James Turner Barclay related that the Temple Mount was in the custody of Mauritanian Africans who assiduously kept all non-Muslims out. What pilgrims saw was largely repugnant. Wrote James Silk Buckingham, "It has no grandeur or beauty or magnificence . . . better ten years in Damascus than five years in Jerusalem."

Chateaubriand wrote that "with the American, everything proclaims the savage who has not yet arrived at a state of civilization; in the Arab, everything indicates the civilized man who has returned to the savage state." What most impressed William Makepeace Thackeray were the mosquitoes, fleas, and lice. Disappointed in just about everything he saw, Sir William Wilde (father of Oscar) was moved at the sight of a Jew mourning over the stones of Jerusalem. Occasionally a more sentimental portrait was painted by such as Dr. T. DeWitt Talmage in his *Palestine Sermons*, but even he advised "only those in robust health attempt to go the length of Palestine and Syria on horseback."[3]

Even with the very modest immigration of early Zionist idealists, the land and the economy were exceedingly barren and bleak. As late as 1913, the British Palestine Royal Commission recounted:

The road leading from Gaza to the north was only a summer track suitable for transport by camels and carts . . . no orange groves, orchards or vineyards were to be seen until one reached Yabna village . . . not in a single village in all this area was water used for irrigation. . . . Houses were all of mud. No windows were anywhere to be seen . . . the ploughs used were of wood . . . The yields were very poor . . . The sanitary conditions in the village were horrible. Schools did not exist . . . the rate of infant mortality were very high . . . The western part, towards the sea, was almost a desert . . . the villages in this area were few and thinly populated. Many ruins of villages were scattered over the area, as owing to the presence of malaria; many villages were deserted by their inhabitants.

The Ottoman Turks were not interested in negotiating with the Zionists. In 1875 they had massacred Christians in their Bulgarian province, and while Queen Victoria and Disraeli downplayed the atrocities because of their fear of the Russians, William E. Gladstone wrote a very influential pamphlet entitled "The Bulgarian Horrors and the Question of the East." Gladstone, Trollope, and Lord Shaftesbury spoke of the Turkish menace at a rally in 1876.[4] Later the Turks would massacre the Armenians.

How World War I and its aftermath eliminated the Turkish menace and opened the door for the Jews is a story to be told. The land made desolate according to prophecy (Leviticus 26:32–33) was to become again like the garden of Eden, to blossom as the crocus (Isaiah 35:1–2).

THE MATRIX

While the nations of Europe are absorbed in political conflicts and worldly business, the sands in their hour-glass are ebbing away. While governments are disputing about secular things, and parliaments can hardly condescend to find a place for religion in their discussions, their days are numbered in the sight of God. Yet a few years and "the times of the Gentiles will be fulfilled." Their day of visitation will be past and gone. Their misused privileges will be taken away. The judgments of God shall fall on them. They will be cast aside as vessels in which God has no pleasure. Their dominion shall crumble away, and their vaunted institutions shall fall to pieces. The Jews will be restored. The Lord Jesus Christ will come again in power and great glory.—Bishop J. C. Ryle on Luke 21:24 (1859)

The Results of War

The carnage and the calamities of World War I were the matrix out of which the State of Israel emerged as a geo-political entity some thirty years later. The Allies suffered some 22,000,000 casualties and the Central Powers had some 15,000,000 casualties. Fought largely with borrowed money, World War I brought inevitable economic dislocation and ultimate disaster to the world economy. The unsatisfactory political settlement of the war sowed the seeds for World War II. The Greeks had a saying, "Whom the gods would destroy, they first make mad." The mindless madness of war is always before us in this narrative but "God makes even the wrath of men to praise Him," and

---

the eye of faith discerns God at work even in the ashes and unspeakable havoc of "man's inhumanity to man."

The first great war resulted from growing nationalism, competition for colonial ascendancy, and the tensions of conflicting diplomatic alliances. The great nineteenth-century contest, known as "the great game," that is, Britain's efforts to keep her way open to India and the East in the face of her rivals (France and Russia), stoked the conflagration in 1914. While the assassination of the Archduke of Austria-Hungary by a Serbian in Sarajevo on July 28, 1914,[5] set off the chain reaction of hostility and declarations of war, the buildup toward confrontation was obvious. Beneath the euphoric optimism of acclerating change, scientific progress, the prospects of "the triumph of the evolutionary vision," and the imminence of the golden age, deep tensions and greed, subjugation and repression, hatred and rivalry, all foamed—the stuff and sin of humankind "writ large."[*]

The stalemates and stories of the war have often been told. The Western front and its incredible fratricide,[6] the Eastern front and the collapse of Russia (she fought for three years and suffered 1,000,000 fatalities), the Southern front and the face-off between Austria-Hungary and Italy[7] all had many long-term consequences. The Allied debacle at Gallipoli on the Dardanelles in 1915 temporarily derailed the career of Winston Churchill. The action in the Middle East affects our story here. Turkey joined the Central Powers in fulfillment of secret treaty commitments and declared war on August 2, 1914, to the great chagrin of the Allies who had desperately hoped for her neutrality.

For 500 years the Ottoman Turks had ruled an empire that extended at its zenith under Suleiman I to almost all of North Africa and the Balkans (in 1566). But Turkey was now "the sickman of Europe." The nineteenth century saw extensive erosion in this colossus astride the Middle East. Torn by wars, outdistanced in modernization, beset by corruption, bedeviled by Muslim fundamentalism, Turkey faced problems not only in the Balkans (known as "the powder-keg of Europe") but throughout her widespread holdings. After the Congress of Berlin in 1878, Turkey's power really began to unravel, and Britain occupied Egypt and Cyprus "for the sultan."

Although Britain, France, Italy, and Prussia had all stood with Turkey against Russia in the Crimean War of 1853–1856 (when the czar moved against Turkey over jurisdictional disputes on sacred sites in the Holy Land), the overall tilt was toward German-Turkish solidarity. Although early backing Zionist aspiration, Kaiser Wilhelm II saw the Middle East as the area in which he might challenge British and French hegemony and possibly cut Britain's lifeline to the Levant. The kaiser visited Palestine. In 1909 Tel Aviv ("The Hill of the Spring") was founded by Arthur Ruppin of Germany as a garden suburb of Jaffa. In 1913 wealthy German Jews financed the building of the Technion in Haifa, the M. I. T. of the *Yishuv*, and intended that German should be its language, but due to the indefatigable efforts of Eliezer Ben Yehuda, modern Hebrew was its language and by 1916 some 40 percent of the Jews in Palestine considered Hebrew as their first language.

The German drive to the Middle East was vigorous and purposive, but Turkey was a wobbly partner. The revolt of the Young Turks in 1908 overthrew the sultan, but the shape of things to come was unclear. The New

◊ ◊ ◊

[*] As Tuchman convincingly argued, the Germans made Darwinian theory national dogma and wed it to Aryan superiority. "Darwinism became the White Man's Burden. Imperialism acquired a moral imperative." War was a necessity.[8]

"Turkism" thought that alliance with Germany could lead to the restoration of lost territory, but it led to the reverse. The "drowsy and negligent sway of the Ottoman Empire," as David Fromkin termed it, was coming to an end. Jews in Palestine during the war were, of course, subjects of the Ottoman Empire. Many were loyal. It must be said of the Germans that they made every effort to protect the Zionists in Palestine. The new Ottoman regime maintained the old attitude: "Autonomy is treason." Attacks on Jewish settlements were not uncommon.

Leaders in the Cause

With rising Arab nationalism in Turkey, Zionist leaders made further contacts with Turkey in 1913. Talit Bey made a proposal for a Muslim-Jewish Alliance but nothing came of it.[9] Further discussions were held in the summer of 1914, but then the war came. Restrictions were reimposed and considerable harassment of the Jews in Palestine began. Vladamir Jabotinsky (born in Odessa, 1880, died 1940), to whom reference has already been made, was a polished European gentleman. He used a rich, mellifluous Hebrew and translated Edgar Allan Poe into Hebrew. He was the ideological mentor of a future prime minister of Israel, Menachem Begin. He felt the future was with the Allies, and he set all of his endeavors to break up the Ottoman Empire and fight against it. He organized the first Zion Mule Corp, led by Joseph Trumpeldor, who was killed subsequently in 1920 in an Arab attack on Jewish settlements. Trumpeldor, a one-armed hero, valiantly supported the Allied cause.[*]

The British objective in the Middle East becomes clear in the career of Horatio Herbert Kitchener (1850–1916), distinguished army engineer, outstanding general and Britain's Secretary of State for War in the early days of World War I. A deeply religious man, Kitchener made a survey of the military geography of Palestine for the War Office under the aegis of the Palestine Exploration Fund in the 1870s. He learned to speak Arabic and was from this time a strong advocate of British influence in the Middle East.[10] He saw the competition as Russia, France, and Germany. An avid student of the Bible, Kitchener had much in common with General Charles Gordon, after whose death at Khartoum, Kitchener was sent by Gladstone on a mission of reconquest. Kitchener's vision in World War I was the dismemberment of the Ottoman Empire.

This vision was behind the secret Sykes-Picot Agreement of 1916 in which Britain and France agreed that after the war Turkey would be divested of its Arab provinces and these would be divided between the big "two" who would then be guaranteed permanent spheres of influ-

◇ ◇ ◇

[*] How Palestinian Jews at great risk supported the British in both world wars is related in Pierre van Paasen's notable work, *The Forgotten Ally*, a volume the British government has sought to repress.

ence in the Middle East. This, of course, took place but the unforeseen discovery of oil in the Middle East and the League of Nations mandate intensified the criticalness of the area, with a resultant influx of both Zionist Jews and a flood of Arabs from other areas who would find in Palestine higher wages and better living conditions. From an Arab standpoint the Sykes-Picot Agreement was just the perpetuation of the Crusades which began in A.D. 1087 and involved only the further division and humiliation of the Arabs. Beyond question the Crusades turned the Arabs in upon themselves and marked the retreat of the Muslim world into isolation.

After Kitchener's tragic death at sea, it was Lord Curzon who took over "the Great Game." David Fromkin argued that the British promises to the Arabs were "sheer dishonesty," and that believing the Arabs were incapable of self-government, they gave them a facade of self-rule but maintained indirect British rule.[11] How the British dealt with the Arabs somewhat parallels their later dealings with the Jews.

Interestingly no one felt more deeply this betrayal of the Arab vassals of the Turkish tyranny (and himself a deep believer in a homeland for the Jews) than did T. E. Lawrence ("Lawrence of Arabia"). This five-foot-tall soldier, lionized largely through the efforts of Lowell Thomas, led a revolt of Arabs in the Hejaz under Hussein of Arabia, theSheriff of Mecca, against the Ottoman Turks and the Germans. When he and Hussein marched into Damascus the war was effectively over for him, but the Damascus Protocol was not to be honored. His unwillingness to sell out was an embarrassment to the British at Versailles where he was an unofficial advocate of Arab independence.[*]

THE MANIFESTO

Ay, the children of the chosen race shall carry and bring them to their place. In the land of the Lord, shall lead the same.—Arthur James Balfour

Justice? There isn't enough to go around.—Robert Browning

The British saw in the collapse of the Ottoman Empire of the Turks the opportunity to pursue their own interests in the Middle East. Sir Henry McMahon, British Commissioner in Cairo, was at the forefront of the action. Just before the outbreak of hostilities, Sheriff Hussein of Mecca, guardian of the holy cities of Mecca and Medina and highly respected in the Arab world, approached Lord Kitchener, then in Egypt,

◊ ◊ ◊

* In his refreshing and massive new "official biography" of Lawrence, Jeremy Wilson meticulously traced Lawrence's post-war influence on Winston Churchill's policy on Palestinian partition and his consistent Zionism."[12]

to see if the British would help the Arabs were they to seek independence from the Turks. Hussein wanted to establish a new Arab caliphate that would include Syria and Mesopotamia. The British were eager not to offend Hussein (the grandfather of the present King Hussein of the Hasemite Kingdom of Jordan), but they felt his demands were exorbitant.

Early Turkish threats to Egypt and the Suez Canal goaded the British to make more lavish promises than they ever intended to fulfill. In order to enlist Arab support against the Turks, the British promised independence for the Arabian Peninsula (although the Wahhabis, the puritanical sect of Muslims led by the Emir Saud of Nejd, ultimately gained total ascendancy in the area) and other Arab territories then controlled by the Turks. McMahon's pledge was made in a letter to Sheriff Hussein dated October 24, 1915, in which it was stated that apart from certain modifications:

> Great Britain is prepared to recognize and support the independence of the Arabs within the limits demanded by the Sheriff of Mecca.[13]

No specific mention was made of Palestine, but there is no question that the British intended the internationalization of Palestine with British dominance. T. E. Lawrence, then doing intelligence work in Cairo, influenced this most controversial pledge when he argued that neither Beirut in Lebanon nor Jerusalem in Palestine were legitimately Arab.

Thus it was that an Arab army, consisting of regulars who had deserted from the ranks of the Turks and numerous Bedouin, fought with the British on their advance out of Egypt. This army was led by Emir Feisal and advised by T. E. Lawrence. Still another force led by two sons of the Sheriff captured Akaba and Taif from the Turks and besieged Medina. Actually the slow pace and inefficiency of the Arab forces in the earlier phases of the war led to the sacking of McMahon, who was always credited by T. E. Lawrence as the man who had done the spadework for the vital cooperation of the Arabs against the Turks.[14]

Further complicating the situation was the secret treaty negotiated in early 1916 between the French and the British. Signed by Sir Mark Sykes for Great Britain and Francois Georges-Picot for France (and known as the Sykes-Picot Agreement),the agreement called for French dominance in Syria and Lebanon and British dominance in Mesopotamia and Transjordan. The essential contradiction between the McMahon Pledge and Sykes-Picot became only too clear as time went on. Sykes-Picot was kept under wraps and became public knowledge only when csarist Russia, who had been kept informed, was overthrown and the Bolsheviks published the document.[15] The Arab world was outraged.

The British advance out of El Arish was headed by Major-General Sir Archibald Murray. When David Lloyd-George took over from Herbert

Asquith as British prime minister at the end of 1916, he is reported to have said: "In Palestine and Mesopotamia nothing and nobody could have saved the Turk from complete collapse in 1915–16 except our General Staff."[16] Two efforts to take the city of Gaza were repulsed, and Lloyd-George unceremoniously removed Murray from command. He wanted General Jan Christian Smuts from South Africa (and an ardent Zionist) to take the command, but Smuts refused, feeling that insufficient support was coming from the War Office. Smuts was subsequently a most distinguished World War II prime minister of South Africa.

The Roles of David Lloyd-George and Sir Edmund Allenby

David Lloyd-George, leader of the British War Cabinet during the last half of World War I, played an important part in the Palestinian question. Born of Welch parentage and raised in a nonconformist home in which he learned all of the biblical imagery, Lloyd-George was a philosemite and a Zionist. Although no devout believer in Christ, Lloyd-George testified: "When Dr. Weizmann was talking of Palestine he kept bringing us place-names which were more familiar to me than those on the western front."[17] He had furthermore imbibed a deep hatred for the Turks from Gladstone, the great leader of his beloved Liberal party. Little wonder then that he proposed decisive action on the Middle-Eastern front, given the horrendous standoff on the Western front.

Lloyd-George chose General Sir Edmund Allenby, whose relationships with the eccentric General Haig on the Western front was deteriorating. The War Cabinet confirmed the appointment on June 5, 1917, and Lloyd-George presented Allenby with a copy of George Adam Smith's *The Historical Geography of the Holy Land*. Allenby, a widely respected cavalryman, became a distinguished British war hero and was given the title, Field Marshal Lord Allenby of Felixstowe and Megiddo. Both the Allenby Bridge and Allenby Road were named after him. Through the marriage of a direct descendant of Oliver Cromwell with Hynman Allenby in the eighteenth century, the family lineage received powerful new blood, and the rumor started that Allenby had some Jewish ancestry (Hynman being the predominant family name). Steeped in biblical studies, he was raised in a home where prayer was made "for the peace of Jerusalem." T. E. Lawrence said of him: "Allenby was so morally great that the comprehension of our littleness came slow to him."

In the film, *The Light Horsemen*, Allenby's senior intelligence officer was Colonel Richard Meinertzhagen, whose daring deceptions of the Turks commanded by German General Von Kressenstein led to the attack on Beersheba, the foiling of the effort to blow up the wells, and the capture of Beersheba. Meinertzhagen was a champion of Zionist aspiration, another example of the extraordinary hand of God in bringing together in this drama so many who by dint of background and conviction looked for a Jewish national homeland in Palestine.

Lloyd-George told Allenby that he wanted to give Jerusalem to the weary British people as a Christmas gift. Seizing his inspiration from Isaiah 31:4–5, Allenby sent planes over Jerusalem in hopes of averting bloody hand-to-hand combat in the Holy City, and indeed the Turks panicked and the city was taken without loss of life, Allenby walking ahead of the troops with his cap doffed, the date being December 11, 1917. T. E. Lawrence walked immediately behind him. The shift into Christian control after 730 years sent shockwaves throughout the Christian world. In London, the leading Baptist minister, Dr. F. B. Meyer and others issued a public manifesto indicating that God's promise to restore the Jew to the land of Palestine was beginning to be fulfilled. Thousands flocked to great services in London to hear exposition of prophetic themes.

The Roles of Chaim Weizmann and Arthur James Balfour

Another very crucial piece in the jigsaw puzzle was added on November 2, 1917, when Foreign Secretary Arthur James Balfour wrote the celebrated letter to Lord Rothschild that contained what has become known as the Balfour Declaration. The World Zionist Headquarters had been moved through the war from Berlin to Copenhagen. The action, however, was with Dr. Chaim Weizmann, president of the English Zionist Federation and a distinguished scientist at Manchester University. Weizmann was born near Pinsk in Russia, had taught in Geneva, and now made England his home. Early interested in Herzl's vision of "a national homeland" for the Jews, he talked to British statesmen relentlessly. Jewish hopes were represented to the cabinet by Herbert Samuel, a late Jewish convert to the Zionist cause. Oddly, opposition came in the main from English-born Jews like Samuel's cousin, Edwin Montagu.

Weizmann, in developing a commercial process for the preparation of aceton, a key ingredient in the manufacture of high explosives, had a few debits to collect from the British government. Weizmann's discussions with Balfour on Palestine go back to 1906. Balfour, nephew of the long-time British prime minister, Lord Salisbury, had been Conservative Prime Minister from 1902–05.[*] Balfour was raised in a devout Christian home. He detested anti-Semitism. Weizmann helped him to see how the British could help the Jews.[†] Balfour pledged his own support,[18] and according to Tuchman, " the motive was biblical not imperial.[19] It was his life-long study of the Bible and his Scottish upbringing that commandeered his whole being.

Balfour's letter, in part, to Lord Rothschild simply stated:

◊ ◊ ◊

[*] Balfour was a brilliant thinker, and his Gifford Lectures of 1922, *Theism and Humanism,* are still worth reading.

His Majesty's Government view with favour the establishment in Palestine of a national home for the Jewish people, and will use their best endeavours to facilitate the achievement of this object, it being clearly understood that nothing shall be done which may prejudice the civil and religious rights of existing non-Jewish communities in Palestine, or the rights and political status enjoyed by Jews in any other country.[20]

Though roundly debated in the War Cabinet, the force of support from the prime minister, the foreign minister, Lord Cecil, Lord Milner, the brilliant Roman Catholic diplomat Sir Mark Sykes, and others carried the day, and the Balfour Declaration was officially sent to Lord Rothschild on November 2, 1917, close in time to Allenby's conquest of Jerusalem.

The Roles of Woodrow Wilson and Louis Brandeis

American support for the Balfour Declaration was secured through President Woodrow Wilson by Supreme Court Justice Louis Brandeis, confidant of Wilson. Brandeis was an early Zionist and the first Jew to sit on the Supreme Court of the United States. His appointment was bitterly fought. One writer on "The Palestine Question in the Wilson Era" observed: "By chance, Louis D. Brandeis, one of the men of 'light and leading' on whom Wilson relied, formally became a Zionist in the year of the Princeton scholar's first election."[21] With the help of Rabbi Stephen Wise and facing the opposition of presidential advisor Colonel House and Secretary of State Lansing, Brandeis obtained Wilson's backing for the Balfour Declaration as early as September 24, 1917. Already we see the negativity of the U. S. State Department to Zionist aspiration which plays out even to the present. The president publicly announced support for the Balfour Declaration on August 31, 1918. The subsequent strength of the Arab opposition to a Jewish homeland seemed to surprise Wilson, and at Versailles he faced a formidable array against him. Yet he stood firmly and the name of Woodrow Wilson belongs among the "fathers" of the new commonwealth of Israel.[22]

The story does not end with the Balfour Declaration in 1917. Unimaginable problems and perils lie ahead.

◇ ◇ ◇

† (previous page) "Weizmann pulled the Zionists through a brief window of opportunity, fated never to open again. Thanks to *Tancred* (Disraeli's novel) and *Daniel Deronda* (by George Eliot) he successfully appealed to the instincts of the British ruling class, and thus received perhaps the last *ex gratia* gift of a great power, which went clean against the arithmetic spirit of the age."—Paul Johnson[23]

THE MOMENTUM

With one step the Jewish causes have made a great bound forward. The declaration of His Majesty's Government as to the future of Palestine in relation to the Jewish people marks a new epoch for our race. For the British government, in accord—it is without doubt assumed—with the rest of the Allies, has declared itself in favor of the setting up in Palestine of a National Home for the Jewish people, and has undertaken to use its best endeavors to facilitate the achievement of that object. The Jew is at last coming to his rights. In place of being a wanderer in every clime, there is to be a home for him in his ancient land. The day of his exile is ended.—Jewish Chronicle (November 9, 1917)[24]

For Zion's sake I will not keep silent, for Jerusalem's sake I will not remain quiet, till her righteousness shines out like the dawn, her salvation like a blazing torch. (Isaiah 62:1).

Euphoria was rampant among Zionistic Jews around the world in the wake of the Balfour Declaration. Some support was given in France, the United States, Italy, and even the Vatican to a degree. While there would be some differences in interpretation at points and while the Declaration itself stated that "nothing shall be done which may prejudice the civil and religious rights of existing non-Jewish communities in Palestine, or the rights and political status enjoyed by Jews in any other country," the document was an immense stride toward the realization of Jewish aspiration for their land the return.

Balfour himself was a somewhat stuffy aristocrat. It was reported that one night he dreamt that he was speaking to the House of Lords. He woke up and found that he was. He had a distinguished career as prime minister, chief secretary for Ireland in a tense time, and foreign minister. His niece and biographer reported that "near the end of his days he said to me that on the whole he felt that what he had done for the Jews had been the thing he looked back upon as the most worth his doing."[25]

Reaction among the Arabs was on the whole predictably negative. Although King Hussein in Mecca welcomed the returning exiles, "the original sons of the country from which their Arab brethren would benefit materially as well as spiritually."[26] Dr. Weizmann went to Akaba in January of 1919 to meet Faisal, son of Hussein. Indication was given that relationships could be cordial between the two peoples and that indeed support would be forthcoming for Jewish aspiration if the promise for an independent Arab state would be kept. Under Arab pressure Faisal very quickly moved to a totally negative position: "The Arabs cannot yield Palestine."

Despite Faisal's reversal, Dr. Weizmann, later to become the first president of the State of Israel, was understandably ecstatic. Nahum Sokolow expressed a widespread feeling when he wrote:

> Mid storm and fire the people and the land seemed to be born again. The great events of the time of Zerubbabel, Ezra and Nehemiah repeated themselves. The Third Temple of Jewish freedom is rising before us.[27]

While doubtless there were complex motives of self-interest on the part of Great Britain, Weizmann stoutly maintained in his memoirs that the sincere Christian beliefs of Balfour, Lloyd-George, and Jan Christian Smuts were more responsible than anything else for the new opening for the Jews in Palestine.

Of course there were strong voices in the British government that were consistently critical of the announced policy, and at Versailles and the peace conference, Lord Curzon and General Henry Wilson worked incessantly for a cutback in British Palestinian involvement. When the Turks collapsed in 1919, apart from France's stake in Northern Syria, Britain hovered over almost all of the Middle East.

Prime Minister Lloyd-George was not about to retreat. When Weizmann visited the prime minister on Armistice Day, "he found him reading the Psalms in tears." Lloyd-George often used to say afterwards that to him "Palestine was the one interesting part of the war."[28]

Exercising the Mandate

At the peace conference Great Britain sought Palestine as a mandate under the League of Nations.* Conflicts between Lloyd-George and Clemenceau, the idealism of Woodrow Wilson and his concern for self-determination, the frustrations of King Faisal and his guide T. E. Lawrence, all postponed the decision until the San Remo Conference where on April 25, 1920, Britain was given the Mandate. Not until the peace treaty with Turkey in 1923 did Britain exercise her rights.

In this time frame, an Inter-Allied Commission on Mandates in Turkey was established to ascertain the will of those to be governed. This was an essential part of Woodrow Wilson's "Fourteen Points." Britain and France would not participate, but the King-Crane Commission began its studies in June of 1919. Charles Crane was a Chicago businessman, and Henry C. King was president of Oberlin College in Ohio. Their studies indicated that 86 percent of those polled wanted a "united

◊ ◊ ◊

* Tuchman is correct in arguing that "the Mandate not the Balfour Declaration gave a footing in public law to the restoration of Israel to Palestine.[29]

Syria" without Mandates. If there were to be a Mandate, the United States was the overwhelming first choice with Britain a distant second. Strong opposition to Zionist aspiration was clear. The findings of the commission were disregarded. As their advisor, Captain Yale tried to show them that promises had been made to the Jewish people.

Felix Frankfurter, working for the Americans and later himself to be a Supreme Court Justice in the United States, wrote the very words of the Balfour Declaration into the Mandate. Sir Herbert Samuel, of a wealthy Liverpool banking family and a leading Liberal politician, was appointed First High Commissioner for Palestine and served 1920–25. Ronald Storrs, the British military governor, described the people in Jerusalem waiting for the new high commissioner as "almost faint with happiness" and "moving as if in the glory and freshness of a dream come true." Yet "almost from that moment the glory began to wear off and the process of deterioration set in, until it reached the day 30 years later when British destroyers fired on the ship *Exodus* bringing Jewish refugees to their 'national home.'"[30]

Highly respected in Britain for his fairness (he introduced the resolution that opened membership in Parliament to women), Samuel took the job as high commissioner with the determination to be even-handed with both Arabs and Jews. While not particularly religious, he was a passionate Zionist from quite early on. He and his wife learned the Hebrew language. While his policies generally disappointed both Arabs and Jews, he was moderate and wise. He built up the economy and attempted to create a viable *modus vivendi* (an arrangement between two nations or groups that affects a workable compromise on issues in dispute without permanently settling them). He wrote insightfully of the problems:

"Unless there is careful steering, it is on the Arab rock that the Zionist ship may be wrecked."[31]

As a representative Jewish organization was set up, the Jewish Agency, (which proved to be so pivotal in Jewish immigration), so a Supreme Arab Council was set up, and Samuel's unfortunate choice to head it up was Haj Amin el-Husseini, the Grand Mufti of Jerusalem, who turned out to be a staunch admirer and a guest of Hitler. Moderation became increasingly difficult for either side in the festering tensions of the Middle East. Herbert Samuel wanted to stay and live in Palestine after his term expired, but his successor, Lord Plumer, did not think this appropriate, and the Samuels returned to Great Britain.

The Mandate was described by one student of the time as the "most important international obligation ever entrusted to a single nation." However, it may be viewed, the fact is Britain failed in her obligation.

The Hashemites, allies of the victors in the Great War, were evicted from the Hejaz by Ibn Saud's warriors between 1924–1926. The sheriff's son, Faisal, was briefly enthroned as king of Syria in 1920 but under the terms of the Sykes-Picot agreement was dethroned by the French, then picked up by the British and made king of Iraq. His brother Abdullah was made emir and later king of Transjordan. The seeds of much misunderstanding and mistrust were sown in these shifts and solutions achieved without any meaningful mutual quest.

Dividing the Land

In 1922 the British evinced some second thoughts on some basic aspects of the Mandate and separated Transjordan from the Mandate and sought to mollify the Hashemites with the arid stretches of desert to the east of the Jordan River. Winston Churchill, colonial secretary at the time, was unbudged from his dream of and commitment to "the creation in our lifetime of a Jewish State under the protection of the British Crown." The move to create a vassal state supervised by the British was unquestionably made to stabilize the anarchy among the Bedouin and to guard against French encroachment. Much of the negotiation with Abdullah was done for Churchill by T. E. Lawrence. While not immediately enthralled with Amman, Abdullah proved to be an able and responsible leader (his grandson, King Hussein of Jordan, has had amazing longevity amid the turmoils of the region). Four-fifths of the land area in the Mandate became the Hashemite Kingdom of Jordan. This was the first partition of Palestine. Amman at this time had only about 2000 inhabitants, most of them Circassians, settled there by the Turks after being driven out of the Caucasus Mountains by the Russians. Britain guaranteed subsidies including support for the Arab Legion to give some clout in the interests of order. The first commander of the Arab Legion was Captain F. G. Peake who was succeeded by the justly renown, Captain John B. Glubb, known as Glubb Pasha.[*]

The problem in all of this talk about immigration and the actual implementation with the Zionists seeking to fill up the land with a growing sense of desperation, was "the unseen question." Palestine was not empty. Half a million non-Jews were in the land. The Zionists had not really thought through how this problem was to be handled. The so-called Passover Riots in 1920 saw six Jews killed and more than 200 wounded, with much destruction of property. A wave of Arab attacks in 1921 killed 95 and seriously wounded 219. The Jews formed their own defense establishment, which they called *Haganah*.

◊ ◊ ◊

[*] According to John Stott, he was a dedicated Christian. See Glubb's superb volume, *A Soldier with the Arabs*, 1957.

The sale of land to the Zionist settlers was prohibited by the Arabs. Leaflets to this effect were mass circulated. Enforcement was difficult. Laqueur admits that "not a few Arab and Druse (a breakoff sect from the Shiites with a very mysterious religious expression) lost their livelihood as the result of Zionist land purchases."[32] The Jews wanted agricultural land. The first kibbutz (communal agricultural colony) was founded in 1911 and the first *moshav* (agricultural cooperative) in 1921.

One-quarter of the Jewish land in Palestine (the Esdraelon Valley) was in fact purchased from "one single absentee landlord, the Christian Arab Sursuq family, which lived in Beirut.[33] A growing landless Arab population was not altogether due to Jewish land acquisition. The objectives of the two population components were irreconcilable. Accelerating Jewish immigration and development triggered the alarm bells and anxieties among the Arab population. Jabotinsky fought the Arabs and was imprisoned. Some like the American Reform Rabbi Judah Magnes, first president of Hebrew University, advocated a binational state of Arabs and Jews.

Stemming from disagreements as to Jewish procedures at the Western Wall, there was great violence in 1929 (with hundreds of Jews killed including sixty-seven massacred in the town of Hebron) and a vicious third wave which must be termed a revolt in 1936. A Royal Commission headed by Lord Peel made inquiry and recommended partition of the land and reduction of immigration. By this time the Arabs as the consequence of the Grand Mufti's relentless agitation refused to sit down with the Jews.

"In the long run, it was the failure to negotiate directly with the Jews, forcing them into unilateral action, which lost the Arabs Palestine."[34]

Beyond question, the Royal Commission concluded, the purpose of the Mandate was to "promote the establishment of the Jewish National Home." This did not immediately result in a Jewish State, but it did commit to "the eventual establishment of a Jewish State." This next step did not come until after the convulsions of World War II. The setting of immigration quotas as early as 1930 was an attempt to obstruct the birth path, but the State of Israel was destined to be born. Irresistible and inevitable forces would push it into the world.

CHAPTER

MIRACLE AT MID-CENTURY—WORLD WAR II AND THE BIRTH OF ISRAEL

So I prophesied as I was commanded.
And as I was prophesying, there was a noise,
a rattling sound, and the bones came together, bone to bone.
I looked, and tendons and flesh appeared on them
and skin covered them, but there was no breath in them.
Then he said to me,
"Prophesy to the breath;
prophesy, son of man, and say to it,
This is what the Sovereign LORD says:
Come from the four winds, O breath,
and breathe into these slain, that they may live."
So I prophesied as he commanded me, and breath entered them;
they came to life and stood up on their feet—a vast army.
Then he said to me:
"Son of man, these bones are the whole house of Israel.
They say, 'Our bones are dried up'
and our hope is gone;
we are cut off."
Therefore prophesy and say to them:
'This is what the Sovereign LORD says:
O my people, I am going to open your graves
and bring you up from them;
I will bring you back to the land of Israel.
Then you, my people, will know that I am the LORD,
when I open your graves and bring you up from them.
I will put my Spirit in you
and you will live,
and I will settle you
in your own land.'"

Ezekiel 37:7–14a

For if their rejection is the reconciliation of the world,
what will their acceptance be but
life from the dead?

Romans 11:15

T HE EARLY IMMIGRANTS TO *ERETZ* ISRAEL from the turn of the
century found life harsh and dangerous in the *yishuv*—"Muck up to their
ankles, flies buzzing around their faces; endless hours of working the
soil, disease."[1] What started as a faint trickle became a steadier stream.
If there were 70,000 Jews in the *yishuv* at the time of the Balfour Declaration, there were approximately 350,000 Jews in the Holy Land in
1935. Was this not the moving of the dry bones of which Ezekiel the
prophet spoke in the sixth century before Christ?

Chapter 37 is doubtless the best-known portion in Ezekiel's great
prophecy. Probably sometime after the destruction of Jerusalem in 586
B.C., Ezekiel was taken from among the exiles by the River Chebar in
Babylon and shown a valley of scattered skeletal remains. Then bones
came together in proper alignment with each other and tendons and
skin formed over the bones and ultimately life came into the corpses and
they stood up on their feet alive![*] The reconstruction was like the shaking of a great earthquake.[†] The breath of God or the spirit of the Lord
accomplished a mighty thing.

Of what then was Ezekiel prophesying? The return of a small contingent of exiles in the days of Ezra and Nehemiah did not really mark
the resumption of national life any more than the brief period of tense
self-rule in the days of the Maccabees. Is this prophecy to be applied in
a spiritual fulfillment to the church irrespective of what Ezekiel and his
contemporaries understood it to mean? While many promises given to
Israel have been enlarged and broadened to include Gentile believers

◊ ◊ ◊

[*] "The graphic imagery of the vision has inspired countless artists through the
ages, from the painters of the ancient synagogue of Dura-Europos in Babylon to
the composers of Negro spirituals in modern America."—Werner E. Lemke[2]

[†] "The coming of the bones together is not by their own action but by the earthquake shaking that follows on the prophetic word. Only then does the miracle of
growth take place."—H. L. Ellison[3]

(Jeremiah 31:31–34), this must not be construed to mean "that the promise has been exhausted in the Church's enjoyment of it."[4] "Unless . . . [expositors] can give full weight both to the transformed land of Israel in Ezekiel 36 and to the national resurrection of Israel in chapter 37, . . . [they have] no right to banish the Israel of the Old Covenant from the picture in favor of the Church."[5]

The graveyard resurrection of the nations is one part of a whole cycle in Ezekiel about restoration—the renewal of the land to Edenic state (36:35); the rebuilding of ruined cities; the growth of God's people in the land (36:37–38); and ultimately a resurgence of witness to the true and living God.

Much scholarly and popular interpretation has insisted that the identification of the bones as "the whole house of Israel" must be taken seriously.[6] First there is to be a physical or national restoration, followed by spiritual renewal. God promised the land and has preserved the Jews in their dispersion. In 1948 the world community established them as a national entity on their native soil. They literally came out of the grave of European tragedy. Tendons and skin have come over them. They have not yet been raised to spiritual life, but that is as sure as their return to *eretz* Israel—now over 4,000,000 of them.

OUT OF THE FURNACE—THE TRAVAIL

Then the LORD your God will restore your fortunes and have compassion on you and gather you again from all the nations where he scattered you. Even if you have been banished to the most distant land under the heavens, from there the LORD your God will gather you and bring you back. He will bring you to the land that belonged to your fathers, and you will take possession of it. He will make you more prosperous and numerous than your fathers (Deuteronomy 30:3–5).

In that day the Lord will reach out his hand a second time to reclaim the remnant that is left of his people. He will raise a banner for the nations and gather the exiles of Israel; he will assemble the scattered people of Judah from the four quarters of the earth (Isaiah 11:11–12).

I will surely gather them from all lands where I banish them in my furious anger and great wrath; I will bring them back to this place and let them live in safety. . . . I will make an everlasting covenant with them; I will never stop doing good to them, and I will inspire them to fear me, so that they will never turn away from me (Jeremiah 32:37, 40).

Almost all of the prophets in the Old Testament promise a coming restoration and return for the ancient people of God in exacting detail. These promises are unannulled. While many Old Testament promises are subsequently enlarged and expanded, these promises about Israel must be understood in their natural and plain meaning. To strip these away from Israel is to invite hermeneutical chaos and to inject uncontrolled subjectivity into the interpretive process.

David Ben-Gurion and Israel's Vision

Personifying and embodying the spirit and courage of the pioneer Zionists is certainly David Ben-Gurion, the "armed prophet" of modern Israel, the nation-builder, and statesman. The man who presided over the birth of the nation came out of the *shtetls* of east central Poland where he was born David Green on October 10, 1886. His father, who was a member of the "Love of Zion" organization, shaped this five-foot-three-inch future prime minister of Israel. While not a traditional Jew in matters religious, David Green (who came to be known as Ben-Gurion or Son of a Lion-cub) was saturated with the Old Testament Scriptures.

"The Bible is our mandate" was his clarion call. He believed that "nothing . . . [could] surpass the Bible at lighting up the manifold problems of our life . . . there . . . [could] be no worthwhile political or military education about Israel without profound knowledge of the Bible.[7] He saw the dispersion as an historical aberration and the new Israel as a "leap across Jewish history." He understood Israel to be a unique nation (*am segulah*) and that her rebirth was part of the vision of "messianic redemption."[8]

Ben-Gurion worked as a teacher in Warsaw and in the face of endemic and vicious anti-Semitism decided to go to Palestine. In September of 1906 he arrived in Jaffa. A convinced socialist, and frequently burning up with malarial fever, he gave himself to the implementation of the Zionist dream. While he lived for brief periods in Salonika, Greece, in Egypt, and the United States, he with Berl Katznelson led in the formation of a Jewish Assembly that early in the 1920s acknowledged as its ultimate aim the establishment of a Jewish state.[9] Making the *Histadrut* (or central labor union) as the cornerstone of his future state, Ben-Gurion was a man of great intellectual capability and with a personal library of 20,000 volumes. He and Jabotinsky could not get along because the latter was committed to the immediate declaration of a Jewish state. Their differences were deep and very divisive in the *yishuv*. They are the basis of the difference between the Labor party and the Likud party in Israel today.

Haj Amin el-Husseini and Arab Revolt

While Churchill in the White Paper of 1922 had wanted only economic considerations to limit Jewish immigration, clearly the mounting opposition of Palestinian Arabs was creating a huge problem for Britain and the Jews. The Arab Revolt of 1936–39 fomented a serious crisis and standoff that only the nightmare of World War II would alter.

Clearly two nationalistic groups were increasingly at each other's throats. Unaccountably the British, in an effort to appease the Arabs, appointed the nationalist extremist, Haj Amin el-Husseini, as the Mufti of Jerusalem (the interpreter of Muslim Law). He was truly a fascist and led a full-scale revolt against Britain in 1936–39. Finally the British had to depose him, and he traveled to Germany where he lectured SS officers in the 1940s and defended the Holocaust. He toured the death camps with Himmler and obtained promise from Adolf Eichmann of post-war help to "solve the Jewish problem in the Middle East." He was in Cairo in 1948 to help in the attacks immediately launched against Israel because of the partition of the land.[10]

The Royal Commission headed by Lord Peel recommended partition as early as 1937, but the Arabs would not hear of it. The Commission spoke of "the irrepressible conflict" between Jew and Arab and proposed separate Jewish and Arab enclaves with a corridor to the sea, including Jerusalem, to be retained under British control.

Orde Charles Wingate and Israel's Army

At this time there came most providentially to the fore a remarkable figure in Palestine, Captain Orde Charles Wingate. Wingate and his father's cousin General Sir Reginald Wingate, who played a prominent role in British policy in Egypt, were both descendants of the Reverend William Wingate of the well-to-do mercantile family in Glasgow. Orde Wingate's grandfather was part of the Scottish missionary effort to the Jews in Hungary. His mother was an avid Bible student and wrote a book on the Jews in the prophet Daniel's interpretation of the great image vision of Daniel 2.

While a somewhat eccentric person, Wingate was a devout believer and an ardent Zionist. After serving in both the Sudan and Libya, he was posted to Palestine in 1936 where for three years he risked his professional career in the British Army by training the Special Night Squads, and thereby laying the foundations of the IDF (the Israeli Defense Force). Tending to be passive in their response to Arab incursion, the Israelis responded well to Wingate's challenge. "Today you are seeing the beginning of a Jewish Army—You are the sons of the Maccabees."[11]

Because he was an irritant to developing British policy, Wingate was ultimately transferred to action in Ethiopia and then to commanding British forces in Burma (the Chindits) where he tragically met his death in 1944. Described by Ben-Gurion's biographer as "a biblical scholar of ascetic experience" and "a mystical Zionist as militant as any Jew and far more aggressive than most Jews in asserting Zionist rights,"[12] Wingate becomes another in a striking succession of British military and political figures* of great Christian persuasion who believed in a future for the Jews in Palestine.

Isaiah and Israel's Resurgence

Despite all of these tensions in Palestine the prophet Isaiah's prediction was coming true:

> They will rebuild the ancient ruins and restore the places long devastated; they will renew the ruined cities that have been devastated for generations (Isaiah 61:4).

Firsthand descriptions from the 1930s detailed the hydroelectric projects, the chemical works at the Dead Sea, the new agriculture, the intellectual and cultural renaissance, and the feats and accomplishments of so many gifted and brilliant emigres—all of which improved living conditions for all who lived in Palestine.[13]

But dark war clouds were lowering over Europe. Ben-Gurion expressed his opinion that "if, God forbid, another world war broke out, a Jewish state would surely bud." What an extraordinary statement. (cf. Luke 21:29–31).[14] The insane machinations of Hitler were driving many Jews to leave Germany (although by no means all), and pressure for more immigration to Palestine was increasing. This was especially true because the United States severely limited immigration to its shores. The approach of war made Britain more skittish about offending Arab interests in the Middle East in light of Arab oil deposits. How could Britain quiet agitation in Palestine? Conferences in early 1939 in which Ben-Gurion and Weizmann led Jewish participation seemed to yield nothing.

Neville Chamberlain and Britain's Betrayal

Britain issued a new White Paper on May 17, 1939, which in effect cancelled the Balfour Declaration. As pushed by then Prime Minister Neville Chamberlain, British policy now called for the limitation of Jewish immigration to 75,000 for the next five years and then an end to it apart from Arab approval; no further purchase of Palestinian land by the Jews without British approval; and the setting up of an independent state with Arab domination within ten years.

The Jews, and particularly Chaim Weizmann, were stunned. Ben-Gurion had been more and more of the persuasion that the British Empire was in decline, and that Britain's involvement in Palestine in the future would not be decisive. It was this line of reasoning that sharply divided Weizmann the Anglophile and Ben-Gurion the gutsy street fighter. The abrogation of the White Paper was, nevertheless, painfully felt by all concerned.

Winston Churchill, always a steady friend of the Jews, wrote:

◊ ◊ ◊

* (previous page) General Gordon, General Allenby, Arthur James Balfour, and David Lloyd-George, to mention but a few.

There is much in this White Paper which is alien to the Balfour Declaration, but I will not trouble about that. I will select one point upon which there is plainly a breach and repudiation of the Balfour Declaration, the decision that Jewish immigration can be stopped in five years by an Arab majority. This is a plain breach of a solemn obligation.[15]

Britain was to pay dearly for this betrayal, but European Jewry, almost devoured in the maw of Hitler's death camps, was to suffer even more greatly. The Evian Conference convened by President Roosevelt in 1938 did nothing substantive. Approximately 150,000 out of 450,000 Jews in Palestine volunteered to fight with the British forces. When three months after the White Paper the war broke out, everything seemed up for grabs.

Ben-Gurion spoke to 600 Jewish leaders in America at the Biltmore Hotel in New York City in 1942 and secured backing for establishment of the State of Israel in Palestine. And while all of this was going on, Hitler continued his resolute steps toward the Final Solution. The Allies were culpably oblivious, and Ben-Gurion himself seemed paralyzed. While a gifted and charismatic leader on so many issues, he was on this inert and tragically defeated.

Viktor Frankl, a survivor of the Holocaust, believed the Holocaust was the final impetus and a necessity for the establishment of the State of Israel.[*] Out of this travail of all travails, a nation was born, "a country born in a day" (Isaiah 66:6).

OF THE FORMATION—THE MIRACLE

"So then, the days are coming,"declares the LORD, "when people will no longer say, 'As surely as the LORD lives, who brought the Israelites up out of Egypt,' but they will say, 'As surely as the LORD lives, who brought the descendants of Israel up out of the land of the north and out of all the countries where he had banished them.' Then they will live in their own land" (Jeremiah 23:7–8).

This is what the Sovereign LORD says: "When I gather the people of Israel from the nations where they have been scattered, I will show myself holy among them in the sight of the nations. Then they will live in their own land, which I gave to my servant Jacob. They will live there in safety and will build houses and plant vineyards; they will live in safety when I inflict punishment on all their neighbors who maligned them. Then they will know that I am the LORD their God "(Ezekiel 28:25–26).

◊ ◊ ◊

[*] How the Holocaust affected Israel's future is striking. Etty Hillesum has left us a legacy out of her oppression and death at Auschwitz.[16]

This is what the LORD Almighty says: "I will save my people from the countries of the east and the west. I will bring them back to live in Jerusalem; they will be my people, and I will be faithful and righteous to them as their God" (Zechariah 8:7–8).

Even so venerable a Victorian pulpiteer as the renowned Charles Haddon Spurgeon of London, "the prince of preachers," opined that "I do not think we attach sufficient significance to the restoration of the Jews. We do not think enough of it. But certainly, if anything is promised in the Bible, it is this."[17]

The highly respected Old Testament scholar, R. B. Girdlestone, of the same era, concluded that Israel's future was clear from Scripture as a whole:

> There is a large unfulfilled element in the Old Testament which demands it, unless we spiritualize it away or relinquish it as Oriental hyperbole. This scattered nation has yet its part to play in the history of the world. There is to be a re-betrothal, a reunion, a liberation, a conversion, a restoration, which shall be like a resurrection, or life from the dead.[18]

In every understanding of this, both Jewish and Christian, "the ingathering of the exiles" is the sure sign of redemption. But redemption is not without *havlei Mashiah* (pangs of the Messianic era).[19]

Immigration Curtailed

"The Holocaust and the New Zion were organically connected."[20] Some 60,000 German Jews had successfully fled Hitler before the outbreak of the war and brought to the *yishuv* in Palestine their skills and assets for the creation of vital infrastructure. After the war Britain was on her knees. Her dependence on Arab good will was stronger than ever, and she began to clamp down even more vigorously on Jewish immigration than was even projected in the White Paper of 1939. The Land Transfer Act of 1940 limited Jews to 5 percent of the total area of western Palestine. So stringent were British pressures to limit immigration that by 1944 only two-thirds of the 75,000 immigration permits had been used.[21]

As World War II unfolded in Europe, the real question, strangely enough avoided by Ben-Gurion, was whether any Jews would be left alive on the continent. General Rommel, the Desert Fox, was advancing on Alexandria in Egypt, and things looked very dark for Britain's interests in the Middle East. Chaim Weizmann described in his autobiography how the Arabs gleefully looked forward to the dividing of the spoils when the Axis Powers occupied *eretz* Israel:

> Some of them were going about the streets of Tel Aviv and the colonies marking up the houses they expected to take over: one Arab, it was reported, had been killed in a quarrel over the loot assigned to him. The correspondent fur-

ther reported that General Wavell had called in some of the Jewish leaders and told them confidentially how deeply sorry he was that the British Army could not do any more for the yishuv: the troops were to be withdrawn toward India, the Jews would have to be left behind, and would be delivered up to the fury of the Germans, the Arabs and the Italians.[22]

The turnabout in North Africa under the brilliant leadership of General Montgomery, a deeply Christian man, surely affected the Middle East. Montgomery, son of a missionary bishop, was a strong believer in and wrote of the bodily resurrection of the Lord Jesus Christ.

Many refugees from the Holocaust were denied entrance to Palestine by the Mandatory power, and 1700 immigrants who had arrived in Haifa on two boats were transferred to the liner *Patria*. Transfer from a third boat had begun when the *Patria* was blown up by Haganah forces with 200 lives lost; the rest allowed to stay. The remaining 1,645 immigrants from the third boat were exiled to Mauritius.[23] Leon Uris's book *Exodus* chronicles the Displaced Persons Camps on Cyprus where Jewish refugees were detained. The British imprisoned forty-three officers of Haganah, the Jewish defense force, for long terms (including Moshe Dayan who was in Acre for sixteen months). The British were intent on seizing all weapons from the Jews thus leaving them defenseless.

After the death of Franklin D. Roosevelt (himself mildly anti-Semitic), President Truman did not know how to balance political realities with regard to the Jewish vote and the consistently anti-Israeli posture of the State Department. He wavered and wobbled on the issues until no one knew where he stood. At one moment he urged Britain to admit 100,000 refugees and in the next moment opposed the Jewish state. American immigration policy was very tight.

The British Labor party, which came to power immediately after the war with Clement Attlee as prime minister, had been fulsome in its promises to the Jews. Labor repeatedly reaffirmed support, as Weizmann has testified.[24] The pacification of the Arabs became the policy of the major powers including the United States, especially after President Roosevelt's visit to King Ibn Saud of Saudia Arabia after Yalta. Promises were made there which if kept would have doomed the State of Israel.

One of Roosevelt's aides is quoted as saying, "There are serious doubts in my mind that Israel would have come into being if Roosevelt had lived."[25]

On November 6, 1945, the Labor government changed course and repudiated its promises and assurances to the Jews. Opting to recommend that the Jews stay in the countries of Europe rather than immigrate, Bevin, the Labor leader, scandalized the Jews with his suggestion, "If the Jews with all their suffering, want to get too much at the head of the queue, you have the danger of another anti-Semitic reaction through it all."[26] So now after failing to address the outrage of what happened before and during the Holocaust, the "friends" of Israel thinly disguised a threat of more anguish.

Jewish Resistance

Not surpising in October of 1945 a Jewish resistance movement was formed and Ben-Gurion ordered the Haganah to attack British forces in Palestine. A sharp ideological split among the Jews of the *yishuv* was now painfully evident. The mainstream or Haganah force was led by David Ben-Gurion. Although Weizmann would ultimately be the first president of Israel, his stubborn holding out for British goodwill led to an irrevocable break with Ben-Gurion.

The primary splinter group was the more ruthless "National Military Organization," Irgun Zvai Leumi, followers of the brilliant revisionist Jabotinsky who had much earlier predicted the Holocaust and urged Jewish armed hostility against the British. Jabotinsky, who died in 1940, had led the Betar youth movement in Poland and there brought under his spell the Jewish lawyer, Menachem Begin. Jabotinsky's personal hero was Garibaldi of Italy. Ben-Gurion labeled him the Jewish Hitler and called the Irgun "Jewish Nazis." Begin, who was born in Brest Litovsk in Poland in 1913, lost his whole family in the Holocaust. He fled eastward and ended up in a Soviet gulag. Finally he found his way to Palestine in 1942 where he came to command in the Irgun, a movement severely shattered by the death of its founder.

An extremist splinter from the Irgun was headed up by Avraham Stern and was called the Stern Gang. Stern refused to obey Jabotinsky's order for a cease-fire with the British during the war, and he himself was killed in 1942. He was succeeded by Yitzhak Shamir (later the prime minister of Israel) and Nathan Yellin-Mor. Both were dedicated to fighting the British wherever and whenever they could. The Irgun under Begin by contrast set themselves to combat with the British military establishment in Palestine. The Stern Gang murdered Lord Moyne, British Minister for Middle Eastern Affairs in Cairo in 1944 and later the Swedish Count Folke Bernadotte, United Nations diplomat after the war.

Begin and the Irgun plotted with Haganah to blow up the King David Hotel where part of the British administration was located. Haganah withdrew but Begin persisted, and in the explosion 28 British, 41 Arabs, 17 Jews, and 5 others were killed. The further murder of two British sergeants by the Irgun tore the *yishuv* apart. The inability of these diverse Jewish elements to work together was a great negative in the whole process, and deep scars have remained. Weizmann condemned the use of terrorism, but there was desperation throughout Jewry. The actual threat of a civil war in the *yishuv* was real. Irgun was like a loose cannon. The demolition of the Arab village of Deir Yassin with over 100 deaths was part of the dark picture. In the Altalena Affair, Begin had to back down and made the concession: "There will be no fraternal strife while the foe is at the gate."[27]

Partition Recommended

In February of 1947 with the failure of an Anglo-American Commission of Inquiry, the British, in an admission of total failure, asked the United Nations to replace the Mandate with a permanent solution. The United Nations at once established a Special Commission on Palestine (*UNSCOP*) with representatives from eleven member states. The Arabs blundered by boycotting the entire process. Israel's lobbying and testimony were tactically brilliant, although many Jews were skeptical. The British were sore and angry. The United States passively awaited a consensus. The Soviet Union was favorable to partition largely out of a desire to humiliate Britain. Judge Sandstrom of Sweden headed the commission, and Dr. Ralph Bunche represented the United Nations.

Indeed "Israel slipped into existence through a fortuitous window in history which briefly opened for a few months in 1947–48. That too was luck; or providence."[28]

In June of 1947 Ben-Gurion testified to *UNSCOP* in the Holy Land:

Who is willing and capable of guaranteeing that what happened to us in Europe will not recur? Can the conscience of humanity absolve itself of all responsibility for that Holocaust? There is only one security guarantee: a homeland, a state.[29]

On September 3, 1947, the commission recommended partition with an internationalized Jerusalem. The vote in the General Assembly was 33 in favor, 13 against, with 10 abstentions (including Britain and China). Truman backed the proposal vigorously and through Weizmann's influence held out for the Negev to be given to Israel. Israel would have 55 percent of the land which would be 58 percent Jewish; the Arabs would have 45 percent of the land with a population 99 percent Arab. The story of the two-thirds vote necessary is an extraordinary story of divine providence.

The United Nations declared:

The Mandate for Palestine shall terminate as soon as possible, but in any case not later than August 1,1948. . . . Independent Arab and Jewish States, and the specific international regime for the city of Jerusalem shall come into existence two months later.[30]

Unquestionably the United Nations' vote for partition was the crossing of the Rubicon for the Zionists. As Abba Eban, later Foreign Minister for Israel observed in a BBC interview: "Partition was the principle which enabled Israel to be born." The Arabs made many critical errors at this time, chief of which was their assumption that the end of Mandate meant an Arab state in Palestine. But the very fact that the United Nations appointed liaisons from both the Jewish Agency and the Palestine Arab Higher Committee showed the legitimacy of Zionist separation was on as solid a footing as that of the Arab viewpoint.

UNSCOP was composed of leading jurists from Sweden, Canada, and India; veteran diplomats from Australia, Yugoslavia, and Iran; a former colonial governor from the Netherlands; a friend of Jan Masaryk from Czechoslovakia; three Latin Americans, one of whom was from Guatemala, which was in tension with Britain over Belize.

The Commission was not afforded customary courtesy by the British in a stopover at Malta enroute to Palestine. By a remarkable coincidence, they saw with their own eyes the British handling of *The Exodus*, the immigrant ship with 4500 Jews on board. They watched British soldiers "using rifle butts, rubber hoses and tear gas on survivors of the death camps." It was clear, if this was the British Mandate, it could not continue.[31]

When the vote to partition was announced, jubilation overflowed among the Jews; the Arabs rioted; and on May 14, 1948, the independence of the State of Israel was declared and the Star of David fluttered over Jerusalem.

INTO THE FUTURE—THE SEQUEL

He gives his king great victories; he shows unfailing kindness to his anointed, to David and his descendants forever (Psalm 18:50).

In your good pleasure make Zion prosper; build up the walls of Jerusalem (Psalm 51:18).

For God will save Zion and rebuild the cities of Judah. Then people will settle there and possess it; the children of his servants will inherit it, and those who love His name will dwell there (Psalm 69:35–36).

Remember the people you purchased of old, the tribe of your inheritance, whom you redeemed—Mount Zion, where you dwelt . . . have regard for your covenant, because haunts of violence fill the dark places of the land. . . . Rise up, O God, and defend your cause (Psalm 74:2, 20, 22a).

In a context of affirming Israel's existence in perpetuity (Jeremiah 31:35ff.) and the divine intention to regather and restore what had been scattered (Jeremiah 31:10ff.), the Lord said to "the clans of Israel": "I have loved you with an everlasting love" (Jeremiah 31:3). The plain and natural meaning of language would seem clearly to indicate that the nation of Israel must exist because of God's everlasting love for her. Everlasting love and everlasting possession would seem to mean everlasting existence as an identifiable entity. The future of Israel cannot be understood as blending into an amorphous ideal people of God or the church (in which there is "neither Jew nor Gentile") but a continuum in which God resumes special dealings with the nation of Israel in what are called "the days of fulfillment." If God's promises and words cannot be taken forthrightly, we have a problem with regard to trust. Can we trust Him in all matters?

"We Christians can only rely upon the loyalty of God to the extent that we confess and testify to this same loyalty extended to Israel."[32]

In the light of Old Testament prophecies, we understand the euphoria of Jewry as David Ben-Gurion read Israel's Declaration of Independence in Tel Aviv on May 14, 1948, under a picture of Theodor Herzl, the founder of modern Zionism and the childhood hero of Ben-Gurion. To the Jews, "the days of fulfillment" were beginning. As two very thoughtful modern Israelis have put it:

> The Jewish people, landless, without a government, without armies, survived many centuries of oppression and persecution. In a nationally critical situation, even a secular Jew cannot overlook the miracles of the Holocaust survival and the rise of the State of Israel. For many hundreds of years there has been a protective hand over this people. It will continue to be held over it, especially now that part of the promise of redemption has been miraculously fulfilled.[33]

Chaos

As soon as the United Nations' vote to partition Palestine was announced, a six-month period of general chaos ensued in which the Arabs attacked and killed many Jews and in which Jewish reprisals took place, among which was the Deir Yassin massacre in April of 1948 by the Irgun. The Arabs made clear that they would not accept nor abide by the United Nations' decision, and six neighboring Arab nations commenced preparations for war. It was Jewish terror against Arab terror, and Jewish terror was more intimidating in this phase and 500,000 Arabs fled their homes. This was the beginning of the problem of Arab refugees that festers to this very day.

The British in a pique announced they would withdraw entirely by the middle of May, 1948. Increasingly tilted toward the Arabs, the British made no real effort to keep Palestine from plunging into chaos. The Arabs were in no mood to compromise. They would win it all on the field of battle. Already the Syrians were helping arm paramilitary groups of Arabs. The Arab Legion of 8000 and the Transjordan Frontier Force of 3000 and the British Palestine Police of 4000 were poised. In walking out of the United Nations meetings, the Arabs made it clear: "The partition line shall be nothing but a line of fire and blood."[34]

The United Nations followed suit with the British and abandoned any plan to implement the United Nations' decision. Even the United States began to shift its weight toward an "international trusteeship" after the end of the British Mandate. President Truman was being swayed by the State Department and others. Dr. Weizmann was not to be admitted to plead the Jewish case with the president.

At this point, Weizmann prevailed on Eddie Jacobson, the Jewish former partner of Truman in the haberdashery business in Kansas City, and through his good offices Truman went contrary to the counsel of General George Marshall and many others and the United States became the first nation to recognize the new State of Israel. The Soviet Union, which had never wavered in support of statehood, was now followed by many others.

As early as January 14, 1948, Arab terrorists goaded on by the British shut down the Jewish section of old Jerusalem. The Arabs attacked the Etzion Bloc of settlements near Hebron and wiped out the Haganah relief force. The Secretary-General of the Arab League announced ominously: "This will be a war of extermination and a momentous massacre."[35] Jewish population totaled only 650,000 against 1,300,000 Arabs in Palestine, and there were the Arab-supporting states. The possibility of another Holocaust was very real. On May 14, 1948, the British left Jerusalem for good, and the key to Zion Gate was handed over by a contrary British officer to Rabbi Mordecai Weingarten.

At this point comes the genius of Ben-Gurion. Immediately with the United Nations' vote, he ordered Mrs. Golda Meyerson (Meir, later prime minister, who had been born in Russia but lived and taught school in Milwaukee) to come to the United States to raise funds. She left with only ten dollars in her pocket and came back with fifty million dollars. This one trip ensured the survival of the newborn nation.

The Soviets continued to be favorable and encouraged their vassal satellite, Czechoslovakia, to send armaments to Israel. Ben-Gurion had only machine guns, rifles, and a few Sten guns, but no armor, no heavy artillery, no aircraft. He ordered the Palmach* (the shock companies of the Haganah) to take control of various centers in Palestine, including Tiberias on April 18, Haifa on April 22, Safed on May 10, Jaffa on May 13, and the Jordan Valley. The various warring factions among the Jews came together to face the foe that was dedicated to her annihilation.

The British had gone and, in the ferment, most middle-class and upper-class Palestinians fled the country, leaving the masses to face the Jews and the new order. Few probably imagined that their abandonment of property would be other than temporary. Curiously, the Arab world never settled its 600,000 Palestinian refugees while little Israel has never stopped absorbing refugees including hundreds of thousands who were forced out of Arab lands with only their clothes on their backs and have never been compensated for their losses.[36] Arab leaders called their people to leave with the prospect of quick return to divide up the Jewish spoils.†

It must surely be recognized that with Israeli acceptance of partition in 1948 there was an implicit recognition of a sovereign Palestinian state, which has long since been forgotten. The desire of King Abdullah of Jordan for Hashemite rule over all of the Arabs made him amenable to the 1949 armistice border that cut Jerusalem in two and gave him control over the West Bank. Of course this sank any hopes for Palestinian Arab statehood, but this whole scenario must be seen as background for the present "land for peace" tension in Israel and her negotiations with the Arab nations. We can also then understand why King Abdullah was assassinated by a Palestinian nationalist in 1951. He was ultimately succeeded by his grandson, King Hussein.[37]

Conflict

The Jews had reluctantly accepted partition as recommended by the Peel Commission as early as 1937. In the five and one-half months of her War of Independence in which she lost 1 percent of her population, she had to use a civilian militia to fight Arab professionals. Early Arab efforts to cut communication lines and isolate the pockets of Jewish resistance seemed effective. Jewish casualties were high. Jerusalem was isolated and in grave danger as the Arab Legion under Glubb Pasha advanced.

◊ ◊ ◊

* They had cooperated during the war with the British to rout out the Vichy French from Syria, in which maneuver Moshe Dyan lost his eye.
† "The Palestinian refugee problem was born of war, not by design, Jewish or Arab. It was largely a by-product of Arab and Jewish fears and of the protracted and bitter fighting that characterized the first Israeli-Arab war."—Benny Morris[38]

As told by Chaim Herzog,[*] later president of Israel and twice director of Israeli Military Intelligence, Arab strategy called for an attack from the north led by Syria, Lebanon, and an Iraqi expeditionary force, an assault on Israel's narrow central "waist-line" which led to the capture of the Jewish old city and the wanton destruction of fifty-eight synagogues, and an Egyptian invasion along two classic routes in the south. Many times Israelis were fighting tanks with Molotov cocktails.

A first truce as proposed by Count Folke Bernadotte was futile. Resumption of hostilities saw heavy losses for the Egyptians and Sudanese on the southern front and the beginning of the collapse of morale. The Lebanese withdrew from the war as the Israelis cleared Galilee. With 4000 men encircled in the Faluja Pocket, Egypt faced the fact that her allies would not come to her aid. Major tactical mistakes and lack of coordination doomed the Arab effort. Armistice was signed with the various Arab nations, but no peace treaty was possible because the Arabs would not recognize Israel as a nation. Approximately 6,000 Israelis were killed, which would be like 2,500,000 Americans being killed in a war.[†]

Israel's survival as a nation has involved her in a series of fratricidal conflicts with the Arabs. This can only be explained in terms of the heroic courage and determination of this ancient people to preserve her "sanctuary" among the nations, massive American aid and support, divisions and enmities among her Arab antagonists, and divine providence. The Sinai Campaign of 1956 was a brilliant "work of art" in terms of military strategy and marked the introduction of a United Nations peacekeeping force in the region.

The Six-Day War of 1967 saw Israel launch a dramatic pre-emptive strike and reap the prize of the Golan Heights, all of Jerusalem and the West Bank, and the Gaza as well as the Sinai Peninsula, a fourfold increase in land assets. What followed, however, was the atrophying "war of attrition" and the almost disastrous Yom Kippur War of 1973, which raised grave doubts among Israelis as to their future and saw the fall of Moshe Dayan and Golda Meir. The Entebbe Raid in 1974 helped shore up Israeli morale along with the Camp David Accords, signed by Menachem Begin, who probably alone could have negotiated this conclusion for the Israelis. But twenty-two Arab states were pitted against Israel, and the "Peace for Galilee" War in Lebanon was clearly a disaster for Israel, in terms of galvanizing world opinion against her, dividing herself internally, precipitating the fall of Menachem Begin, and failing to resolve the issue of the P. L. O.

◇ ◇ ◇

[*] Herzog was an emigrant from Ireland whose father was appointed Chief Rabbi of Palestine.

[†] Our deaths in Vietnam were about 35,000.[39]

While all of this action was on the front burner, Israel as the premier "immigrant society" of the world continued to draw Jews from all over the world, from over 100 different nations.* The stories are in many instances almost beyond belief—as the Kurds helped Iraqi Jews to escape (a community which once numbered 130,000), the flight of Jews from Yemen, the rescue of Jews from Egypt after the Six-Day War (with the help of the Spanish ambassador), liberation for the bulk of Romanian Jews, the exodus of the black Jews (Falashas) from Ethiopia, and then the mass movement of Soviet Jews more recently.[40]

After all this immigration, what will the future for Israel will be? What is meant by the prophet Ezekiel's prayer, "Come from the four winds, O breath, and breathe into these slain that they may live"?

◊ ◊ ◊

* More Jews have come to Israel from Morocco than from any other nation.

CHAPTER

JEWS INSIDE
AND OUTSIDE ISRAEL—
ASSESSMENT AND
ANTICIPATION

What is a Jew?
This question is not at all so odd as it seems.
Let us see what peculiar kind of creature the Jew is,
which all the rulers and all the nations have together and separately
abused and molested,
oppressed and persecuted,
trampled and butchered,
burned, and hanged,
and in spite of all this, is yet alive . . .
the Jew is the emblem of eternity.
He whom neither slaughter nor torture
of himself for years could destroy;
he whom neither fire nor sword, nor inquisition
was able to wipe off the face of the earth;
he who was the first to produce the oracles of God;
he who has been for so long a time the guardian of prophecy,
and who has transmitted it to the rest of the world—
such a nation cannot be destroyed.
The Jew is everlasting as eternity itself.

Count Leo Tolstoy

From the rocky peaks I see them,
from the heights I view them.
I see a people who live apart
and do not consider themselves
one of the nations.
Who can count
the dust of Jacob
or number
the fourth part
of Israel?

Balaam in Numbers 23:9–10a

"I

F YOU WILL IT, IT IS NO DREAM," said Theodor Herzl, and indeed after so many long centuries and anguished prayer and desperation, the Jews had a homeland.

For 2000 years they had prayed: "And to Jerusalem, thy city return in mercy and dwell therein as Thou hast spoken, rebuild it soon in our days, as an everlasting building . . . as in the days of old, and as in ancient years" (*The Prayer Book*).

No wonder President Harry S. Truman spoke of himself as "another Cyrus," that is, a servant of the Lord who helped the Jews. No wonder that the Jews facing the question as to who would be the dead or the displaced—Jew or Arab—rose up to defend *eretz* Israel again and again and successfully!

Israel with the occupied territories is about the size of the state of New Jersey (9,000 square miles). She has repeatedly faced 22 Arab countries with 5,000,000 square miles and 144,000,000 people who are supported and aligned with the whole Muslim world of a billion people and an area twice the size of the United States and 672 times the size of minuscule Israel. The current population of Israel is about 5.1 million including 4 million Jews.

The Jewish phoenix rising up out of the ashes of the Holocaust has faced unbelievable problems and odds. Yet the influx of immigrants relieved something of this grim prospect. From fall of 1989 to March of 1992, 395,000 Soviet Jews came to Israel, among whom are 8,000 physicians. Israel has the highest number of physicians per capita in the world, yet a high percentage of the immigrants are unemployed. Immigrants have also come from Yugoslavia, and 14,000 Ethiopian Jews came last year bringing the total to 45,000, among whom there is great unrest and intermittent strikes and protests. Half a million Israeli citizens live in the United States, and tensions have been exacerbated between Jews in Israel and Jews in the Diaspora. Called in Scripture both "the holy land" (Zechariah 2:12) and "the Beautiful Land" (Daniel 11:41), Israel sees almost daily violence and the bloodshed seems to presage a horrible bloodbath. The land which had been desolate became what the prophet said:

> This is what the sovereign LORD says: When I gather the people of Israel from the nations where they have been scattered, I will show myself holy among them in the sight of the nations. Then they will live in their own land, which I gave to my servant Jacob. They will live there in safety and will build houses and plant vineyards; they will live in safety when I inflict punishment on all their neighbors who maligned them. Then they will know that I am the LORD their God (Ezekiel 28:25–26).

Some of these promises have been fulfilled but others obviously have not.

Israel, as Lawrence Meyer has demonstrated, is a nation deeply troubled.[1] Her standard of living is made possible by huge foreign debt, but the benefits and privileges are available to mainly Jewish citizens. Israel has one of the highest accident rates in the country, a serious organized crime problem, and much rowdyism and disrespect for law (Hebrew has no word for gentleman). Its government employs three out of ten workers, spends five times per capita what the United States spends on defense, taxes its people more heavily than any in the world. In addition Israel has growing internal tensions among various ethnic groups, possesses virtually no natural resources, loses more days to strikes than any other Western country, faces serious water shortages, and still is without a written constitution because of disagreement over the role of religion internally.

The beach game, *matcote,* which is a cross between ping-pong and paddleball is distinctively Israeli in that it has no rules, no winner, no end. It is, perhaps, a symbol of Israel's quandary and dilemma in the modern world.[2]

As Israel has become increasingly isolated, some thoughtful observers like Moshe Leshem have raised the question as to whether or not Israel has lost her way.[3] One might ask the question, has she ever found her way?

THE VITALITY OF ISRAEL

Israel is no more—epitaph used by Mnepthah, Pharaoh in Egypt thirty centuries before Israel was reborn as a nation in 1948.

When the LORD brought back the captives to Zion, we were like men who dreamed. Our mouths were filled with laughter, our tongues with songs of joy.

Then it was said among the nations, "The LORD has done great things for them. The LORD has done great things for us, an we are filled with joy" (Psalm 126:1–3).

Reflecting something of the ambivalence Israelis felt at the time of Independence, Moshe Dayan recalled:

"We were happy that night, and we danced, and our hearts went out to every nation whose UN representative had voted in favor of the resolution . . . We danced, but we knew that ahead of us lay the battlefield."[4]

Notwithstanding the conflicts and seemingly insoluble problems of the fledgling state, the very existence of Israel is a miracle and her persistence a continuing miracle. Her national life is characterized by a series of extraordinary vitalities.

Sanctuary

While serious tensions continue in Israel between Ashkenazic and Sephardic Jew and between secular and observant Jews, given the fact that immigrants have come from over 100 countries and from very primitive as well as very technologically advanced nations, the degree of assimilation has been remarkable. Tiny Israel has been a haven in the storm for hosts of oppressed and tyrannized people. The relatively effective absorption is quite striking considering the rate of immigration and the compressed time factor.

Militarily Israel is the strongest force in the Middle East and one of the most formidable in the world. Her patience in Operation Desert Storm only pointed the way to the kind of sophisticated warfare Israel is well able to develop. Doubtless Israel has nuclear capability emanating from her research facility at Dimona. The pioneering Zionist ethos has all but disappeared, and the country is largely run by a managerial class recruited "from the top ranks of what is now an advanced consumer society."[5] The Arabs in Israel have themselves benefited from a standard of living generally higher than in other Arab lands.

In the first forty years of her existence Israel's population multiplied six times; she built a million houses and apartments; became a world center for medical and biotechnical research; added 800,000 more students in her schools, and established 800 new settlements. Israel is an agricultural miracle. The deserts of the Negev blossom. Her society is increasingly into high-tech. Brilliant thinkers from all over the world have found a congenial environment at places like the Technion in Haifa, the Hebrew University in Jerusalem, and the Weizmann Institute in Rehovot.

Democracy

While Israel is the most open society in the Middle East, democratic opportunity is altogether different for the Jews than it is for the Arabs. Existing side by side as "intimate enemies," 90 percent of the cultivable land, 75 percent of the water, and all the infrastructures are really dedicated to the Jews. Yet an amazing right of self-determination and individual freedom are possible in Israel. When the socialists who largely founded the State of Israel, did not find the capitalism of the House of Rothschild greatly to their liking, the Rothchilds quietly disengaged but gave to the nation the magnificent Knesset Building. Here Arabs, the Orthodox, and the right and left wings exhibit democracy in action.

The mayor of Jerusalem from 1965 until 1993, Teddy Kollek, typified those who have made a difficult coexistence work. "In times of war, and continuing wars," says the modern Hebrew poet Yehuda Amichai, "Teddy has made Jerusalem work, not by making it something different, but by making it work as it is."[6] With 102 different Jewish groups and 42 Christian bodies plus the Arabs, both Christian and Muslim, Kollek (who was born near Budapest and raised in Vienna) was faced with a Solomonic balancing act.[7] Kollek did not hesitate to denounce the government when he felt they were unfair, as when Israeli nationalists moved into Arab districts of East Jerusalem. To use his words:

"We are driving the Arabs crazy and forcing them to hate us."[8]

Dependency

Galling as it is to many Israelis, the fact is that up to now Israel would not have made it without the largess of the United States government. Many millions also are raised from the American Jewish community. The current budget is about $30 billion dollars. The servicing of Israel's massive foreign debt (largely to the United States) has given rise to a debilitating inflation. Long regarded as America's most reliable ally in the Middle East, Israel's strategic importance to the United States has greatly decreased since the collapse of the former Soviet Union. With one-third of the Israeli operating budget coming from American money, the Israelis view the future with some trepidation under American pressure to move more away from the socialistic welfare state to which she has become accustomed to more of a free-market economy. The disaster of the war in Lebanon almost put them under (with inflation soaring to 1000 percent), but recovery also has been impeded by the inability to pare down military expenditure significantly in the light of Israel's security risks.

Diversity

The richest resource in Israel is her variegated population. Israel is a finely textured tapestry of cultures. Visit Israel with an Israeli guide or visit Israel with an Arab guide and you see and feel the throbbing pulse of millennia of colorful history.[9]

Walk with Amos Elon, the well-known writer, as he explores Jerusalem, "city of mirrors," almost like Alice stepping through the looking-glass.[10] Or see Jerusalem* as "the end of days" through the eyes of the American Jew, Samuel Heilman, as he meets an Argentinian-Jewish cowboy who has recorded his every impression of Jerusalem for forty years; a womanizing monk; a German tour guide who will never leave; a gentle Arab schoolteacher who writes English poetry about his native city; a mystical rabbi; a suspicious shopkeeper; a fanatical archaeologist; and a pious woodcarver.[11] Or examine the people, passions, and politics with Abraham Rabinovich, who has watched the changes take place since reunification in 1967.[12] Israel is like a giant theme park.[13] Listen as one of Israel's finest writers interviews Israelis—Jews and Arabs—on the battlefield of divergent beliefs."[14] Such convulsive surges of contrasting feeling and faith. This is Israel today.

THE INSECURITY OF ISRAEL

We have neither taken any other man's land, nor do we hold dominion over other people's territory, but only over the inheritance of our fathers. On the contrary, for a certain time it was unjustly held by our enemies; but we, seizing the opportunity, hold fast the inheritance of our fathers (1 Maccabees 15:33–34).

Hear my prayer, O LORD, listen to my cry for help; be not deaf to my weeping. For I dwell with you as an alien, a stranger, as all my fathers were (Psalm 39:12).

Jews are like other people, only more so.—Aphorism of Bernard Malamud

When Israel struck pre-emptively at Egypt in 1967 and won the sweeping victory over her enemies on every hand, a tremor of excitement went through world Jewry. The occupation of the West Bank, East Jerusalem, Gaza, and the Golan brought well over 1,000,000 additional Palestinians under the Israeli umbrella, there being 700,000 Arabs already citizens of Israel. Now Israel had to face greater uneasiness and tension from within as well as the massive forces poised from without.

The Palestinian Liberation Organization
The Palestine Liberation Organization was founded in 1964 in Kuwait as a recognition of the unresolved issue of Palestinian refugees. Yasser

◊ ◊ ◊

* Even Sigmund Freud considered moving to Jerusalem at one time, briefly in 1922.

Arafat and his networking of underground cell organizations called Fatah took over the P.L.O. in 1969 and incorporated a number of desperate groups under its aegis. Arafat was born in Cairo in 1929. He was a relative of the infamous Nazi collaborator Haj Amin Husseini, the Grand Mufti of Jerusalem. He was given military training by a German officer.[15] Murders and massacres have been his agenda, and mutinies from within have been his constant peril. Backed by oil-rich Arab nations and supported by wealthy Palestinian interests abroad, Arafat has built a strong terrorist organization. Known as "the Old Man" within the inner circle, Arafat has survived many attempts on his life but like the proverbial cat with nine lives always seems to land right-side-up.

The Palestinian National Covenant is dedicated to the abolition of the Jewish state, and billions of petro-dollars have been poured into the effort.[16] Yet King Hussein's suppression of the "Black September" movement in 1971 in Jordan (where 80 percent of the population is Palestinian), the collapse of world oil prices and chaos in OPEC, and Arafat's futile backing of Saddam of Iraq in 1991 have caused endless splintering in his movement and a great weakening of his power. The rise of Hamas or Muslim Fundamentalism in Palestine itself threatens to ultimately displace Arafat and the P.L.O. His problems with President Asad of Syria are typical of the mercurial nature of his support.[17]

Endless butcheries such as at Munich in the Olympics and at the El Al counters in the Rome and Vienna airports are typical of the strategy of the P.L.O. These acts dramatize the depth of the hatred and passionate antipathy underlying Israeli-Palestinian relationships. This is the milieu of Israel's life and hopes.*

The Yom Kippur War of 1973

The brilliant strategies and daring of the Israeli Defense Force tended to make the Israelis feel they were invincible. No Israeli peace initiatives seemed necessary. Even though the Egyptians had been humiliated militarily, Israel did not seem to understand the inevitability of further conflict. The United Nations passed Resolution 242/67 calling for Israeli withdrawal, recognition of Israel, and amelioration for the Palestinians. Nasser's "War of Attrition" was nagging. With the death of Nasser in

◊ ◊ ◊

* Israel of course has sought to penetrate all Palestinian groups, and Patrick Seale goes so far as to argue that Abu Nidal, the notorious independent operator now out of Libya, has been a cooperator with Israel.[18] This is difficult to accept, but what may be possible in the always murky and intrigue-filled world of spying and terrorism in the Middle East? Two rather crass but immensely revealing spy pieces are John LeCarre's *The Little Drummer Girl* and David Ignatius's *Agents of Innocence*.

Chapter 12

1970 and the accession of Anwar el Sadat, Egypt began to skillfully play the Russians and the Americans against each other.[19]

In the Khartoum Conference, the confrontive Arab states adamantly insisted: no peace, no negotiation, no recognition.

Although Israel made careful stipulations regarding Temple Mount policy and although Moshe Dayan as Chief of Staff encouraged the "open bridges" policy with Jordan, an overlay of religious rhetoric tended to make Israel overconfident and even swaggering. Dayan's premise was: "The Arabs will not dare to attack Israel again."[20] Creeping annexation was leading inexorably to permanent annexation, and Dayan fell victim to his own policy. In a non-urgent atmosphere with the fact that a fully mobilized Israel would be labeled an aggressor, Israel was caught offguard in 1973. Had Nixon and Kissinger not faced up to the Soviets and gone on full alert, the outcome might have been even more disastrous. Israel counterattacked but Dayan was unimaginably changed. He made apocalyptic remarks about "the destruction of the Third Temple," and while the Agranat Commission in seeking "who created this feeling in Israel" did not finally blame either Dayan or Prime Minister Meir; they were both done. The disaster of unpreparedness haunted the nation. Another consequence was ultimately the nation's turning at last from Labor to the right-wing Likud and Menachem Begin (prime minister 1977–83). Even though Begin signed the Camp David Accords that established a framework for peace in the Middle East and set up peace between Israel and Egypt, the loss of Sinai and the assassination of Sadat in 1981 made Israel very uneasy.[21]

The War in Lebanon

After King Hussein crushed the P.L.O. in Jordan, terrorism found a new cradle in Lebanon, increasingly destabilized from her long balancing act between Christian, Druse, Sunni, and Shi'ite Muslims. Syria's intervention in the bloody internecine conflict in Lebanon was especially alarming to Israel. Israeli support for a private Christian army and her encouragement to several Christian warlords did not avert the terrorism on her northern borders. Syria's quest for hegemony in Lebanon and the presence of Syrian missiles in the Beka Valley inclined Israel to take aggressive action. The war lasted from June to September, 1982. What initially was to be a limited war soon expanded to the siege of Beirut and the expulsion of the P.L.O. from Lebanon. The war was a failure and unmitigated disaster for Israel.[22]

Israel's image was severely tarnished in "Operation Peace for Galilee." Although early on the Israelis were welcomed by the populace, the Israeli presence was soon too heavy and oppressive and was resented by all, especially by the fast-growing Shi'ites. On September 17, 1982, Christian Phalangists entered the Palestinian camps of Chatila and Sabra and brutally massacred 1000 helpless civilians. All decent people found this utterly repugnant. The Kahan Report, published in February of 1983, found Israel "indirectly responsible for the massacre and Ariel Sharon in particular most responsible." He was forced to resign, but he did not leave the cabinet.[23]

The cost to Israel involved very high casualties, the fall of Menachem Begin, isolation among the nations, a changed attitude on the part of Israel's 50,000 Druse, and perhaps most significantly, deep divisions within Israel. This was the first Israeli war in which some Israeli soldiers refused to fight. Jacobo Timerman, whose sufferings in Argentina were so vividly chronicled in *Prisoner Without a Name, Cell Without a Number*, wrote a powerful and devastating indictment of the Lebanese debacle.[24] The whole saga of the hostages in Lebanon and the incredible nightmare of that once beautiful country and anyone who became embroiled in its conflicts, left everyone absolutely ill and in shock.[25]

The Intifada

Many in Israel began to raise the question as to whether Israel was not altering the vision and losing its way. Significant Israeli thinkers agonized over their appraisal of what direction Israel ought to take.[26] Who should govern and how should governance take place?[27]

The seeming intractability of the Jewish/Arab problem in Israel has been evidenced by "the days of rage" seen in the intifada or Palestinian uprising.[28] The Palestinians were hopeless and finally agreed that armed force alone would obtain their rights to a Palestinian homeland.

In 1980 there were 10,000 Jews living on the West Bank and Gaza while now there are 100,000 with more and more immigrants coming.

Beginning on December 9, 1987, after four Gazans had been killed and seven others injured by an Israeli road vehicle, what started as a youth revolt soon became a war. Two premier Israeli journalists have argued that Israel's strategy is really to decouple the Jewish State from the Palestinian population.[29] This thesis holds that what radical Meir Kahane sought overtly, Israeli tacticians are in fact seeking more covertly.[30]

American and other Christians in their empathy for Israel have sometimes failed to recognize certain unfair conditions for Arabs and others in Israel. There is a crescendo of Jewish protest in Israel against some of these policies. And with the Intifada and the collapse of the Soviet Union, there is a change in Washington's posture on certain key issues.

Israel will always be a special ally, but the road has been rough occasionally and doubtless will be from time to time. The development of the Israeli nuclear capability,[31] Israel's liaison with South Africa,[32] and the Israeli use of Jonathan Pollard for the theft of American secrets have all placed a strain on this old and still very viable relationship[33] The Peace Accords with the P. L. O. and negotiations with Jordan and Syria have been pursued by the Rabin government. Much progress has been made but great uneasiness remains.

THE SPIRITUALITY OF THE JEWS

When the Most High gave the nations their inheritance, when he divided all mankind, he set up boundaries for the peoples according to the number of the sons of Israel. For the LORD's portion is his people, Jacob His allotted inheritance (Deuteronomy 32:8–9).

This is what the Sovereign LORD says: This is Jerusalem, which I have set in the center of the nations, with countries all around her (Ezekiel 5:5).

Judaism was born in a corner and has always lived in a corner . . . History has not yet satisfactorily explained how it came about that a tiny nation in Asia produced a unique religious and ethical outlook, which, though it has had so profound an influence on the rest of the world, has yet remained so foreign to the rest of the world.— Ahad Ha'am (Asher Ginzberg)

Obviously Jewry and Judaism are not coextensive. Although the preponderance of Jews in Israel and in the Diaspora are secular and not observant in a religious sense, any study of the Jews today would be grossly incomplete without reference to the Jewish soul. Spiritual Zionism is as much part of the mix as political Zionism. Although the "religious" draw from 6 percent to 15 percent of the vote in Israel, these small splintered parties are often those who determine the balance of power in the very unique proportional system used in Israel. Ben-Gurion himself, although not a practicing Jew, turned to the "religious" to cement his coalition. The vision of Israel as a spiritual center has been but dimly realized even in the sense of reviving Jewish national culture. Yet the Bible reveals such a vision for Israel (Isaiah 2:2–4), and the church has not superseded Israel in this regard but rather become part of an expanded and enlarged fulfillment of the promises not always clearly seen by the prophets of old.

The Parties

Judaism as a religious expression has four main branches. Orthodoxy or "true-Torah" commitment has not been as numerically significant in the United States but is seeing something of a renewal at the present time and is the dominant expression in Israel, where *halachic* law (the sum total of Scriptural and Talmudic teaching) really runs the country. Only Orthodox marriages are allowed; El Al, the state airline, does not operate on Sabbath. The Rabbinic Courts in Israel are Orthodox and the Chief Rabbis are Orthodox, and marriages other than by an Orthodox Rabbi are not registered with the Interior Ministry. The Israeli Supreme Court has upheld the Orthodox monopoly in marriage.

The Orthodox *yeshivot* (learning academies) are subsidized by the Israel government and, most controversially, *yeshiva* students are exempt from Israeli National Service. Considering how large an armed force Israel has (with her large reserve component), it is not difficult to see that this arrangement works some hardship on others.

At the time of the founding of the Jewish state in 1948 the Ashkenazic or Western Jews comprised 85 percent of the Jewish population. Now with the immense Sephardic or Oriental immigration, the Oriental Jews are more than 60 percent of the population and they tend to be more traditional in their religious outlook. The 45,000 Ethiopian Jews have variant customs but are extremely orthodox.[34]

The Ultra-Orthodox split into three main groups:

(1) the "Lithuanians" perpetuate Rabbinic schools from Eastern Europe;

(2) the Sephardim from North Africa, Middle Eastern lands, and the Balkans, and like the Lithuanians generally wear modern dress but always with a head-covering for men and boys and women cover their hair as a sign of modesty; and

(3) the Hassidim or "holy ones" who trace back to eighteenth-century Poland and a miracle worker-teacher named Baal Shem Tov or "Master of the Good Name." Rooted in Talmudic and Kabbalistic teachings (mystical interpretations of Torah with much speculation on the Hebrew letters and numerology) this movement is almost like a Jewish charismatic expression with joyous dancing and singing.[35] Countless sects following different *rebbes* (rabbis or spiritual leaders) have dresscodes going back 300 or 400 years. Walk through sections of Brooklyn or in parts of Jerusalem on Shabbat and see the Satmar or Belz Hassids wearing fur hats or the Breslau Hassids who do not touch the *payot* (or side curls or earlocks). Many see the Ultra-Orthodox or Haredi ("Fearful") and their fervor as representing protest against the secularization of Israel. Never in history have so many young men been studying Torah as presently.

Reformed Judaism is liberal Judaism, and although quite popular in the United States, it has been restricted in Israel. Conservative Judaism, a kind of middle ground and also quite popular in the United States, often observes *kashrut* (the kosher food laws) and other scruples and yet has not taken great root in Israel. Reconstructionism, mentioned in a previous chapter, is not widespread anywhere and scarcely found in Israel.[36] Most American Jews do not believe in an active or personal God and only 26 percent believe that religion is "important."[37] Although many more American Jews will participate in the High Holidays or a Bar Mitzvah or Bas Mitzvah, all Jews of the Diaspora are facing an increasing danger of cultural assimilation.

Politics

Many of the Haredi are actually anti-Zionist and oppose the existence of the State of Israel. The most extreme groups are the Eda Haredit of Jerusalem and the Neturei Karta with about 15,000 adherents who boycott Israel by refusing to take government subsidies and who regularly voice their support for the P. L. O. and Arab rule in Palestine. The Orthodox generally have gained many benefits as bargaining chips in the difficult Israel problem of governance, given the relative parity of Labor and the Likud parties. Amending the Law of Return by limiting it to those born Jewish (born of a Jewish mother) or those who have an authentic conversion would effectively rule out Conservative or Reform conversions and would be an unspeakable affront to many American Jews.

Minuscule groups such as Agudat Yisrael (the seven sages), Shas, and Degel Hatora exert an influence far disproportionate to their small numbers because of their strategic importance in forming governmental coalitions. The Agudat, for instance, justifies its sitting in a Knesset of "heretics" because it has been able to thereby hold the crucial chairmanship of the all-important Knesset finance committee for the last fifteen years. Much money and patronage derive from these liaisons to the total disgust and horror of the secular Jewish community. The political profile of the Orthodox community in the United States is also developing as certain surges of vitality are in evidence within these circles.[38]

While the Israeli Proclamation of Independence in 1948 declared "equality of social and political rights for all its citizens, without distinction of creed, race or sex" and that "freedom of religion and conscience, of language, education and culture" are guaranteed, it is not clear to all Jews that they enjoy such rights as stones are hurled at their cars when they drive on Shabbat, nor is it at all clear to Muslims, Druse, Bahais, or Christians that they have rights and freedom. Protestant organizations seem to face increasing restriction on their activities.

Prospects

Giving up any land at all is now seen by some as high treason. The death of Rabbi Kahane has not lessened the appeal of his "catastrophic Zionism." All Orthodox Jews believe in the future establishment of an *Halachic* state, a Jewish theocracy. For many this includes the reinstitution of the ruling House of David and the Sanhedrin as well as the rebuilding of the Temple and the restoration of animal sacrifice.

Rabbi Kook, whose father was the first Ashkenazic Chief Rabbi in Israel, believed that the Zionist state was the first step and was indeed the instrument in God's scheme of messianic redemption. As spiritual leader of the *Gush Emunim* ("The Block of the Faithful"), Rabbi Kook taught that three *mizvot* are required of the Jews as they enter the land: (1) anoint a king; (2) rebuild the temple; and (3) destroy Amalek.

Most of the Orthodox see the meaning of the Jerusalem Talmud to be clear: an Israelite kingdom, or an independent state, will arise and the Temple be rebuilt before the Messiah comes. The present State of Israel is an interim stage between the Age of Exile and the Messianic Age. The stir over the Lubavitcher Rebbe's strong pronouncement after Operation Desert Storm that the Messiah-Redeemer is soon to come has been widespread.

Rabbi Menachem Schneerson of Brooklyn, their rebbe who died in June 1994, was seen by some to be the Messiah.[39] Rabbi Eliezer Schach of Degel Hatora has spoken for many when he blasted the Habadic rebbe as a false messiah. Yet many in Israel and elsewhere in the Jewish world would agree with the respected Sephardic scholar Rabbi Professor Leon Ashkenazi of Jerusalem, who has argued that beyond question the "ingathering of the exiles" has begun and the Messianic Era has been launched.[*]

THE VULNERABILITY OF THE DIASPORA

The LORD will drive you and the king you set over you to a nation unknown to you or your fathers. There you will worship other gods, gods of wood and stone. You will become a thing of horror and an object of scorn and ridicule to all the nations where the LORD will drive you (Deuteronomy 28:36–37).

So I will throw you out of this land into a land neither you nor your fathers have known, and there you will serve other gods day and night, for I will show you no favor (Jeremiah 16:13).

◊ ◊ ◊

[*] With Jewish spiritual renewal has steadily come a new interest among the Jews in scholarly studies of Jesus. "The Jewish reclamation of Jesus," i.e. a new perception of the Jewishness of Jesus and "the emergence of a positive attitude toward Jesus and his teaching . . . [seems] nothing less than astonishing.[40] A prominent Orthodox Rabbi from Europe has come out with a book favorable to the resurrection of Christ while denying the messianic mission of Jesus.[41]

D'Israeli [Isaac] contributed liberally to synagogue funds and had certainly caused Benjamin to be given instruction in the Jewish faith, but he was not ardent in his religious observances. Accordingly, the governors of the synagogue, as a call to order and much to his annoyance, elected him as Warden; when he refused, they tried to fine him 40 pounds. This appears to have been the reason why Benjamin Disraeli was baptized at the age of twelve.—Anthony Powell of Disraeli[42]

More than three times as many Jews live in the Diaspora than live in Israel. More Jews live in the United States than live in Israel by quite a margin. The changing scene in Israel,[43] the fact that a high percentage of the Soviet emigres are unemployed gives poignancy to present restlessness. So 25,000 Jews from the Commonwealth of Independent States (the former Soviet Union) have applied to immigrate to Germany.[44] What's happening?

Prosperity! We are well warned not to typecast the Jewish people.

Sammy Davis, Jr., once observed: "After I decided to become a Jew only then did I learn that Jews don't really have all the money. When I found out Rockefeller and Ford were goyim, I almost resigned."

There are among the Jews what is not often discussed—the *Heimishe mensch*, or the familiar, down-home regular guy.[45] However, what cannot be gainsaid is that the Jewish people as a whole are a remarkably gifted and brilliant people. Their experience in the Diaspora is demonstrative of that.

The Jews came to the United States (to speak of the largest Diaspora population) in three waves:

(1) The Sephardic (or Spanish) Jews who started coming in 1654;

(2) the great wave of German Jews from 1815 to 1890 spreading over the entire nation;

(3) the great stream out of the ghettos of Eastern Europe—2,000,000 strong—between 1881 and the quota laws of 1920–21.

Of the 5,750,000 Jews in the United States only 10 percent attend synagogue on a given Sabbath; 70 percent attend only 4 times a year; 11 percent are Orthodox; 30 percent are Reform; 40 percent are Conservative. About 30 percent of the Jews in this country are married to Gentiles.[46]

The American Jewish community has met innumerable obstacles and emerged nonetheless as a powerful influential force in our common life.

Jewish professionalism is reflected in *Who's Who in America?* where the Jews are over-represented by 308 percent in the medical professions (one in five doctors is Jewish); 283 percent in mathematics; 231 percent in nonmedical sciences; 108 percent in contemporary literature, and 89 percent in art and music.[47] "Like their European-Jewish predecessors earlier in the century, the second and third generations of American Jews craved a soul-satisfying blend of economic security and intellectual creativity. In the post-World War II era, they achieved it."[48]

Yet as good as conditions frequently were, American Jews retained loyalty to and sympathy for the downtrodden Jews in distant lands. The American Jewish identification with the establishment and perpetuation of the Jewish state has been emotional and somewhat cyclical (stronger and more intense in the earlier wars, especially the Six-Day War of 1967). Narrative studies disclose both cultural continuities and discontinuities in the American Jewish community.[49] The political motifs are also well-woven into the fabric of our national life right up to the present.[50]

Pressures

The Jews in America continually face a not-so-subtle underlying anti-Semitism. A jealous and envious nativism delights to rub in "the Shylock image."* But it is not only latent anti-Semitism that has created pressure but also the criticism by Jews who felt all Jews should make *aliyah* to Zion.

Had not the Talmud said that "whoever dwells outside the Land is unclean?"

Michael Greenstein looses a broadside from Jerusalem at the very term *American Jew,* calling it contradictory. Jews, he argued, must not

◊ ◊ ◊

* Howard M. Sachar has listed representatives of anti-Semitism in American life, who to a greater or lesser degree have expressed stereotypes which hurt, including Walt Whitman, Jack London, Henry Cabot Lodge, Henry Ford, Charles Lindbergh, Thomas Wolfe, William Faulkner, Theodore Dreiser, Willa Cather, F. Scott Fitzgerald, Ernest Hemingway, Edith Wharton, Walter Lippmann (an instance of "Jewish self-hatred"), Truman Capote, Richard Nixon, Spiro Agnew, James Baldwin, and Jesse Jackson. We have not spoken of the infamous lynching of Leo Frank in Cobb County, Georgia in 1915, which gave rise to the Bnai Berith and the Anti-Defamation League, nor have we referred to the pre-World War II isolationists and their opposition to the "Jewish cabal" leading the United States to war (including Senators Ernest Lundeen, Gerald Nye, Burton Wheeler, George Norris, and such neo-fascist types as Gerald Winrod and Gerald L. K. Smith).

allow the tumult of Babylon to deaden the words of Cyrus, King of Persia: "Whosoever there is among you of all the people that the Lord His God be with him—let him go up."[51]*

Defensively the American-Jewish leader, Philip Klutznick has replied: "It is false and mischievous for the Israelis to predict the disintegration of American Jewish life."[52] American Jews have a difficult time buying into Rabbi Riskin's thesis: "In theological terms, the difference between the Diaspora and Israel is that the former is transitory, a passing stage in the realization of our historical role, while the latter is eternal, the raison d'être of our existence."[53]

Further pressure on Jews of the Diaspora comes through the overly muscular Israel lobby, the pro-Israel PACs. Clearly a reappraisal of American Jewish largess is taking place in the face of certain Israeli policies, the shrill tendency to label any opposition to Israeli direction as anti-Semitic and the awkward issue of dual loyalties emblazoned large in the Pollard case. Rabin of Israel calls Israelis living in the United States "the fallen among the weaklings."[54]

The fact is since 1985, 52 percent of marriages involving Jews are inter-faith; 12 percent of American Jews attend Christian churches. Is the Diaspora being assimilated? These pressures moved Howard M. Sachar himself to a somewhat repressed but wistful final quote from Adam Myer: "Israel is my home—there I know who I am."[55]

◊ ◊ ◊

* Not putting it quite so strongly but with a stiletto nevertheless, Borowitz entitled his book *The Masks Jews Wear: The Self-deception of American Jewry (1973)*. His thrust is that American Jews are Marranos in reverse and his advocates what he calls "creative alienation."

THE PROPHETICAL
FUTURE

For the Israelites will live many days without king or prince,
without sacrifice or sacred stones, without ephod or idol.
Afterward the Israelites will return and seek
the Lord *their God and David their king.*
They will come trembling to the Lord
and to his blessings
in the last days.

Hosea 3:4–5

THE FULLNESS OF THE GENTILES AND THE EXIT OF THE CHURCH

But I see that Christian religion wherein prophecies are fulfilled; and that is what everyone cannot do . . . the prophecies are the strongest proof of Jesus Christ . . . Here is a succession of men during 4000 years, who consequently and without variation, come one after another, to foretell this same event. Here is a whole people who announce it and who have existed for 4000 years, in order to give corporate testimony of the assurances which they have and from which they cannot be diverted by whatever threats and persecutions people may make against them.

Blaise Pascal in Penseés, Xi. 693, 706, 710

About the Time of the End, a body of men will be raised up who will turn their attention to the Prophecies and insist on their literal interpretation, in the midst of much clamor and opposition.

Sir Isaac Newton, 18th century

For the revelation awaits an appointed time;
it speaks of the end and will not prove false.
Though it linger, wait for it; it will certainly come and will not delay.

Habakkuk 2:3

Jerusalem will be trampled on by the Gentiles
until the times of the Gentiles are fulfilled.

Luke 21:24b

Israel has experienced a hardening in part until the full number of the Gentiles has come in. And so all Israel will be saved.

Romans 11:25b–26a

SIR FRANCIS BACON RIGHTLY SAID that "the spirit of man coveteth divination," that is, the human desire to know the future is so powerful as to have virtually the strength of an innate instinct. The ancients used a variety of methods in an effort to ascertain the shape of things to come. We moderns spend vast sums of money in a vain effort to obtain some clue as to what is impending. Sometimes charlatans, pundits, savants and astrologers have by chance hit on some vague or indefinite future aspect, but the fact is we don't know the future. The *Dialogues* of Plato do not contain predictive prophecy. Our most expert futurologists must hedge their prognostications.

The Bible has a unique corpus of predictive prophecy. Roughly 25 percent of the Bible was predictive prophecy when written.[*] The prophets of the Lord in the Old Testament, called speakers, seers, watchmen, and "men of God," were entrusted with the message of God (Exodus 7:1; 1 Kings 18:12; 2 Kings 2:16; Amos 3:7). Jesus Christ is not only the fulfillment of many prophecies (Luke 1:69), but also the climactic prophet (Deuteronomy 18:15; Isaiah 11:2ff.).

A substantial part of prophetic revelation is in the form of predictive prophecy.[†] The fulfillment of prophecy is proof for the reliability and trustworthiness of Scripture. Fulfilled prophecy in Scripture vindicates God (cf. Joshua 3:9–10; Isaiah 41:22–23; 46:9–11), and is based on His omniscience (Acts 15:18). He knows the end from the beginning and all of the contingencies.[1] Jesus unveiled future events during His ministry on earth and indicated that the Holy Spirit would "tell [them] what is yet to come" (John 16:13).

Many hairbrained and ridiculous schemes of prophetic interpretation have been foisted upon patient and longsuffering listeners and

◊ ◊ ◊

[*] Prophecy is "an oral or written disclosure in words through a human mouthpiece transmitting the revelation of God and setting forth His will to man."—Gleason Archer[2]

readers across the centuries, but that does not give us license to discard one-quarter of the Bible's own material. God has seen fit to give us information about the future, particularly the wrap-up of human history (2 Peter 1:20–21), and this has immense practical relevance (cf. 2 Peter 1:19). The book of Revelation consists in large part of "what must soon come to pass," and this has great import for the lives of all believers (Revelation 1:3). There are false prophets on every side, and we are given tests with which to identify them (Deuteronomy 18:21–22).

Predictive prophecy often specifies names, places, events, and dates—the 120 years until the flood (Genesis 6:3); the 400 years until Israel entered the land (Genesis 15:13); the 40 years of wandering in the wilderness (Numbers 14:33); the 65 years until Ephraim would be broken (Isaiah 7:8); the 70 years during which Judah was to be in captivity (Jeremiah 25:11–12; 29:10); the great chronological prophecy of the 490 years in (Daniel 9:24–27), and many others.[3] Although many passages do not yield their interpretations easily, the natural and plain sense of prophecy is preferred to the spiritualizing, allegorical approach.[*]

The fact that hundreds of biblical prophecies have been so exactly fulfilled can only embolden us to expect exact fulfillment of those prophecies we shall now inspect which relate to the Jew, the Gentile and the church of God (1 Corinthians 10:32).[4] All praise and glory be to God!

THE PROGRESSION OF THE CHURCH AGE

What I mean is this: The law, introduced 430 years later, does not set aside the covenant previously established by God and thus do away with the promise (Galatians 3:17).

◊ ◊ ◊

† (previous page) In his discussion of predictive prophecy, Payne used Fairbairn's definition of prediction: "An announcement, more or less specific, of the future—a miracle of knowledge, a declaration or representation of something future, beyond the power of human sagacity to discern or to calculate."[5] The word *miracle* is well chosen. The anti-supernatural bias that has vitiated Christendom since Schleiermacher, Ritschl, Fosdick, and essentially controlled modern higher criticism has no place for predictive prophecy. Like David Hume's dictum, "Miracles do not happen," this approach will insist on a late date for Daniel primarily because any notion of predictive prophecy is inadmissible (the old logical fallacy of *petitio principii*).

* "The literalist (so-called) is not one who denies that figurative language, that symbols, are used in prophecy, nor does he deny that great spiritual truths are set forth therein; his position is, simply, that the prophecies are to be normally interpreted—that which is manifestly literal being regarded as literal, that which is manifestly figurative being so regarded."—John Peter Lange[6]

That is not, of course, to say that in the New Testament the church has simply taken the place of Israel as the people of God, as if Israel had lost the priority given to her by God. This is perhaps the major problem Paul wrestles with in Romans. His conclusion is that Israel is and remains God's people, and has not been rejected by God.— H. Beitenhard [7]

[Paul's present mission as "apostle to the Gentiles"] does not negate Israel's historical mission to the world. . . . Israel's strategic position in salvation-history is not confined to the past, as if Israel is now absorbed by the church. Israel remains a distinct entity in the future of God's purpose. Thus . . . Paul simply refuses to equate the Gentile church with the true Israel.—J. Christian Beker [8]

The spectacular failures of Israel do not abrogate the promises of God to her. Even Israel's coming under judgment for her sin does not do away with the promise of grace. "If you, O LORD, kept a record of sins, O Lord, who could stand?" (Psalm 130:3). In Balaam's oracle he claims "He (the LORD) has not looked on Jacob's offenses or on the wrongs found in Israel" (Numbers 23:21, margin). How faithful and merciful is God in the face of human failure?

The prophetic indictments of the nation are to the mark. God did send His ancient people into captivity and bondage. He chastened and disciplined them in the forty years of wandering in the wilderness and in the Assyrian, Babylonian, and Persian exiles. He sent the Romans as an instrument of punishment. Indeed when the builders rejected the cornerstone, Jesus clearly said:

Therefore I tell you that the kingdom of God will be taken away from you and given to a people who will produce its fruit (Matthew 21:43).

Israel became a discarded branch. The natural branches were to be cut off (Romans 11) and replaced by the wild olive branches grafted in to "share in the nourishing sap from the olive root," (Romans 11:17). But Gentiles are not to boast or to be arrogant, "For if God did not spare the natural branches, He will not spare [them] either" (11:21). How the Lord has treated Israel is how He will treat us.

The Mission of Israel

God's glorious purpose has always been salvation for all nations (cf. Genesis 12:3). From the beginning "all peoples" have been within the purview of His gracious redemption, and Israel was called to be the prime instrument. God's sovereign wisdom worked for "the reconciliation of the world" even in Israel's rejection (Romans 11:15), just as He will work wonders through their acceptance (Romans 8:28), when the natural branches are grafted in again. But of course there is a condition set forth for their enjoyment of new life and their employment once again in His work—"if they do not persist in unbelief, they will be grafted in, for God is able to graft them in again" (11:23). How will this grafting take place? What then is the relationship between Israel and the church?

God's call to Israel was to be a nation apart in order that she might bear effective witness to the nations. While even her dispersion and tragic history among the nations will be a real plus in her ultimate testimony and witness, her restoration as a nation and her "resurrection" from among the nations (Ezekiel 37:1–14) will become the fulcrum for her worldwide effectiveness at the end of the age. With her captivity and only a remnant in the land, Israel was facing an extended period of time called by Jesus "the times of the Gentiles" (Luke 21:24), during which Jerusalem would be "trampled on by the Gentiles." This prolonged period is the scope of the dream of the great image that God gave to the Babylonian King Nebuchadnezzar in Daniel 2 (and repeated to Daniel himself in the vision of the four beasts in Daniel 7). Through this extended period of many centuries, Babylon, Medo-Persia, Greece, and Rome (in an earlier, continuing, and later form) will dominate world history until Jesus Christ comes back to reign (cf. the stone smiting the image in Daniel 2:44–45 and the coming of the Son of Man as described in Daniel 7:13–14).

The Mystery of the Church

We are living in "the times of the Gentiles." The salvation of Gentiles in great numbers was certainly anticipated through the Old Testament (as Paul himself argued in Romans 9:23 ff.; 15:9ff.), but the inclusion of both believing Jews and Gentiles in a new spiritual community was a mystery not disclosed in the Old Testament (see Romans 16:25–27; Ephesians 3:2–6). This spiritual community (the *ecclesia*, or "called-out ones," i.e. drawn out of all the nations) is one and the wall separating Jews and Gentiles was broken down (Ephesians 2:11ff.), as believing sinners are incorporated into the body of Christ (1 Corinthians 12:13; Galatians 3:28). Although initially the early church came out of the believing remnant in Israel (Joseph and Mary, John the Baptist, Simeon and Anna, the Twelve, and others), it was not always easy for these early Jewish-Christians to see that Christianity was not an adjunct of Judaism— new wine in the old wineskin or a new piece of cloth patching the old garment . For example, Peter's struggle with the inclusion of Gentiles and the deeper issue of the principle of grace, (cf. Acts 10; Galatians 2:11ff.).

The church then consists of all those who have believed on Christ from the Day of Pentecost. Of course there are similarities between God's ancient covenant people, Israel, and God's New Covenant people, the church, but there are also significant differences. Christ in the gospel of Matthew spoke of the church that is to be built (Matthew 16:18–19) and of discipline in the church (Matthew 18:17). The Lord Jesus had concern about other sheep which were not of Israel's fold. Yet He gave special attention to His kinsfolk after the flesh (as in Matthew 10:5–6; 15:24; 23:37ff. and Paul spoke of Him as "a servant of the Jews" in Romans 15:8). Special blessings yet await Israel as an identifiable entity in the eschatological climax to human history and on into eternity. The church will not in this age Christianize the world or bring everyone to faith in the gospel. But when "the full number of the Gentiles has come in" (Romans 11:25), then God will turn once again to Israel.

God's plan for Israel is not any reflection on the glory of the church of Christ but rather to recognize and rejoice in the extraordinary diversity within God's magnificent unity. To say that Israel is Israel and different from the church is not unlike declaring cherubim are cherubim and different from seraphim. Both cherubim and seraphim are ministering spirits, and Israel and the church both make up the believing humanity. The writer to the Hebrews seems to revel in the variety of the intelligences who comprise the joyful assembly. The book of Revelation has different spiritual groups.

Rather than representing regression in turning back to bless the Jews, God is manifesting His fidelity to His immutable oath (Hebrews 6:17–18).* The church age is an interval or intercalated period of time (not clearly seen in the prophetic telescoping of the Old Testament just as the difference between the two advents of Christ was not clearly seen). The church is never called Israel in the New Testament. Israel has an earthly, ethnic, and national character. The church has an heavenly, non-ethnic, and universal character. Salvation for all who are saved is based on the mediatorial work of Jesus the Messiah, before or after the Cross; now, in the Tribulation, or in the Millennium.

During this interadvent period, the "church which is [Christ's] Body" is "the fullness of him who fills everything in every way" (Ephesians 1:23). Many students of Scripture have felt that the interval is foreshadowed in the Feasts and Celebrations of ancient Israel.[9] The prophetic parables of Matthew 13 set forth the kingdom in its mystery during this age.†

The seven churches of Asia Minor (Revelation 2–3) were actual congregations in the first century with real problems and churches through the ages have experienced these problems; however, a case can be made for seeing in the seven churches of Revelation the essential outlines of the history of the church from apostolic days, through persecution and into imperial favor, on through the Middle Ages and past the Reforma-

◊ ◊ ◊

* "The oath that insures our eternal salvation is no more valid than the oath that insures the perpetuity of David's House, David's Kingdom and David's Throne."— Ford C. Ottman[10]

† I agree with Arthur Pink that Israel is the treasure hid in the field and the church is the pearl of great price.[11]

tion and the missionary church even to the church of the Last Days.[12] But then comes the consummation of the age—and the exit of the church.

THE EXPECTATION OF THE BRIDAL CHURCH

The hope that Jesus would soon come again . . . it was this hope which more than anything gave its color to primitive Christianity, its unworldliness, its moral intensity, its command of the future even in this life. That attitude of expectation is the bloom of Christian character. . . . the Christian who does not look upward wants one mark of perfection.— James Denney in Expositor's Bible

Those who believe in the reality of the resurrection of Jesus Christ must also look for His return.— Bishop Hans Lilje[13]

And if I go and prepare a place for you, I will come back and take you to be with me that you also may be with me where I am (John 14:3).

Whereas the Greeks and many of the ancients had a cyclical view of history with eternal recurrence (thus tending to look backwards and be quite pessimistic),[14] the Judeo-Christian or biblical philosophy of history is linear. For Christians history has a beginning in the creation *ex nihilo*, a decisive midpoint in the death, burial, and resurrection of Christ, and is moving on inexorably to the omega point, what the Bible calls "the consummation of the age" (Matthew 28:20).

The focus in three-fourths of the Scripture is upon Israel. Old Testament believers, coming before the Cross, were saved through the mediatorial work of Christ in forward-looking faith (John 8:56; Romans 3:25–26). Not appropriating what it means to be "in Christ" or the fullness of the Holy Spirit as those under the New Covenant, the last two Old Testament prophets "sensed that they themselves stood at the close of an era of special revelation (see Zechariah 13:2–5; Malachi 4:5)."[15] Indeed, "the division of the canon into two testaments . . . [signaled] a massive change."[16]

Israel and her testimony were to be laid aside but only temporarily.

God can always do more than He promises but never less than He promises.

God enlarges the field in which grace operates and objectifies His sovereign purpose[*] (cf. Ephesians 3:2; Colossians 1:25–27).

The Day of the Lord

The "times of the Gentiles" during which Israel is basically sub-merged under the aegis of the nations is moving full-tilt toward cata-clysmic judgment, what Sauer called "a multiplicity of ruins"[17] (Daniel 2:35) or what the prophets of the Old Testament spoke of as "the Day of the Lord." Immediate judgments and traumas (like the locust plague in Joel's time) were seen as foreshadowings of the ultimate day of the judgment of a holy God. The literal locusts were prophetic (Joel speaks of the Day of the Lord five times) and that in the end time both God's jealousy and His pity would be manifest (Joel 2:18)—jealousy in judg-ment on the nations and pity for His ancient covenant people , home-less and godless.[18] Amos spoke only twice of the Day of the Lord (Amos 5:18–22) but saw in connection with the eschatological upheavals the emergence of an Israelitish remnant (Amos 9:8–10) along with the reha-bilitation of David's house and throne.[19] This is consistently borne out by James's use of the Amos passage in the Jerusalem Council where he holds that after "taking from the Gentiles a people for himself," the Lord would "rebuild David's fallen tent" in order that many Gentiles might be saved (Acts 15:13–18).

The Day of the Lord is not a day of twenty-four hours but a complex of events beginning with "the coming of Christ as a thief in the night" through to the recreation of a new heaven and a new earth.[*] The primary events in this scenario are the Parousia (the Second Coming of Christ), the Tribulation period, and the Millennium.

Although derided as "the lunatic fringe in religious life" because of their belief in the Second Coming of Christ, Christians through the ages have confessed their confidence in keeping with both Testaments that Christ will appear in the flesh "a second time" (Hebrews 9:28). One verse in four in the New Testament speaks of the Second Advent. The angels at the ascension of our Lord unequivocally spoke of His return (Acts 1:11). The earliest of Paul's epistles, the Thessalonian letters, are filled with references to the return of Christ. This hope cannot be explained as an oblique reference to the coming of the Holy Spirit on the Day of Pentecost, the destruction of Jerusalem in A. D. 70 (the "blessed hope!"), or the coming of Christ for the believer in death. As surely as He came

◊ ◊ ◊

* (previous page) "In horizontal time God calls out two peoples successively, so that there is always one people of God at a given time, representing Him on earth."—Ramesh P. Richard[20]

* Using Zephaniah 1:14–18 as his platform passage, Dwight Pentecost has shown the importance of this designation of the final seismic events in space-time history (the phrases "that day," "the day," or "the great day" occurring seventy-five times in the Old Testament).[21]

to earth the first time so He will come back to earth a second time, but the Parousia will be in two stages.

The Rapture of the Church

Just as those "who were looking forward to the redemption of Jerusalem" (Luke 2:38) did not always clearly discern the interval between Christ's coming in humiliation and His coming in glory (inasmuch as sometimes the two events separated by several millennia are found in the same verse with no indication of the interval, cf. Isaiah 61:1–2), so it would seem not all perceive the seven-year interval between Christ's coming to take the church out of the world and His subsequent return with His saints and angels to set up His kingdom and reign for 1000 years. How the interval is perceived defines the differences between the pretribulation, midtribulation, and posttribulation views of the Rapture. The word *rapture* is not found as such in Scripture but is taken from the Latin *rapturo* or to be "caught up" as translated in 1 Thessalonians 4:13–18.

If Israel and the church are different spiritual entities, then it would logically follow that the church must exit the world scene before Israel can once again return to center-stage. No position on the relationship of the church to the Tribulation period is explicitly stated in Scripture. If it were, there would be no discussion. Any position on this highly controversial and finely nuanced issue is inferential, but that does not mean the issue is unimportant. The word *trinity* is not found in Scripture either, and Trinitarian theology is largely inferential; yet we take our stand on it.* Inferences are important and obviously can be true or false. The rapture of the church, a very important inference, is the next event on the prophetic agenda for the following reasons:

(1) The momentary or "any moment" rapture of the church would seem to be a fair inference from what Jesus taught His disciples (Luke 12:35–40 is typical).

In contrast to Christ's coming in power and glory to set up the Kingdom when "every eye shall see Him," now He comes as "like a thief." We are not to say, "My master is taking a long time in coming" (Luke 12:45). No intervening events are necessary although in hindsight we can see historic fulfillments, but these were not necessary before the Rapture. Jesus raised the possibility that John might be living when He returned (John 21:22), and Paul and the apostles clearly lived on the tiptoes of

◊ ◊ ◊

* There are significant practical implications of the stand we take on doctrinal matters. Covenantal theologians who see the church as fulfilling the promises made to Israel tend to infer infant baptism from the circumcision of infants in the Old Testament.

expectancy believing they would live to see Christ come back (1 Thessalonians 4:17). There is a vast difference between "could come in this generation" and "could come at any moment."[22]

In the words of Archbishop Trench, the Second Coming is "possible any day, impossible no day."

---

(2) When Jesus promises to come for His own, He says He will take them to where He is (John 14:1–3) and since He has spoken of the Father's house and the many abiding-places He is presently preparing for them, I infer He is taking the church back to heaven.

There they will experience the judgment seat of Christ and the Marriage Supper of the Lamb. Indeed an interval for these events is necessary. This is in sharp contrast to Christ's coming with His own to the Mount of Olives (Zechariah 14:3ff.).

(3)The Tribulation period has a definite Jewish cast.

It involves the outpouring of the wrath of the Lamb in such a way as to preclude the participation of the church.[23]

(4) In the book of Revelation, the church is promised absolute immunity to "the hour of future tribulation" (Revelation 3:10 ALFORD) and the "saints" as depicted are Jewish and Gentiles saved in the Tribulation.

Revelation 4–5 shows the direct results of the Rapture with the twenty-four elders representing those now in heaven (Old Testament saints and the church, cf. Revelation 21:12,14). The elders wear the crowns of the victors (*stephanos*) and sing (as is never alleged of angels). The church is not mentioned in the events of 4:1–19:5 because the church is raptured home to heaven. The twenty-four elders probably represent the people of God, Israel, and the church in heaven."[24]

(5) Careful exegesis of the Thessalonian correspondence supports the idea of a great apostasy and the removal of the restrainer before the dreadful wrath the Thessalonians feared.[25]

(6) The Olivet discourse, though overwhelmingly Jewish in texture hints at the Rapture.

So what gripped the early church and Christians down through history—"the blessed hope" (Titus 2:11–14)—should now be our fervent expectation. With the ending of the "times of the Gentiles," the church will make her exit.

THE TRANSLATION OF THE BRIDAL CHURCH

We cannot claim to know the end and goal of history. Therefore the question of meaning in history has become meaningless.—Rudolf Bultmann

Man is like a convoy lost in the darkness on an unknown rocky coast, with quarreling pirates in the chartroom and savages clambering up the sides of the ship to plunder and do evil as the whim may take them.— H. G. Wells

Has not the Lord Jesus in despite of Satan's malice, carried up our flesh into heaven? And shall He not return? We know He shall return, and that with expedition.—John Knox

Hasten, O my Savior, the time of Thy return. Send forth Thine angels and let that dreadful joyous trumpet sound. Thy desolate bride saith come. The whole creation saith come. Even so, come, Lord Jesus.— Richard Baxter

He who testifies to these things says, "Yes, I am coming soon." Amen. Come, Lord Jesus (Revelation 22:20).

In sharp contrast to the heaviness and hopeless of the ancient world, the early believers were amazingly hopeful and buoyant about the future. Those who were "without God and without hope" couldn't understand the vibrancy of the often maligned Christians. This was part of the appeal of the early church. As Alexander Maclaren put it:

"The primitive church thought a great deal more about the coming of Jesus Christ than about death; thought a great deal more about His coming than about heaven."

The full-orbed Christian life involves significant reference to past, present, and future, as the apostle stated it so lucidly:

You turned to God from idols to serve the living and true God, and to wait for his Son from heaven, whom he raised from the dead—Jesus, who rescues us from the coming wrath (1 Thessalonians 1:9–10).

Christians are the people of the future, the sons and daughters of the resurrection, those who have been given "new birth into a living hope through the resurrection of Jesus Christ from the dead" (1 Peter 1:3). "For in this hope we were saved," Paul observed as he sketched the deliverance God will bring to the whole creation (Romans 8:24). Contrast this hopefulness to the gloom of modern atheistic existentialism, of nihilistic deconstructionism, of vapid "new age" humanism. Christians are the people before the time, already participating in the "powers of the coming age" (Hebrews 6:5).

Christians are the premature ambassadors of the court of heaven. Seeking to avoid an arrogant triumphalism, believers in Christ cry "Maranatha" (The Lord is coming!) and are confident of ultimate victory (Matthew 16:18). We know that we are on the winning side because "Our Lord God Almighty reigns" (Revelation 19:6).

C. S. Lewis put it well:"We must always be ready for Him!"

William Barclay quoted from a play about the Irish potato famine in 1846 in which the starving were given makeshift work in building roads which had no purpose. One day young Michael came home and said with a kind of "poignant disillusionment": "They're makin' roads that lead to nowhere!" As Barclay says: "the doctrine of the Second Coming is the final guarantee that life is not a road that leads to nowhere."[26]

The return of Christ for His own is an immensely practical and powerful truth calculated to modify behavior.

Christ is coming before the Tribulation period to take His chosen bride to be with Him in glory (John 17:24)—like Enoch who was translated before the flood came. The morning star rises before "the sun of righteousness [rises] with healing in his wings" (Malachi 4:2).

The *locus classicus* of the Rapture is undoubtedly 1 Thessalonians 4:13–18. Here we have a description of the meeting in the air, not to come down to earth, but to go back to heaven.

The Certainty of Christ's Coming (4:13–14).

To the grieving and apprehensive Thessalonians, Paul affirmed Christ's return and their reunion with loved ones. This coming event could be based on their confident assurance that "Jesus died and rose again." With the interment of the mortal bodies, spirits of deceased believers go into the immediate presence of the Lord Jesus Christ (2 Corinthians 5:6–9; Philippians 1:21–24). These spirits "will God bring with Jesus" when He returns to receive the completed bride.

The Sequence of Christ's Coming (4:15–17a).

"According to the Lord's own word," Paul has assured us, there will be living believers on earth when Christ returns, but this does not put deceased believers at any disadvantage. "The Lord himself will come down from heaven."[27] No surrogate is employed. Like a magnet drawing iron filings to itself, the Lord Jesus will draw first the dead in Christ (they've got six feet farther to go) and then living believers, and in that moment, in the "twinkling of an eye," all believers will receive new bodies made like our Lord's resurrection body (cf. 1 Corinthians 15:51–53;

Philippians 3:20–21; 1 John 3:1–3). The phrase "caught up together with them in the clouds" is the source of the expression "rapture."

The Solace of Christ's Coming (4:17b–18).

This great truth is an immense comfort for Christians, a strong inducement for evangelism and mission, and a powerful incentive for godly living. Prophetic truth was never intended to gratify curiosity.

How many hairs are on the beard of the he-goat in Daniel or how many spots on the nose of the beast in Revelation are not matters of concern.

What does this wonderful hope entail for our own lives and the lives of others? This is the relentless focus and frame-of-reference for prophetic truth in Scripture.

No system of interpretation is without its difficulties, but the pretribulation rapture does justice to what the Bible teaches about Israel and the church. Any discussion with those who disagree should avoid emotional, personal attacks, and be done in a spirit of humility to maintain the unity of the church (Ephesians 4:1–6). My model in this has always been my teacher, Dr. Wilbur M. Smith, who, although he held strongly to the pretribulation rapture, could analyze and discuss opposing views with civility.[28]

Different Views of Christ's Coming

Views of Rapture Other Than Pretribulationism			
View	**Proponents**	**Concept**	**Analysis**
Partial Rapture	R. Govett G. H. Lang	"The elite of the elect" will be taken.	This view has the problem of the nature of the church itself and the principle of divine grace that constitutes the church.
Midtribulation Rapture	N. B. Harrison G. L. Archer	The church will be exempt from the outpouring of the wrath of God in the last 3 1/2 years of the Tribulation period.	In giving up immineency and making the rapture datable (essentially taking away any element of surprise), much seems to have been lost and little gained.[29]

Prewrath Rapture	M. Rosenthal	Christ comes for His church at the three-fourths point of the Tribulation.[30]	In a rather complex argument people lose sight of the glorious appearing of Christ.
Posttribulation Rapture	A. Reese G. E. Ladd	The church is true Israel and includes all the saints of the ages.[31]	Although there are many variations, posttribulationists have surrendered or radically redefined imminency.[32]

I recall asking a question of one of my teachers, Dr. George E. Ladd, a most gifted and forceful expositor of God's truth yet a man whose writings on eschatology have influenced many to move away from the pretribulational view. I asked, "Dr. Ladd, do you believe Jesus Christ could come back today?" He replied without hesitation: "No, that is not possible. Many things must occur before Christ comes back."

This denial of imminency as ordinarily and commonly understood and the problem of equating Israel and the church present some systems of eschatology with their greatest difficulties.[*]

The heavenly Bridegroom is coming for His bride.[33] Jesus said in light of this: "Therefore, keep watch, because you do not know the day or the hour" (Matthew 25:13). The church could be translated at any moment.

THE INCREASING DISINTEGRATION OF SOCIETY AND CULTURE

Four chief moments dominate the eschatological expectation of early Christian theology—the return of Christ, known as the Parousia, the resurrection, the judgment, and the catastrophic ending of the present world-order. In the primitive period they were held together in a naive, unreflective fashion, with little or no attempt to work out their implications or solve the problems they raise.—J. N.D. Kelly in Early Christian Doctrines[34]

◊ ◊ ◊

* Understandably liberals from within their presuppositions have an unmitigated hostility toward the Lord's return.[35] Several exceedingly brash assaults on the pretribulation return of Christ have been suitably answered.[36] The resurgence of old postmillennial theology in the form of the new Dominion theology or reconstructionism, of course, has no place for Israel (even though classical postmillennialists like Charles Hodge believed there would be a great people movement to Christ in Israel at the end of the age).

> He [Jesus] replied: "When evening comes, you say, 'It will be fair weather for the sky is red,' and in the morning, 'Today it will be stormy, for the sky is red and overcast.' You know how to interpret the appearance of the sky, but you cannot interpret the signs of the times. A wicked and adulterous generation looks for a miraculous sign, but none will be given it except the sign of Jonah" (Matthew 16:2–3).

> But you, brothers, are not in darkness so that this day should surprise you like a thief. You are all sons of the light and sons of the day. We do not belong to the night or to the darkness (1 Thessalonians 5:4–5).

Readiness for the Future

There will come for Israel a time "for God to restore everything, as he promised long ago through his holy prophets" (Acts 3:21). In contrast the bridal church is to be in constant readiness now for the return of her Bridegroom. The writers of the New Testament seem to have taken Jesus' admonition to watch with great seriousness. Paul said that "the time is short" (1 Corinthians 7:29) and that "the night is nearly over; the day is almost here" (Romans 13:12) and that "the Lord is near" (Philippians 4:5b). How could Paul be so mistaken?[*] He was not mistaken in that He was only reflecting the readiness Jesus urged upon His followers.[37]

The promise of the Messiah was given as early as Genesis 3:15. Believing souls expected the Messiah (Luther argued that Eve hoped her firstborn would be the "seed of the woman" who would retrieve their fallen estate, see Genesis 4:1). As we look back over "salvation-history," we see God working out many things until at last "the time had fully come and . . . [He] sent His Son" (Galatians 4:4).

If the Rapture is imminent it must be essentially a signless event, that is, no one can say that this or that must happen before Christ comes back for His church. To assert that the temple must be rebuilt or that there must be a worldwide revival before Christ comes back is erroneous. It is to assert that the "Lord delays His coming." But did not Christ state that Peter would die in old age, that an extended interval would be required for the fulfillment of the Great Commission (Matthew 25:14–30, 13:1–50; 28:18–20; Luke 19:11–27; and Acts 15:16–17) and that Jerusalem would be destroyed? All of these difficulties dissolve upon close inspection. In the atmosphere of martyrdom (as seen in the death of James in Acts 12) "the difficulties of communication would leave

◇ ◇ ◇

[*] The early church had not systematized its understanding of last things. This was to await a subsequent period of church history just as in the case of clarifying the critical Christological, trinitarian, and soteriological issues.— J. N. D. Kelly

most of the church with no knowledge on a given day whether Peter was alive or not."[38] Even by the writing of the Thessalonian correspondence, Paul indicated that the Thessalonian's faith in God had "become known everywhere" (1 Thessalonians 1:8). How the destruction of Jerusalem related to the Rapture was not a matter of finely calibrated disclosure.

Nonetheless, while there is a carnal pandering after miraculous signs that Jesus finds reprehensible (Matthew 16:2–4), Jesus does urge upon His own a thoughtful and diligent consideration of "the signs of the times." The signs are chiefly related to the Tribulation period, but our Lord spoke of "the beginning of birth pains" (Matthew 24:8) and those trends that would only accelerate as the age draws toward its consummation. Obedient believers who are waiting and watching would not be surprised if Christ returned.

One or several of the signs of the end have been present in any age. So Tertullian wrote early in his *De Spectaculiis* (*Concerning the Shows*) that the Roman gladiatorial shows should have no appeal to Christians because they are expecting the most brilliant and dazzling display of the Lord's power and glory at the Parousia. Lactantius in the fourth century expressed the same sense, and during the Middle Ages many were influenced by a piece entitled, "The Fifteen Signs Before Doom's Day." Luther believed Christ's coming was at hand; Cotton Mather preached that "the church is shortly to be gathered"; and John Fletcher believed "we are come to the last times."

While our whole age from Pentecost on is known as "the last days" (cf. Acts 2:17ff.; Hebrews 1:1–3; 1 Corinthians 10:11) or the time of fulfillment, it would be a mistake to think of all the signs as being fulfilled in the midst of history. The last things are never events lying in the distant future. There is an actual end of history coming, and as the close of history approaches there will be a confluence of signs that will quicken the hope of believers and solemnize their sense of the world task.

Apart from a spasm of intense interest in "the signs" during the Persian Gulf War, Christians today have a generally reduced level of interest in these things. With new age eschatology the rage and apocalyptic Marianism widespread, we must not miss what Scripture teaches. Garry Wills, from outside evangelical ranks, observed in his widely read *Under God* that "an understanding of Christian prophecy will be more needed, not less, in the next few years as 'signs of the time' are read by everyone under the impending deadline of a millennium." Precursory signs of Messiah's coming are cited in Orthodox Judaism in our time, as the "era of redemption" or the "messianic era." A prominent former chief rabbi speaks of now as the "days of the foot of the Messiah."[39]

Merrill Tenney showed "the increasing imminency of the Lord's coming as reflected in His utterances of correction" to the seven churches in Revelation (and hence increasing the probability of their forecasting the development of the historic church):

THE SEVEN CHURCHES AND THE LORD'S COMING	
Ephesus	"or else I come to thee and will move thy candlestick" (2:5)
Smyrna	(none)
Pergamum	"or else I come to thee quickly" (2:16)
Thyatira	"Hold fast till I come" (2:25)
Sardis	"I will come as a thief, and thou shalt know what hour I will come upon thee" (3:3)
Philadelphia	"I come quickly" (3:11)
Laodicea	"I stand at the door and knock" (3:20) [40]

Signs of the Future

And what are the signs?

(1) The physical signs

There will be earthquakes, famine, demographic explosion, celestial phenomena, and wars. These have always been present to some degree but there will be an intensification at the end of the age.[*]

(2) The intellectual signs

Daniel 12:4 would seem to indicate an opening of the prophetic word in "the time of the end."[†] There has been an increase in rapid travel and general knowledge. Some 90 percent of the scientists who have ever lived are alive today, and 75 percent of the medicine practiced today has been developed since 1950. "The days of Noah" (Luke 17:26–27; cf. Matthew 24:36–39) were (a) days of accelerated progress; (b) days of moral looseness; (c) days of aggravated violence; and (d) days of granite indifference. These days are to be duplicated.

◇ ◇ ◇

[*] "The signs preceding the first stage of the Second Advent are all of such a nature that they appear, more or less, in every generation" —George N. H. Peters. What we should expect to see is a greater magnitude of the signs as the age concludes.

[†] H. A. Ironside wondered if "the midnight cry" of Matthew 25:6 might not be the recrudescence of prophetic interest and study that began in the last century.

(3) The ethical signs

The end time will see the increasing moral decomposition of society and what Charles Colson aptly termed the descent "into the dark ages." Wickedness will abound (Matthew 24:12) and "evil men and imposters will go from bad to worse" (2 Timothy 3:13). The lights seem to be going out in our world and the "perilous times" of 2 Timothy 3 seem to be upon us. These indices of depravity have been manifest since the Fall— but "lovers of themselves," "lovers of money," and "lovers of pleasure" are to be seen in the narcissism, the materialism, and the hedonism of our times as never before.

(4) The ecclesiastical signs

Jesus asked, "When the Son of Man comes, will he find faith on the earth?" (Luke 18:8). There will be a Laodicean condition of lukewarmness, ignorance, and indifference prevailing in the church of the last days (Revelation 3:14–21), a growing disinterest in sound doctrine (2 Timothy 2:22 ff.), and a great increase in false teaching and deception (2 Peter 3:3ff). The North American church seems particularly hard bitten by a compromising spirit which would be "user-friendly" even at the price of emasculating the gospel, betraying the Word of God, and accommodating the spirit of the age.

(5) The Israel signs

Add to the previous signs what no other generation of Christians has ever seen—the return of Jews in great numbers to the land promised to their forebears and the establishment of the State of Israel (Luke 21:29–31). Notice Ezekiel 20:34:

> I will bring you from the nations and gather you from the countries where you have been scattered—with a mighty hand and an outstretched arm and with outpoured wrath.

That is a description of what we have seen in our own times (cf. Jeremiah 16:14–16).[41]

"Coming events cast their shadow before them," the old adage says. If the final wrap-up of history is signified in a constellation of signs,[*] then the church should be aroused to eager expectancy for the Lord's return, signs or no signs. But is this what we see?

The late A. W. Tozer wrote about what he called "The Decline of Apocalyptic Expectation" in the contemporary church:

◊ ◊ ◊

* Compare Matthew 24:33: "When you see all these things, you know that it is near, right at the door" and Luke 21:28: "When these things begin to take place, stand up and lift up your heads, because your redemption is drawing near."

A short generation ago, there was a feeling among gospel Christians that the end of the age was near, and many were breathless with anticipation of a new world order about to emerge. This new order was to be preceded by a silent return of Christ to earth, not to remain, but to raise the righteous dead to immortality and to glorify the living saints in the twinkling of an eye. These He would catch away to the marriage supper of the Lamb, while the earth meanwhile plunged into its baptism of fire and blood in the Great Tribulation. This would be relatively brief, ending dramatically with the battle of Armageddon and the triumphant return of Christ with His Bride to reign a thousand years.[42]

Used only for the declaration of war or the assassination of a president of the United States, the largest size of type in newspaper composing rooms before modern type technology was often called *Second Coming Type*. Even in a secular setting, the most stupendous, momentous event imaginable was the Second Coming of Jesus Christ! This is next on God's agenda on a day and at an hour unknown to any of us. But we need to be right with God and ready for Christ's imminent return.

CHAPTER

CONVULSIONS OF THE END TIME AND THE NEW WORLD ORDER

Nowhere in the New Testament do we find any expectation that in the course of the centuries mankind will become Christian, so that the opposition between the world and the Church will be overcome in historical time. But the contrary is true: the Christian community or Church will be a minority to the end, and therefore the battle between the dark powers and the power of Christ goes on until the day of judgment. If there is any truth in the apocalyptic pictures which we find in the New Testament, we have to say even more. The apocalyptic visions are unanimous in depicting the end of time, the last phase of human history before the coming of the day of Christ, as a time of uttermost tension between light and darkness, the Church and the world, Christ and the devil.

Emil Brunner in *The Scandal of Christianity*

Things fall apart; the centre cannot hold;
Mere anarchy is loosed upon the world,
The blood-trimmed tide is loosed.
Surely some revelation is at hand;
Surely the Second Coming is at hand.

William Butler Yeats in "The Second Coming"

For then there will be a great tribulation,
such as has not occurred since
the beginning of the world
until now, nor ever shall.

Matthew 24:21 NASB

But immediately after the tribulation of those days, the sun will be darkened, and the moon will not give its light, and the stars will fall from the sky, and the powers of the heavens will be shaken, and then the sign of the Son of Man will appear in the sky, and then all the tribes of the earth will mourn, and they will see the Son of Man coming on the clouds of the sky with power and great glory.

Matthew 24:29–30 NASB

THE APOCALYPTIC TIMES in which we live lend a kind of credibility to Karl Barth's familiar claim, "I read the Bible in one hand and the newspaper in the other." The overwhelmingly critical nature of the events in our world and the approach of the end of the second millennium after Christ (of which we shall hear more and more) have moved not only Christians but Jews and Muslims to think about the end of time. The "doom boom" as it is called is not so much the province of clergy (who by and large ignore eschatology leaving it to the cults and the kooks), but actually sociologists, philosophers, and other physicians of our culture are increasingly using the language of the end time.

Influenced by the Hegelian synthesis, the brilliant young thinker, Francis Fukuyama has rattled many a cage with his controversial article, "The End of History?"[1] Again *Time* magazine has used biblical vocabulary in speaking of "Stumbling Toward Armageddon?" in analyzing events in the Middle East.[2] Quoting Isaiah 13:6, "Wail for the day of the LORD is near; as destruction from the Almighty it will come!") John Elson in *Time* raises the question: "Apocalypse Now?"[3] All these articles and titles reveal humanity's fear of a world gone awry—a planet headed for destruction. They open the door for Christians to talk about how the world will really end, as the prophets of old did.

The prophets in Israel spoke repeatedly of a final outpouring of divine wrath and judgment known as "The Day of the Lord." The Lord Jesus picked up this imagery in the Olivet discourse. He spoke of unparalleled distress to come upon the earth at the end of the age, of which the destruction of Jerusalem in A. D. 70 was but a faint foreshadowing. This awesome time is described in the book of Revelation as the time when "the wrath of the Lamb" is poured out on the "inhabitants of the earth" and a series of dreadful cataclysms falls upon rebellious humankind to the point that "blood [flowing] out of the press, rising as high as the horses' bridles for a distance of [180 miles]" (Revelation 14:20). This succession of woes unfolded, through the 7 seals, the 7 trumpets, and the 7 bowls of "God's wrath on the earth," climaxes in the great eschatological conflict at the Battle of Armageddon (Revelation 16:16). This is "the day of vengeance" as set forth in the Old Testament (cf. Isaiah 63:4; Deuteronomy 32:41).

Surely Christians face tribulation as such in all ages (John 16:33; Acts 14:22), but the very nature of the end-time tribulation is different. The final opposition to Israel will culminate and the nations will be judged. Before the final convulsive spasm in "the times of the Gentiles" and the Tribulation begins, the church will be translated out of the world. John, the writer of Revelation, details the prominence of the Jews in these events and notes the benefits of their testimony for the Gentiles (Revelation 7:13–14). This will be "the time of Jacob's trouble" but the pattern of blessing-judgment-blessing will be literally and powerfully re-enacted on the stage of human history. We shall see the principle of 1 Thessalonians 5:9 ("For God did not appoint us to suffer wrath but to receive salvation through our Lord Jesus Christ") in full force in relation to Christ's church.

It will be as Thomas Chalmers used to say, "You may talk as you please, but the Scriptures make it clear that this dispensation is going to end with a smash."[4]

"It stands out clearly that the world is beyond doubt moving on to meet the most tragic of ends. The words of the prophet announcing grace and salvation have literally been fulfilled;[*] it is certain that all the rest will be fulfilled in the same manner."[5] The point is that Christ's return is to be visible and the events surrounding it are to be literal, historic actual happenings in time-space. The Parousia is not metahistorical any more than is Christ's bodily resurrection from the dead. Both are actual events.

The witness to Christ's First Advent by the prophets was strikingly literal in its fulfillment (Acts 10:43). Twenty-seven prophecies were fulfilled on the day Christ died. Over 300 prophecies about Jesus the Messiah have been fulfilled. It is not unreasonable, therefore, to predicate similar fulfillment respecting Christ's Second Advent and correlative events. This does not necessitate understanding that the ancient engines of war will be reinstated or that a "king" cannot represent a president or a prime minister. To allege that "the sea of glass" in Revelation is not the translucent product made by Owens-Illinois or Corning does not take away an iota of the reality of a glasslike substance shining and glimmering for all to see.

◊ ◊ ◊

* This horrifying literality is the bane of a liberal scholar like Paul Minear who protests that "this sort of literalness would destroy faith in the invisible."

THE TIME PARAMETERS

And we have the word of the prophets made more certain, and you will do well to pay attention to it, as to a light shining in a dark place, until the day dawns and the morning star rises in your hearts (2 Peter 1:19).

Light then, and not darkness, is the true character of all the inspired prophecies. But the description applies most fully to those which predict the past desolation and future glory of Israel. They reveal to us a counsel of God plainly fulfilling itself on the face of the earth. They show us a country marked off, a people sep-arated as visible witnesses, first of His just severity against sin, and then of His overflowing mercy and unchangeable goodness. With a variety of fullness of truth, which opens a boundless field for hope, meditation and prayer, there is in these predictions a simplicity which the meanest Christian can understand.
—Professor T. R. Birks of Cambridge[6]

The darkest place in human history is doubtless the great Tribulation period of which Jesus spoke these most ominous words: "If those days had not been cut short, no one would survive, but for the sake of the elect those days will be shortened" (Matthew 24:22). The "elect" here, as throughout the Olivet discourse (24:24, 31), refer not to the church, which has been translated to heaven, but to Jews and Gentiles saved during the Tribulation period.

"The times of the Gentiles" culminate in judgment as portrayed by the prophet Daniel's metallic colossus (Daniel 2). The structure of Gen-tile world power persists to the end of the age and ultimate ruination when struck by "the rock cut out of a mountain, but not by human hands—a rock that broke the iron, the bronze, the clay, the silver and the gold to pieces" (Daniel 2:45). The metals while decreasing in value, increase in sheer strength until we come to the mixed iron and clay in the feet and the ten toes. Corresponding to the great image are the four beasts of Daniel 7, out of the last of which creatures come ten horns (Daniel 7:7ff.). Among these ten horns arises a "little horn" of a partic-ularly devious sort who wages war against the saints (Jews who are saved during the Tribulation period) and indeed inflicts great duress upon them "until the Ancient of Days came and pronounced judgment in favor of the saints of the Most High, and the time came when they pos-sessed the kingdom." This time of suffering for "the saints," the Jewish "messianic woes," is the trauma preparatory to the establishment of the Messianic Kingdom. The "little horn" should be seen as the Antichrist.

Revived Roman Empire

To speak of "the revived Roman Empire" at the end of the age is some-what imprecise, since as Dwight Pentecost pointed out, "The fact that the ten horns rise 'out of' the fourth kingdom seems to suggest that the fourth is not viewed as having passed out of existence, to be resurrected again, but rather, to have continued in some form until the ten horn condition emerges."[7] The two legs may then be seen either as the split of the eastern and western empires in the fourth century or the division between the eastern and western churches in A. D. 1054, probably the latter. As Goldwin Smith observed in *The Heritage of Man*, "the rule of the Caesars ended; the power of the Bishops survived." That is to say, the Roman Catholic Church and the Holy Roman Empire persisted.

Samuel Johnson wrote: "all religion, almost all our laws, almost all our art, all that sets us above savages, has come to us from the shores of the Mediterranean."

Toynbee held that "the history of Europe is the effort to reunite the Roman Empire."

Such a reunification of the Roman Empire will be effectively accomplished as the age draws to a close. We have seen in our own time the fascinating evolution of the European Common Market, a movement toward an economic, cultural, social, and political union of countries, roughly the geographical area of the ancient Roman state. Progress toward a "European supernation" is not untroubled, but few question the potential of an economic force greater than either the United States or Japan. The parliament sitting now in Strasbourg symbolizes a prophetic fulfillment in embryonic development. Into Rome the ancient world was absorbed; out of Rome modern Europe has evolved.

Seventy Sevens

Daniel the prophet[*] was an intense student of unfulfilled prophecy as it related to his own people, the Jews (Daniel 9:1ff.). The close intertwining of prayer and prophecy is to be seen in this passage as it represents Daniel's understanding from 2 Chronicles 36:21, Jeremiah 25:11–12 , and 29:10 that the captivity and exile would extend to 70 years (606–536 B.C.). It is clear that the computation of the seventy years was carefully done—penal servitude was exacted in order that the land might have its Sabbath rest. As those 70 years ticked off, Daniel wondered how God would restore His people. His magnificent prayer is a model for God's people in all ages (Daniel 9:4–19). It is most significant that the seventy-year prophecy was fulfilled precisely. Should we not always expect the same of our great God?

◊ ◊ ◊

* We hold unabashedly to a sixth-century date and the genuinely prophetic nature of Daniel with the support of the Lord Jesus on this matter (cf. Matthew 24:15 et al.)

Then it is that the angel Gabriel comes with that most remarkable "backbone of biblical prophecy," the prophecy of the seventy sevens (Daniel 9:24–27). Although there has been much discussion and debate about when the prophecy commences and when it concludes, there is general agreement that it projects a period of 490 years (70 x 7 years).* As the text explicitly says, "Seventy 'sevens' are decreed for your people and your holy city" (Daniel 9:24). "What is to be accomplished in these seventy sevens of years related exclusively to the fortunes of Israel as a nation† and to their city and state."[8]

The following three ideas are essential in prophetic theology:

1) Israel in prophecy is not merely a type of the church;

2) Israel has yet a future; and

3) Before the Last Judgment there shall be a time of a glorious kingdom of God.[9]

Josephus, the first-century Jewish historian, makes a remarkable observation about Daniel:

> The several books that he [Daniel] wrote and left behind him, are still read by us till this time, and from them we believe that Daniel conversed with God, for he did not only prophesy of future events as did the other prophets, but he also determined the time of their accomplishment (*Antiquities of the Jews*, X, 11, 7).

Daniel learned that six objectives would be accomplished during the 490 years:

1) to finish transgression

2) to make an end of sins

3) to make reconciliation for iniquity

4) to bring in everlasting righteousness

5) to seal up vision and prophecy

6) to anoint the most holy ‡

◊ ◊ ◊

* "This prophecy is a prophecy for Daniel's people and Daniel's city."—Robert Culver[10]

† We must reject the notion advanced by Keil and Leupold that it is the church that is in view here.

‡ Even Keil, the amillennialist, sees the last of these as not fulfilled until the Second Coming, "to anoint a most holy place," i.e. the Temple at the time of the end, contra E. J. Young.[11]

If we start the reckoning with the decree to rebuild and restore the walls of Jerusalem (Nehemiah 2:5–8), the first seven sevens brings us to the completion of the second temple or the end of the Old Testament canon with Malachi.

The 483 years bring us to the life of Christ and most particularly to Palm Sunday and Messiah's public presentation.[12] No wonder Simeon and Anna and company were "waiting for the consolation of Israel" (Luke 2:25ff).[13] They read and understood this chronological prophecy!

But this leaves one week or seven years left unfulfilled. The church age is intercalated after the death and resurrection of Jesus Christ (indeed as can be shown from the Old Testament itself time does not count for Israel while they are in captivity).[14] As Daniel is informed, "After the sixty-two 'sevens,' (i.e., the 483 years en toto are finished), the Anointed One will be cut off and have nothing. The people of the ruler who will come (a reference to the Antichrist) will destroy the city and the sanctuary" (a reference clearly to the destruction of Jerusalem in A. D. 70). "The end will come like a flood: War will continue until the end, and desolations have been decreed" (9:26). What will transpire during the seven-year period of Tribulation is then detailed. Momentous events for Daniel's people and Daniel's city will take place as here prophesied. This is future for us today.

When the church is taken home, the Israel-clock will resume ticking. There will be only seven more years to be fulfilled until "the end."

The earliest extant commentary on Daniel[*] by Hippolytus (c. A.D. 170–325) separates the seventieth seven or seven-year period in the manner we have just concluded. In his *Treatise on Christ and the Anti-Christ* he stated:

> In the one week remaining, Elijah and Enoch will appear, in the midst, the abomination of desolation will be manifested, who is the Anti-Christ.[15]

The remaining seven year segment is of immense importance, inasmuch as 3 1/2 years (time, times and half a time) and 1,260 days are critical factors in prophetic chronology. And as Seiss well points out, "It is thus included in the very texture of this fore-showing of the angel that

◇ ◇ ◇

* In Hippolytus's discussion of the feet of mixed iron and clay in Daniel 2, he indicated that this diluted sovereignty "signifies the democracies [Greek-democratia; Vulgate-democratinae] which are to come."

the Jewish people will be largely regathered again from their present dispersion to their ancient land, with their temple rebuilt and their worship restored."[16]

THE DRAMATIS PERSONAE

The 70 sevens are an outline of the philosophy of universal history, and the almanac of the ages. They reveal to us an organic unity and theological end of history such as Herodotus and Thucydides never dreamed of, simply because they were unable to understand Israel's place in 'the times foreappointed' (Acts 17:26), and Israel's relation to the nations, a problem that baffled even the genius of a Hegel. . . . The 70 sevens cover the entire times of the Gentiles from the fall of Babylon in the past to the fall of the greater Babylon in the present. They begin with Cyrus. They end with Christ at His Second Coming. They are decreed upon the Jews and Jerusalem. They belong to Palestine alone, and involve in their outcome, the solution of what politicians call the 'Eastern question.' And, so the 69 sevens have been literally fulfilled upon the Jews and Jerusalem in their own land, so will the 70th seven be fulfilled upon the same people, in the same land, and according to the law of their own Sabbatic seven.— Nathaniel West in 1880[17]

The ruler of the great confederacy of the end time (the ten toes of the image of Daniel 2 and the 10 crowns on the fourth beast in Daniel 7) will "confirm a covenant with many for one 'seven'" (Daniel 9:27). I take this to mean that Israel back within her borders will join the whole world in submission to and adulation for the world ruler, "the beast" of Revelation 13, the Antichrist. A decisive rupture occurs at the half-way point of the seventieth seven when the Antichrist "puts an end to sacrifice and offering" and erects "an abomination that causes desolation, until the end that is decreed is poured out on him"(9:27b). In other words, the whole identity and destiny of restored Israel are established in the tensions and turmoil of the Tribulation period.

The Prime Mover

The book of Daniel makes clear that God is the Sovereign of historical process. "His kingdom is an eternal kingdom; his dominion endures from generation to generation" (Daniel 4:3b). To Nebuchadnezzar, "contented and prosperous" (4:4) and puffed up with the pride of power, God made it dramatically evident that the Babylonian king was not in control. At last Nebuchadnezzar was moved and humbled to praise the Most High and to declare:

All the people of the earth are regaded as nothing. He does as he pleases with the powers of heaven and the peoples of the earth. No one can hold back his hand or say to him: "What have you done?" (Daniel 4:35).

The prophet Zechariah likewise showed how God's patrols maintain surveillance over the whole earth (Zechariah 6:1–8). The book of Revelation depicts "the throne" of God a dozen times amid the ferment. God is the prime mover.

Satan

He is called "that ancient serpent . . . the devil, or Satan, who leads the whole world astray" (Revelation 12:9), a liar, a murderer from the beginning, deceiver, accuser of the brothers. He is the original sinner whose fall implicated one-third of the angels of heaven (Revelation 12:4) and brought humankind into his revolt against God (cf. Isaiah 14; Ezekiel 28; 1 Timothy 3:6). As an avid student of Scripture, he knew he is a goner, but such is the nature of evil that he is bent resolutely on thwarting God's redemptive purpose. Satan sought to destroy the Lord Jesus at every turn but was hurled back and decisively defeated at the Cross. He continues to fight and defy righteousness as "the prince of this world" (as Jesus called him three times) orchestrating his demon hoards to perpetrate his nefarious schemes . His doom is surely sealed (cf. John 12:31; 14:30; 16:11), but he is undeterred in his evil genius and exceedingly powerful.[18]

Luther once wrote that "*Diabolos est simia dei,*" or "the devil is God's ape." Satan is the great imitator who delights in presenting counterfeits of the real. Just as there is a Holy Trinity (Father, Son, and Holy Spirit), so there is an malign trinity (the dragon, the beast, and the false prophet). During the seven years Satan seeks to create a facsimile of the Millennium (1 Thessalonians 5:3). The pure bride of Christ, the church, is paralleled by the great whore or the false, apostate ecclesiastical monstrosity of the end time.

The Antichrist

This infernal being is Satan's masterpiece, his effort to deceptively reduplicate the person and work of Christ. Half-demon and half-human, performing "all kinds of counterfeit miracles, signs and wonders" (2 Thessalonians 2:9) and even performing a pseudo-resurrection (Revelation 13:3), this "man of sin" will climax the sin of humanity (2 Thessalonians 2:3 ff.). Jewish eschatology has an "anti-Messiah" figure who will be operative in the time of great distress for Israel (cf. Daniel 12:1).[19] Twenty different titles are used in Scripture to describe this being. He is the "little horn" of Daniel 7 who has a mouth that speaks boastfully and who subdues three kings (Daniel 7:24). Daniel described him:

> He will speak against the Most High and oppress his saints and try to change the set times and the laws. The saints will be handed over to him for a time, times and half a time [three-and-one-half years] (7:25).

The tyrannical Antiochus Epiphanes (168 B.C.), a prophetic picture of the Antichrist (cf. Daniel 8:9ff.; 11:21–35, which gives an extraordinary prevision of the suffering of the Jews under Antiochus; 1 Maccabees for a non-canonical description of this carnage), joins with Cain, Lamech, Nimrod, the seducer Balaam, Goliath, Herod, Nero, Mohammed, Napoleon, Hitler, and Stalin as embodying aspects of the character and career of the Antichrist.

In Daniel 11:36ff. we go beyond the typical picture of the Antichrist to the Antichrist himself, in the nightmarish personality who "will exalt and magnify himself above every god and will say unheard-of things against the God of gods" and who "will be successful until the time of wrath is completed" (Daniel 11:36).[20] He will seek worship. Jesus spoke of "false Christs and false prophets [who would] appear and perform great signs and miracles to deceive even the elect" (Matthew 24:24). Paul indicated that "the man of lawlessness" is not to be revealed until "the one who now holds it back . . . is taken out of the way" (2 Thessalonians 2:7).

The restrainer is the Holy Spirit indwelling the church in His dispensational fullness.[*] When the church is raptured, then the "man of lawlessness" is revealed, "whose coming" (Parousia) will be dramatic, daring, and diabolic (2:9). The Holy Spirit will continue to be in the world as before Pentecost and people will be saved, but not in the same manner as has been the case while He has been incarnated in the church.[†]

The Beast out of the Sea

This would seem to be both a system and a person (Revelation 13:1–9). Here is the serpent's seed with a vengeance, for the beast like the dragon has seven heads and ten horns. The drama in the Apocalypse pits the Beast against the Lamb. As Christ is set forth in four Gospels, so the Beast is set forth on the four horsemen of Revelation 6. The ten-kingdom confederacy gives "the beast their power to rule, until God's words are fulfilled" (Revelation 17:17). The self-deified Antichrist is worshiped (13:4, 8). This picture is largely prophetic.[21] This is the world ruler of the end time, the gravedigger of this age, who will spearhead Satan's "final effort to frustrate God's purpose by destroying God's people,"[22] by "mak-

◊ ◊ ◊

[*] George Ladd and F. F. Bruce felt the restrainer was government. While government may exert an inhibitory influence against evil, many times government espouses and fosters evil (as in the case of Roe vs. Wade in our country).

[†] "Only a supernatural person can truly frustrate the supernatural workings of Satan."[23] As Hiebert has pointed out, the identification of the restrainer with the Holy Spirit in the church and the removal of the church before the revelation of the "man of lawlessness" imply a pretribulation rapture.

ing war with the saints," and by turning upon "the woman who had given birth to the male child" (Revelation 12:13). This woman must be Israel who gave birth to Christ (Isaiah 9:6). Israel becomes the object of the hostility and venomous hatred of the Antichrist during the Tribulation period. In the way in which Judas Iscariot betrayed Jesus, the Antichrist will betray Israel.[24] This is the Antichrist who will come (1 John 2:18). He is one of the principal players in the revolt that will climax at the Battle of Armageddon.

The False Prophet

The second beast, the one out of the earth (Revelation 13:11–18), is the religious henchman of the beast out of the sea. He is a parody of Christ. The False Prophet and the Antichrist are not the same (cf. 19:20). What Menelaus was to Antiochus, the False Prophet will be to the Antichrist.[25] He has "two horns like a lamb, but he [speaks] like a dragon" (13:11). This is the agent of the unholy trinity who shapes the final apostasy into a gargantuan religious amalgam (the great whore of Revelation 17), which will reinforce the Beast's desperate challenge to God and His people. Counterfeiting the Holy Spirit's faithful testimony and witness to Christ, the False Prophet points unceasingly to the Beast, performs mighty wonders, and successfully imprints the mark of the Beast (666, the number of man, humanism with a vengeance) on the deceived "inhabitants of the earth" without which they can neither buy nor sell (13:16–18).[26]

This Christless, wordless, bloodless, and powerless religious sham will sweep the vulnerable "inhabitants of the earth" off their feet in the greatest hoax of all history. As Jesus described it:

> At that time many will turn away from the faith and will betray and hate each other, and many false prophets will appear and deceive many people. Because of the increase of wickedness, the love of most will grow cold, but he who stands firm to the end will be saved (Matthew 24:10–13).

But God is never without a testimony, and even in this dark time Israel will be His witness. Though sorely persecuted, martyred and hated "by all nations because of [Christ]," Israel will preach the gospel of the kingdom "in the whole world as a testimony to all nations, and then the end will come" (Matthew 24:9, 14).

THE PREPARATORY PROCESS

> There will arise THE MAN, strong in action, epigrammatic in manner, personally handsome, continually victorious. He will sweep aside parliaments, carry civilization to glory, reconstruct them into an empire and hold it together by circulating his profile and organizing further successes. He will codify everything, galvanize Christianity, organize learning into meek academies of little men and

prescribe a wonderful educational system, and the grateful nations will deify a lucky and aggressive egotism.—Harpers in 1902

The whole world was astonished and followed the beast (Revelation 13:3b).

The stage for the Beast and his religious cohort, the False Prophet, is the Tribulation period, "the hour of trial that is going to come upon the whole world" (Revelation 3:10) or the time of "messianic woes" as the Jews have spoken of them. In this time frame certain gigantic collectivisms will arise to form the driving wedge of Satan's massive effort to frustrate God's purpose. Problems on earth seem insurmountable; no human leadership seems competent to address the complexity of the issues. A demographic explosion with moral, social, economic, ecological, and political ramifications baffles the think tanks of the world. Humankind's vaunted self-sufficiency evaporates in the face of insoluble questions. The church, notwithstanding her frequent impotence and perennial failure, is now gone, and the salt and light she has afforded are missing. *Homo sapiens* are adrift, rudderless.

"Nature abhors a vacuum," the old adage has it. The Scriptures depict a brilliant, charismatic personality, a demagogue of the first order, striding dramatically onto the stage of human history. It is George Orwell's *1984* and Aldous Huxley's *Brave New World*. So desperate is the human race for solutions and answers that freedom easily becomes a casualty in the panic for security. As the late Paul-Henri Spaak, prominent Belgian diplomat and astute European strategist put it so baldly:

"We do not want another committee—we have too many already. What we want is a man of sufficient stature to hold the allegiance of all people and to lift us out of the economic morass into which we are sinking. Send us such a man be he god or devil, we will receive him!"

The mood of helplessness is by no means isolated. The distinguished European economist-banker, Paul M. Mazur, has stated that

> the large number of governmental bureaus that will have their orbits in the atmosphere of our planet cannot be allowed the freedom to compete and collide with one another. So, in order to control the diverse bureaucracies required, a politburo will develop, and over this group organization there is likely to arise the final and single arbiter—the master of the order, the total dictator.

The French-Russian philosopher, Alexandre Kojeve, has argued that a world state would be established, if necessary, by a tyrant who would end our struggle for domination.[27] Since the biblical scheme of the end time sees the Antichrist figuring so prominently in events relating to

Israel and the Jews, it is critical to demonstrate the feasibility and appropriateness of the picture presented in Holy Scripture. This is not some whacko, off-the-wall discussion inasmuch as these themes have been widely discussed and held in Christendom down through the centuries. For example, "Catholic theologians have been nearly unanimous in maintaining that the Antichrist is preserved for 'the last times,' his tyranny to extend to the Second Coming of Jesus Christ," who will "vanquish and obliterate him and set His Kingdom on earth." This statement is faithful to the Scriptural sources, and this devious personality is at the apex of movement against God and Israel.

The Coming World Government

Because of the global management capabilities of the Antichrist and the power of an United Europe, the nations of the earth will stampede toward a political collectivism.

In 1940 the late Wendell L. Wilkie wrote his famous *One World*, a cause of the United World Federalists and a hope of many for the United Nations. Many have dreamt of it, including Plato in his *Republic*, Thomas More in *Utopia*, and Immanuel Kant in 1790 in his work *Toward Universal Peace*, in which he advocated "a society of all nations, which would ostensibly embrace all the nations of the earth."

As Tennyson in "Locksley Hall" expressed it:

Till the war-drums throb no more
And the battle flags unfurled
In the parliament of man, the Federation of the World.[28]

Pope John XXIII in *Pacem Terris* (*Peace on Earth*) called for "a supernational world authority able to cope with the realities that today threaten the whole of mankind."

No effort could be more misguided than theories advanced to identify the Antichrist. Although he will be alive while the church is still on earth, his identity will not become clear until the church is translated. This crafty character will seize the imagination of a desperate world.

As someone has described him, he will have the savagery of Nero; the hypocrisy of Torquemada; the bloody frenzy of Robespierre; the insatiable appetite of Napoleon; and the insane wrath of Hitler.

With a strong arm he will bring into coalition the peoples of earth, and Satan's mock millennium will be in force. "While people are saying, 'Peace and safety,' destruction will come on them suddenly, as labor pains on a pregnant woman, and they will not escape" (1 Thessalonians 5:3).

Certainly the plausibility of such a collectivism becomes increasingly clear in our own time:

1) there is an increasing hue and cry for world government and a solution to the scourge of tribalism and hyper-nationalism;

2) the technological explosion makes one world very plausible in terms of data base and communication;

3) the evolutionary vision dominates in modern education[*] in which the "cultural elite" continue to argue that despite temporary setbacks, human progress is linear, automatic, and upward; and

4) the accelerating tendency is toward a world religion with the surrender of biblical supernaturalism in favor of a syncretistic pluralism.

Such a vast merger of competitive nationalism is indeed formidable.

Where will the United States find itself in all of this? The United States is not to be found in biblical prophecy as such, probably because weakened by the departure of the church and reeling under the deserved judgment of God for its self-indulgence, the nation will become a negligible quantity in the end-time equation.

The preliminary battle described in Ezekiel 38–39 when an invader from the north comes down into Israel but is roundly defeated becomes part of the Antichrist's road to coalescing power. The identity of the northern invader (a familiar theme in Old Testament prophecy) has been widely discussed—many have thought Russia but this rogue power could be Russia with militant Islam.[29] "The Kings from the East" (Revelation 9:14–16; 16:12) are the massive numbers who come out of the Orient and threaten to be a destabilizing factor, but ultimately are narcotized by the skill of "the ruler who will come" (Daniel 9:26). Feisty little Israel herself becomes a part of the world state.

The Coming World Religion

All politicians understand the adhesive qualities of religion. The Antichrist's religious advisor (who I believe will be a Jew) will grease the skids for Israel's early acceptance of the world ruler (John 5:43, "I have come in my Father's name, and you do not accept me; but if someone else

◊ ◊ ◊

* This is despite catastrophism's solid case against uniformitarianism and the disintegration of classical Darwinianism.[30]

comes in his own name, you will accept him.). Under the aegis of the False Prophet, religion will join the Antichrist. This superchurch is described in Revelation 17 as Babylon. She lords it over the nations of the earth, displays great pageantry, and sits upon the beast. This ecclesiastical and ecumenical bigtop will have brief usefulness and serviceability to the world ruler, but her doom is sealed because she is unfaithful and untrue to the Lord. Her spiritual adulteries are infamous.[31]

In the "newspeak" of *1984*, Orwell epitomized the sloganeering that controls thought: "War is peace; freedom is slavery; and ignorance is strength." The "doublethink" of the tyrant destroys the nonconformist, and what Thomas Hobbes visualized as the ultimate surrender to the great central directing authority—the Leviathan—is upon us. What Erich Fromm feared in *Escape From Freedom* is here. G. H. Lang used Daniel 3 and the experience of the three young Hebrews as a picture of the pressure for conformity to an apostate and idolatrous system, "You have issued a decree, O king, that everyone . . . must fall down and worship the image of gold" (Daniel 3:10). There is a commercial Babylon (Revelation 18) in collusion with religious Babylon. Lang characterized the attractiveness and appeal of this "religion":

1) it is external and visible;

2) it is magnificent;

3) it is seductive to the senses;

4) it is impressive;

5) it is united;

6) it is orderly; and

7) it is dignified—the Head of State is present.[32]

Professor Hocking from Harvard, in his *The Coming World Civilization*, predicted: "Thus there will eventually emerge one religion for this one world, in which tradition is fused together into an inseparable whole." Ralph Barton Perry spoke for many aspirants when he wrote: "We need a world religion. The essence of a world religion is its equal and undiscriminating appeal to all men. It joins the Christian doctrine of regeneration, the Buddhist doctrine of recurrent desire and its conquest through self-denial, and the more homely wisdom of Confucius."

Totally forsaking "the narrow way" and "Christ who is the way," this watered-down, lowest-possible-common-denominator religion will have a broad appeal. One ecumenical theologian has said, "Our superiority complex regarding Christianity must go if religion is not to further divide the world." Toynbee in his Gifford Lectures spoke from the vantage point of ecumenical inclusivism in saying: "Christianity is a fragment, animism a fragment—put them all together and you still only have a fragment of the truth."

In diametric contrast is biblical Christianity that says that the truth is not a circle that includes all error. But increasingly every viewpoint and life-style must be accommodated and included by the broad-minded and tolerant or else! Eschatological Babylon is upon us. Satan will be allowed to do his worst. And it is all moving toward the climactic eschatological battle with little Israel who will be at the eye of the storm. The end is at hand. The call is to depart from Satan's ecclesiastical Babylon, then and now.

THE PENULTIMATE PAROXYSM

There shall be at the last time, about the waning of the moon, a world-convulsing war deceitful in guilefulness. And there shall come from the ends of the earth a matricide fleeing and devising sharp-edged plans in his mind. He shall ruin all the earth, and gain all power, and surpass all men in the cunning of his mind. That for which he perished he shall seize at once. And he shall destroy many men and great tyrants, and shall burn all men as none other ever did.—Sybylline oracles, 5:361—368 (Second century A.D., H. H. Rowley)

The times are out of joint.—Hamlet, Shakespeare

We are looking now at the nightmare of human history, the harvest of human rebellion against God, the climacteric of our complicity in Satan's assault on righteousness. The book of Revelation is the book of outcomes, and chapters 6–19 describe the inevitable judgments of God upon all that is raised up against Him. This scenario goes far beyond any historic persecution. In this seven-year period, mercifully brief but very severe, the issues in the invisible spiritual world are focalized for the whole universe to behold.

The First Half of the Tribulation

The first three-and-a-half years of the Tribulation period (Daniel's seventieth seven) see the Antichrist and his entourage consolidate power. Upon his denouement, he goes away and comes back again (Revelation 13:3; 17:8). After some initial skirmishes and his successful rescue of Israel from the invader out of the north (Ezekiel 38:13ff.), the Antichrist is virtually unchallenged in his hegemony over earth. Here is vintage Machiavellianism. Social engineering proceeds to pinnacles never before imagined.

Fifty verses in Revelation describe Babylon. As suggested by many, Revelation 17 gives us ecclesiastical Babylon, the false religious system in cahoots with the world ruler; Revelation 18 gives us political and economic Babylon. While some[*] see ancient Babylon resurrected, passages such as Jeremiah 50–51 would seem to militate strongly against seeing any future for the literal Babylon in Mesopotamia.[33] John in Revelation is speaking about "mystery Babylon"—political and economic titan of Revelation with enormous strength and resources to back up the Antichrist. What Daniel said of Antiochus will be all the more accurate in speaking of the anti-type: "It prospered in everything it did, and truth was thrown to the ground" (Daniel 8:12b).

God is not without a witness even in this spiritually sterile environment, and Revelation 11 narrates the ministry of two witnesses. The Jewish texture of this chapter is very striking with its references to the temple, Jerusalem, and the two witnesses (perhaps Moses and Elijah)."The coming special activity of the Messiah [is] in Israel, an activity which shall have as its end their restoration for the fulfillment of age-long purpose."[34][†]

JEWISH STRANDS IN REVELATION	
Chapter 7	The sealing of the 144,000 Jews
Chapter 11	The two apparent witnesses, clearly Jews, will be sent to Israel to bring about her conversion.[35]
Chapter 12	The mother of the man-child who is hidden in the wilderness for three-and-a-half years
Chapter 21	The reference to the "twelve tribes of the children of Israel"

At the half-way point in the seven years the smoldering and latent anti-Semitism of the world ruler bursts into a flame of fury. In a frenetic rage "he will put an end to sacrifice and offering. And on a wing of the temple he will set up an abomination that causes desolation" (Daniel 9:27). Something happens among the Jews in Israel in response to the testimony of the two witnesses of Revelation 11. In the great hatred that Antiochus Epiphanes had for the Jews in the second century B.C., there

◊ ◊ ◊

[*] Certain editors of the Scofield Bible, some present students of prophecy, and Arnold Toynbee felt historical Babylon would become the world center.[36]

[†] "He who once was so active in the chosen nation, but who for so long has assumed a passive attitude, is once again, according to many Scriptures in both Testaments, to resume his dealings with it and fulfill His covenants of promise."—W. Graham Scroggie

is a fore-glimpse of the Antichrist's vicious aggression toward the Jews in the Tribulation period (Daniel 8).[*] The world ruler will then turn his evil genius to "the final solution," to do what Hitler and all the anti-Semites of history have been unsuccessful in doing. The little land of Israel and Jerusalem become the objects of universal scorn and hostility. But this is to be no rerun of the Holocaust.

The presupposition in all of this action in the end times is that great numbers of Jews have returned to *eretz* Israel and that a Jewish geopolitical entity had been established (as indeed our generation has seen with its own eyes). Zephaniah 2:1–3 picks up these elements:

> Gather together, gather together, O shameful nation, before the appointed time arrives and that day sweeps on like chaff, before the fierce anger of the LORD comes upon you, before the day of the LORD's wrath comes upon you. Seek the LORD, all you humble of the land, you who do what he commands. Seek righteousness, seek humility; perhaps you will be sheltered on the day of the LORD's anger.

Here we see a regathering of the people of God and a clarion call to repentance in a context of impending and imminent wrath and judgment.

The Second Half of the Tribulation

The drama of the last three-and-one-half years of the tribulation period is called "the time of Jacob's trouble." Compare Jeremiah 30:7:

> How awful that day will be! None will be like it. It will be a time of trouble for Jacob, but he will be saved out of it.

Daniel described the same time period in a passage we have already examined:

> There will be a time of distress such as has not happened from the beginning of nations until then. But at that time your people—everyone whose name is found written in the book—will be delivered (Daniel 12:1).

The Old Testament predicts one great siege of Jerusalem that has never taken place. Already Jerusalem has been besieged twenty-seven times, and it will happen once more, the twenty-eighth time. Just as little Finland so remarkably held the Russian bear at bay for such an unex-

◊ ◊ ◊

[*] Of this passage Luther himself observed: "These chapters of Daniel, as all expositors unanimously decree, refer to Antiochus and to the Antichrist of the last times, in which we are now living."[37] Jerome reported that the Jews of his day saw more than Antiochus in this prophecy, of which Jerome said: "This is also our understanding concerning the Antichrist whose shadow has thus been projected before."[38]

pectedly long time, so little Israel will fend off the world police force, the representative military arm of the Antichrist when he makes his final move against Israel. Joel described it:

> I will gather all nations and bring them down to the Valley of Jehosaphat. There I will enter into judgment against them concerning my inheritance, my people Israel, for they scattered my people among the nations and divided up my land (Joel 3:2).

The prophet Zechariah likewise spoke of the final siege:

> I am going to make Jerusalem a cup that sends all the surrounding peoples reeling. Judah will be besieged as well as Jerusalem. On that day, when all the nations of the earth are gathered against her, I will make Jerusalem an immovable rock for all the nations. All who try to move it will injure themselves (Zechariah 12:2–3; 14:2).

Zechariah, whose name means "God remembers," elaborated on the truth that Almighty God will always remember Israel. God has a great passion for His elect Israel (Zechariah 8:3), and although the false shepherd (the Anti-Messiah) does his utmost to dissolve the Jewish state, in this time of unparalleled trouble (Zechariah 11:15–17), Israel turns to the Lord. There is a great national cleansing, a transformation of the land, and the establishment of the Messianic Kingdom as predicted in the age-spanning prophecies of both Testaments.[39]

Christ's last great utterance before His passion, the Olivet discourse, can be better understood if we ponder the questions asked by the followers of Jesus. Having spoken of the destruction of the temple, Jesus received three questions from His own:

> "Tell us," they said, "when will this happen, and what will be the sign of your coming and of the end of the age?" (Matthew 24:3).

Jesus dealt sequentially with all three questions.[40] He described the fall of Jerusalem in A.D. 70 (at greatest length in Luke 19 and 21). But then beyond the intercalated interval of the present age, the Savior went on to describe the signs of the end of the age. Jesus spoke to the disciples as representative of the Jewish remnant of the Tribulation period (as was not uncommon; cf. Matthew 10:23; 23:39; other Gospels). The Jewish tone of Matthew 24 is not surprising for it is not simply an extrapolation of Jesus' own Jewish particularity, but the realistic expectation that Jews restored to their land and living in Jerusalem and its environs will face a fierce siege. He addressed those who will actually see "the abomination that causes desolation" standing in the holy place (Matthew 24:15; cf. Daniel 9:27).

Christ urged those who see these events as prophesied to seek refuge (Revelation 12:13ff.), for behind the insane wrath and rage of the world ruler is the age-long animosity against the Jews which lodges in Satan himself, who now cast out of the vestibule of heaven, vents his spleen against "the woman who gave birth to the male child," that is , Israel. Only the intervention of heaven averts the annihilation of Israel. The Lord Himself will go forth to war and do battle (Revelation 19:11–21). Christ will descend with His saints and angels and "His feet will stand on the Mount of Olives, east of Jerusalem" (Zechariah 14:4). A great day is coming for Israel as all the prophets foretold.

CHAPTER

THE REBUILDING OF THE TEMPLE—ISRAEL AND THE ANTICHRIST

The great event of Israel's return to God in Christ, and His to Israel, will be the signal and the means of a vast rise of spiritual life in the Universal Church, and of an unexampled ingathering of unregenerate souls from the world. When Israel . . . fell, the fall worked good for the world merely by driving, as it were, the apostolic preachers out from the Synagogue to which they so much longed to cling. The Jews did anything but aid the work. Yet even so they were made an occasion for world-wide good. When they are "received again," as this Scripture so definitely affirms that they shall be received, the case will be grandly different. . . . A national and ecclesiastical return of Israel to Christ will of course give occasion over the whole world for a vastly quickened attention to Christianity, and for an appeal for the world's faith in the facts and claims of Christianity, as bold and loud as that of Pentecost.

Bishop H. C. G. Moule on Romans 11

"Return, faithless people," declares the LORD,
"for I am your husband.
I will choose you—
one from a town
and two from a clan—
and bring you to Zion."

Jeremiah 3:14

Therefore say: "This is what the Sovereign LORD says:
'I will gather you from the nations
and bring you back from the countries
where you have been scattered, and
I will give you back the land
of Israel again.'"

Ezekiel 11:17

AFINAL SEVEN-YEAR PERIOD becomes decisive as Israel, regathered and restored back to her land in unbelief, moves front and center with the church removed. In a final gathering of the nations before Jerusalem (Zephaniah 3:8; Micah 4:12), Satan's pawn, the Antichrist, Nietzsche's Superman climactically actualized, seeks to exterminate the Jews but is foiled by Christ's coming in glory and great power with ten thousand thousands of His saints and angels. This is the time of suffering for Israel which the Talmud speaks of frequently as "the birth-pangs of Messiah" or "the messianic travail." Brutal ravaging gives way to the blessings of redemption.

The experience of the prophet Jonah pictures the experience of Israel. Called to bear testimony to Gentiles who are under divine judgment, Israel like Jonah was resistant and disobedient. Consequently overtaken by a storm of disaster, the nation is thrown into the sea of the nations. Storm after storm beats over the hapless prophet (Jonah 2:3) in the deep and he says: "I have been banished from your sight; yet I will look again toward your holy temple" (Jonah 2:4). Ultimately vomited up on the land, Jonah hears the call of God a second time (3:1), and great masses are turned to God in Nineveh through the preaching of the restored servant of God. The picture is that of "life from the dead" (Romans 11:15).

How are we to understand God's future dealings with Israel? Will there be a literal temple during the Tribulation and an actual abomination of desolation? In answering these and all biblical questions, David L. Cooper has put it well: "When the plain sense of Scripture makes common sense, one is to seek no other sense."[1]

The plain sense of Scripture as it relates to Israel's future can be seen in the Minor Prophet. The pattern of Pentateuchal curses and blessings underlies the book of Hosea. The blessings for Israel are essentially eschatological. "God's overall plan of blessing for his chosen nation still prevails."[2] God's love is both punitive and restorative, and there is a pattern of blessing-cursing-blessing. In Joel "the long-established covenantal centrality of Jerusalem" seems unassailable. "The guarantee of eventual vindication is a great sustenance to God's people to remain faithful and to continue to trust."[3] In Amos the covenantal perspective dominates, and very literal punishments are paralleled by promises of restoration (5:4–6, 14–15; 9:11–15). There is "a persistent belief in a Davidic empire in the prophets" and "the permanent reoccupation of the promised land."[4] How then is the ultimate fulfillment of the promises of restoration in the church? At the end of this commentary on Hosea the church inherits "the restoration promises of Hosea and the rest of the Old Testament"[5] and at the end of Amos the recipients of the blessing package becomes "the Christian remnant," i.e., "all faithful believers," and ultimately "the Church."[6]

Concerning Obadiah's prophecy of the messianic kingdom (v. 17), the late Frank E. Gaebelein, inveighed strenuously against "the tendency to spiritualize these predictions and identify the Messianic kingdom of the prophets with the Church of the New Testament" and quoted some very striking words from the poet Robert Louis Stevenson:[*]

> I cannot understand how you theologians and preachers can apply to the Church Scripture promises, which, in their plain meaning apply to God's chosen people, Israel, and to Palestine; and which consequently must be future. . . . The prophetic books are full of teachings which, if they are interpreted literally, would be inspiring, and a magnificent assurance of a great and glorious future; but which, as they are spiritualized, become farcical . . . as applied to the Church they are a comedy.

Why should the plain and natural sense of a text be jettisoned? In Luke 1:31–33 seven promises were given to Mary. Five of them have already been literally fulfilled. "By what rule of interpretation are we authorized to say that the remaining two will not be also fulfilled?"[7] Christ shall indeed receive the throne of His father David, and He shall rule over the house of Jacob forever, literally.

WHAT THE SCRIPTURES INTIMATE

The world is like an eye. The white of the eye is everywhere else. The iris is Israel. The pupil is Jerusalem. But, ah, the gleam in the center of the pupil, that is the Temple Mount—that is Mount Moriah.—Saying of the old rabbis

◇ ◇ ◇

[*] "From his belief in the prophetic books of the Old Testament, the teaching of Christ, and the apocalyptic portions of the New Testament, he [i.e. Stevenson] possessed the fullest, and clearest conception of the Second Coming of Christ, and the establishment of His Kingdom upon earth of all the men I knew."—missionary in *The Atlantic Monthly* [8]

May it be Thy will that the temple be speedily rebuilt in our days.—Daily prayer of Orthodox Jews

It is beautiful in its loftiness, the joy of the whole earth. Like the utmost heights of Zaphon is Mount Zion, the city of the Great King. God is in her citadels; he has shown himself to be her fortress (Psalm 48:2–3).

The LORD will roar from Zion and thunder from Jerusalem; the earth and the sky will tremble. But the LORD will be a refuge for his people, a stronghold for the people of Israel. Then you will know that I, the LORD your God, dwell in Zion, my holy hill. Jerusalem will be holy; never again will foreigners invade her . . . Judah will be inhabited forever and Jerusalem through all generations (Joel 3:16–17, 20).

Temples of the Past

Jerusalem! What sacred associations cluster about it for Jews, Christians, and Muslims. First mentioned Scripturally in connection with Melchizedek, "King of Salem," in Genesis 14 and finally captured by David from the Jebusites, Jerusalem became the site of the central sanctuary of Israel (as anticipated in Deuteronomy 12). From the gathering of all of Israel on the occasion of its dedication (1 Kings 8:1–5), the temple in Jerusalem was the citadel and seat of the worship of the Lord (cf. Amos 1:2; 1 Kings 12:27, 32).

The old rabbis said of Jerusalem: When God created beauty, He created ten parts of it and gave nine to Jerusalem; when He created knowledge He did the same; and the same when He created suffering.

Isaiah the prophet makes 223 references to Jerusalem in his masterful prophecy and uses seventeen different titles for the city. Zion, for instance, is used forty-eight times in Isaiah. Another is Ariel, an Akkadian word that means "mountain of God" (Isaiah 29:1–2,7).[9]

Yet Jerusalem, "the city of peace," or "the city of the God of peace," has been a city of war and siege and bloodshed without parallel during its 3000-year history.[*] Jerusalem has truly been "a burdensome stone" or "an immovable rock for all the nations" (Zechariah 12:3) and is to this day.

The Temple Mount was the location of two monumentally significant edifices in the history of Judaism. Every aspect of this history is fraught with significance and controversy. King David wanted to build the temple but was bypassed by God in favor of his son Solomon because David was a man of blood. The first temple was some twenty stories high and took 150,000 workmen years to build. Because the temple directly succeeded the tabernacle of Israel, we know the general layout, but we do not know the exact appearance of the temple (although Shick's model or Steven's reconstruction present plausible possibilities). This temple was destroyed by Nebuchadnezzar and the Babylonians in 586 B.C. and was succeeded by the Second Temple built by the returnees from captivity. Although the cornerstone was laid in 536 B.C., construction was delayed until 520 B.C. with completion and dedication in 516 B.C. (as described in Ezra, Nehemiah, and the prophets Haggai and Zechariah). Inferior in quality and appearance because of the deprivation of materials, this temple was enlarged and essentially rebuilt under the aegis of King Herod in the days of the Lord Jesus Christ. It too was destroyed (as we have seen) in A. D. 70 after a five-month siege with 1,000,000 Jews killed in action (cf. 55,000 Americans killed in Vietnam over an eight-year period). Interestingly both temples were destroyed on the ninth day of the Hebrew month Av, 656 years apart.

Thus for 2000 years the Jews have had a religion without a central sanctuary, a liturgy without a sacrifice, a remnant without a haven of return, and pilgrims with no place to go (cf. Hosea 3:4). Christians cherish every scrap of knowledge about the temples because of the biblical associations and the ministry of Christ in the court of the Second Temple, or Herod's Temple as the reconstructed edifice was commonly called.[10] Great interest attaches to the present Eastern Gate or Golden Gate on the Temple Mount, through which Jesus entered on Palm Sunday. Blocked up since the days of Suleiman the Magnificent, the Ottoman Turk, in the sixteenth century, this gate had special fascinations for both Jews and Christians who believed Messiah would use this gate when He appeared (cf. Ezekiel 43:1, 4; 44:1–3).[11] In the fourth century, the Roman Emperor Julian (called the Apostate, A. D. 361–363) "aspired to restore the ancient glory of the temple of Jerusalem," chiefly in order to contradict the words of Jesus and show Him to be a false prophet, but also to cater to the Jews, of whom Gibbon spoke:

"The desire of rebuilding the temple has in every age been the ruling passion of the children of Israel."

◊ ◊ ◊

* (previous page) Jerusalem has enthralled poets and songwriters, artists and craftsmen, religious zealots and students and scholars through all the years. William Blake's visionary poem "Jerusalem" or Selma Lagerlöf's novel *Jerusalem*, the story of some Swedish peasants who are caught up by the Zionist ideal and immigrate to Jerusalem, are but samples of a vast literature. Emanuel Swedenborg, the bizarre Swedish mystic of the eighteenth century, established a religious movement called to this day "The Church of the New Jerusalem." Swedenborg's published output is forty times the volume of the Old and New Testaments.

But a terrible earthquake interdicted the building process, and a letter from Ammianus Marcellinus who had been placed in charge related that "balls of fire came out of the ground and scorched and burnt the workmen, so that the work had to be abandoned."[12] But the longing for a temple has persisted.

Temples of the Future

A credible body of evidence in both Testaments would seem to support the expectation that there will be another temple built and functioning during the Tribulation period (and indeed still another future temple for the millennial reign of Christ). Daniel 9:24–27 can only find complete fulfillment in a future seven-year period of Jewish history. Reference is made in this passage to Daniel's city, Daniel's people, the Messiah, the Romans who destroyed Jerusalem and the sanctuary in A.D. 70, and the Antichrist or world ruler who stands in continuity with the Romans of the first century and who makes a covenant for seven years. This is the world ruler's seven-year plan to address the needs of humankind. The Jews go along with the whole world, but the inference is quite clear that they have a temple in which "sacrifice and offering" are taking place (Daniel 9:27). With ferocity the world ruler puts an end to these religious rites in the temple and brazenly erects a statue of himself in the holy precincts, thus further harassing the Jews. That this is something totally beyond anything that Antiochus Epiphanes did in 168 B.C. (as prophesied in Daniel 8 and 11) is clear from the fact that Jesus used this passage to speak of something yet future to His own time. What Antiochus did foreshadows what the Antichrist will do (cf. Daniel 11:31–32; 12:11). Notice there are three references to "the abomination" in Daniel.

Malachi 3:1ff. speaks of the First Advent of Messiah who heralded by the ministry of John the Baptist, the forerunner, will "suddenly come to His Temple." But both the First and Second Advents of Christ seem to blend together here and to be seen in parallel. Augustine himself wrote: "The first and second advents of Christ are here brought together." Indeed Elijah is to come before the Day of the Lord (and John the Baptist would have been seen as Elijah had the offer of the kingdom been received, cf. Matthew 11:14; 17:11–13). The Jews have understood this prophecy quite literally and preserve a chair for Elijah at the Passover. Many of the Fathers and others through history have understood Malachi 4:5 to be a prophecy of "the real, literal, personal Elijah" coming before the Second Advent. That Malachi 3:1ff. refers to a future temple does not seem to be an unreasonable inference.

The words of our Lord in the Olivet discourse assign the fulfillment of Daniel's prophecy to the placing of "the abomination that causes desolation" in "the holy place" during the sequence of events just prior to Christ's coming in glory (Matthew 24:15; Mark 13:14). The existence of a "holy place" necessitates a temple. This temple could be built before, during, or after the translation of the church (for which event it is not a sign). In its precincts a crowning act of impiety and idolatry will be perpetrated by the world ruler.

Further evidence is in 2 Thessalonians 2:4 where we read about "the man of lawlessness," "the man doomed to destruction," and how "he will oppose and will exalt himself over everything that is called God or is worshiped, so that he sets himself up in God's temple, proclaiming himself to be God." At the zenith of the Antichrist's career will come this shocking bid for worship, and the milieu is a temple in Jerusalem.

The final capstone of scriptural revelation concerns literal Jerusalem (Revelation 11:8) and a literal temple that can be measured (11:1–2), in relation to which the two witnesses conduct their ministry during the first half of the Tribulation period. The anger of the Antichrist is aroused when a body of faithful Jews refuses to be part of the idolatrous worship required. This rupture between the Jews and the Antichrist will inaugurate "the time of Jacob's trouble," the time of immense pressure, but a glorious epoch of effective witness as well. The question rises as to how these Scriptural intimations fit into the situation developing today with regard to Israel's restoration. It would appear to be hand in glove.

WHAT THE SITUATION IMPLIES

Hear us, O Shepherd of Israel . . . Restore us, O God; make your face shine upon us, that we may be saved (Psalm 80:1a, 3).

He has set his foundation on the holy mountain; the LORD loves the gates of Zion more than all the dwellings of Jacob. Glorious things are said of you, O city of God (Psalm 87:1–3a).

But he took note of their distress when he heard their cry; for their sake he remembered his covenant and out of his great love he relented. He caused them to be pitied by all who held them captive. Save us, O LORD our God, and gather us from the nations, that we may give thanks to your holy name and glory in your praise. Praise be to the LORD, the God of Israel, from everlasting to everlasting. Let all the people say, "Amen!" (Psalm 106:44–48).

If the LORD had not been on our side—let Israel say—if the LORD had not been on our side . . . they would have swallowed us alive; the flood would have engulfed us, the torrent would have swept over us, the raging waters would have swept us away (Psalm 124:1–2a, 4).

Understanding the prophetic plan of God is like putting together the pieces of a gigantic crossword puzzle or laying the tiles of an exquisite mosaic. God in His sovereign wisdom did not see fit to give us a precise picture in any one place in Scripture, but drawing on Scripture in its totality and making reasonable inference we find a satisfying whole. This seems to be true of the data regarding the Tribulation temple.

Regaining the Temple Mount

Much scholarly archaeological attention has centered on the ancient Temple Mount in recent years. After all, here is where Abraham prepared to offer his son Isaac; this is the site of the ancient Jewish temples; here is where the Lord Jesus taught; and here is the place from which the Muslims believe Mohammed ascended through the seven heavens into the presence of Allah. Here shortly after 1000 B.C. Solomon built the First Temple in a somewhat rounded shape to match the contour of the hilltop site purchased by King David. The Second Temple was very similar, but in enlarging it King Herod virtually doubled its size and embellished it, making it one of the architectural wonders of the ancient world. In fact, one of the great blocks used by Herod weighed 415 tons.[*]

The Muslims took Jerusalem in the seventh century, and apart from the brief period when the Christian Crusaders controlled the site, the Temple Mount has been under Muslim control until the present. The Dome of the Rock or the Mosque of Omar, dating from A. D. 691 and the adjacent Al Aksa Mosque, built later, constitute Islam's third holiest site. From the thirteenth to fifteenth centuries the Mameluke rulers embarked upon an extensive building program on the Temple Mount. The Jews were not allowed any access to the Temple Mount through the intervening centuries other than to the Western Wall or Wailing Wall, the principal ruin of the temple destroyed in A. D. 70 in which not one stone was left upon another (Luke 19:44). Jewish efforts to claim ownership even of the Wailing Wall were rebuffed, and attempts to constitute the site as a synagogue in 1929 resulted in serious Arab riots. An International Commission found that the Wall did indeed belong to the Muslims but that Jews had a right to pray there.

When the Arab Legion of Jordan occupied the old walled city in 1948 all Jews were banned from the Wailing Wall. For nineteen years no Jew could come to the Wailing Wall. Jordanian officials often required certificates of church membership in visa applications in order to exclude any Jewish person from the area. As self-proclaimed "protectors of the Holy Land," the Jordanians allowed the Old Jewish Quarter to molder and they systematically destroyed old Jewish cemeteries, making urinals for soldiers out of the headstones.

◊ ◊ ◊

[*] The megaliths at Stonehenge weigh forty tons and the blocks for the pyramids weigh fifteen tons.[13]

As R. M. Kneller remarked, "For a Jew, the uniqueness of Jerusalem is beyond understanding; it lies in the realm of the mysterious." In a special publication marking the twenty-fifth anniversary of the reunification of Jerusalem, Nahum Rabinovitch points out that poets have sung of the glory that was Athens and the grandeur that was Rome but that Jerusalem is the city of promise and the tangible model of hopefulness.[14]

As the ancient rabbis said, "If Jerusalem is built, know that the ingathering of the exiles of Israel is nigh."

With surging emotion the Jews on June 7, 1967, repossessed the temple area in the course of the Arab-Israeli Six-Day War. For the first time in 1,897 years the Jews possessed the area, and for the first time in over nineteen years they had access to their Wailing Wall.

More than half a million Jews walked to the Wailing Wall during the first week of its occupation, 200,000 coming on one day, the Shabuoth Holiday, or Pentecost on the Christian calendar. General Moshe Dayan ordered all the gates of the Old City opened (except the Eastern Gate) and walked to the Western Wall, proclaiming: "We have returned to our holiest of holy places, never to be parted from it again. We earnestly stretch our hands to our Arab brethren in peace, but we have returned to Jerusalem never to part from her again" (June 7, 1967). All Orthodox Jews are forbidden by their own scruples from any accessing of the Temple Mount beyond the Western Wall. Years ago when Baron Rothschild visited the site he insisted upon being carried in a chair lest he inadvertently walk on the location of the Holy of Holies. Dayan ordered all Israeli flags taken down from Islamic buildings on the Mount and entrusted control to a Muslim political/religious trust, the Waqf, "which does not permit members of other religions to pray on the Temple Mount."[15] Dayan gave the Waqf the key to all gates to the Temple Mount except the Mograbi Gate adjoining the Western Wall. While a small police outpost on the Mount symbolizes Jewish sovereignty, the Muslims are permitted to govern the site and are not required to adhere to Jerusalem Building Codes.*

Rebuilding the Temple

Predictably and most understandably the legal Israeli possession of the Temple Mount has aroused a fever pitch of excitement about the possibility of rebuilding the temple. Reflective of this interest was the

◊ ◊ ◊

* The very enlightened and generous Israeli treatment of the Temple Mount with great sensitivity to Muslim feelings and anxieties must be seen in stark contrast to Jordanian policies respecting the Jews up to 1967.

article in *Time* magazine within a month of the retaking of the site: "Should the Temple Be Rebuilt?"[16] "Rebuild the Temple" signs began to appear in Israel almost immediately. Messianic speculation reached a new peak among the Orthodox. Even in the face of the most wretchedly complex political and religious problems, many observant and some secular Jews are in accord with former Chief Ashkenazic Rabbi Shlomo Goren who sounded the shofar in June of 1967 and announced that "the days of the Messiah have begun." Maimonides himself taught that the generation that recovers the site must rebuild the temple. Rabbi Mendel Lewittes says, "The rebuilding of the Temple* will be the acme of the Redemption process." Rabbi Shabtai Rappoport rightly claims that

---

"the Temple is the very foundation of the Jewish people's existence in *eretz* Israel. It is the very backbone of our history."[17]

The Waqf deny that the Jews ever existed on the Mount and have pursued many efforts to obliterate evidence of a Jewish presence in antiquity.[18] And Jews have responded in kind. Several maniacal efforts have been made to torch the mosques on the Mount, one by an Australian follower of Herbert W. Armstrong.[19] In 1983 more than forty Jews were arrested for plotting to seize the Temple Mount, and in 1984 Israeli security foiled an assault on the Mount by the Lifta Band (apparently financed in part by money from American Christians).[20] In 1986 a prominent group of Israeli rabbis called for the building of a synagogue on the Temple Mount and for the building of a Third Temple "in the immediate future."[21]

Meanwhile extensive digging in the area of the Western Wall has disclosed that the whole Temple Mount sits above an intricate networking of tunnels and passages, some of which have been extensively investigated by the Israelis, much to the anger of the Muslims. What is called "the Rabbinical Tunnel" has been particularly fascinating and its excavation has led to the discovery of a buried gate almost 200 feet below street level. The name "Rabbinical Tunnel" has come because Israel's most venerated rabbis began worshiping at this gate, closest to the Temple Mount, upon its discovery.[22]

The positioning of this gate with respect to the Temple Mount has led some to believe that the location of the Ark of the Covenant in the temple was on the bedrock beneath what is commonly called The Dome of the Tablets, considerably to the side of the Dome of the Rock, and there-

◊ ◊ ◊

* A torrent of evangelical articles in *Eternity, Christianity Today,* etc. and books like McCall and Levitt's *Satan in the Sanctuary* proved how deeply sympathetic the true friends of Israel in fact are.

fore opening the possibility of rebuilding the temple without having to touch the Dome of the Rock.[23] In an interview, Rabbi Shlomo Goren indicated his opinion that the diggers should concentrate on the east side of the Temple Mount because "the debris from the destroyed Second Temple was pushed over the east side of the Temple mount." Goren added that no further excavation was currently being done in the area because of a Muslim cemetery that now covers the area.[24] In one underground cavern, a plaque has been placed on the wall which reads:

> With every stone revealed we come to know better how the western wall links the last days of ancient kingdom with the beginnings of our future. This wall which survived as a remnant of the holy Temple will be the first wall of the rebuilding of the next Temple, "the house of prayer for all peoples."—the inscription attributed to the "Ministry of Religious Affairs"[25]

"Time for a New Temple?" was the title of a in 1989 *Time* article reporting that two Talmudic schools near the Western Wall were teaching students "the elaborate details of Temple service."[26] Orthodox Jews are buying up Arab houses in the Old City. More recently the project known as "Treasures of the Temple" under the guidance of Rabbi Ysrael Ariel has a goal to recreate all the artifacts and music of the temple service. Thirty-eight out of 103 ritual implements needed for animal sacrifice have been made.[27]

Garments for the priesthood are ready, and identification of Cohens, Levis, and others who might claim legitimacy in a priestly line is being pursued. A publication from The Temple Institute, the sponsoring agency, states:

> The dream of rebuilding the Temple spans 50 generations of Jews, five continents and innumerable seas and oceans. The prayer for the rebuilding is recited in as many languages as are known to humanity . . . with the rebirth of a Jewish state by the nation Israel. . . . With God's help we will soon be able to rebuild the Temple on its holy mountain in Jerusalem, ushering in an era of peace and understanding, love and kindness, when "God will be king over all the earth."[28]

The *Ateret Cohanim* (The Priest's Crown) *Yeshiva* located near the Temple Mount is training priests for temple service. Careful study is being given to the practice of animal sacrifice. Torah scholar Menahem Burstin has extensively researched incense for offering, published a book on the bluish dye used on fabric derived from a sea-creature called the hilazon, and led the search for the red heifer needed for ritual purification before any temple service could begin. A Swedish herd of red cattle is being studied to ascertain suitability.[29] Burstin is searching with the Texan Vendyl Jones for the ash of the red heifer[*] used previously and for the lost Ark of the Covenant.[30]

An ultraconservative and very controversial movement in Israel called The Temple Mount Faithful achieved some considerable notoriety in October of 1990 when they announced and indeed went to the Temple Mount to lay the foundation for the Third Temple. This action fomented riots, and the police reacted very violently to thousands of frenzied Arab stone-throwers with the result that nineteen Arabs were killed and 150 wounded. In a revealing interview, Gershom Salomon, leader of the movement, indicated the group favored removal of the Muslim presence from the Temple Mount. The Temple Mount Faithful have a four-ton marble stone hewn without metal tools at Mitzpe Rimon near the Old City. Salomon sees the battle over the Temple Mount and Jerusalem as absolutely central, and that is the reason why his own name is number one on the hit-list by the leaders of the intifada.[31]

Now after the observance of the twenty-fifth anniversary of the reunification of Jerusalem and the celebration of the Covenant of Jerusalem, a pledge and prayer relating to the indivisibility of the Holy City, the Jews face hard issues. Yet moderate a person as Ruth Brin, Minneapolis Jewess, has asserted:

"Jews may expect a new Messiah . . . because of signs that appear with increasing frequency."[32]

WHAT THE SCENARIO INVOLVES

He has remembered his love and his faithfulness to the house of Israel; all the ends of the earth have seen the salvation of our God (Psalm 98:3).

You will arise and have compassion on Zion, for it is time to show favor to her; the appointed time has come. For the LORD will rebuild Zion and appear in His glory. So the name of the LORD will be declared in Zion and his praise in Jerusalem when the peoples and the kingdom assemble to worship the LORD (Psalm 102:13, 16, 21–22).

He provides food for those who fear him; he remembers His covenant forever. He provided redemption for his people; he ordained his covenant forever—holy and awesome is his name (Psalm 111:5, 9).

◊ ◊ ◊

* Numbers 19:1–22 stipulates that the heifer must be pure red.

Those who trust in the LORD are like Mount Zion, which cannot be shaken but endures forever. As the mountains surround Jerusalem, so the LORD surrounds his people both now and forevermore (Psalm 125:1–2).

Even if the fig tree is sprouting (Luke 21:29ff.) and our generation is seeing signs that precede the wrap-up of human history, any date-setting is altogether improper and impossible. The imminent return of Christ for His church is essentially a signless event. We are to look for Him every day! But signs of the approaching end time and of all of the pieces coming together alert us to greater readiness. One generation of believers will not see death but be taken. "What if it were today?"

Even the Lord Jesus when on earth revealed:

No one knows about that day or hour, not even the angels in heaven, nor the Son, but only the Father (Matthew 24:36).

How foolish and ill-advised are those human efforts to predict a date on the basis of examining the bells on the Pope's cap, or American currency, or measuring the passages in the pyramids of Egypt, or consulting astral formations. Seeking to find prophetic significance in the alignment of planets or the Jupiter Effect is irrelevant and futile. The tip-off is, of course, that any date-setting[*] denies imminence.

Jesus admonished:

So you also must be ready, because the Son of Man will come at an hour when you do not expect him (Matthew 24:44).

After the church is removed, the lawlessness of the ages will come into dynamic focus in a tyrannical political and religious monolith headed up by the Antichrist, George Orwell's "Big Brother" incarnate. This deification of man is the sum and substance of the humanism and narcissism that increasingly characterize modern society. The music of our time, "Everything's going my way," or "I've done it my way" or "I believe

◊ ◊ ◊

* The mistaken interpretation of Hal Lindsey and David L. Cooper which understood "generation" in Luke 21:32 as a prediction that Christ would return within the generation born at the time of the establishment of the Jewish state has brought obvious discredit to prophetic study as we have moved out of the 1980s into the 1990s. Christ has not come and the generation has passed. Edgar C. Whisenant's *88 Reasons Why the Rapture is in 1988* created quite a stir but is riddled with unproved premises and faulty chronologies. Nothing in Scripture indicates that Christ will return on the Feast of Trumpets.

in me—that is reality," reveals the attitude underlying the move to the world ruler. Billy Graham has aptly remarked that

---

"the trend of world events is the psychological preparation for the Antichrist."

Graham is right in stating that the rider on the white horse in Revelation 6 is not Christ but the Antichrist.[33] He has said :

> The hoofbeats of the white horse are at this moment being heard louder and louder up and down the streets of our troubled world.[34]

The first horseman leads a procession that brings disaster and judgment, but he comes as "an angel of light." In contrast will be Christ's return at the end of the Tribulation period to judge and set up His kingdom as represented by the rider on the white horse of Revelation 19 who has a sharp sword and whose vesture is dipped in blood.

The Antichrist, as one of the four horsemen, must be seen as one of the agents of demoniac destruction "who leads the whole world astray" (Revelation 12:9). The riders that follow bring slaughter and bloodshed, famine, pestilence, and disease, rather than the peace and prosperity that are promised. But his advent is with alluring words; he sells a bill of goods.

The hero of William Golding's *Lord of the Flies* says to the victims of war and struggle: "There isn't anyone to help you. Only me. And I'm the Beast."[35]

The world is waiting to be led by this brilliant strategist, financial wizard, superecumenist but false messiah. His number is 666, which is the number of man generically, not a man specifically. Anyone's name can add up to 666. First try Hebrew letters, then Greek, and then Latin. If it still doesn't come out right, just don't be too fussy about spelling.

The Temple Mount Plan

The Antichrist will dominate the world, but the irresolvable problem will continue to be the Middle East and Jerusalem. This is the "burdensome stone" that lacerates the nations. But the Antichrist has a peace plan. Might his solution resemble some projected sharing arrangement on the Temple Mount? Skillfully the world ruler pressures both sides to concessions and to the amazement of the whole world, his seven-year plan is a howling success! The unachievable is achieved! Or so it seems. And he is "given authority over every tribe, people, language and nation" (Revelation 13:7b). A worldwide coalition congeals around him:

Who is like the beast? Who can make war against him? (Revelation 13:4b).

The true character of this monstrous manipulator and Satan who devises him, will ultimately come out, and the locale for this crucial revelation will be no other than the Third Temple in the Tribulation period. The Jews have gone along with the new world order (as Prime Minister Begin, under pressure, went along with President Carter in entering into the Camp David Peace Accords with Sadat of Egypt). Israel historically rejected "the Good Shepherd" (Zechariah 11:1–14) and came into great grief. But the worthless shepherd to whom they turn (John 5:43), the Antichrist, as commended by his John the Baptist, the False Prophet, is a total disappointment.*

The Temple Mount Rebellion

As McCall and Levitt have portrayed the scenario:

> The Jews will have put up with the Antichrist until he gets around to the Temple. They will have been thankful for his handling of their political situation, and they will render him such allegiance as doesn't interfere with their normal worship of God.[36]

Remember that sacrifice and offering are going on in the temple. The only fly in the ointment is the noisy and irritating testimony of the two witnesses who "will prophesy for 1,260 days, clothed in sack cloth" (Revelation 11:3). Using the imagery of Zechariah 4 and the two olive tree (a picture of Israel's candlestick among the nations), John the Revelator showed how God will preserve these two witnesses alive even under great duress until their testimony is given (Revelation 11:7). Their prophecies call Israel to stiffen their resistance to the increasingly bold intrusions of the Antichrist.

Infuriated by the prophetic ministry of the two witnesses, Moses and Elijah perhaps, the Antichrist resents the idiosyncratic worship of the Jews and determines to have decisive confrontation. He breaks covenant with them and sets himself up as God to be worshiped in the temple (2 Thessalonians 2:4). He orders that this climactic idolatry be perpetuated by having a robot-like representation of himself ("the abomination which causes desolation") set up in the temple to perpetuate the worship of himself (Revelation 13:14–15). This the Jews refuse to do, bringing down upon themselves the wrath of the Antichrist. This horrendous break in world solidarity becomes focal, as the Antichrist is

◊ ◊ ◊

* Zechariah 11:15–17 prophesies of the personal Antichrist of the end time (following Baron, Dennett, Pusey, Feinberg, and Unger). This hireling shepherd only seeks to fleece and mutilate the flock.

determined to liquidate Israel. Imagine CNN Headline News presenting these spectacles to the whole world (cf. Revelation 11:9–10)!

But God will not stand idly by. He has made covenant promises to Israel and they will be fulfilled. God's righteous character is on the line.

"Israel is the clue to God's plan and the sign of God's faithfulness to His plan."[37]

The velocity of this devilish rebellion lead the Antichrist and his hoards straight to Armageddon and the end. Although former President Reagan was mocked for his references to Armageddon, the Scripture speaks of how demonic spirits will draw "the kings of the whole world, to gather them for battle on the great day of God Almighty . . . to the place that is called in Hebrew Armageddon" (Revelation 16:14, 16).[38] The Antichrist has great resources out of which to draw his representative force as he moves to battle.[39] The Oxford English Dictionary defines Armageddon as "the place of the last decisive battle of human history." Indeed what Napoleon called "the most natural battleground of the whole earth" will be where the forces of the Antichrist gather. But then as John has borne witness:

> I saw heaven standing open and there before me was a white horse, whose rider is called Faithful and True. With justice he judges and makes war. . . . His name is the Word of God. The armies of heaven were following him. . . . Out of his mouth comes a sharp sword with which to strike down the nations. "He will rule them with an iron scepter." Then I saw the beast and the kings of the earth and their armies gathered together to make war against the rider on the horse and his army. But the beast was captured, and with him the false prophet who had performed the miraculous signs on his behalf" (Revelation 19:11ff.).

This is the grand finale of which Enoch early prophesied:

> See the Lord is coming with thousands upon thousands of his holy ones (Jude 14).

This is what Jesus spoke of when He said:

> Immediately after the distress of those days . . . at that time the sign of the Son of Man will appear in the sky, and all the nations of the earth shall mourn. They will see the Son of Man coming on the clouds of the sky, with power and great glory. And he will send his angels with a loud trumpet call, and they will gather his elect from the four winds, from one end of the heavens to the other (Matthew 24:29a, 30–31).

The prophet Zechariah foretold this event:

Then the LORD will go out and fight against those nations, as he fights in the day of battle. On that day his feet will stand on the Mount of Olives, east of Jerusalem, and the Mount of Olives will be split in two from east to west . . . . the LORD will be king over the whole earth (14:3–4, 9a).

When the total annihilation of the Jews seems unavoidable, then the one whose name is King of Kings and Lord of Lords will intervene, will challenge the final effort to block the divine plan.

And He shall reign forever . . . and ever!

One additional, very essential factor has yet to be added to this picture—and it is the dimension of salvation which is always part of God's intention—and it is glorious!

CHAPTER

THE CONVERSION, AGONY, AND GLORY OF ISRAEL

Israel has a call to salvation, independent of the church, which remains to the end. This thesis was mentioned by "salvation historical" theology, which extends from the Reformation theologian Johannes Cocceius, by way of Pietism and the 19th century Lutheran school at Erlangen, down to the present day . . . this salvation-historical thesis is closely connected with millennarianism, the hope that Christ will rule for 1000 years in history before the end. . . . Israel will only be converted to the Lord through the direct and special intervention of Christ before the end. . . . Israel's conversion in the last days will be the external sign of the transition from messianic world mission to the messianic kingdom. It is not Pepuza or Munster, not Rome or Geneva that will be the place of Christ's second coming; it is Jerusalem.[1]

Jürgen Moltmann

Paul is completely convinced that Israel will be converted when the full number of Gentiles is won for Christ. He reverses the prophetic promise according to which the Gentiles come and worship when Zion is redeemed from earthly humiliation in the endtime. The mission of the apostle is a colossal detour to the salvation of Israel, whereby the first become the last.[2]

E. Kasemann

The church of Jesus Christ has not grown to its full stature, nor has the kingdom of God arrived at its full manifestation, until Israel has been brought back to its Messiah (when and how God alone knows), so that Israel and the world of the nations both learn to acknowledge the free grace of the one who has consigned all men to disobedience, that he may have mercy on them all.[3]

Dutch Reformed Church of 1949

THE GUINNESS BOOK OF RECORDS lists the Jews as the oldest minority in the world. The longevity of this people is no fluke or accident. God says they are a brier bush but they survive. Moses turned aside to see the burning bush in the wilderness and God spoke to him (Exodus 3:3ff.). The little nondescript shrub was ablaze but it was not consumed. "So Moses thought, 'I will go over and see this strange sight—why the bush does not burn up' "(Exodus 3:3). What is the significance of the burning bush? In calling Moses to his vocation, the Lord said:

> I have indeed seen the misery of my people in Egypt. I have heard them crying out . . . and I am concerned about their suffering (Exodus 3:7).

Though in the furnace of affliction, Israel was not consumed. God providentially preserved His people notwithstanding Pharaoh's dastardly determination to obliterate them (cf. Exodus 1:8–22).The God of Abraham, Isaac, and Jacob would keep his promises, and he assured Moses of that. (Exodus 3:5–6).

The restoration of Israel as a nation has great import in the fulfillment of the divine plan, but there is something further on the horizon. There is a spiritual renewal coming. "When we begin to hear, as even now we do hear occasionally, of a concern on the part of the Israeli government for the rebuilding of the Temple, the reestablishment of the priesthood, and the restoration of their ceremonial worship in Jerusalem—then I think we may indeed say, 'The coming of the Lord draweth nigh.'"[4] Many Bible students with diverse backgrounds have come to the identical conclusion with regard to Israel's future.[*]

◊ ◊ ◊

[*] The late Marshall McLuhan, the brilliant communications theorist from Canada and a staunch Roman Catholic, believed that the Parousia of Christ was to be the omega point of history and that Israel was the decisive sign of the end of human history.[5]

Does God keep His promises? Or does He fulfill His purposes in such a way as to make His words and His language meaningless and contradictory? The fidelity of God to His ancient people becomes the joyful basis for our undying confidence in His fidelity to us.

The book of Deuteronomy, a covenant-renewal document, strongly emphasizes the "chosenness" of Israel (14:1–2) and the obligations related thereto. Israel was to be a missionary nation to the pagan world. The land had been given "for all time" (4:40), but Israel's enjoyment of prosperity and plenty in the land and her employment in the Lord's service were contingent upon her obedience (27:1–28:68). The outcome was no surprise to God ("I know what they are disposed to do, even before I bring them into the land I promised them on oath" 31:21b).

Moses, looking down the corridor of time, saw a restoration[*] coming (beyond anything fulfilled in the sixth century B.C.):

> When you are in distress and all these things have happened to you, then in later days you will return to the LORD your God and obey him. For the LORD your God is a merciful God; he will not abandon or destroy you or forget the covenant with your forefathers, which he confirmed to them by oath (4:30–31).

The promise of the Lord to circumcise their hearts (30:6) has yet to be fulfilled but that therein is the character of God exonerated from any and all aspersion and we therefore praise Him and worship Him (32:4–5) as "a faithful God who does no wrong, upright and just is he."

WHAT?

No other phenomenon in history is quite so extraordinary as the unique event represented by the Restoration of Israel. At no other time in world history, so far as it is known, has a people been destroyed, and then come back after a lapse of time and reestablished itself. It is utterly out of the question to seek a parallel for the recurrence of Israel's restoration after 2500 years of former history.[6]— William Foxwell Albright of Johns Hopkins

And I will pour out on the house of David and the inhabitants of Jerusalem a spirit of grace and supplication. They will look on me, the one they have pierced, and they will mourn for him as one mourns for an only child, and grieve bitterly for him as one grieves for a firstborn son. On that day the weeping in Jerusalem will be great. . . . On that day a fountain will be opened to the house of David

◊ ◊ ◊

[*] J. Ridderbos correctly sees the promise of blessing contingent on Israel's conversion, but most inexplicably reads Israel literally for the curses but the church for the blessings.[7]

and the inhabitants of Jerusalem, to cleanse them from sin and impurity (Zechariah 12:10–11a; 13:1).

The miracle of Israel's national restoration is closely tied into the promise of the land. Israel is God's earthly people and the promises to her involve a physical, earthly, and temporal component. The church as the heavenly people of God who are "blessed in the heavenly realms in Christ Jesus with every spiritual blessings" (Ephesians 1:3) has promises that are spiritual and extraterrestrial. But the disjunction is not total, for the temporal and the spiritual can never be altogether disengaged. The church prays for daily bread (Matthew 6) and draws upon the promises of every provision from God (Philippians 4:19). Similarly, there is a spiritual contingency for Israel's ultimate realization of her earthly destiny in God's plan (cf. Deuteronomy 30:1–6). When Israel repents and obeys the Lord with all her heart, then the Lord will pour out His blessing.

But the prophets not only lay out the conditions for spiritual recovery, they predict that the nation will turn back to God in one of the most amazing spiritual revivals ever seen on planet earth. The purpose of our God is salvation, and that salvation will be extended to the Jewish people in one of the most extraordinary spiritual outpourings in history! As the prophet exclaimed:

Who has heard such a thing? Who has seen such things? Can a land be born in one day? Can a nation be brought forth all at once? As soon as Zion travailed, she also brought forth her sons (Isaiah 66:8 NASB).

The physical and national restoration of Israel is but the beginning of what God will do. This turning back to God is the commencement of a worldwide ministry of witness and testimony by the Jews in which all of God's original purpose for His ancient people will be fulfilled.

The principle of God's "second" is seen here with Israel, as with Jonah. The first experience is negative; the second is glorious.[8]

This massive people-movement to the Messiah at the end of human history is a reiterated theme in the prophets of the Old Testament. We hear its strains in the promise of a new covenant "with the house of Israel and with the house of Judah" (Jeremiah 31:31ff.). This new covenant is one of forgiveness, spiritual internalization and, it is implied, the priesthood of all believers. But the identity of Israel is not obliterated under the terms of the new covenant (Jeremiah 31:35–37), and indeed to fortify this impression, we have seen Jerusalem built today just as predicted by the prophet Jeremiah (Jeremiah 31:38–40).[9]

Ezekiel heralds the spiritual resuscitation that will take place in Israel in relation to the regathering from among the nations. God promises:

> I will sprinkle clean water on you, and you will be clean; I will cleanse you from all your impurities and from all your idols. I will give you a new heart and put a new spirit in you; I will remove from you your heart of stone and give you a heart of flesh. And I will put my Spirit in you and move you to follow my decrees and be careful to keep my laws" (Ezekiel 36:25–27).

This stirring chapter describes something that has never taken place to this date in Israel. And while the bones have come together in the land promised to Abraham, Isaac, and Jacob, we have yet to see regeneration on anything like this scale.

In other words, there is not yet "life from the dead" in which the corpses stand on their feet as a great army (Ezekiel 37:14). The program is further elaborated in the same chapter:

> I will take the Israelites out of the nations where they have gone. I will gather them back into their own land. . . .. I will save them from all their sinful backsliding, and I will cleanse them. They will be my people and I will be their God (Ezekiel 37:21, 23).

The reign of the Davidic King and shepherd is also promised and will be fulfilled.

The prophets abound with pregnant promises of return and rejoicing that cannot be stretched to mean the church. Passages like Isaiah 35:5–10 and Isaiah 51:9ff. are examples. Here we see the redeemed of the Lord returning with singing to Zion. T. B. Baines has incisively pointed out:

"When will the Church come to Zion? Or if Zion be spiritualized into heaven, how can the Church 'return' where it is has never been?"[10]

Verses 17 and 22–23 of Isaiah 51 aptly describe Israel and not the church. Hosea 1:9–10 speaks of something glorious for Israel as does Joel 3:16–17 and Micah 7:14 ff. What kind of hermeneutic is it that allows us to strip Israel of what manifestly belongs to her in the promises of God?

The prophet Zechariah was particularly occupied with the long-range future of Israel and early on affirmed the intention of the Lord:

> "Shout and be glad, O Daughter of Zion. For I am coming, and I will live among you," declares the LORD. . . . The Lord will inherit Judah as his portion in the holy land and will again choose Jerusalem (Zechariah 2:10 ff.).

Zechariah, whose name means "Whom God Remembers," stressed the covenant faithfulness of God. He depicted Joshua the high priest and Zerubbabel the prince, "the sons of oil," as two witnesses empowered to serve God. They embodied Israel. Before luminous witness can be borne, there must be cleansing. The promise of God is plain:

> I will remove the sin of this land in a single day (Zechariah 3:9).

Israel's candlestick shall yet shine![11] Out of the fire of worldwide suffering (3:2), God will raise up a testimony to the nations. Israel will fulfill her destiny as "a kingdom of priests and a holy nation" (Exodus 19:6), but in order to do so she must replace the filthy garments with "rich garments" and a clean turban and then be empowered. The consummation will come, when "the man whose name is the Branch," clearly the Messiah, "will branch out from his place and build the temple of the LORD" (Zechariah 6:12).

God's great passion for His ancient people resonates through the entire prophecy of Zechariah. It will indeed be marvelous in the eyes of all but God is committed:

> I will save my people from the countries of the east and the west. I will bring them back to live in Jerusalem; they will be my people, and I will be faithful and righteous to them as their God (8:7–8; see also 10:6–7).

In a time of unparalleled difficulty, there will be a mega moral and spiritual shift (12:10 ff.; 13:1). Israel has a climactic Yom Kippur as she turns to Messiah, and the crucified One will purify the land (13:2 ff.).

This is what the New Testament describes as "all Israel" being saved (Romans 11:26–32). This will be the day when the Jews say: "Blessed is he who comes in the name of the Lord" (Matthew 23:39). This is the promised time "for God to restore everything, as he promised long ago through his holy prophets" (Acts 3:21), but Israel must listen to Messiah first. There will be first the conversion of a vanguard of the Jews during the Tribulation period (Revelation 7:1–8). The winds of judgment are temporarily suspended in order that certain persons may be sealed (meaning salvation and protection, cf. Ezekiel 9:4; 2 Timothy 2:19). The 144,000 come "from all the tribes of Israel"[*] (Revelation 7:4). and are on Mt. Zion with the Lamb in vision of Revelation 14:1–5.[†]

◇ ◇ ◇

* When it says "children of Israel" it must mean "children of Israel" and that here is prima facie evidence that God is not through with the Jews.—J. A. Seiss [12]

† While recognizing that the most natural way to interpret them (the 144,000) is to see them as the Jewish people and to find in this symbolism "the salvation of Israel," and while admitting that God's promises to the Jews are not annulled and that the Jews are still "a holy people" (Romans 11:16), George Ladd chooses to identify the 144,000 as the church.[13] The natural and plain interpretation is waived because of the system's uneasiness with the implication. Ladd cites the listing of the tribes as problematic, but each biblical listing has its challenges (cf. Genesis 49, Deuteronomy 33, Revelation 7).

Following many earlier and more recent students of Revelation 7,[*] it would seem best to understand the 144,000 as a vanguard of Jewish converts saved in the Tribulation period. This is the beginning of a great people-movement among the Jews who will turn to the Messiah. Vast numbers will follow and through their witness "a great multitude" of palm-waving Gentiles will be converted (7:9–17). The New Testament only confirms what the Old Testament presents—a climactic spiritual awakening in the nation established again in "the glorious land."

WHEN?

"Come now, let us reason together," says the Lord. "Though your sins are like scarlet, they shall be as white as snow; though they are red as crimson, they shall be like wool" (Isaiah 1:18).

"The Redeemer will come to Zion, to those in Jacob who repent of their sins," declares the LORD (Isaiah 59:20; cf. Romans 11:25–26).

God will convert them like Saul when He throws them to the ground.—Count Zinzendorf

If we confess our sins, he is faithful and just and will forgive us our sins and purify us from all unrighteousness (1 John 1:9).

And the survivors were terrified and gave glory to the God of heaven (Revelation 11:13b).

That God has something spiritually special for Israel is quite generally conceded.[†] As someone has well put it,

---

"While Japheth is entitled to share the tent with Shem, he has no right to steal the tent and turn Shem out, robbed of his promises and his inheritance."[14]

But the issue is, at what point in the unfolding of the prophetic panorama does Israel turn to the Lord?

Many have argued that Israel turns to Messiah at the Second Coming of Christ in glory, quoting Revelation 1:7:

◊ ◊ ◊

[*] Such as Irenaeus, Bullinger, Grotius, Bossuet, Bengel, B.W. Newton, Tenney.
[†] Even Charles Hodge the postmillennialist and William Hendricksen the amillennialist admit that in Romans 11 Israel means the nation Israel.

> Look, he is coming with the clouds, and every eye will see him, even those who pierced him; and all the peoples of the earth will mourn because of him. So shall it be![15]

The connection with Zechariah 12:10 is apparent, but this linkage does not prove that this is the first time Israel looks to the crucified One. The passage is of course obviously far broader than Israel. If Israel is not converted until the very end of the Tribulation period, then there is no witness after the death of the two witnesses of Revelation 11 (during the last three-and-a-half years of the Tribulation) and then we are puzzled as to whose testimony leads to the conversion of the great palm-waving multitude of Revelation 7:9–17. The 144,000 will be Jewish evangelists pursuing a magnificent ministry during the "time of Jacob's trouble" and with a mighty outpouring of the Spirit.*

It would seem then that the turning of Israel to Messiah will come at the midpoint of the seven years of Tribulation. During the first half of that period the two witnesses, probably Moses and Elijah (Revelation 11:1–14) bear faithful witness in Jerusalem, the Holy City. Notice the identification of the two witnesses with the two olive trees of Zechariah 4. They represent that remnant in Israel that is according to grace (Romans 11:5).[16] The steady witness of these two charismatic figures is a thorn in the side of the world ruler and his cohorts, but an impression is being made on the Jews. Notice then, the conditions at the beginning of the seven years (with the church gone) are very similar to those before the first appearance of Israel's Messiah:

> Israel will be back in the land; the sacrificial system will be in force because of the rebuilt temple; the nation will be reconstituted as a homogeneous national entity with its leaders, who will be able to negotiate contracts with foreign powers, specifically the Roman Prince; and the Sabbath (and by implication all the religious calendar which was interrupted by the crucifixion of Christ and the scattering of Israel worldwide) will be in force again (cf. Matthew 24:16–21).[17]

Then the ministry of Elijah calling the nation to repentance takes place (Malachi 4:5–6) and this ministry is very fruitful. How can this be?

The two witnesses are martyred after their testimony has been zealously delivered (Revelation 11:7) and their bodies are exposed on a street in Jerusalem. The whole world views the corpses and gloats (11:8–10).

◊ ◊ ◊

* Joel 2:28–32 seems to point to cataclysmic celestial phenomena at this very time and an indication of salvation, "And everyone who calls on the name of the LORD will be saved."

Robert Govett wrote in 1864 about "every people, tribe, language and nation" gazing on these bodies: "The word *blepo*, that is to look upon, denotes not merely the nations seeing them but their directing their eyes to this great sight and gazing upon them. But how is it conceivable that men all over the earth should be rejoicing in the news when only three and a half days intervene between their death and resurrection? . . . Is it not perfectly conceivable if the electric telegraph shall then have extended itself at the rate it has of late years?"[18]

Think how plausible the literal fulfillment of this prophecy has become with television and telestar communications satellites.

Spectators then behold the resurrection and the ascension of the two witnesses (11:11–12). Immediately these awesome events are followed by a severe earthquake with great damage and many fatalities. The impact on the Jews is significant. I mark the words, "And the survivors were terrified and gave glory to the God of heaven" (11:13b) as description of a turning from enmity to worship. Some have wanted to understand this as a reflex of fear, but the phenomenon goes beyond that.[*]

The saints in glory rejoice (11:16–18), and a frequently overlooked reference to the ark of the covenant in heaven is made (11:19).

> The ark contains the covenant made with Israel. This is now remembered and connected with it are the manifestations of coming wrath for those who oppress His people. God is now taking up the interests of His earthly people and as of old the ark is the token of His presence with them and the coming victory.[19]

Revelation 11 describes how the 144,000 are converted, and with their conversion a great multitude of Gentiles comes to Christ during the Tribulation. The Tribulation period is a time of salvation, as every period must be, because of our great God's gracious and loving plan of salvation. He wants people to be saved! (cf. 1 Timothy 2:3–7; 2 Peter 3:8–9).

The Jews have long awaited the Messiah. Out of the rich tapestry of messianic prophecy, the Jews in the first century fixated on political rulers rather than suffering servants . Indeed, as the apostle Paul wrote:

> For to this day the same veil remains when the old covenant is read. It has not been removed, because only in Christ is it taken away. Even to this day when Moses is read, a veil covers their hearts. But whenever anyone turns to the Lord, the veil is taken away (2 Corinthians 3:14b–16).

◊ ◊ ◊

[*] Here I follow Fausset, Alford, Dusterdiek, and Weidner.

There is a remnant in Israel who see Jesus as Messiah; there are others who are in a quandary.*

Dr. Arnold T. Olson, long-time president of the Evangelical Free Church of America and a great lover of Israel, reported talking about the coming of the Messiah to a leading religious figure in Israel who said: "When Messiah comes, I will ask Him—is this your first coming or your second coming?"[20]

Orthodox Jews await Messiah's coming and daily recite their creed,† saying: "I believe with complete faith in the coming of the Messiah; and even though he tarry, I will wait for him every coming day."[21] Yet many do not believe in a coming Messiah.‡ Hence, this great turning of Jews to Christ in the Tribulation period, beginning with the 144,000 and continuing with many more ("all Israel"), is going to be, as all conversions are, a glorious miracle of God's grace!

Paul wrote:

Christ Jesus came into the world to save sinners—of whom I am the worst. But for that very reason I was shown mercy so that in me, the worst of sinners, Christ Jesus might display his unlimited patience as an example for those who would believe on him and receive eternal life" (1 Timothy 1:15b–16).

Paul's conversion is a pattern for all (in terms of theology) but for Israel especially (in terms of its pattern):

The conversion of Saul my be suggestive of much that will take place after the rapture of the saints when the Lord Jesus comes for His own who are in the world. The blindness and hatred which Saul held for the church of God, which was evidenced by his persecution of it, came to an end after the Lord had returned to heaven. The blindness of Israel's eyes will be terminated after the Lord has completed the work of calling out a people for His name from all nations and has come for them and returned to heaven. The conversion of Saul resulted in his going forth as a flaming evangelist with the gospel . . . such will be the position taken by the apostles of the gospel of the seventieth week of Daniel."[22]

◇ ◇ ◇

* How difficult a decision about the Messiah can be is evident in the epistle to the Hebrews where the author wrote to Hebrew Christians under relentless attack and argued for the incomparable uniqueness of Jesus Christ .

† Traced back to the medieval philosopher and rabbi, Maimonides.

‡ While such a distinguished Jewish thinker as Joseph Klausner stated his view that Israel's legacy to the world consisted of monotheism, a refined ethic, the prophets of truth and righteousness, and belief in the Messiah,[23] he himself did not believe in a personal Messiah.[24]

Conversion to Christ is always a miracle.[25] Paul's argument in Romans is that Jews as well as Gentiles are guilty before God and need what Christ's sacrificial death can alone provide (Romans 3:9–20). This salvation is received by faith alone just as Abraham and David experienced (Romans 4:1–25). Converted Gentiles in the Old Testament were most frequently added to Israel as proselytes. Converted Jews in this age are made one with Gentiles in the church (Ephesians 2:11–22). The outwardly near (Jews) and the outwardly far (Gentiles) are both brought near "through the blood of Christ" (Ephesians 2:12–13). Those who come to Christ in the Tribulation will face unspeakable pressure and persecution, but with the church gone, there is no evidence of a differentiation between Jew and Gentile.

WHY?

The fourth beast is a fourth kingdom that will appear on earth. It will be different from all other kingdoms and will devour the whole earth, trampling it down and crushing it (Daniel 7:23).

When the dragon saw that he had been hurled to the earth, he pursued the woman who had given birth to the male child. The woman was given the two wings of a great eagle, so that she might fly to the place prepared for her in the desert, where she would be taken care of for a time, times and half a time out of the serpent's reach. . . . Then the dragon was enraged at the woman and went off to make war against the rest of her offspring—those who obey God's commandments and hold to the testimony of Jesus (Revelation 12:13–14, 17).

Back of hatred of the Jews is Satan himself. If anything proves the existence of a personal devil, anti-Semitism does. Satan knows that Israel gave us the Book he most despises, the Book that foretells his undoing. Satan knows that a Jewish womb gave body to our Lord and Savior when He came into this world. Satan well knows that the precious blood that flowed for the sinner's cleansing came from the wounds and the open side of a Jew (John 4:22). Satan knows that the scepter has not departed from Judah and that it is the Lion of the tribe of Judah who will yet rule over all the earth.—Dr. Harry A. MacArthur

The conversion of the Jews begins significantly at the midpoint of the Tribulation period.* This will be a disruptive development for the world

◊ ◊ ◊

* George Ladd sees the two witnesses of Revelation 11 as two "eschatological personages who will be sent to Israel to bring about her conversion." Ladd argues that "the conversion of Israel is to be accomplished by a miracle of resurrection." This and the ascension of Revelation 11:12 are seen by Ladd as "describing the final conversion of the Jewish people as a whole."[26]

ruler and the immense final syncretism he has catalyzed with the help of his religious cohort. Related to and conflicting in time with the Jewish refusal to worship the image of the beast, the conversion of the Jews marks the beginning of a violent move against the Jews and those Gentiles who come to Christ through their testimony (Revelation 12:17).

A player of immense importance now comes on the scene. John saw "a great and wondrous sign . . . in heaven . . . a woman . . . about to give birth" (Revelation 12:1–2). The woman is not the Virgin Mary or the church or Mary Baker Glover Patterson Eddy (as Christian Science holds) but Israel and the male child is Messiah, Jesus Christ (cf. Isaiah 9:6–7; Micah 5:2; Romans 9:5). Her antagonist is Satan whose primal revolt implicated one-third of the angels of heaven (who are the demonic hoards spoken of in Scripture and functioning in our world today). God has preserved Israel (Isaiah 54:6–7), and He will do so again in the climactic hour of her greatest peril.

In analyzing time-space events, we see only the external, but the Bible shows us that there is intense spiritual warfare taking place in the unseen spiritual realm of reality (Daniel 10:1–21).

Because Michael the archangel ejects Satan from access to heaven, satanic persecution of the Jews intensifies (Revelation 12:7–10). Michael is called Israel's "prince" in Daniel 10:21 and 12:1 and has had a special ministry in relation to Israel. The only two angels named in Scripture are Gabriel, the messenger of God, and Michael, "the great prince of Israel."[27] The immediate result of Satan's expulsion from any access to the vestibule of heaven is his frenetic rage against the woman, Israel.

Indeed the dirge is sounded:

Woe to the earth and the sea, because the devil has gone down to you! He is filled with fury, because he knows that his time is short (Revelation 12:12b).

Note that the heavens are to rejoice "and you who dwell in them!" (12:12a). The latter is probably a reference primarily to the bridal church that has now appeared before the judgment seat of Christ (1 Corinthians 3:11–15; 2 Corinthians 5:10), and notwithstanding Satan's accusations against the saints, the precious blood of Christ is proven efficacious (Romans 8:1) and Satan is expelled. He is outraged and goes after "the woman." Not only the Antichrist turns against Israel but also Satan, whose smoldering anger now bursts into an inferno of hatred. Satan becomes apoplectic. He sees his defeat in Christ's cross demonstrated in the salvation of the believers in heaven; and when he is hurled down by Michael and his angels (Revelation 12:9), he can only vent his spleen against the believers on earth—the Jews, especially the 144,000. He also, as an astute student of Scripture, realizes he has three-and-a-half years, i.e., forty-two months or 1,260 days and then he is finished.

During this time the woman is protected (Revelation 12:6). Believing Jews are given sanctuary and refuge just as were Christians in A.D. 70 at Pella. This is not to say there are not heavy casualties in the population as a whole (Zechariah 13:8–9), but of the believing remnant it must be said, Satan's nefarious opposition is frustrated. Help comes from a number of quarters (Revelation 12:16) as God acts to protect His own. Even in this great suffering, many more come to Messiah. This is what Moses described as "the day of their calamity" (Deuteronomy 32:35 KJV). The prophet Jeremiah spoke of this time:

> How awful that day will be! None will be like it. It will be a time of trouble for Jacob, but he will be saved out of it (Jeremiah 30:7).

So the message the prophet carries away from this consideration is clearly:

> "So there is hope for your future," declares the LORD. "Your children will return to their own land" (Jeremiah 31:17).

Reinforcing this understanding is Daniel 12:1ff., set in the context of the Antichrist's invasion of "the beautiful land," his brazen self-exaltation, and his blasphemy (11:41ff.). This is a reference to the determination of the world ruler to subdue all nations and to go after the dissident Israel. He is sorely frustrated but climactically he moves to Armageddon in an abortive final attempt to solve the Jewish problem. So we read:

> At that time Michael, the great prince who protects your people, will arise. There will be a time of distress such as has not happened from the beginning of nations until then. But at that time your people—everyone whose name is found written in the book—will be delivered (Daniel 12:1).

Scripture elsewhere calls this a time of unparalleled agony for the elect (Matthew 24:21ff.; Revelation 13:5–10).

A greater deliverance than the Exodus will come (cf. Jeremiah 16:14–15). After another wilderness experience, the Lord acts on behalf of His own.[28] In the first three-and-a-half years of Daniel's seventieth week, the Jews share in the prosperity; then come three-and-a-half years of oppression and bitterness (cf. the three-and-a-half years of public ministry of the Lord Jesus). God wants to break the stubbornness of Israel (Daniel 12:5–7; Ezekiel 20:34–38). But in this time of unexampled distress,[*] Israel will realize her destiny in the evangelistic purpose of God, and she will develop the character to do her task.

When the apostle Paul was on trial, he maintained that

it is because of my hope in what God has promised our fathers that I am on trial today. This is the promise our twelve tribes are hoping to see fulfilled. . . . Why should any of you consider it incredible that God raises the dead? (Acts 26:6–8).

Daniel 12:2 speaks of resurrection. This is a reference to national resurrection in the sense of Ezekiel 37:1–14 with some who are part of that national renaissance coming to faith (which means everlasting life) and some not coming to faith (meaning shame and everlasting contempt). The emphasis here[*] is not on the physical resurrection of the Tribulation martyrs but on spiritual resuscitation.[29] Confirming this is Daniel 12:3, which presents the ministry of the believing remnant.

Another interval of intense suffering for the Jews is hard to consider with any equanimity, but we must remember that their suffering is ongoing. They with the other "inhabitants of the earth" in the Tribulation period will face the menace of the Antichrist, but in that time of "messianic woes," as their own rabbis have always termed it, "the nation will be born spiritually and have their finest hour" of spiritual witness and testimony.[†]

WHEREFORE?

Come, let us return to the LORD. He has torn us to pieces but he will heal us; he has injured us but he will bind up our wounds. After two days he will revive us; on the third day he will restore us, that we may live in His presence. Let us acknowledge the LORD; let us press on to acknowledge him. As surely as the sun rises, he will appear; he will come to us like the winter rains, like the spring rains that water the earth. (Hosea 6:1–3).

◊ ◊ ◊

* (previous page) "A mighty sea of ills and judgments, tears and recompenses for sin, still lies between Israel and that continent of peace and glory. God will put them in the crucible, and sit as a refiner and purifier of silver, to purify the sons of Levi and purge them as gold and silver, that they may offer unto Jehovah an offering in righteousness. By the fires of unexampled trial He will purge away their dross and take away all their tin, that He may restore their judges as at the first, and their counsellors as at the beginning."—J. A. Seiss [30]

* Following Carl Armerding, H. A. Ironside, and A. C. Gaebelein.

† Even now Christian organizations have established depositories of spiritual literature, Bible commentaries, scholarly and popular works which will be resources for this brilliant and resourceful people to make up lost time in getting hold of New Testament material. What will it be like to hear "All Hail the Power of Jesus' Name" coming from *yeshivas* and synagogues?

Those who are wise will shine like the brightness of the heavens, and those who lead many to righteousness, like the stars for ever and ever. (Daniel 12:3).

As for long life, the Jews live—the same peculiar people—today, long ages after the Phoenicians and the Philistines have lost their identity. Their ancient Syriac neighbors have gone into the melting-pot and have been reminted, with new images and superscriptions, while Israel has proved impervious to this alchemy—performed by history in the crucibles of universal states and universal churches and wanderings of the nations—to which we Gentiles all in turn succumb.—Arnold Toynbee [31]

One would not expect so tiny a territory to play a major role in history, or to leave behind an influence greater than that of Babylonia, Assyria, or Persia, perhaps greater than even that of Egypt or Greece. But it was the fortune and misfortune of Palestine that it lay midway between the capitals of the Nile and those of the Tigris and Euphrates. This circumstance brought trading to Judea, and it brought wars; time and again the harassed Hebrews were compelled to take sides in the struggle of the empires, or to pay tribute, or be overrun.—Will Durant [32]

The purpose of God with respect to Israel is to bless them in order to make them a blessing, and indeed, "all peoples on earth will be blessed through [them]" (Genesis 12:2–3). This blessing is through Messiah, the Lord Jesus Christ, and in this age "the church which is Christ's body" is the agency. During the Tribulation period after the exit of the church, Israel is once again the appointed vehicle. Then converted Jews will be God's witnesses as had originally been projected (Isaiah 43:10; 44:8).

God never leaves Himself without a witness, and it is His divine design to incorporate and utilize Israel in the day of great indignation for His glory and for humankind's greater good.

Some 144,000 apostle Pauls will spearhead an impact that will reach not only the Jewish people in their extremity, but masses of Gentiles.[*]

The "wise" will "lead many to righteousness" (Daniel 12:3). In the face of the unmitigated hostility and hatred of the world government and the world religious amalgam, these Jews will stand defiantly . They will not take the mark of the beast (Revelation 13:16–17). Visualize the unfolding of the judgments described in the Apocalypse. The seals, the trumpets, and the bowls tell of this time of unequaled conflict. The four

◊ ◊ ◊

[*] Even secular writers like Toynbee and Durant see even the geography of Israel as giving them a unique influence and their history attesting to a unique durability.

horsemen lead it off (Revelation 6:1–17) and humankind cries out to the mountains and the rocks: "Fall on us and hide us" (6:16). The release of the demonic hoards exacerbates the anguish of the inhabitants of the earth, and "during those days men will seek death, but will not find it; they will long to die, but death will elude them" (9:6). But there are those in all of this who keep "themselves pure," who "follow the Lamb wherever He goes," who are the "firstfruits to God and the Lamb," of whom it is said, "No lie was found in their mouths; they are blameless" (14:4–6). These are the 144,000. Of their situation it is said: "This calls for patient endurance on the part of the saints who obey God's commandments and remain faithful to Jesus" (14:12).

Is there any word of hope or salvation for those who are embittered, hardened, impenitent, and blasphemous? In the scenes of death, pain, frustration, and misery there are messengers of hope and truth. When the blood of battle rises as high as the bridles of the horses (14:20), there are emissaries of peace. In this "the day of the vengeance of God" there are those entrusted with the gospel. Indeed like a host of John the Baptists they will fearlessly proclaim God's truth:

> And this gospel of the kingdom will be preached in the whole world as a testimony to all the nations, and then the end will come (Matthew 24:14).

Who could be better equipped and qualified when endued with the Spirit to share Christ among the nations than the Jews. Brilliant, aggressive, multilingual with roots in over 100 nations of the Diaspora, salespersons par excellence!

Israel knows from Scripture there are just three-and-a-half years until Christ comes in glory with thousands of His saints and angels to judge the nations and set up the Kingdom. Yet, so dreadful are those days, "If [they] had not been cut short, no one would survive, but for the sake of the elect, those days will be shortened" (Matthew 24:22). Yet many will be saved. This will be one of the greatest revivals in the history of this planet. As the apostle Paul made plain:

> But if their transgression means riches for the world, and their loss means riches for the Gentiles, how much greater riches will their fullness bring? (Romans 11:12).

The Lord's gracious intervention is intended to "provide for those who grieve in Zion—to bestow on them a crown of beauty instead of ashes, the oil of gladness instead of mourning, and a garment of praise instead of a spirit of despair. They will be called oaks of righteousness, a planting of the LORD for the display of his splendor" (Isaiah 61:3b). The Jewish people are an expressive people—what marvelous witnesses they will be for Christ! So the prophet exulted in the tone of praise that will doubtless characterize those who have come to faith:

Sing for joy, O heavens, for the LORD has done this; shout aloud, O earth beneath. Burst into song, you mountains, you forests and all your trees, for the LORD has redeemed Jacob, he displays his glory in Israel (Isaiah 44:23).

The Lord has made a promise to Israel which He will honor:

The LORD will make you the head, not the tail. If you pay attention to the commands of the LORD your God that I give you this day and carefully follow them, you will always be at the top, never at the bottom (Deuteronomy 28:13).

Israel was created for God's glory (Isaiah 43:7) and the great fulfillment of promise is yet to come:

I will grant salvation to Zion, my splendor to Israel (Isaiah 46:13).

Some of these passages spill over from the Tribulation period to the Millennial Kingdom in all its fullness, but the Tribulation period is the inception of the usefulness that eventuates in a cloudless sky of divine largess. Zechariah pictured the scene:

This is what the LORD Almighty says: "In those days ten men from all languages and nations will take firm hold of one Jew by the hem of his robe and say: Let us go with you, because we have heard that God is with you (Zechariah 8:23).

This is a time of "worldwide revival."[33] With Jerusalem and Israel as the base, messengers of the gospel go out into all the world notwithstanding the opposition and tyranny of the Antichrist. In great deprivation, they nonetheless as "the Lord's brethren" find hospitality and food and clothing from Jews and Gentiles; there are those courageous enough to visit them in prison (cf. Matthew 25:34–46). The issue of their ministry is eternal life or eternal punishment (Matthew 25:46). And many will be saved.

A passage like Isaiah 24:14–16 has a tribulational context:

They raise their voices, they shout for joy; from the west they acclaim the LORD's majesty. Therefore in the east give glory to the LORD; exalt the name of the LORD, the God of Israel, in the islands of the sea. From the ends of the earth we hear singing: "Glory to the Righteous One.

The great promise of the Lord to Solomon concerning revival contains the principle that believers in any age can rightly tap into for renewal, but as it stands it is literally for Israel:

If my people, who are called by my name, will humble themselves and pray and seek my face and turn from their wicked ways, then will I hear from heaven and will forgive their sin and heal their land (2 Chronicles 7:14).

And then in the darkest and most dangerous hour of the Tribulation, the world ruler moves against beleaguered little Israel—and Christ will come in power and great glory!

CHAPTER

17

THE SMITING STONE AND THE COMING OF THE KINGDOM

In the time of those kings, the God of heaven will set up a kingdom that will never be destroyed, nor will it be left to another people. It will crush all those kingdoms and bring then to an end, but it will itself endure forever.

Daniel 2:44

In my vision at night I looked, and there before me was one like a son of man, coming with the clouds of heaven. He approached the Ancient of Days and was led into his presence. He was given authority, glory and sovereign power; all peoples, nations and men of every language worshiped Him. His dominion is an everlasting dominion that will not pass away, and His kingdom is one that will never be destroyed.

Daniel 7:13–14

Then the sovereignty, power and greatness of the kingdoms under the whole heaven will be handed over to the saints, the people of the Most High. His kingdom will be an everlasting kingdom, and all rulers will worship and obey him.

Daniel 7:27

*Deliverers will go up on Mount Zion
to govern the mountains of Esau.
And the kingdom
will be the
Lord's.*

Obadiah 21

*The Lord will be king over the whole earth.
On that day there will be one Lord,
and his name the only name.*

Zechariah 14:9

THE KINGLY RULE OF GOD IS THE FINAL GOAL of salvation's history, "that God may be all in all" (1 Corinthians 15:28).[1] With the church translated and glorified, and with Israel's long night of weeping over and this ancient people converted and protected, and with the cohorts of the Devil defeated, Christ now sets up His kingdom and rules on earth for 1000 years (Revelation 20:1–6). This is Nebuchadnezzar's vision of "the rock cut out of a mountain, but not by human hands" smiting the structure of Gentiles world power and pulverizing it into powder (Daniel 2:45). This rock that strikes the statue becomes "a huge mountain and [fills] the whole earth" (Daniel 2:35). Bringing in everlasting righteousness, sealing up the vision and the prophecy, and anointing the most Holy Place will be accomplished by and at the end of Daniel's seventieth week (see Daniel 9:24).[2]

Beyond any question the premillennial or chiliastic understanding of the end of history was dominant in the early church.[*] In contrast to amillennialism that spiritualizes the one-thousand-year reign of Christ making it the present experience of the church[†] or postmillennialism that over-optimistically sees the church as triumphing in history and ushering in the kingdom,[‡] is the premillennial system advocated in this

◇ ◇ ◇

[*] Although holding to a posttribulational view, Robert Gundry is squarely with the facts when he says: "Until Augustine in the fourth century, the early church generally held to the premillennarian understanding of biblical eschatology. This chiliasm entailed a futuristic interpretation of Daniel's seventieth week, the abomination of desolation, and the personal Anti-Christ."[3]

[†] This is consistent with its view that the church has replaced and superseded Israel.

[‡] Postmillennialism largely went out the window because of our century's wars and genocide; it has found new life in the current movement known as theonomy, or reconstructionism.

book. No one has stated more crisply and clearly what premillennialism is than Charles Ryrie:

> Premillennialists believe that theirs is the historic faith of the church. Holding to a literal interpretation of the Scriptures, they believe that the promises made to Abraham and David are unconditional and have had or will have a literal fulfillment. In no sense have these promises made to Israel been abrogated or fulfilled by the church, which is a distinct body in this age having promises and a destiny different from Israel's. At the close of this age Premillennialists believe that Christ will return for His church, meeting her in the air, which event, called the rapture or translation, will usher in a seven-year period of tribulation on earth. After this, the Lord will return to the earth to establish His kingdom on the earth for a thousand years, during which time the promises to Israel will be fulfilled.[4]

The early historian Eusebius related the very typical view of Papias, a bishop of the second century and widely honored in his time:

> Among other things he declares that after the resurrection of the dead, a thousand years would follow during which Christ's kingdom would exist corporeally upon this earth.

Eusebius was not happy with these ideas. He was already showing the influence of the neoplatonism that had made Augustine domesticate the kingdom as a synonym for the church.

John Calvin would be another example of how Platonic thinking led to the abandonment of a consistent hermeneutic. Calvin discounted the historical significance of the conquest of the Promised Land in favor of seeing the land as a figure of the church's heavenly inheritance. This led Calvin to assert that "the Jews were separated from other nations, not for their own sakes, but for ours, that the Christian Church might have an image, in whose external form they could discern examples of spiritual things."[5] In contrast is the understanding of the disciples of Jesus (Acts 1:6) and Papias.*

Resistant to Platonic spiritualization and its aversion for the physical and consistent with belief in the bodily resurrection, Jews and Christians have looked forward to a golden age. For the Greeks, the golden age was *retrospect*; for the Jews and Christians the golden age is *prospect*. Then the Lord will rule and "the knowledge of the LORD" shall cover the earth as "the waters cover the sea" (Habakkuk 2:14).†

At the birth of Jesus, the angels acclaimed "on earth peace to men on whom his favor rests, good will among those with whom God is well pleased" at the birth of Jesus (Luke 2:14). And when the Prince of Peace

◊ ◊ ◊

* "Papias's conception of the temporal messiahship is in all essential points that of the New Testament itself."[6]—Edward H. Hall

comes to rule and reign, then creation itself will be set free from the scars and slavery of sin (Romans 8:18–27). The deliverance effected by the conquering Christ will be resplendent in all dimensions of the created order. And yet, the millennial reign of Christ is a further and expanded overlap of the powers of the age to come. It is an interim kingdom.[7] It is the initial stage of the everlasting kingdom.[*]

THE ESTABLISHMENT OF THE KINGDOM

What did he mean by the Kingdom? A supernatural heaven? Apparently not, for the apostles and the early Christians unanimously expected an earthly Kingdom. This was the Jewish tradition that Jesus inherited; and he taught his followers to pray to the Father, "Thy kingdom come, thy will be done on earth as it is in heaven."—Will Durant [8]

In a certain sense, every branch of literature may be regarded as auxiliary to the study of the history of the Kingdom of God.—John Peter Lange

I saw heaven standing open and there before me was white horse, whose rider is called Faithful and True. With justice he judges and makes war. . . . Out of his mouth comes a sharp sword with which to strike down the nations. "He will rule them with an iron scepter." He treads the winepress of the fury of the wrath of God Almighty. On his robe and on his thigh he has this name written: KING OF KINGS AND LORD OF LORDS (Revelation 19:11, 15–16).

The Kingdom will be restored to Israel. This is as sure as her ultimate salvation.[†] The Tribulation period and Satan's vendetta against the Jews will end at Armageddon when the Lord Jesus will descend from heaven in power and in great glory to judge the nations and set up His Kingdom (Revelation 19:11–21). It would seem that when Christ descends to the Mount of Olives He sets up His Kingdom (Zechariah 14:4ff.). The additional month beyond the 1,260 days (Daniel 12:11) is for the judgment of the living nations (Matthew 25:31–46), and considering the carnage

◊ ◊ ◊

† (previous page) We see the great longing for a perfect society in Plato's *Republic*; or in the imaginary utopia of Aristophanes' *Birds*; or in Virgil's *Fourth Eclogue*; where he hails a great personage who would inaugurate "a great order of ages begun wholly new" ("*Magnus ab integro seclorum nascitur ordo*"); or in the utopias of Thomas More, Samuel Butler, Edward Bellamy, as well as Henry David Thoreau, Robert Owen, and Leo Tolstoy. [9] We also see it in Marx' vision of a classless society.

* "In the zenith of the power of anti-Christ, Jesus will be revealed from heaven with the whole company of His saints, coming to set up His own blessed reign upon the earth."—G. Campbell Morgan[10]

and consequent collapse of Gentile world power, indeed "blessed is the one who waits for and reaches the end of the 1,335 days," that is , who lives on into the millennial rule of Christ after the debris of the vanquished nations is blown away by the wind (Daniel 12:12).

Daniel the prophet concluded concerning those who are saved during the whole traumatic ordeal: "Many will be purified, made spotless and refined, but the wicked will continue to be wicked. None of the wicked will understand, but those who are wise will understand" (Daniel 12:10). The purpose of God is always salvation and will be in the Tribulation period and as we shall see will be also in the millennial reign of Christ.

The Lord Jesus Christ will personally and powerfully reign over the whole earth and all who have part of the first resurrection will rule with Him (Revelation 20:1–6). Christ will express His glory in time-space order before the endless eternities.

The Millennium is "the consummating link between history and the eternal order."

In Greek philosophy, especially Plato, we find a deep antipathy to the physical, as for instance that the body is the prison of the soul. The Hebrews were by contrast an earthy people because God pronounced good the physical order He created. Hence matter is good but it has been defiled and debased by human sin. The created order needs and will obtain redemption (Romans 8:18 ff.). Christ will rule for 1000 years with Jerusalem His earthly center. This is the golden age the prophets foretold. Thus we are not surprised that the earthly reign of Christ has a Jewish cast.[*]

Even though in this book the view of Christ's earthly reign has had many proponents through the centuries[11] and something of a resurgence in recent years and in some very unexpected places,[12] the whole system does not rest on six references to the 1000 years in Revelation 20:1–7.[†] The whole bulk of Old Testament prophecy points to the estab-

◊ ◊ ◊

† (previous page) Even George Ladd conceded that "It cannot be denied that Jesus offered the Kingdom to Israel. . . . The Kingdom was theirs by right of election, history and heritage . . . the Jews as a whole refused this new relationship . . . the Kingdom in its new manifestation was taken away from Israel and given to a new people . . . this does not mean that God has for ever cast off Israel after the flesh . . . Israel will recognize Christ as her Messiah and will say, 'Blessed is he who comes in the name of the Lord' . . . Israel is yet to be saved . . . the salvation of Israel is an essential part of God's single redemptive purpose."[13]

lishment of a kingdom of peace upon earth when the law will go forth from Mount Zion (Isaiah 2:1–4; Micah 4:2–5).[*] Micah 3:8–12 tells about judgment on Jerusalem (literal and actual Jerusalem); then immediately following is the picture of the establishment of the Mountain of the Lord in Jerusalem during the Millennium (Micah 4:1–7).[14] How possibly could the latter not be as literal and actual as the former?[†] "The millennial reign on earth does not rest on an isolated passage, but all the Old Testament prophecy goes on the same view."[15]

The New Testament saints who constitute the church and the angels will rule with Christ (cf. Matthew 19:28, "Judging the twelve tribes of Israel"; 1Corinthians 6:2–3; 2Timothy 2:11–13). Somewhere in this universe there exists the New Jerusalem, the city of God (Hebrews 11:10), which will descend from heaven and exist like a gigantic space module in relation to earth (Revelation 21:1–5).[‡] As described in the Revelation, the garden city of God will be like a huge chandelier over the earth (Revelation 21:10).[16] The saved nations will walk in the light of it (Revelation

◊ ◊ ◊

* (previous page) J. Sidlow Baxter aptly characterized the situation: "Jerusalem will indeed be the geographical center, and a regenerated Israel the nucleus of that coming reign . . . the 'kingdom' will be a global dominion over all lands and peoples; the climax-era of our race's history."[17] J. Oliver Buswell in his *Systematic Theology* mounted a strong defense of historic premillennialism in which he stated: "That the future kingdom of Christ is in a real sense Jewish and Davidic should be clear to every student of the Bible." He cited numerous biblical quotations from both Testaments and asserted: "The Davidic kingship of Christ is not a matter of favoritism to one people above another, but 'they were entrusted with the oracles of God' (Romans 3:2). Just so the future kingdom of Christ is to have historical continuity with the chief channel of revelation" (cf. Romans 9:6; 11:25–36).[18]

† (previous page) Were there only a single reference in Scripture that would suffice of course, as in the case of the Virgin Birth of our Lord, mentioned overtly only in two places in the New Testament.

* Gordon Lewis has most helpfully pointed out that even Kromminga who had problems with a specifically Jewish character to the Millennium admitted: "It is not inconceivable that in the millennium the people that sprang from Abraham were to render some spiritual service to the rest of the nations, as in consequence of and by their conversion to Christ."[19] He also quoted Pache to the point: "The millennium will not be heaven, but rather a theocracy, an authoritarian reign of God upon earth. It will therefore be useful that Israel in a holy and spiritual fashion be at the head of the people to submit them to the Lord."[20]

† Godet strenuously argued that Luke 1:31–33 (concerning the throne of David) requires a natural and literal sense: "It is, indeed, the theocratic royalty and the Israelitish people, neither more nor less, that are in question here."[21]

‡ Louis T. Talbot was the first in my experience to give this understanding.

21:24). This is literally the rule of the heavens over the earth. This is not heaven through all eternity, it is the New Jerusalem in time-space. It is the interim kingdom. Christ will not be sitting on a throne in Jerusalem for twenty-four hours at a time, but rather our Lord with His bride will be back and forth during the 1000 years.[22]

Other crucial components in the inauguration of the Kingdom will be setting King David up for special earthly responsibility (Jeremiah 30:9; Ezekiel 34:23–24; 37:24); the binding of Satan for.1000 years (Revelation 20:1–3); the judgment of the sheep and goat nations (Matthew 25:31–46); the resurrection of the Tribulation martyrs and the total recasting of the topography of the Holy City, and the building of the millennial temple (Ezekiel 40–48).

THE ARRANGEMENT OF THE KINGDOM

In earlier books of the Bible we have glimpses of phases of the Millennial Kingdom or of the return of Christ. At the end of the Bible, in Revelation 19 and 20, a picture is given to gather them together and show their arrangement in the pattern of God's plan. . . . It is so clear that one marvels that anyone should misunderstand it.—Allan A. MacRae

Righteousness and justice are the foundation of your throne; love and faithfulness go before you (Psalm 89:14).

The moon will be abashed, the sun ashamed; for the LORD Almighty will reign on Mount Zion, in Jerusalem, and before its elders, gloriously (Isaiah 24:23).

In that day I will restore David's fallen tent. I will repair its broken places, restore its ruins, and build it as it used to be (Amos 9:11).

He will proclaim peace to the nations. His rule will extend from sea to sea and from the River to the ends of the earth (Zechariah 9:10b).

If some have underplayed the present sense of the Kingdom (Colossians 1:13–14), then certainly others have underplayed the future sense of the Kingdom in devaluing the eschatological dimension. The stone of Daniel 2 strikes the great image while there were feet and toes to be struck and before it began to grow into a great mountain. The Stone Kingdom has not yet come because the stone has not yet fallen. It is difficult to imagine how anyone can seriously argue that the Millennium has come and that we are now in it.

If Satan is now bound ("to keep him from deceiving the nations," Revelation 20:3), he has a mighty long chain, as Wilbur M. Smith used to say.

Surely Christ breaks the power of Satan over individuals (Matthew 12:29), but the binding in Revelation 20:3 has to do with the nations and is millennial and future. For 1000 years Christ will rule. The blessings for Jew and Gentile are indescribable.[*]

Spiritual

The church which reigns with Christ is clothed with immortal bodies, but the living nations admitted to the Millennium as sheep are yet in their mortal bodies and procreate. Among the latter there is death (although anyone dying at 100 is like the death of a youth in our time, (Isaiah 65:20–25). In other words, there is a need for evangelism among these offspring. Despite the total immobilization of Satan, some are resistant to the gospel and many join in a final revolt against the Lord when Satan is released at the end of the 1000 years (Revelation 20:3, 7–10). Israel will be at the very center of spiritual impact (cf. Isaiah 4:3; 11:9; Zechariah 14:20–21). Then will be fulfilled the prophecy:

> And the ransomed of the LORD will return. They will enter Zion with singing; everlasting joy will crown their heads. Gladness and joy will overtake them, and sorrow and sighing will flee away (Isaiah 35:10).

Ethical

"And the crooked shall be made straight" (Isaiah 40:4). The increasing moral anarchy of our times has been fomented by the total rejection of authority and absolute standards. But Jesus Christ will embody truth, and the written exposition of that truth will naturally flow from Him (Isaiah 8:20). Impartiality and fairness prove to be elusive in many courts of law,[†] but in the Kingdom there will be immediate and just redress for all wrongs (Isaiah 11:2–5).

Social

"They will neither harm nor destroy on all my holy mountain" (Isaiah 65:25b). Children will be unthreatened (Zechariah 8:4–5). The streets will be safe. The aged will be afforded the dignity due them. There

◊ ◊ ◊

[*] In my judgment, no one has more richly and fully expounded the range and scope of the blessings of the Kingdom than Alva J. McClain in his classic, *The Greatness of the Kingdom.*[23] The outline of blessings is his.

[†] Charles Dickens wrestled with a corrupt judiciary in his time in the novel *Bleak House.*

will be no threats of war or the wastes of military budgets. The curse will be lifted. There will be no discrimination against minority populations.

Economic

Not only is there peace but there is prosperity as well. "Every man will sit under his own vine and under his own fig tree, and no one will make them afraid, for the LORD Almighty has spoken" (Micah 4:4). "They will build houses and dwell in them; they will plant vineyards and eat their fruit. No longer will they build houses and others live in them, or plant and others eat. For as the days of a tree, so will be the days of my people; my chosen ones will long enjoy the works of their hands. They will not toil in vain or bear children doomed to misfortune; for they will be a people blessed by the LORD, they and their descendants with them" (Isaiah 65:21–23). The grievous and growing gulf between the "haves" and the "have nots" will be obliterated.

Political

The balance of power and the balance of terror endemic to world political history will yield to the righteous reign of Jesus Christ (Isaiah 9:7). Jerusalem will be the capital of the world (Isaiah 2:2–4; Ezekiel 43:1–7). Christ is not yet ruling from the throne of David (cf. Psalm 110:1ff.) but He will do so.*

Physical

Some very striking geographical and topological changes will take place when Christ returns in glory to set up His Kingdom. A great earthquake will rend the Mount of Olives (Zechariah 14:3–4) and the Mount of the Lord will be sufficient in size for the building of the millennial temple described in Ezekiel 40–48.[24] From its summit will flow the life-giving stream depicted in Ezekiel 47:1–12, which will reach to the Dead Sea with its rejuvenating qualities. Then indeed "Jerusalem will be raised up and remain in its place," and the promise will be kept:

> It will be inhabited; never again will it be destroyed. Jerusalem will be secure" (Zechariah 14:10–11).

In this time the ferocity of animal life will revert back to Edenic harmony, before nature was "red with tooth and claw." Climatic conditions will again be antediluvian when a reimposed canopy will give uniformly mild conditions and a "greenhouse effect."

◊ ◊ ◊

* "Many passages likewise refer to Christ's rule over the entire earth of which Zechariah 14:9 may be taken as representative. Gentiles, although in a subordinate role in relation to Israel, will nevertheless be greatly blessed in the millennium and share in the prosperity of the period."[25]—John F. Walvoord

Ecclesiastical

"For my house will be called a house of prayer for all nations" (Isaiah 56:7). Jesus Christ is the priest-king on His throne (Zechariah 6:12–13). He is not yet on the throne of His Father David but He will be (Psalm 110:1ff.). A central sanctuary will be built in Jerusalem on the Mount of the Lord (Ezekiel 40–48), and it will be used by all people. This will fulfill the prophecy:

> I will put my sanctuary among them forever. My dwelling place will be with them; I will be their God, and they will be my people. Then the nations will know that I the LORD make Israel holy, when my sanctuary is among them forever (Ezekiel 37:26b–28).

Obviously this has never yet been fulfilled, but it will be fulfilled along with innumerable prophecies given by our God. The Shekinah Glory will once again take its proper place in the sanctuary (Ezekiel 43:1–7). God's sovereign purpose for His ancient people will be realized, as Isaiah stated it:

> And you will be called priests of the Lord, you will be named ministers of our God (Isaiah 61:6a).[26]

The fulfillment of the New Covenant will not make teachers unnecessary then any more than now (Jeremiah 31:31ff.), but human beings will know, to the praise and glory of God. The Jews will be the expositors with us.

A major question regards mortals and immortals in contact with each other. The "first resurrection" (Revelation 20:6; cf. John 5:28) is in phases, consisting of those saints raised immediately after Christ's resurrection (Matthew 27:52–53); saints at the Rapture; the two witnesses and other Tribulation martyrs; saints who die during and who are alive at the end of the Millennium.[27] Those raised up from the dead will headquarter in the New Jerusalem hovering over the earth; mortals will live on earth, but they will intermingle, "the heavenly and the earthly, the Jerusalem above and the Jerusalem in the earth, and the ladder, so to speak, will be Mt. Zion."[28]

THE ACCOMPLISHMENT OF THE KINGDOM

Thus there is during the Kingdom period a well-ordered system of government, embracing the whole earth, administered by Christ, through those whom He appoints; a system adapted to meet the needs of all its inhabitants in all their varied conditions and degrees of intellectual development.—Samuel J. Andrews[29]

The preservation of Israel as a racial entity and the resurrection of Israel as a political entity are twin miracles of the twentieth century which are in perfect accord with the premillennial interpetation. The doctrine of Israel remains one of the central features of premillennialism. —John Walvoord [30]

Only in a literal millennium do we have a meaningful culmination of world history. —James Montgomery Boice [31]

Is earth simply a failure, abandoned by God to the power of the enemy, the scene of divine judgment, and not the scene of the vindication and triumph of righteousness? We believe that He will come, and with Him the Kingdom, and with the Kingdom the fulfillment of the prayer, "Thy Will Be Done on Earth as it is in Heaven."—Adolf Saphir

The advancement of God's sovereign purpose is often in phases as many have taught through the ages such as Johannes Cocceius in the seventeenth century who argued for "distinct temporal stages" in the unfolding of God's plan. In our present evil age, we see the powers of the age to come breaking into time-space; in the Millennium there will be a further and far more extensive overlap, with Christ visibly at the center of all things and converted Israel bearing effective witness, as indeed Philip did in the first century:

We have found the one Moses wrote about in the Law, and about whom the prophets also wrote. Jesus of Nazareth (John 1:45).

Purpose of Kingdom

But why the 1000 year reign of Christ? This manifestation of the Kingdom becomes one of the capstones in our philosophy of history. The fact is God has chosen the earth to be "the theater for the manifestation of His Name!" (Psalm 8:l ff.; Isaiah 30:27; John 17:6–26). Hebrews 2:5–9 speaks of "the world to come" and sees Jesus Christ fulfilling the role God chose Adam and Eve to fulfill, ruling as viceregents and regents over planet earth (cf. Genesis 1:28ff).

"Yet at present we do not see everything subject to him. But we see Jesus" (Hebrews 2:8–9a). Indeed, Paul showed that "then the end will come, when He hands over the kingdom to God the Father after He has destroyed all dominion, authority and power. For He must reign until he has put all his enemies under his feet" (1 Corinthians 15:24–25). This is the essential action of the millennial reign.

Some have protested that premillennialism is gross carnality and materialism and flies in the face of Romans 14:17:

For the kingdom of God is not a matter of eating and drinking, but of righteousness, peace and joy in the Holy Spirit.

Of course the Kingdom of God and entrance thereto is essentially spiritual (John 1:12–13; 3:3, 5), but it is Greek philosophy, not Scripture, that disallows the spiritual reality to translate into the time-space order.

The resurrection of the body is just a further extension of the principle in which the very coarse mantle of flesh will be transformed and will express the glory of God (Philippians 3:20–21). Indeed earthly elements can convey and carry deep and powerful spiritual meaning as in Christian baptism and the Lord's Supper. J. Oliver Buswell, long-time president of Wheaton and distinguished Christian scholar, put it beautifully:

"With the vindication of God's creative purpose in mind, the Christian has a different attitude toward physical and material things. Every blade of grass, every grain of sand is seen in a different perspective. Every tree and flower and fruitful thing is seen in the light of God's good purpose for man as created in His image. Every noxious weed and venemous reptile is contemplated in the light of the fall of man. Every fault and failure of the visible church in the course of history is seen in cosmic perspective in the light of the future visible kingdom of Christ."[32]

If history culminated with cataclysm and judgment, the Second Coming of Christ in power would be only "a walk through the ruins." The stone which becomes a mountain will "fill all the earth" (Daniel 2:35). "They will reign on earth" is the promise (Revelation 5:10).[33] The venue of the Kingdom is to be on earth before we come to the final expression of the Kingdom in "the new heaven and the new earth" (2 Peter 3:13; Revelation 21–22). The new millennial temple portrayed in Ezekiel 40–48 is an ideal vision of the perfected Kingdom of God and every detail and facet disclose how spiritual truth and doctrine are enshrined and embodied in physical form and shape.

Worship in Kingdom

The new millennial temple (Ezekiel 40–43) is considerably larger than any previous temple and more vast than could be built on the existing site given its present topography. This will all be changed to accommodate the new sanctuary. This structure is not for the New Jerusalem because in it there is no temple, for the Lamb is the temple (Revelation 21:22).[34] Very exact and specific dimensions are given, further reinforcing the impression that this is to be a literal and actual sanctuary. Many have pointed out that only the table is in the Holy Place and no reference is made to the Ark of the Covenant in the Holy of Holies. It is a new order of worship, unique and appropriate to the millennial reign. The suggestion is typically made that there is no laver of bronze as in the tabernacle nor brazen sea as in Solomon's temple because of the great river that gushes up in the Holy of Holies and flows under the door of the new temple. [35] The climax of the book of Ezekiel really comes when the glory of the Lord returns to the house (Ezekiel 43:1–3; cf. 11:23 when the Shekinah left the first temple).

There are differences in worship between the prescriptions of Moses and the descriptions of Ezekiel.[36] These differences include matters of size, arrangement, furnishings, the insistence on a Zadokite priesthood (one branch of Aaron's progeny), their consecration, the cleansing of the altar, etc. Allocation of territory in the land is made on a new basis (Ezekiel 45:1–12; 47:13–48:35) and a somewhat modified sacred calendar is presented (Ezekiel 45:13–46:29). Everything in the temple passages in Ezekiel hinges on a restoration of Israel in the end time.[37]

But is not a return to literal animal sacrifice retrogression and indeed contrary to the message of the book of Hebrews in the New Testament? (cf. Hebrews 10:1–8, 14, 18). That the finished work of Jesus Christ for the sins of the world on the cross is completed and that no more sacrifice for sin is necessary or possible does not rule out the perpetuation of symbolism or sacramental witness. As we observe the Lord's Supper, we look back and remember the atoning work of Christ.[38] Yet the Supper is more than memorialization. Alexander concluded that the Lord's Supper will continue for believers in Christ during the Millennium (Matthew 26:29; Mark 14:25; Luke 22:18): "If the Lord's Table is a memorial and the sacrifices of the Ezekiel system are memorials, the two should not in any way conflict with each other but should be able to coexist . . . the Lord's Table is the primary memorial to those believers of the church age while the sacrifices in Ezekiel would be the primary commemoration of the Jews."[39] Physical and material emblems do bear spiritual meaning and significance. This is the real meaning of the millennial reign of Christ.

One further facet of what the Millennium accomplishes will be apparent when we consider the loosing of Satan and the revolt at the end of the 1000 years. We are but further sure thereby that the Millennium leads to the eternal order but is not to be identified with it. The 1000 years are a final and decisive test (cf. Deuteronomy 8:2) of immense import.

THE ABATEMENT OF THE KINGDOM

The remaining two chapters (Revelation 21–22) describe the eternal and consummated kingdom of God upon the new earth. As the world of nations is per-

vaded by Divine influence in the millennium, so that of nature shall be, not annihilated, but transfigured, in the subsequent eternal state. The earth was cursed for man, but is redeemed by the second Adam. Now is the church; in the millennium shall be the kingdom; after that shall be the new world wherein God shall be all in all . . . God's works are progressive. The millennium, in which sin and death are much restricted, is the transition state from the old to the new earth. The millennium is the age of regeneration. The final age shall be wholly free from sin and death.—A. R. Fausset

Arise, shine, for your light has come, and the glory of the LORD rises upon you. See, darkness covers the earth and thick darkness is over the peoples, but the LORD rises upon you and his glory appears over you. Nations will come to your light, and kings to the brightness of your dawn . . . Your sun will never set again, and your moon will wane no more; the LORD will be your everlasting light, and your days of sorrow will end. Then will all your people be righteous and they will possess the land forever" (Isaiah 60:1–2, 20–21a).

He who was seated on the throne said, "I am making everything new!"(Revelation 21:5).

Supporting the understanding that the millennial reign is transitional[*] not terminal is the loosing of Satan at the end of the 1000 years and the subsequent epochal last battle (Revelation 20:7–10). For 1000 years Satan will be incarcerated in the Abyss or the bottomless pit. He is totally unable to tincture the triumph of the Lord Jesus Christ. None of his demon hoardes will be roaming over the earth to create misery, envy, jealousy, or acrimony. What a relief! But at the conclusion of the munificent regime of the Son of God, Satan will "be set free for a short time" (Revelation 20:3c). Satan will return to earth (this could rightly be called the Second Coming of Satan), and he will go forth to deceive the nations. He is the ultimate recidivist, lapsing into his former mode of behavior. Thus we see how incorrigible sin and rebellion are. No consideration has fazed Satan's determination to foil God's purpose. How futile is any thought of rapprochement with Satan or his minions.

The absolutely flabbergasting development is his amazing success in gathering a vast aggregation, "in number they are like the sand on the seashore" (20:8c). Once again Satan leads a vast array against the center of the Lord's authority on earth:

◊ ◊ ◊

[*] The course of human history is often represented in literature as a journey, as in Dante's *Divine Comedy* (echoed in C. S. Lewis's *The Great Divorce*) or Bunyan's *Pilgrim's Progress.* Yet again history is often seen as proceeding to a great conflict or war, such as in Bunyan's *The Holy War* or in Lewis's *Narnia,* where the Last Battle is seen as the Apocalypse.

They marched across the breadth of the earth and surrounded the camp of God's people, the city He loves (20:9a).

Again we are impressed with the significance of literal Jerusalem, not only in the Tribulation period (11:8) but in the millennial reign as well. This final, flagrant assault on the Lord and the Lord's people surely comes to nought. It is the absolute end of the Devil who now joins the Beast and the False Prophet in everlasting torment (20:10). Here is most evidently the consummate disclosure of the unmitigated meanness and destructiveness of sin and Satan. But there is more.

Why is Satan released in this manner and at this time? The successive periods of God's dealings with humankind all put certain hypotheses and theories to a test. Human conscience or government cannot fully answer our problems; the law cannot provide salvation, and the hardened human heart often resists the gospel of the grace of God. But lurking down in human hearts and expressed in many a treatise on the human condition is the notion that were only human beings economically self-sufficient, if only we were spared the graft, crookedness, and prejudice of public officials, if only we did not have to face the insecurity of hostile threat and war, we would do well.

God is determined to demonstrate to the whole universe and to all created beings His "manifold wisdom" (Ephesians 3:10). For 1000 years humankind lives under the direct and just reign of the Son of God. No one lacks any good thing; Satan can be no excuse. No one can say, "the devil made me do it." Yet, at the end of such a time, unregenerate human hearts are ready to follow the evil genius of Satan in revolt against God. Thus is disclosed the depths of the depraved heart, the intransigent, and debilitating reality of sin. God's insistence that only redemption and regeneration can address the sin problem is unequivocal. On a grand scale, God has conclusively proved social planners and do-gooders are absolutely mistaken. No sociological scheme however well intentioned can truly address the need of the human heart. Only the new birth can change the deep-dyed sinfulness we all share.

Even when Christ is visibly and powerfully involved in human history for 1000 years there are those who will not yield or submit to Him. Ezekiel intimated as much in his magnificent portrait of millennial bliss. He pointed out that the miracle stream that emanates from the new temple on the Mount of the Lord does prove to be efficacious in all instances, "but the swamps and marshes will not become fresh; they will be left for salt" (Ezekiel 47:11). Even in the Millennium not all respond to the Lord's grace. Some of the children born in the Millennium do not seek the Lord, and they are those who then follow Satan in his abortive crusade to defeat the living God.[*] "The elaborate measures taken to insure his custody are most easily understood as implying the complete cessation of his influence on earth (rather than a curbing of his activities)."[40]

There are sinful mortals in the Millennium (Isaiah 2:4; 65:20; Zechariah 8:4, 23), and this sin eventuates in complicity with Satan in his final rebellion. Thus the Millennium becomes as all history must, and the history of the Jews most especially, a theodicy, a "justification of the ways of God to man" (and the whole universe, for that matter).

When all evil is thus eradicated from the earth, and there is a purging of every trace of sin and rebellion and "a new heaven and a new earth" (2 Peter 3:13) and after the judgment of all of the dead at the Great White Throne (Revelation 20:11–15), the eternal state will be inaugurated. The millennial reign of Christ is an "initial stage in the everlasting kingdom of Jesus Christ."[41] Both Old Testament saints and New Testament saints reign with Christ. They will continue to do so throughout eternity.[†]

There will be no ultimate fusion of the people of God. Israel and the church share the same sphere, but Israel is forever to be on the new earth and the church will be forever in the new heaven in the closest but yet distinct tangency, as the New Jerusalem (Revelation 21–22) and the new earth will exist eternally as it existed during the Millennium, in a symbiosis with heaven which glorifies God forever. Jews stand together in Mount Zion, in the heavenly Jerusalem, in the city of the living God, not forfeiting their identities anymore than do the "thousands upon thousands of angels in joyful assembly" (Hebrews 12:22–24) and the object of all praise and worship is "Jesus the mediator of a new covenant."

However we paint the future, "we must," as John Calvin said, "hunger after Christ till the dawning of that great day when our Lord will fully manifest the glory of His Kingdom. The whole family of the faithful will keep in view that day."

◊ ◊ ◊

[*] Arthur H. Lewis in his rather curious work entitled *The Dark Side of the Millennium.* [42] argued that we are now living in the Millennium and that in our age "the nations are no longer deceived by a Satanic ruler," which is certainly news as we look at what is happening about us.

[†] "The millennium is 'like a 'first-fruits' of the eternal state . . . a preview of the eternal messianic kingdom that will be fully revealed in the eternal state. Therefore, because the two are alike in nature, they share distinct similarities. . . . they likewise reflect some dissimilarities."[43]

OUR FAITHFUL GOD AND THE RESPONSIBILILITY OF THE CHURCH

This Israel was no "love-child," where the "love" only accounts for the origin of the child; Israel's whole existence—present and future as well as past—depended on God's continuing love and the perpetual election expressed in Covenant. The chosen people live forever only with the patient, long-suffering love of God.[1]

H. D. Beeby in *Grace Abounding*

It seems to be the roll of the Jews to focus and dramatize these common experiences of mankind, and to turn their particular fate into a universal moral. But if the Jews have this role, who wrote it for them? If the earliest Jews were able to survey, with us, the history of their progeny, they would find nothing surprising in it. They always knew that Jewish society was appointed to be a pilot-project for the entire human race.[2]

Paul Johnson

Those who trust in the LORD are like Mount Zion,
which cannot be shaken but endures forever.
As the mountains surround Jerusalem,
so the LORD surrounds his people
both now and forevermore.
The scepter of the wicked will not remain
over the land allotted to the righteous.

Psalm 125:1–3a

He shows unfailing kindness
to his annointed, to David and his descendants forever.

Psalm 18:50b

T

HE "IDEA OF HISTORY AS JUDGMENT," wrote Professor Butterfield of Cambridge, in speaking of Jewish history, "was superimposed
on the idea of history of Promise, but without superseding the earlier
idea—without actually cancelling the promise. . . . The judgments
might be terrible, but for the children of God, the Old Testament view
of history was always one of hope."[3] This hope has filled the chapters
of this book.*

History is "His story." God has been working in history and the experience of the Jews corroborates our understanding and interpretation of
the biblical material. After all, Judaism and Christianity are historical
religions. The natural sciences cannot "safely be left to determine our
views on human destiny." Israel's destiny and the wrap-up of human
history are intertwined. Israel is a special case in history. Hopefully there
will be more than just agreement with these ideas. If they are true, then
they should change our attitudes and actions.

What should be the Christian position as the quest for some kind of
a political settlement in the Middle East proceeds? What shall we say
about Christian Zionism? Can it go too far on certain issues and "out-
Israel Israel" itself? What shall we say about Christian witness and evangelism in the wake of Vatican II, *Nostra Aetate,* and the mood for Jewish-
Christian dialogue? What about messianic Judaism? How should the
Christian react to continuing and new forms of anti-Semitism? How

◊ ◊ ◊

* The veracity of Scripture and the worthiness and fidelity of God have been at
stake in our argument. God is greater than any of our systems, and we must be
very cautious not to advance from an *a priori* that the character of God being
what it is necessitates that God must do this or that. What God does, after all,
defines what is good and right, and while through the *imago dei* we can to some
degree think God's thoughts after Him, we must not push this line of reasoning
too far (Isaiah 55:8–9). Nevertheless, the shape of our argument here has been
impacted theologically by our doctrine of God.

does the church's own eschatological posture influence its attitude toward the Jews and the State of Israel?

In making this literary trek across the centuries, we have been heartened at the variety and virility of the companions who have shared the essential burden of this work. Certainly some earnest believers have not been able to identify with the argument at key junctures. Others who have made more significant concessions to modern presuppositions part company because they feel the whole idea of a literal, visible, personal return of Jesus Christ to this earth is obsolete.* However, supernaturalism must undergird both the beginnings in special creation and the conclusions in the Second Coming. From start to finish God acts in Christ miraculously, uniquely, and powerfully, and these "wonders of God" (Acts 2:11) should move us to praise Him and motivate us to live according to His purpose.

AN INVITATION TO JUSTICE

Follow justice and justice alone, so that you may live and possess the land the LORD your God is giving you (Deuteronomy 16:20).

He has showed you, O man, what is good. And what does the LORD require of you? To act justly and to love mercy and to walk humbly with your God (Micah 6:8).

The God of the Bible is upright and just. God demonstrates this in his concern for the oppressed and downtrodden. God undertakes for widows and orphans and the disenfranchised of society. The stranger was welcomed in ancient Israel. The principles of divine judgment strongly emphasize impartiality and truth (Romans 2:1–16). Therefore in legitimately standing up for "Jewish" rights in *eretz* Israel, the Christian friends of Israel must not lose a balanced and fair concern for Palestinian rights. We can undercut our case for the hope of Israel by disregarding justice.

To be sure, even the designation "Palestine" riles many Jews. The land was known as Israel or Judea from time immemorial, and it was the Romans who renamed the land "Palestine" in A. D. 70 as part of their effort to "de-judaize" the land and erase every vestige of the 1500-year Jewish presence in the land. As Jonathan Kellerman pointed out in a letter to the *New York Times Book Review*, "Palestine was chosen with mal-

◊ ◊ ◊

* Douglas Clyde MacIntosh admitted that the teaching is to be found in the Bible but that it is "incredible" that anyone in today's world would actually believe in it![4]

ice—recalling the Philistines, a tribe,whose vicious and chronic hatred of the Jews was well known and whom King David had vanqished."

He went on:

> The revisionist name endured through several other non-Jewish conquests and has since been adapted by the Arab movement of the 20th century, with a similar political agenda: recasting the return of the Jewish people to their homeland as colonial settling, and promulgating the fiction that the Arabs who migrated to the region several centuries after the Jews were conquered predated their cousins.[5]

The propriety and inevitability of the establishment of the Jewish state in the land should not be denied; indeed, there has always been a Jewish "presence" in the land through all centuries since the days of Moses and Joshua. But there has always been a non-Jewish "presence," also. Joshua and the children of Israel did not totally expel the Canaanites from the land. Through centuries of conquests and migrations other ethnic groups found representation. With the Roman destruction and expulsion of the bulk of the Jewish population, a vacuum was created into which many wandering Beduins entered. And with Jewish immigration in this century and increasing prosperity, many Arab peoples have come to benefit from the enlarging economic base in Israel, and their numbers have steadily increased. Notwithstanding the Arab-Israeli wars and the departure of many Palestinians, there remain 700,000 (832,000 if we include East Jerusalem) Arabs in Israel proper and well over 1,000,000 in the "occupied territories."

Debate over the land will continue and will not be easily solved, but Israel does not have a right to confiscate Arab land. Yet control of land that is seized in war is undeniable, and Americans would no more return Texas and California seized from Mexico in war than would Jews the land of the original borders of the United Nations partition of 1948. Yet some go so far as to state or imply that since God has given the land to the Jews in perpetuity, they have the right to take it all now. The doctrine of "greater Israel" is based on the original promise of God to give the offspring of Abraham a vast holding in the Middle East (cf. Genesis 15:18–21). In the Millennium Israel will possess this territory from Egypt to the Euphrates, but actual possession of the land promised is contingent on obedience and holiness (Deuteronomy 30:1–10).

Abraham, promised the whole land by God, nevertheless purchased property for the burial of Sarah (Genesis 23:1–20). David purchased land for an altar of praise from Araunah the Jebusite (2 Samuel 24:18ff.). He did not expropriate the land on the basis of God's promise to Abraham. Jeremiah purchased land as a testimony (Jeremiah 32).

Approximately 80 percent of the original land was taken and given for the establishment of the Hashemite Kingdom of Jordan in 1922 (an action recognized in international law by the League of Nations Mandate and also by a joint resolution of the United States Congress on September 21, 1922). The "Jordanian Option" as the solution to the "land" problem is advocated by some, but there never has been a "Palestinian State" as such west of the Jordan. Even when King Hussein and the Jordanians had opportunity, they never set a "Palestinian State" on the West Bank, nor the Egyptians, nor any Palestinian sovereignty in the Gaza, nor the Syrians on the Golan. The accords between Israel and the P. L. O are being pursued because of the collapse of the Soviet Union and the impossibly high price of continuing violence and tension. Yet it is difficult to be very optimitic about the long-term prospects. The Jews will never yield an inch on Jerusalem nor will the Arabs.

But whatever the shape and configuration of these negotiations and any agreement, all sides must seek justice. The rights of none should be abridged. If we argue for a Jewish right of return, we should recognize the right of Palestinian return. The Israelis have been at times overaggressive in their encroachments in the Arab section of the Old City and in East Jerusalem where even former Mayor Teddy Kollek has been at times alarmed at Israel's seizure of Arab land. *Christianity Today's* headline "Christians fear Jewish takeover of Old City."[6] perhaps reveals the potential for Jewish injustice. This is not right, and Christians with all others should stand for due process under law.

Many Israeli Jews recognize with regret that Israeli Arabs are second-class citizens. Some 50 percent of the Arabs in Israel are beneath the poverty line (compared with 17 percent of the Jews in Israel). The Arab dropout rate from school is five times the Jewish rate. Yosef Goell has written sensitively in the *Jerusalem Post* of "Israeli Arabs monumentally neglected."[7] Economically and politically they are subjugated. The souring relationship between the Jews and their Arab minority becomes all the more ominous when we realize that 50 percent of the Palestinians are under age 15, and 60 percent are under 20. Factors in economic deprivation are certainly security considerations in the light of the intifada and the massive Russian immigration. In a particularly awkward position are the Christian Arabs who feel really caught in the middle. Of special concern must be the Druse and Circassians, who have on the whole been very loyal to Israel and have fought in the IDF. [8]

The first president of Israel, Dr. Weizmann, used to say that how Israel treated her non-Jewish minorities would be a major judgment on the Jewish state. All of us must be concerned about our minority populations—this is an on-going reflection of our real commitment to biblical justice.

Some scholars seem to be in virtual despair about the problem.[9] Danny Rubinstein, a noted Israeli, has written movingly of the roots of the resurgence of Palestinian nationalism. He has theorized that short of returning to their original homes, many Palestinians might be satisfied were there the acknowledgment of their right to have a home ("an eerie reflection of the Zionist dream").[10] The growing "Peace Now" element in Israel continues to call for a two-state settlement. The typical Palestinian theology of liberation affords no hope for settlement.[11] Prominent Israelis see the perils of simply drifting on as things are.[12]

My concern is that Christians out of loyal identification with the fortunes of the Jewish state (which I profoundly share) cease to be concerned about justice for all. Read the almost daily accounts—the mounting tensions in Jerusalem,[13] the strife between old Arab and Jewish families,[14] and the struggles of any Palestinian family in Israel[15]—*and weep.* We do not honor our God by deprecating and despising any people—Jew or Arab. To treat others justly; that is our calling.

AN INVITATION TO HOPEFULNESS

Redeem Israel, O God, from all their troubles! (Psalm 25:22).

He provided redemption for his people; he ordained his covenant forever—holy and awesome is his name (Psalm 111:9).

Give thanks to the LORD, for he is good. . . . [he] brought Israel out from among them . . . and gave their land as an inheritance—his love endures forever. An inheritance to his servant Israel; his love endures forever (Psalm 136:1, 11, 21–22).

I understand Scripture and Christian theology to support Jewish aspiration for a national homeland in their historic and ancestral place of origin, and in the realpolitik of the Middle East I believe it imperative to stand with Israel in the defense of her borders and national security. In drawing upon a millennia of Jewish and Christian apocalyptic and prophecy, I stand as a premillennialist who would see developments with respect to a restoration of the nation of Israel in our time as having more than incidental significance for the unfolding of God's sovereign plan of the ages.

Theologically I have greatly treasured the Old Testament and the historic Christian moorings in the Old Testament. What James Adams said of the Puritans is true also in a limited sense of those who value the Old Testament:

> In spirit they may be considered Jews. Their God was the God of the Old Testament, their laws were the laws of the Old Testament, their guides to conduct were the character of the Old Testament.

I love the Jewish people, my spiritual forebears, and I'm delighted to see the beginnings of what David Baron wrote about in 1918:

It seems from Scripture that in relation to Israel and the land there will be a restoration, before the second advent of our Lord, of very much the same state of things as existed at the time of his first advent, when the threads of God's dealing with them nationally were—finally dropped, not to be taken up again"until the times of the Gentiles be fulfilled. So it will be again. There will be at first, as compared with the whole nation, only a representative minority in Palestine and a Jewish state will be probably formed, either under the suzerainty of one of the Great Powers, or under international protection. . . . Around this nucleus a large number more from all parts of the world will in all probability soon be gathered.[16]

The premillennial position pulsates with hopefulness. Although it takes seriously the sinfulness of man (and failure in both Israel and the church), premillennialism vibrates with hope because the last word for both Israel and the church is a divine "yes!" Both Testaments resonate with hope. Through the centuries chiliasm has pointed to the divine intervention of the Second Advent as the polestar of eager Christian expectation and motivation.* As deeply millennarian, Christian Zionism is upbeat on the future because the sovereign God is on His throne![†]

Though an ardent Christian Zionist, I have been called anti-Semitic for taking exception to Israeli government policy. The Millennium has not yet come, and some Israeli policy even in the eyes of many Israelis can be short-sighted and mistaken. Support for Israel should not be blind, sentimental, mindless support. To make American recognition of Jerusalem as the Israeli capital or to make the issuance of loan guarantees the litmus test of love for Israel, is extreme. Solidarity with Israel does not require allegiance to any particular political faction in Israel, and no Christian can pretend to speak for Israel.

What political scientist Daniel Elazar called "Israelotry" can be a peril for those of us who dearly love Israel. The nation of Israel can be and has been reprehensible at points, as has the United States. The Arabs made a serious mistake from the standpoint of their interests and rights

◊ ◊ ◊

* "Christianity had a well-developed millennialist doctrine by the second century, one that presented a picture of a future earthly paradise in the richest colors, of a heaven come down to earth. No other element of Christian thought has had as profound and far-reaching effect upon the whole world, not merely the West, as has its millennialist vision."—Robert Nisbet[17]

† Miliast enthusiasm has had critical significance in American history. Garry Wills argued in *Under God* that the mainstream of American religious life has always been evangelical, and that a recurring theme has been the hope of Israel. In characterizing Christian Zionism, however, *Christianity Today* has rightly raised the question as to whether some Christian Zionists are not in danger of running the "Israel—right or wrong" position into the ground. The point is well-taken.[18]

in a truculent opposition to any partition. Strong Zionists like Winston Churchill and T. E. Lawrence gave vigorous support to both Jewish and Arab claims for a sovereign state. Subscription to bottom-line hopefulness for Israel's future does not require an unreasoning or exclusive attachment to Israel. Commitment to fairness and justice will make hopefulness even more credible and convincing. Former President Nixon argued in his recent volume *Seize the Moment*, that Israelis and Arabs will keep on hating each other no matter what happens. As a Christian Zionist I rejoice—there is coming a day!

AN INVITATION TO VIGILANCE

He who watches over Israel will neither slumber nor sleep (Psalm 121:4).

They have greatly oppressed me from my youth. . . . May all who hate Zion be turned back in shame (Psalm 129:2a, 5).

For the LORD has chosen Jacob to be his own, Israel to be his treasured possession. The LORD will vindicate his people and have compassion on his servants (Psalm 135:4, 14).

The Lord God has committed Himself to continual surveillance over His ancient people. Such a promise has never entailed exemption from suffering or tragedy, but it does involve ultimate and eternal certainties, be it for nations or individuals. Christians, like God their Father, must be on the alert. They must steadfastly oppose this vicious plague of anti-Semitism wherever and whenever it rears its ugly face.

Recent reading has deeply impressed me with how endemic anti-Semitism really is. Peter Costello's biography of Jules Verne, the father of science fiction, who wrote 103 volumes in the last century, indicates how deeply anti-Semitic he was. A cradle Catholic, he left the church and was more of an anarchist, living an increasingly bleak life tinged with anti-Semitism.[19] The widely read Dutch-American historian of this century, Hendrik Van Loon, was very anti-Semitic.[20] Holocaust revisionists seem to be having a heyday. Research is uncovering how involved the Vatican and the Nazis were in opening escape routes for the most virulent anti-Semitic war criminals.[21]

Anti-Semitic computer games are being sold in Europe. In these games the players assume the role of Nazi commandant of a concentration camp and then amass points for torture of prisoners, extracting gold from their teeth, making their skin into lampshades, and selling their remains for soap.

The press tells us of the skinheads and the KKK in America. In his thoroughly documented study of Christian complacency and complicity in the years of Jewish persecution in Europe, Robert Ross of the University of Minnesota laid bare a lamentable history. He showed that the liberal *Christian Century* never seemed to grasp what was happening despite the evidence which was forthcoming. Rabbi Stephen Wise took exception to the *Century's* dismissal of Holocaust reports as "propaganda" in the strongest words:

> It would appear that you are more interested in seeking to prove that figures which I gave out in the name of five important Jewish organizations of America are inaccurate in respect to Jewish mass massacres in the Hitler-occupied countries than you are in making clear to American Christians how unspeakable has been the conduct of Hitlerism against the Jewish people.

Ross also has shown that evangelical and conservative publications were very slow and also tended to be unresponsive to the facts.[22]

Christians must take the lead in sensitivity to anti–Semitic behavior. We must publicly take our stand against anti-Semitism in any form. We must be concerned about media accuracy in reportage from the Middle East.

There are stirring examples of those who have paid a great price to befriend the Jews. Maximilian Kolbe was a Roman Catholic priest who died at Auschwitz. He was one of ten German prisoners who was deliberately starved to death in retaliation for helping one Jewish prisoner to escape. *Time* magazine carried the story of a Jewish cantor who reached out in his community to the Grand Dragon of the KKK who had been hounding him and ultimately transformed this enemy into a friend. [23]

Christians need to challenge hate and prejudice wherever it is found. In this we only emulate our Jewish Messiah.

AN INVITATION TO WITNESS

Peace be upon Israel (Psalm 128:6b).

O Israel, put your hope in the LORD, for with the LORD is unfailing love and with him is full redemption. He himself will redeem Israel from all their sins (Psalm 130:7–8).

O Israel, put your hope in the LORD both now and forevermore (Psalm 131:3).

Highly critical of the New England Puritans for their efforts to "proselytize" the Jews, Howard Y. Sachar disapprovingly quoted a prayer from Cotton Mather's diary in which he desires "the conversion of the Jewish nation, and for . . . [his] own having the happiness . . . to baptize a Jew, that should by . . . [his] ministry be brought home unto the Lord."[24] The very idea of seeking to win the Jews to Christ is unthinkable to some in the climate in which much modern ecumenism takes place. But unacceptable as it may be in some circles, it is only consistent with the premises of this study that the church of Jesus Christ takes with utmost seriousness the commission of her living Savior, "Make disciples of all nations" (Matthew 28:19). If Christianity is true and Christ is who He says He is (John 14:6; Acts 4:12), then the church has the joyous privilege to bear witness of Jesus Christ to the Jews. Christianity not only rose out of the same matrix as Judaism, it rose out of Judaism.[*] In recent years there has been deepening appreciation for the Jewishness of Jesus and the influence of Rabbinic Judaism with fewer voices stressing discontinuity and the marginality of Jesus' Judaism.[25]

The earliest followers of Jesus were all Jews and they were evangelists to their own people. Indeed Paul said:

> I am not ashamed of the gospel, because it is the power of God for the salvation of everyone who believes: first for the Jew, then for the Gentile (Romans 1:16).

The gospel is "first" for the Jew, not only historically and methodologically, but theologically.[26] Frans Delitzsch put it well: "For the church to evangelize the world without thinking of the Jews, is like a bird trying to fly with one broken wing."

Hudson Taylor used to begin each New Year by sending a check to the Hebrew Christian Testimony to Israel in London, marking it "to the Jew first." David Baron who received the gift always responded by sending his personal check to the China Inland Mission, of which Taylor was the founder, with the annotation: "and also to the Gentile."

There is an order here that local churches and denominations are obliged to observe.

The Holocaust and Paul Van Buren's argument that evangelism of the Jews is "theologically impossible" are all part of the same piece of cloth. The new Archbishop of Canterbury has declined to be patron of the church's Ministry Amongst the Jews in the interest of "trust and friendship between different faith communities."[27] The Archbishop participates in the interfaith Commonwealth Day Observance in Westminster

◇ ◇ ◇

[*] James Dunn well argued that Christianity and Judaism are siblings, with "contemporary Judaism the heir of a new non-Temple-centered interpretation of the covenant tradition developed at the same time the basic split occurred with Christianity."[28]

Abbey that omits the two stanzas in "All Creatures of our God and King" which refer to Jesus. Such is a pretty steep price to pay for congeniality at the expense of "the faith." The surrender of theological integrity cannot be an option however affable the atmosphere.

It is estimated that there are about 40,000 Jewish followers of Jesus in North America, 80 percent in Christian churches and the balance to be found in approximately 100 Messianic Jewish congregations. There is both a small overt group of Jewish believers in Israel proper and an underground church. [29]

A. A. Berle predicted that the establishment of the State of Israel would rejuvenate Judaism. He wrote: "One of the first results of the establishment of a Jewish state will be the rehabilitation of the religion of Israel throughout the world."[30] This has not taken place. Although there has been some stirring among the Orthodox Jews (primarily led by the Lubavitchers who are themselves proselytizers), the fact is that Jews are overwhelming non-religious.[31] Massive disaffiliation is in evidence in this country. Intermarriage has increased by five times in the last thirty years. Some Jews are moving toward "new-age Judaism" and the Aquarian Minyan.[32] In the face of this and the untrue caricatures of Christianity in circulation,[33] it would be a moral travesty for Christians not to share Christ and the gospel with our Jewish friends. Archimedes in ancient Greece could not repress announcing his discovery—eureka! eureka!—nor can we whom Christ has saved!

Jewish Christians are not stepchildren of God. Many Jews including rabbis have come to know Jesus as their Moshiach (Messiah).[34] Interestingly premillennial evangelicals have tended to spearhead Jewish missions.[*]

The road for the follower of Jesus is not an easy one. A rabbi told one young woman who had turned to Christ: "By converting, you have allowed Hitler to win another victory posthumously." But she could not move from Christ and His resurrection.[35]

When we are asked for bread, shall we give a stone? When asked for meat shall we give a serpent?

Sensitive and loving witness is mandatory. Arthur Kac, the articulate Hebrew Christian, put it this way:

◇ ◇ ◇

[*] Louis Meyer has chronicled the histories of some of the eminent Hebrew Christians of the last century, including Theodore J. Meyer, J. A. W. Neander (the great historian), Alfred Edersheim, A. A. Saphir, Joseph Wolf, and others.[36]

Israel is a remarkable people. Its history, perhaps —more than the history of any other nation— is a demonstration of the working out of God's faithfulness. If the Christian church will remain loyal to its Master, true to its confession and faithful to its commission, the Jew will continue to be reminded of his Jewishness, as long as Jewishness will be what it has come to be, a way of life from which God is left out. But the church must do more than this. She needs to search her heart and see in what areas she has failed in relation to Israel. She needs to stretch out her hand to Israel and, in a fresh outpouring of Christian love, seek for ways of a possible reconciliation. Then she may hasten the dawn of the day when Israel as a nation shall return to Jehovah and to its spiritual heritage. [37]

The methods and means of this essential witness should be lovingly and graciously and prayerfully focused. Our miracle-working God can change human life whether it be Jewish or Gentile. This is our confidence and this is our trust. To fail to bear such witness to our Jewish friends would be culpable and anti-Semitism.

AN INVITATION TO READINESS

Let Israel rejoice in their Maker; let the people of Zion be glad in their King (Psalm 149:2).

If Jesus returns tomorrow, then tomorrow I'll rest from my labor. But today I have work to do. I must continue the struggle until it's finished.— Dietrich Bonhoeffer

The Lord is near (Philippians 4:5b).

A final duty is incumbent on believers everywhere. In the light of Christ's commands to live in constant readiness for His return and in view of the constellation of signs of the approaching end of the age, particularly in relation to Israel, we need a strong and growing sense of spiritual urgency in the mission and ministry our Lord has entrusted to us.

We need to identify with Luther's passion: "I ardently hope that, amidst these internal dissensions on the earth, Jesus Christ will hasten the day of His coming." John Wesley was one with the Reformer at this point: "The spirit of adoption in the bride in the heart of every true believer says with earnest desire and expectation: COME AND ACCOMPLISH ALL THE WORDS OF THIS PROPHECY." It was as well the ardent longing of the saintly Samuel Rutherford: "Oh, that Christ would remove the covering, draw aside the curtains of time, and come down. Oh, that the shadows and the night were gone."

Although warned, American forces were unready when the Japanese attacked Pearl Harbor. Many Christians today live unprepared lives. A zeal in witness, holiness in life, living on the tiptoes of eagerness characterized the early believers. We are to be a "Maranatha" people who exude hope—"The Lord is coming!"

His coming is imminent, and we must assist others in boarding the ark of safety before the deluge of judgment falls. The promise stands: "The LORD swore an oath to David, a sure oath that he will not revoke: 'One of your descendants I will place on your throne' "(Psalm 132:11). THE KING IS COMING! As John Donne, the celebrated preacher of seventeenth-century England asked: "What if this present were the world's last night?"

APPENDIX

KEY STATEMENTS ABOUT THE
COVENANT CONCEPT IN THE OLD TESTAMENT

Johannes Behm	"There is no firmer guarantee of legal security, peace or personal loyalty than the covenant."[1]
Walter Eichrodt	The "covenant" is the central or unifying theme of the Old Testament.
Jacob Jocz	"According to the text the Abrahamic covenant is absolutely conditionless."[2]
Walter Kaiser	Genesis 17:1ff does not impose conditions upon the promissory covenant but parallels Genesis 12:1–3 (two imperatives are followed by two cohortative imperfects).[3]
Meredith Kline	Covenant in the Old Testament covers all such agreements and the book of Deuteronomy should be seen as such a covenant renewal document.[4]
Dennis McCarthy	The promissory covenant with Abram is unilateral and without "conditional elements."[5] Genesis 12:1–3 is like the bridal blessing of Numbers 24:9—there is an unconditional quality to the patriarchal blessing.[6]
Thomas McComiskey	The promise of Genesis 12 is placed in a covenant form in Genesis 15.[7]
George Mendenhall	"It is not often enough seen that no obligations are placed upon Abraham."[8]
J. Barton Payne	The promise of the land was unconditional (indeed the conquest by Joshua was seen as dependent on covenantal rights as in Nehemiah 9:8 and repossession after the exile similarly, of Nehemiah 9:32, 36).[9]
John A. Thompson	Studies have shown the parallels between the vassal treaties of the ancient Near East and the biblical covenants. Parity treaties and suzerainty treaties are to be distinguished, with possible stipulatory sections in the latter.[10]

NOTES

INTRODUCTION

1. Garry Wills, *Under God: Religion and American Politics* (New York: Simon and Schuster, 1990), 124.
2. Marvin Wilson, in "Christian Zionism— Israel Right or Wrong," *Christianity Today*, 9 March 1992, 50.
3. B. A. Asbury, "The Revolution in Jewish-Christian Relations: Is It To Be Found in Christian Theological Seminaries?" in *Theological Education*, Spring 1992, 60–73.
4. Wills, 24.

CHAPTER 1

1. For a beautiful study into the meaning of Israel as "the apple of his eye," see Charles Lee Feinberg, "Israel, the Apple of God's Eye," in *Israel in the Spotlight* (Wheaton, Ill.: Scripture Press, 1956), 19–23.
2. II am here assuming the substantial identity of those people known in ancient, medieval, and modern history as the Jews. Only a very few thinkers have argued otherwise, mainly anti-Semites influenced by an Austrian anthropologist and other very idiosyncratic writers like the Hungarian-born Jewish émigré, Arthur Koestler, who sought to show that contemporary Jews are descendants of the medieval Khazars from Russia, see *The Thirteenth Tribe* (London: Hutchinson, 1976). Koestler is well-known for his novel on communism entitled *Darkness at Noon* and for his *The Strange Case of the Mid-wife Toad*.
3. Barbara W. Tuchman, *Bible and Sword* (New York: Ballentine Books 1956), ix–x.
4. Paul Johnson, *A History of the Jews* (New York: Harper and Row, 1987), 2–3.
5. Martin Buber, *The Writings of Martin Buber* (New York: Meridian Books, 1956), 161. Buber's essay "Upon Eagle's Wings" (172–180) about the Jewish people is a classic.
6. Abraham Joshua Heschel, *Israel: An Echo of Eternity* (New York: Farrar, Straus and Giroux, 1967), 133ff.
7. George Ernest Wright, *The Old Testament Against Its Environment* (London: SCM, 1957), 47. This quotation is cited in William Klein's intriguing but not altogether convincing argument in *The New Chosen People* (Grand Rapids: Zondervan, 1990) that election is essentially corporate and not individual (somewhat after Karl Barth as critiqued in G.C. Berkouwer, *The Triumph of Grace in the Theology of Karl Barth* (Grand Rapids: Eerdmans, 1956), 89–122.
8. Sir Leonard Wooley, *Ur of the Chaldees* (London: Penguin, 1928, 1938, rev. 1950).
9. Johnson, 19.

10. The Hebrew word *segullah* is very rich and suggestive, see Franz Delitzsch, *Biblical Commentary on the Old Testament,* vol. 2 (Grand Rapids: Eerdmans, 1951), 96ff.

11. H. H. Rowley, *The Biblical Doctrine of Election* (London: Lutterworth, 1950).

12. Ibid., 39.

13. David L. Cooper, *Messiah: His Final Call to Israel* (Los Angeles: Biblical Research Society, 1962), 2ff.

14. Erich Sauer, *From Eternity to Eternity* (Grand Rapids: Eerdmans, 1954), 26-27. An older but very rewarding study is Henry Ostrom, *The Jew and His Mission* (Chicago: Bible Institute Colportage Association, 1923).

15. Sholom Aleichem, *Favorite Tales of Sholom Aleichem* (New York: Avenel Books, 1983).

16. See Donald E. Gowan, "The Centrality of Zion in Old Testament Theology," in *Eschatology in the Old Testament* (Philadelphia: Fortress, 1986), 4–20.

17. Claus Westermann, *The Promises to the Fathers: Studies on the Patriarchal Narratives* (Philadelphia: Fortress, 1960); Walter C. Kaiser, Jr., *Toward an Old Testament Theology* (Grand Rapids: Zondervan, 1978).

18. Jurgen Moltmann, *The Theology of Hope* (New York: Harper and Row, 1967), 105.

19. Arthur Kac, *The Rebirth of the State of Israel* (Chicago: Moody Press, 1958), 20.

20. Sauer, 122.

21. Thomas B. McComiskey, *The Covenants of Promise: A Theology of the Old Testament Covenants* (Grand Rapids: Baker, 1985), 59ff.

22. Walter C. Kaiser, Jr., *Toward Rediscovering the Old Testament* (Grand Rapids: Zondervan, 1962), 99.

23. Three relevant articles from *Bibliotheca Sacra* should be noted: Cleon Rogers, "The Covenant with Abraham and Its Historical Setting," July, 1970, 24lff.; Walter C. Kaise, Jr., "The Promised Land: A Biblical-Historical View," October-December 1981, 302ff.; Jeffrey L. Townsend, "Fulfillment of the Land Promise in the Old Testament," October-December 1985, 320ff.

24. Kaiser, 93.

25. McComiskey, 207, 209.

26. J. H. Kurtz, quoted in Wilbur M. Smith, "Prophecies Regarding Israel," in *Moody Monthly,* December 1958, 37.

27. Theodore Mueller, "Luther and the Bible," in *Inspiration and Interpetation,* ed. John F. Walvoord (Grand Rapids: Eerdmans, 1987), 87ff.

28. Smith, 39.

29. Barton Payne, *Encyclopedia of Biblical Prophecy* (Grand Rapids: Baker, 1973) p.137, 292. The whole matter of the apologetic value of ful-

filled prophecy will be dealt with later, but suffice it in passing to refer to Bernard Ramm, *Protestant Christian Evidences* (Chicago: Moody Press, 1953), 81-124; Josh McDowell, *Evidence That Demands a Verdict* (San Bernardino: Campus Crusade, 1972), 277–335.

30. Patrick Fairbairn, *The Prophetic Prospects of Jews* (Grand Rapids: Eerdmans, 1930). This is the basis for the famous "Fairbairn versus Fairbairn," by Albertus Pieters.

31. Sauer, 122.

32. Michael Wyschogrod, "But God Promised," *Context*, 1 June 1960, 1–2.

33. Gowan, 52.

34. Kaiser, 205.

35. Smith, 40. Note also the modern Hebrew scholar, Dr. Cyrus Gordon's words on Amos 9:14-15, as quoted in Wilbur M. Smith, *Israeli/ Arab Conflict and the Bible* (Ventura, Calif.: Gospel Light Press, 1968), 146: "These are the great words that make history. Centuries later in the time of Ezra and Nehemiah, people thought that these words were being fulfilled. But history has shown that the Second Commonwealth was not the fulfillment of Amos's prophecy. Yet Amos's immortal words will continue to cry out for fulfillment until every promise comes true. His words are inseparable from the vigor of Israel down to the present time; and his message of hope has encouraged Israel to survive millennia of disaster." (From his *Introduction to Old Testament Times*, 1953, 215).

CHAPTER 2

1. O. Palmer Robertson, *The Christ of the Covenant* (Grand Rapids: Baker, 1980); cf. also John S. Feinberg, ed., *Continuity and Discontinuity: Perspectives on the Relationship Between the Old and New Testaments* (Wheaton, Ill.: Crossway, 1988).

2. For reference on the prophets generally, see Edward J. Young, *My Servants the Prophets* (Grand Rapids: Eerdmans, 1952); H. L. Ellison, *Men Spake from God* (London: Patermoster, 1952).

3. Charles C. Ryrie, *The Basis of the Premillennial Faith* (Neptune, N.J.: Loizeaux, 1953), 44.

4. R. E. Clements, "The Messianic Hope in the Old Testament," in *Journal for the Study of the Old Testament* 43 (1989), 3–19.

5. H. L. Ellison, *The Centrality of the Messianic Idea for the Old Testament* (London: Tyndale, 1953), 6.

6. The classic work is E. W. Hengstenberg, *Christology of the Old Testament*, 4 vols. (Grand Rapids: Kregel, 1958)—the reprint of the British edition of 1872–78); see also the well-known study by the Hebrew Christian, Alfred Edersheim, "List of Old Testament Passages Messianically Applied in Rabbinic Writings," Appendix IX,

The Life and Times of Jesus the Messiah, II, (Grand Rapids: Eerdmans, 1953), II, 710–741.

7. J. Barton Payne, *Encyclopedia of Biblical Prophecy* (Grand Rapids: Baker, 1973), 665–668.

8. John Bright, *The Authority of the Old Testament* (Nashville: Abingdon, 1967), 78, 112.

9. "Scrolls mention 'piercing' of a Messiah," in *The Jerusalem Post*, 16 November 1991.

10. Willem Van Gemeren, *Interpreting the Prophetic Word* (Grand Rapids: Zondervan, 1990), 371. This is a superlative and compendious study.

11. Robert P. Lightner, *The Last Days Handbook* (Nashville: Thomas Nelson, 1990), 141. The *Scofield Reference Bible* also teaches that both Israel and the church are beneficiaries of the new covenant (see p. 1297 on Hebrews 8:8). For a helpful discussion see Craig A. Blaising, "Doctrinal Development in Orthodoxy," in two parts, in *Bibliotheca Sacra* (April–June 1988 and July–September 1988), 277–278. For a substantial critique of "Covenantal Theology," note Renald E. Showers, *There Really is a Difference! A Comparison of Covenant and Dispensational Theology* (Bellmawr, N.J.: Friends of Israel, 1990), 19–25.

12. Geerhardus Vos, *Biblical Theology* (Grand Rapids: Eerdmans, 1948), 321.

13. Van Gemeren, 82–83.

14. Erich Sauer, *The Dawn of World Redemption* (London: Patermoster, 1951), 97.

15. William E. Blackstone (W.E.B.). *Jesus is Coming* (Old Tappan, N.J.: Revell, 1898), 20, 46.

16. Paul D. Feinberg, "Hermeneutics of Discontinuity," in John S. Feinberg, ed., 118–199.

17. Richard N. Longenecker, *Biblical Exegesis in the Apostolic Period* (Grand Rapids: Eerdmans, 1975).

18. R. B. Girdlestone, *The Grammar of Prophecy* (Grand Rapids: Kregel, 1955), 138.

19. Ibid., 57.

20. E. F. Scott in George E. Ladd, *Crucial Questions about the Kingdom of God* (Grand Rapids: Eerdmans, 1952), 31.

21. Ladd, 81. As Ladd shows, the kingdom of God is the sovereign rule of God. Ladd is superb in his delineation of both the present and future forms of the kingdom, the now, and the not yet aspects of God's rule. Yet Ladd is perhaps too skittish about seeing kingdom as also involving sphere and domain. In his strong insistence that the kingdom is soteriological (and since the work of God is ultimately one, all of its calibrated nuances share a dynamic unity),

Ladd may well be faulted for underemphasizing the governmental aspects of the kindgom, i.e. the political and theocratic dimensions.

22. Erich Sauer, *The King of the Earth* (Grand Rapids: Eerdmans, 1962).
23. For thoughtful surveys of the history of the kingdom, cf. Ray B. Baughman, *The Kingdom of God Visualized* (Chicago: Moody, 1971); Herbert VanderLugt, *God's Plan in All Ages* (Grand Rapids: Zondervan, 1979.
24. A. B. Bruce, *The Kingdom of God* (Edinburgh: T & T Clarke, 1891).
25. George E. Ladd, 80.
26. For serious and rewarding studies of the mediatorial kingdom, cf. Alva J. McClain, *The Greatness of the Kingdom* (Grand Rapids : Zondervan 1959); John F. Walvoord, *The Millennial Kingdom* (Grand Rapids: Zondervan, 1959); J. Dwight Pentecost, *The Shape of Things to Come* (Findley, Ohio: Dunham, 1958).
27. McClain, 217–54.
28. Erich Sauer, *The Triumph of the Crucified* (London: Patermoster, 1951), 22.
29. Robert L. Saucy, "The Presence of the Kingdom and the Life of the Church," in *Bibliotheca Sacra*, January–March 1988. Cf. also Lewis Sperry Chafer, *The Kingdom in History and Prophecy* (Findlay, Ohio: Dunham, 1915).
30. Alphin C. Conrad, "The Kingdom Hope of Israel in the Old Testament," in *Bethel Seminary Quarterly*, Winter 1958, 4–12.
31. Herman A. Hoyt in Robert G. Clouse, *The Meaning of the Millennium* (Downers Grove, Ill.: IVP, 1977), 67–68.
32. Ibid., 67.
33. Desmond Ford, *The Abomination of Desolation in Biblical Eschatology* (Washington, D.C.: University Press of America, 1979), 25, 73, 112, 1121, 156.
34. A. T. Pierson, *Many Infallible Proofs* (London: Morgan and Scott, n.d.), 48–78. For an important treatment of what may appear to be unfulfilled prophecies, see Walter Kaiser, Jr. *Back Toward the Future* (Grand Rapids: Baker, 1989), 61–68.
35. Charles Gore in A. E. J. Rawlinson, *The Gospel According to St. Mark,* Westminster Commentaries (London: Methuen, 1949), 180.
36. Albert Schweitzer in Ford, 7.
37. H. T. Andrews, "The Significance of the Eschatological Utterances of Jesus," in *London Theological Studies*, 1911.
38. Ford, 9.
39. For contrasting viewpoints but helpful exegetical studies, see Arno C. Gaebelein, *The Olivet Discourse* (Grand Rapids: Baker, 1969); J. Marcellus Kik, *Matthew Twenty-Four* (Swengel, Pa.: Bible Truth Depot, 1948).
40. G. R. Beasley-Murray, *Jesus and the Future* (London: Macmillan 1954), 104.

41. Ford, 117.
42. I follow Lohmeyer, Schniewind, Michaelis, and many others.
43. Henry Alford, *The New Testament* (Chicago: Moody, n.d.), 169.

CHAPTER 3

1. John Urquhart, *The Wonders of Prophecy, 2 vols.* (New York: The Christian Alliance Publishing Co., 1925) and George T. B. Davis, *Fulfilled Prophecies That Prove the Bible* (Philadelphia: Million Testaments Campaign, 1931).
2. Elmer A. Martens, *Motivations for the Promise of Israel's Restoration to the Land in Jeremiah and Ezekiel* (Ph.D. dissertation, Claremont Graduate School, 1972).
3. Ibid.
4. Hans LaRondelle and others hold this view.
5. This view has long been associated with C. H. Dodd. See Hans K. LaRondelle, *The Israel of God in Prophecy* (Berrien Springs, Mich.: Andrews University Press, 1983).
6. J. Barton Payne retained the ethnic and geographical points of reference.
7. Frank M. Cross, *The Ancient Life of Qumran* (Garden City, N.Y.: Doubleday, 1958), 78, n. 36a.
8. We are not imposing a Jewish application on Matthew as R. H. Gundry alleges. In contrast see W. D. Davies, *The Gospel and the Land: Early Christianity and Jewish Territorial Decline* (Berkeley: University of California, 1974).
9. Victor Gordon, "Eschatology as the Structure of New Testament Theology," in *Theology News and Notes*, June 1983, in the Tribute to George Ladd, 12.
10. Mandell Lewittes, *Religious Foundations of the Jewish State: The Concept and Practice of Jewish Statehood from Biblical Times to the Modern State of Israel* (New York: Ktav Publishing House, 1977).
11. R. H. Charles, *Eschatology: the Doctrine of a Future Life in Israel, Judaism and Christianity* (New York: Schocken, 1963), 103–104.
12. Conzelman argued this view of Luke's writings.
13. Davies, *The Gospel and the Land*, 184.
14. Ibid., 275.
15. C. K. Barrett sharply differentiates Platonic idealism from eschatological emphases in Hebrews which have as their premise that what the prophets spoke remains steadfast.
16. Eadie, Ellicott, Zahn, and Burton support the references to ethnic Israel.
17. W. D. Davies, *Paul and Rabbinic Judaism* (London: SPCK, 1948), 82.
18. Ibid., 367.

CHAPTER 3

19. Henry J. Cadbury in W. D. Davies and D. Daube, *The Background of the New Testament and Eschatology* (Cambridge: Cambridge Press, 1964), 315.

20. This is important substantiation for our thesis in view of the widespread influence in our times of C. H. Dodd who contemporized eschatology (in his so-called "realized eschatology") and was allergic to apocalyptic.

21. Barrett, 374.

22. Charles Lee Feinberg, *Hosea: God's Love for Israel* (New York: American Board of Missions to the Jews, 1947), 20. For a splendid exegetical treatment, see John A. Battle, "Paul's Use of the Old Testament in Romans 9:25–26," in *Grace Theological Journal* 2:1 Spring 1981.

23. Peter C. Craigie, *Twelve Prophets* in *Daily Study Bible Series* (Philadelphia: Westminster, 1984), I, 17.

24. Davies, *Paul and Rabbinic Judaism*, 85.

25. Tom Schreiner, "Israel's Failure to Attain Righteousness in Romans 9:30–10:3," in *Trinity Journal*, n.s., 12, (1991), 209–220.

26. George E. Ladd, *The Last Things* (Grand Rapids: Eerdmans, 1978), 25.

27. C. I. Scofield and others may have claimed too much for this passage, but it does help us understand how the early church viewed Old Testament prophecy.

28. Even Adam Clarke concedes this.

29. Charles Zimmerman, "To This Agree the Words of the Prophets" in *Grace Theological Journal*, 4:3, 28–40.

30. F. F. Bruce thought it was the resurrection of Christ.

31. John F. Walvoord, *The Millennial Kingdom* (Grand Rapids: Zondervan, 1959), 205.

32. Yehuda Bauer, in "Last Word" by Prof. Clement Graham in *Christian Witness to Israel Herald*, December 1988–February 1989, 20.

33. Johannes Munck, *Christ and Israel* (Philadelphia: Fortress, 1967), 12; Munck agrees with Bernard Weiss that the promise of the Second Coming presupposes the conversion of Israel; See also William Sanday and Arthur C. Headlam, *Epistle to the Romans* (New York: Scribner's 1896), ICC, 264.

34. Ibid., 21.

35. Ladd, 28.

36. S. Lewis Johnson, "Israel's Covenant and History," Founder's Lectures at Trinity Evangelical Divinity School, February 1987.

37. Munck, p. 66.

38. Willem Van Gemeren, "Israel as Hermeneutical Crux in the Interpretation of Prophecy," *Westminster Theological Journal*, Spring 1984, 256.

39. Charles Hodge, *Epistle to the Romans* (Grand Rapids: Eerdmans, 1953).

40. H. L. Ellison, *The Mystery of Israel* (Grand Rapids: Eerdmans, 1966), 11.

41. G. C. Berkhouwer, *The Return of Christ* (Grand Rapids: Eerdmans, 1972), 331.

42. Karl Barth, *Church Dogmatics III,* 3, 199, 218.

43. Martyn Lloyd-Jones, *"The Future of the Jews"* in *Israel Herald,* 7.

44. Martyn Lloyd-Jones, *"Life from the Dead,"* 12.

45. John Murray, *Romans* (Grand Rapids: Eerdmans, 1967), NICNT II, 99.

46. C. E .B. Cranfield, *Romans,* (Edinburgh: T. and T. Clark, 1979), ICC; C. K. Barrett, *Romans* (New York: Harper, 1967).

47. Elliott E. Johnson, *Expository Hermeneutics: An Introduction* (Grand Rapids: Zondervan, 1990), 251.

48. Hendrikus Berkhof, *Christian Faith* (Grand Rapids: Eerdmans, 1979), 340.

49. Erich Sauer, *The Triumph of the Crucified* (London: Patermoster, 1951), 153.

50. George E. Ladd, *The Gospel of the Kingdom* (Grand Rapids: Eerdmans, 1959), 42–43.

51. In notes of J. Barton Payne, *Encyclopedia of Bible Prophecy* (Grand Rapids: Baker, 1973), 548; cf. Geerhardus Vos, *Paulines Eschatology* (Grand Rapids: Eerdmans, 1953), 226ff.

52. This is the terminology of Vos.

53. Daniel T. Taylor, *The Voice of the Church on the Coming Kingdom* (New York: H. L. Hastings, 1855), 23.

54. Ibid., 10.

55. Alva J. McClain, *The Greatness of the Kingdom* (Grand Rapids: Zondervan, 1959), 443.

56. G. H. Pember, *The Great Prophecies Concerning the Gentiles, the Jews, and the Church of God* (Miami Springs, Fla.: Conley and Schoettle, 1984), 450.

57. McClain, 442.

58. Nathanial West, *The Thousand Years in Both Testaments* (New York: Revell, 1880), 380ff. For a survey of competing millennial options, see Robert G. Clouse, *The Meaning of the Millennium* (Downers Grove, Ill.: IVP, 1977); for a lucid and convincing treatment from a premillennial perspective, see Robert D. Culver, *Daniel and the Latter Days: A Study in Millennialism* (Westwood, N.J.: Revell, 1954).

59. Henry V. Frost, *Matthew Twenty-four and the Revelation* (Oxford: Oxford University Press, 1924).

60. J. Marcellus Kik, *Revelation Twenty* (Philadelphia: Presbyterian and Reformed, 1955), 46.

CHAPTER 4

61. Jack S. Deere, "Premillenialism in Revelation 20:4-6," in *Bibliotheca Sacra*, January–March 1978, 58–73.
62. Philip B. Hughes, "The First Resurrection: Another Interpretation" in *Westminster Theological Journal*, 39, Spring 1977, 315–18.

CHAPTER 4

1. Paul Johnson, *A History of the Jews* (New York: Harper and Row, 1987), 3.
2. Gerhart Riegner in Howard M. Sachar, *Diaspora* (New York: Harper and Row, 1985), 1.
3. Johnson, 13.
4. John W. Wright, "Who is a Jew?" in *Biblical Research Monthly*, July–August 1978, 18–19.
5. Erich Sauer, *From Eternity to Eternity* (Grand Rapids: Eerdmans, 1954); 27ff.
6. Proponents of British Israelism are Adam Rutherford, N. J. Fuller-Good, Edward Hine, F. R. A. Glover, W. H. Poole, J. H. Allen, Howard B. Rand.
7. R. B. Girdlestone, *The Grammar of Prophecy* (Grand Rapids: Kregel, 1955), 126.
8. For a significant refutation of British-Israelites, see Allen H. Godbey, *The Lost Tribes—A Myth* (New York: Ktav Publishing House, 1974); Anton Darms, *The Delusion of British Israelism* (Neptune, N.J.: Loizeaux Brothers, 1938); Richard DeHaan, *British-Israelism* (Grand Rapids: Radio Bible Class, 1969).
9. For helpful historical resources on this period, see William Fairweather, *The Background of the Gospels* (Edinburgh: T. & T. Clark, 1908); Stewart Perowne, *The Life and Times of Herod the Great* (Nashville: Abingdon, 1958); *The Later Herods* (Nashville: Abingdon, 1958).
10. Michael Grant, *The Jew in the Roman World* (New York: Scribner's, 1973), 189.
11. Primary source material is Flavius Josephus, *Antiquities of the Jews* and *Wars of the Jews*.
12. H. Graetz, *Popular History of the Jews* (New York: Hebrew Publishing Co., 1919), 232.
13. Emil Schurer, *A History of the Jewish People in the Time of Jesus* (1891; reprint, New York: Schocken, 1961), 275.
14. Graetz, 367.
15. Berl Locker, *Covenant Everlasting: Palestine in Jewish History* (New York: Sharon Books, 1947), 109, 113.
16. Edward Gibbon, *The Decline and Fall of the Roman Empire*, vol. 1 (Chicago: Great Books, 1952), 354.
17. Schurer, 308.
18. Locker, 78.

19. Schurer, 417.
20. Diane and Meier Gillon, *The Sand and the Stars: The Story of Jewish People* (New York: Lothrop, Lee and Shepard Co., 1971), 100.
21. Stanley A. Ellisen, *Who Owns the Land?* (Portland, Ore.: Multomah, 1991), 33.
22. Johnson, 149.
23. John Phillips, *Exploring the World of the Jew* (Chicago: Moody, 1988), 54.
24. I am indebted to my good friend, Rev. Harold McClure, for referring me to Joseph Wolff, *Narrative of a Mission to Bokara in the Years* 1843-1845 (New York: Harper, 1945), 26ff.
25. *The World History of the Jewish People*, vol. 2, ed. Cecil Roth, "The Dark Ages," (Jerusalem: Jewish History Publications, 1961), 14. This is an epochal set of books.
26. Leo Rosten, *The Joys of Yiddish* (New York: Pocket Books, 1968), 338.
27. Eugene Sue, *The Wandering Jew* (New York: The Modern Library, n.d.).
28. Gibbon, 607.
29. A well-researched historical novel on the Marranos is Lilane Webb, *The Marranos* (New York: Pocket Books, 1980).
30. Will Durant, *Rosseau and Revolution,* The Story of Civilization, X (New York: Simon and Schuster, 1967), 632.
31. Johnson, 236ff.
32. Ibid., 258.
33. For authentic samples of life in the shtetls of eastern Europe, see the novels by Isaac Bashevis Singer, such as *Scum* (New York: Farrar, Strauss & Giroux, 1990) and also the novels by his brother, I. J. Singer. They were raised on Krochmalna Street in Warsaw.
34. Phillips, 75–87. For a most informative overview, of "History of the Jews in the USSR," in *The Chosen People*, July, September 1990.
35. Abraham Rabinovich, "Following the Apostate Messiah," in *Jerusalem Post*, 27 July 1991, 16.
36. For enlightening insights into Jewish-Chinese life, see Pearl S. Buck's carefully prepared novel entitled *Peony* and also Jonathan D. Spence, *The Memory Palace of Matteo Ricci* (New York: Penguin, 1983), the admirably researched study of a Jesuit priest who went to China in the sixteenth century at the time of the Ming Dynasty and had extensive contacts with the Jews there at the time.
37. Sachar, *Diaspora*, 374ff.
38. Max I. Dimont, *The Indestructible Jew* (New York: New America Library, 1971), 22ff.
39. Ibid., 439ff.
40. For glimpses into Argentine Jewry's mottled experience, see Jacob Timerman, *Prisoner Without a Name, Cell Without a Number* (New

York: Random House, 1981); "Despite Changes, Town Remains a Haven for Jews," *Chicago Tribune*, 3 May 1991, 6.

41. Lawrence Meyer, *Israel Now: Portrait of a Troubled Country* (New York: Delacorte, 1981).

CHAPTER 5

1. Rolfe Humphries, trans., *Satires of Juvenal* (Bloomington, Ind.: Indiana University Press, 1978), XIV, 94.

2. David A. Rausch, *A Legacy of Hatred* (Grand Rapids: Baker, 1984, 1990), 36.

3. Bernard Lewis, *Semites and Anti-Semites* (New York: W.W. Norton, 1986), 46.

4. Gavin I. Langmuir, *Toward a Definition of Anti-semitism* (Berkeley: University of California Press, 1991).

5. Quoted in David A. Rausch, 97.

6. Flavius Josephus, *Antiquities,* trans. William Whiston (Philadelphia: David McKay, n.d.), XI, 8.

7. Richard E. Gade, *A Historical Survey of Anti-semitism* (Grand Rapids: Baker, 1981), 12. For the best and most thorough work in this area, see the multivolume work of S.W. Baron, *A Social and Religious History of the Jews* (New York and Philadelphia: Columbia University Press and The Jewish Publication Society of America, 1973).

8. Dennis Prager and Joseph Telushkin, *Why the Jews? The Reason for Anti-semitism* (New York: Simon and Schuster, 1987).

9. Samuel Sandmel, *The First Christian Century in Judaism and Christianity: Certainties and Uncertainties* (Oxford: Oxford University Press, 1969), 22.

10. Jacob Neusner, *The Ecology of Religion: From Writing to Religion in the Study of Judaism* (Nashville: Abingdon Press, 1989). Neusner has written more than 200 books, including the definitive multivolume history and analysis of Babylonian Jewry.

11. Nancy Rubin, *Isabella of Castille: The First Renaissance Queen* (New York: St. Martin's Press, 1991), 178. An outstanding treatment.

12. Ibid., 7.

13. Ibid., 204. For evaluation of Columbus and the current controversy on the 500th anniversary of the commencement of the voyage, see "Debunking Columbus," by Stephen Gode, in *Insight*, 21 October 1991, 10–17; also "The Columbus Controversy" by John Maust and some analysis of his very devout *Book of Prophecies* given by Kay Brigham in *Latin American Evangelist*, January–March 1992 6–11. The definitive denial that Columbus was a Marrano is in Samuel Eliot Morrison's superb *Admiral of the Ocean Sea* (Boston: Little, Brown and Co., 1942). Two fine historical novels on the Expulsion are Mayer Abramowitz' *Sacred Sword* and the Mexican novelist Homero Aridjis' *1492: The Life and Times of Juan Cabezon of Castile.*

A helpful analysis of Ladino (and comparison with Yiddish) is Eli Kenan, "A Jealously Guarded Tongue," *Jerusalem Post*, 12 October 1991, 19.

14. Edward H. Flannery, *The Anguish of the Jews: Twenty-three Centuries of Anti-semitism* (Mahwah, N.J.: Paulist Press, 1987).

15. Rosemary Reuther, quoted in Joseph B. Tyson, ed., *Luke-Acts and the Jewish People* (Minneapolis: Augsburg, 1988), 11.

16. Leon Poliakov, *The History of Anti-semitism* (New York: Vanguard, 1965) II, 272. This multivolume work translated from the French is indispensable.

17. F. F. Bruce, "Are the Gospels Anti-Semitic?" in *Eternity*, November, 1973, 11ff.; in the same issue—Paul Maier, "Did Anti-Semitism Distort the Crucifixion Story?" These articles show the efforts of responsible evangelicals to wrestle with these issues. See also Louis A. Barbieri, Jr., "That Incredible Mistrial," *Moody Monthly*, April 1973.

18. Poliakov, III, 472.

19. Tyson, 28, 34, 54.

20. Lewis, 106.

21. Poliakov, II, 165ff.

22. Littell, *The Crucifixion of the Jews* (New York: Harper, 1975), 2.

23. Heiko A. Oberman, *Luther: Man Between God and the Devil* (New Haven, Conn.: Yale, 1982), 296.

24. Poliakov, III, 280.

25. Ibid., 181.

26. Ibid., 42.

27. Ibid., 75.

28. "Israel Philharmonic to Play Wagner," *Chicago Tribune*, 16 December 1991; "The Case of Wagner—Again," in *Time*, 13 January 1992, 57.

29. Yakov Rapoport, *The Doctor's Plot of 1953* (Cambridge, Mass.: Harvard University Press, 1991).

30. Daniel Wattenberg, "A Venomous Tree Grows in Brooklyn," in *Insight*, 7 October 1991, 18–20.

31. Richard K. Tucker, *The Dragon and the Cross: The Rise and Fall of the Ku Klux Klan in Middle America* (Hamden, Conn.: Archon Books, 1991).

32. William F. Buckley, Jr., "In Search of Anti-Semitism," in *National Review*, 30 December 1991, 20–62.

33. Littell, 82, n. 29.

34. Paul Johnson, *A History of the Jews* (New York: Harper, 1987), 246.

35. Gabriel Sivan, "Abrabanel on Pirke Avot," In *Jerusalem Post*, December, 1991, 16.

36. Rubin, 302.

37. Ibid., 310, 422.

38. Bernt Engelmann, *Germany Without Jews* (New York: Bantam, 1984).
39. Paul R. Carlson, *O Christian! O Jew!* (Elgin, Ill.: David C. Cook, 1974). This is a very splendid little book, and Carlson quotes the quatrain but may have indeed written it.

CHAPTER 6

1. Charles Krauthammer, "Judging Israel" in *Time*, 26 February 1990, 77.
2. For a very well-researched, fictionalized series of historical studies, the superb work of Bodie Thoene cannot be surpassed. The six volumes of *The Zion Covenant* series treat the road to the Holocaust, and the five volumes of *The Zion Chronicles* deal with the establishment of the State of Israel. The *Shiloh Legacy* series describes events on the American side of the Atlantic. These books are published by Bethany House Publishers.
3. Yehuda Bauer in M. S. Littell, *The Holocaust: Forty Years After* (Lewiston, N.Y.: Edwin Mellen Press, 1989), xi.
4. "Holocaust toll higher, papers show," in *Chicago Tribune*, 16 December 1991, 12.
5. From a 26 January 1992 *Doonesbury* strip. For the appalling documentation of such hate instances, see David A. Rausch, *A Legacy of Hatred: Why Christians Must Not Forget the Holocaust*, 2d ed. (Grand Rapids: Baker, 1990), 8ff.
6. "Holocaust survivor wins his battle" in *Jerusalem Post*, 28 September 1985.
7. "Court approves suit in Holocaust Issue" in *The Los Angeles Times*, January 25, 1992, Bl; "Holocaust" in *Chicago Tribune*, 8 May 1990, 5; "The moral truth of the Holocaust" in *Chicago Tribune*, 26 February 1992, 17.
8. Yehuda Bauer, *The Holocaust in Historical Perspective* (Seattle: University of Washington Press, 1978); Lucy S. Dawidowicz, *The Holocaust and the Historians* (Cambridge: Harvard University Press, 1981).
9. Rausch, 8.
10. Lawrence L. Langer, *Holocaust Testimonies* (New Haven, Conn.: Yale University Press, 1990).
11. Dawidowicz, 22ff.
12. "Red Cross to catalog, clarify Holocaust victims' fate" in *Chicago Tribune*, 12 February 1992.
13. Tamar Vital, "Jewish Hero, Polish Saint" in *Jerusalem Post*, 15 February 1992, 12.
14. Elie Wiesel, "Some Words for Children of Survivors," in M. S. Littell, *The Holocaust: Forty Years After*, 15.
15. Paul Johnson, *A History of the Jews* (New York: Harper and Row, 1987), 483.

16. Gordon J. Horowitz, *In the Shadow of Death: Living Outside the Gates of Mauthausen* (London: I. B. Tauris, 1919).
17. Tom Segev, *Soldiers of Evil: The Commandants of the Nazi Concentration Camps* (New York: McGraw-Hill, 1987).
18. Helen Epstein, *Children of the Holocaust* (New York: Penguin, 1979, Another very moving series of case studies is Peter Sichrovsky, *Abraham's Children: Israel's Younger Generation* (New York: Pantheon, 1991).
19. Raul Hilberg, *The Destruction of the European Jews* (New York: New Viewpoints, 1973). This is the *locus classicus* of documentation. Professor Hilberg is from the University of Vermont.
20. Siegfried Jagendorf, *Jagendorf's Foundry*: *Memoir of the Romanian Holocaust 1941–1944* (New York: HarperCollins, 1991).
21. Alexander Stille, *Benevolence and Betrayal: Five Italian Jewish Families Under Fascism* (New York: Summit Books, 1991); Fabio Della Sea, *The Tiber Afire* (New York: Marlboro, 1991).
22. George M. Kren and Leon Rappoport, *The Holocaust and the Crisis of Human Behavior* (New York: Holmes and Meier, 1980), 89.
23. David A. Rausch, 15.
24. Samuel Willenberg, *Surviving Treblinka* (Oxford: Blackwell, 1991); Azriel Eisenberg, *Witness to the Holocaust—150 Eyewitness Accounts* (New York: Pilgrim Press, 1975); George Topas, *The Iron Furnace: A Holocaust Survivor's Story* (Lexington: University of Kentucky Press, 1991).
25. Peter Sichrovsky, *Strangers in Their Own Land: Young Jews in Germany and Austria Today* (New York: Penguin, 1986).
26. Tom Segev, *The Seventh Million: The Israelis and the Holocaust* (Jerusalem: Domino Press, 1991).
27. Emil L. Fackenheim, *To Mend the World* (New York: Schocken, 1982).
28. David A. Rausch, 130.
29. J. Willard O'Brien in M.S. Littell, *The Holocaust*, 49.
30. Michael Aronson, *Troubled Waters: Origins of the 1881 Anti-Jewish Pogroms in Russia* (Pittsburgh: University of Pittsburgh Press, 1919); Don Levin, *Tekufa Besograim* (The Period in Brackets): *The Jews in the Soviet Territories* 1939–1941 (Jerusalem: Hebrew University Institute for Contemporary Jewry, 1990).
31. Sholom Aleichem, *The Bloody Hoax* (Bloomington: Indiana University, 1919).
32. Paul Johnson, *Birth of the Modern* (New York: HarperCollins, 1991), 142.
33. Otto Pflanze, *Bismarck and the Development of Germany*, 3 vols. (Princeton: Princeton University Press, 1991).
34. George M. Kren and Leon Rappoport, 20.
35. S. S. Prawer, *Heine's Jewish Comedy* (Oxford: Clarendon, 1983).
36. Yehuda Bauer, 78.

37. Edwin S. Gaustad, *Liberty of Conscience: Roger Williams in America* (Grand Rapids: Eerdmans, 1919), 96, 140, 176, 219.
38. Stephen Goode, "The Unequivocal Heavy of Being," in *Insight*, 9 March 1992, 12ff.
39. Yehuda Bauer, 78.
40. David S. Wyman, *The Abandonment of the Jews: American and the Holocaust* 1941–1945 (New York: Pantheon, 1984).
41. Paul Johnson, *A History of the Jews*, 504.
42. Jan Karski in M.S. Littell, *The Holocaust*, 34.
43. "Church ends pogrom rite" in *Jerusalem Post*, 15 February 1992.
44. Rolf Hochmuth, *The Deputy* (New York: Grove Press, 1964).
45. Irving Halperin, "Victim, Fighter, Martyr: Literature of the Concentration Camps," in *The Christian Century*, 25 July 1962, 907ff.
46. Viktor E. Frankl, *Man's Search for Meaning* (New York: Washington Square, 1963). See also Auschwitz victim Etty Hillesum's moving *An Interrupted Life* (New York: Washington Square, 1985).
47. Jean Amery, *At the Mind's Limits: Contemplation by a Survivor of Auschwitz and its Realities* (New York: Schocken, 1986). This volume interacts with the thinking of the notable Italian survivor of Auschwitz, Primo Levi, whose point-of-view is quite in contrast.
48. John Bierman, *Odyssey* (New York: Simon and Schuster, 1984).
49. Yaffa Eliach, *Hasidic Tales of the Holocaust* (New York: Avon, 1982).
50. Quoted by Paul Tillich, *The Shaking of the Foundations* (New York: Schribner's, 1948), 165.
51. Johnson, 514.
52. Rausch, 15.
53. Alan Adelson and Robert Lapides, eds., *Lodz Ghetto: Inside a Community Under Siege* (New York: Viking, 1990); Leni Yahil, *The Holocaust: The Fate of European Jewry* (New York: Oxford University Press, 1991). In my experience, probably the most moving of all the eyewitness accounts is that of Martin Gray, *For Those I Love*. This is the account of one who survived the Warsaw ghetto.
54. Ehud Sprinzak, *The Ascendance of Israel's Radical Right* (New York: Oxford University Press, 1991), 123.
55. Ibid., 165.
56. Ibid., 270.
57. Ibid., 273.
58. Dawidowicz, *The Holocaust and the Historians*, 18.
59. Stephen Larsen and Robin Larsen, *A Fire in the Mind: The Life of Joseph Campbell* (New York: Doubleday, 1991).
60. Martin P. Marty in *Context*, 15 October 1991, 2.
61. F. Burton Nelson in M. S. Littell., 89.
62. Franklin H. Littell in M. S. Littell, 5.
63. Alan L. Burger in M. S. Littell, 67ff.

64. Henrik Bering-Jensen, "A Nation Haunted Still," in *Insight*, 20 March 1989, 13ff.
65. Wolfgang Gerlach in M.S. Littell, 103.
66. Ibid., 101.
67. Ibid., 95.

CHAPTER 7

1. "Muscovites protest TV fare," in *St. Paul Pioneer Press*, 2 March 1992.
2. Robert P. Ericksen, *Theologians Under Hitler* (New Haven, Conn.: Yale University Press, 1985), see particularly his probing analysis of Gerhard Kittel's attitude toward the Old Testament.
3. K. Schilder, *Christ on Trial* (Grand Rapids: Eerdmans, 1939), 264.
4. Nathaniel West, *The Thousand Years in Both Testaments* (New York: Fleming H. Revell, 1880), 56. Interestingly, West (1826–1906), a Presbyterian minister and former professor at Danville Theological Seminary and director of the 1878 Niagara Conference, speaks of Governor Henry H. Sibley of Minnesota in his preface as a particularly dear and faithful friend.
5. Seock-Tae-Sohn, *The Divine Election of Israel* (Grand Rapids: Eerdmans, 1991).
6. Ibid., 194.
7. Ibid., 244.
8. Emil Schurer, *A History of the Jewish People in the Time of Jesus*, vol. 2 (1891; reprint, New York: Schocken, 1961), 440–464.
9. Samuel J. Andrews, *Christianity and Anti-Christianity* (Chicago: Bible Institute of Colportage Association, 1898).
10. Kenneth Scott Latourette, *A History of the Expansion of Christianity: The First Five Centuries*, vol. 1 (Grand Rapids: Zondervan, 1937), 121.
11. R. S. MacLennan, "Texts in Content: Were the Second-Century *Adversus Judaeos* Preachers Anti-Jewish?" in *Explorations*, volume 5, number 2, 1991, 1, 4.
12. *Epistle of Barnabas* in *Apostolic Fathers*, trans. Kirsopp Lake (Cambridge, Mass.: Harvard University Press, n.d.), I, 49ff., 81, 355ff.
13. *Clement* in *Epistle of Barnabus*, 23.3–5, 42.3.
14. Michael Green, *Evangelism in the Early Church* (Grand Rapids: Eerdmans, 1970), 276.
15. Henry C. Thiessen, *Introductory Lectures in Systematic Theology* (Grand Rapids: Eerdmans, 1949), 477.
16. Daniel T. Taylor, *The Voice of the Church on the Coming and Kingdom of the Redeemer* (New York: H. L. Hastings, 1855), 23.
17. J.B. Lightfoot, *The Apostolic Leaders* (Grand Rapids: Baker, 1956), 266.
18. A. Skevington Wood, "Prophetic Witness Pioneers—Justin Martyr" in *Your Tomorrow*, May 1991, 11.
19. Irenaeus, *Adversus Haereses* (Paris: du Serf, 1965), 5.33–35.

20. Terullian, *Adversus Marcion*, vol. 7 (London: T. & T. Clark, 1868), 5.9.

21. Brian E. Daley, *The Hope of the Early Church* (Cambridge: Cambridge University Press, 1991), 60.

22. Larry V. Crutchfield, "Israel and the Church in the Ante-Nicene Fathers," in *Bibliotheca Sacra*, July–September, 1987, 263.

23. A. Skevington Wood, "Prophetic Witness Pioneers—Hippolytus" in *Your Tomorrow*, August 1991, 14. Wood cites Leroy E. Froom whose massive four volume history of eschatology, while veering to certain idiosyncratic Adventist interests, stands as the most complete ever done: *The Prophetic Faith of our Fathers* (Washington, D.C.: Review and Herald, 1950). I recommend careful perusal of Froom from beginning to end.

24. Wood, 15.

25. F. F. Bruce, *The Spreading Flame* (Grand Rapids: Eerdmans, 1958), 279 ff.

26. Jerome, *Esaiam* (Paris: J. P. Migne, 1845), 66.20.

27. Gleason L. Archer, trans., *Jerome's Commentary on Daniel* (Grand Rapids: Baker, 1958), 94ff.

28. Froom, *The Prophetic Faith of our Fathers.*

29. West, 7.

30. Salo Wittmayer Baron, *A Social and Religious History of the Jews,* vol. 1(New York: Columbia University Press, 1966), vii–ix, as cited in Douglas J. Culver, "National Restoration of the Jewish People to Palestine in British Non-conformity" 1585–1640 (Ph. D. dissertation, 1970), 32.

31. Christopher Dawson, "St. Augustine and His Age," in *St. Augustine: His Age, Life, and Thought* (New York: Meridian Books, 1957), 73. Another contemporary of Augustine whose brilliant preaching and vicious anti-Semitism should be noted is treated in Robert L. Wilken, *John Chrysostom and the Jews: Rhetoric and Reality in the Later Fourth Century* (Berkeley: University of California, 1983).

32. Ibid., 66.

33. Augustine, *The City of God* (New York: Modern Library, 1950), 20.30, 757.

34. F. W. Farrar, *History of Interpretation*, vol. 1 (Grand Rapids: Baker, 1961), 245.

35. Leroy E. Froom, as cited in Douglas J. Culver, 65.

36. Robert E. Lernerm, "Joachim of Fiore's Breakthrough to Chiliasm," in *Cristianesimo Neloa Storia 6* (October 1985), 489–512.

37. Marjorie Reeves, *Joachim of Fiore and the Prophetic Future* (New York: Harper, 1976).

38. Culver, 26.

39. Gottlob Schrenk, *Gottesreich Und Bund Im Aelteren Protestantismus Vornehmlich Bei Johannes Coccejus* (Frankfort: C. Bertelsmann, 1923); privately translated by Richard P. Clarke.

40. Ibid., 314.
41. Bernard Weiss, *Biblical Theology of the New Testament*, vol. 1(Edinburgh: T. & T. Clark, 1892), 102–103, cited in C. S. McCoy, *The Covenant Theology of Johannes Cocceius* (New Haven, Conn.: Yale University Press, 1957).
42. West, *The Thousand Years*, opposite the title page.
43. Barbara W. Tuchman, *Bible and Sword: England and Palestine from the Bronze Age to Balfour* (New York: Ballantine Books, 1956).
44. Culver, "National Restoration of the Jewish People to Palestine in British Non-conformity."
45. Peter Toon, ed., *Puritans, the Millennium, and the Future of Israel: Puritan Eschatology 1600 to 1660* (Cambridge: James Clarke, 1970); Iain Murray, *The Puritan Hope* (London: Banner of Truth, 1971).
46. Wilbur M. Smith, *World Crises and the Prophetic Scriptures* (Chicago: Moody Press, 1950), 186.
47. Manasseh Ben Israel of the Netherlands (1604–1657), authored the book *The Hope of Israel*, and implored Cromwell to readmit the Jews. He did not live to see it.
48. Edward Gibbon, *The Decline and Fall of the Roman Empire*, vol. 2 (Chicago: Great Books, 1952), chap. 58.
49. Toon, ed., *Puritans, The Millennium, and the Future of Israel: Puritan Eschatology 1600 to 1660*.
50. Tuchman, 168.
51. Ibid., 239ff.
52. Ibid., 185.
53. Ibid., 186.
54. John Pollock, *Shaftesbury: The Poor Man's Earl* (London: Hodder and Stoughton, 1985), 53.
55. Tuchman, 175.
56. Michael J. Pragai, *Faith and Fulfillment: Christians and the Return to the Promised Land* (London: Vallentine, Mitchell, 1985), 54ff.
57. Robert A. Peterson, "An Early Scottish Mission to the Jews," in *Israel My Glory*, June–July 1989, 22–24; John S. Ross, "A Pioneer in Jewish Mission: Rabbi Duncan" in *Christian Witness/Israel Herald*, June–August 1991, 10–12,19.
58. Tuchman, 239.
59. *Call to America to Rebuild Zion* (New York: NYT Arno Press, 1977), 1–50.
60. M. M. Noah, *Discourse on the Restoration of the Jews,* 1–55.
61. Quoted in Pragai, 56.
62. *Christian Protagonists for Jewish Restoration* (New York: NYT Arno Press, 1977), 1–23.
63. David A. Rausch, *Zionism Within Early American Fundamentalism* (New York: Edward Mellen Press, 1979).

CHAPTER 8

1. G. Frederick Owen, *Abrahamto the Middle-East Crisis* (Grand Rapids: Eerdmans, 1939, 1957), 284.
2. John Freidman, *The Redemption of Israel* (New York: Sheed and Ward, 1947), 94ff.
3. Arthur Hertzberg, "A Lifelong Quarrel with God," in *New York Times Book Review*, 6 May 1990, lff.
4. Owen, 284.
5. Shlomo Avineri, *The Making of Modern Zionism* (New York: Basic Books, 1981), 3.
6. Owen, 285.
7. Walter H. Price, *Next Year in Jerusalem* (Chicago: Moody Press, 1975), 13.
8. Ibid.
9. Peter Gay, *A Godless Jew: Freud, Atheism and the Making of Psychoanalysis* (New Haven, Conn.: Yale University Press, 1987), 121ff.
10. Anthony Allfrey, *Edward VII and His Jewish Court* (London: Weidenfeld and Nicholson, 1991).
11. Barbara W. Tuchman, *Bible and Sword: England and Palestine from the Bronze Age to Balfour* (New York: Ballantine, 1956), 163.
12. Gad G. Gilbar, ed., *Ottoman Palestine 1800–1914: Studies in Economic and Social History* (Leiden: E. J. Brill, 1990).
13. Paul Johnson, *History of the Jews* (New York: Harper and Row, 1987, 374.
14. Walter Laqueur, *A History of Zionism* (New York: Holt, Rinehart, and Winston, 1972), 46–55.
15. Harold M. Sachar, "The Rise of Zionism," *The Zionist Movement in Palestine and World Politics*, N. Gordon Levin, Jr,. ed. (Lexington, Mass.: D.C. Heath, 1974), 304.
16. Avineri, 61.
17. Neville J. Mandel, *The Arabs and Zionism Before World War* I (Berkeley: University of California, 1976), 36ff.
18. Ben Siegel, *The Controversial Sholem Asch* (Bowling Green, Ohio: Bowling Green University, 1977).
19. Avineri, 85. The most readable description of Ben Yehuda's extraordinary dedication is Robert St. John's *Tongue of the Prophets* (North Hollywood, Calif.: Wilshire Books, n.d.).
20. Sachar, 5.
21. Laqueur, xiii.
22. Ernst Pawel, *The Labyrinth of Exile: A Life of Theodor Herzl* (New York: Farrar, Straus, and Giroux, 1989).
23. Ibid., 47.
24. Ibid., 126.
25. Ibid., 206.

26. Alfred Dreyfus in his diary describes Bernard Lazare as "a young writer, a Jew turned evangelical Christian, who published a pamphlet, 'A Judicial Error,' " 15.
27. Pawel, 165.
28. Sachar, 10.
29. Avineri, 87.
30. Sachar, 12.
31. Johnson, 399.
32. Laqueur, 98.
33. Isaiah Friedman, *Germany, Turkey and Zionism* (Oxford: Oxford University Press, 1977), 95.
34. The amazing career of "Chinese Gordon," an eccentric but dedicated Christian and great student of the Bible and lover of Palestine (Gordon's Calvary and the Garden Tomb) is best told in my opinion in John A. Waller, *Gordon of Khartoum* (New York: Atheneum, 1988).
35. Abba Eban, *My People: The Story of the Jews; the World of the Jew* (Chicago: Moody, 1981, 1988), 135.
36. Pawel, 336.
37. Sachar, 20–21.
38. Tuchman, 308.
39. Pawel, 487.
40. Walter L. Wilson in *Hastening the Day of God,* John Bradbury, ed. (Wheaton, Ill.: Van Kampen, 1953), 185.
41. Johnson, 423.
42. Pawel, 530.
43. Joyce R. Starr, *Kissing Through the Glass: The Invisible Shield Between Americans and Israelis* (Chicago: Contemporary Books, 1990).
44. Jacob Neusner, *Death and Burial of Judaism: The Impact of Christianity, Secularism and the Holocaust on Jewish Faith* (New York: Basic Books, 1987), 225.
45. Noam Chomsky, *The Fateful Triangle: The United States, Israel and the Palestinians* (Boston: South End Press, 1983).
46. Isidore Epstein, *Judaism: A Historical Presentation* (London: Penguin, 1959), 50.
47. Laqueur, 142.
48. Mandel, 47.
49. Sergio I. Minerbi, *The Vatican and Zionism: Conflict in the Holy Land,* 1895–1925 (Oxford: Oxford University Press, 1990).
50. Hertzel Fishman, *American Protestantism and a Jewish State* (Detroit: Wayne University Press, 1973) cf. also Ya'akov Ariel, *On Behalf of Israel: American Fundamentalist Attitudes Toward Jews, Judaism and Zionism, 1865–1945* (Brooklyn: Carlson Publishing, 1991).
51. Iain Murray, *The Puritan Hope* (London: Banner of Truth, 1971), 214, and quoting from *Sword and Trowel,* 1891, 446.

CHAPTER 9

52. Timothy Weber, *Living in the Shadow of the Second Coming, 1875-1982* (Grand Rapids: Zondervan, 1983).

CHAPTER 9

1. Saul Bellow, *To Jerusalem and Back: A Personal Account* (New York: Avon, 1976), 216.
2. Negib Azoury in "Ishmael and his brother" in the *Jerusalem Post*, 22 April 1985, 11.
3. G. Frederick Owen, *Jerusalem* (Grand Rapids: Baker, 1972).
4. John J. Robinson, *In Dungeon, Fire and Sword* (New York: M. Evans, 1991).
5. David Pryce–Jones, *The Closed Circle: An Interpretation of the Arabs* (New York: Harper, 1989), 188ff.
6. James Parkes, *Whose Land? A History of the Peoples of Palestine* (Oxford: Oxford University Press, 1949).
7. H. A. R. Gibb, *Mohammedanism* (New York: Mentor, 1949, 1955), 44.
8. Samuel M. Zwemer, *The Moslem Doctrine of God* (Edinburgh: Oliphant, Anderson and Ferrier, 1905), 28, 63.
9. Gibb, 32.
10. Henry Munson, Jr., *Islam and Revolution in the Middle East* (New Haven: Yale University Press, 1988), 14–15.
11. Bernard Lewis, *The Jews of Islam* (Princeton, N.J.: Princeton University Press, 1984), 11. This book is the classic in the field!
12. Zwemer, 114.
13. Gibb, 43; see also the masterful Geoffrey Parrinder, *Jesus in the Quran* (New York: Oxford University Press, 1977).
14. John H. Waller, *Gordon of Khartoum: The Sage of a Victorian Hero* (New York: Atheneum, 1988), 158ff.
15. Robert T. Lacey, *The Kingdom: Arabia and the House of Saud* (New York: Harcourt, Brace, Jovanovich, 1981); Sandra Mackey, *The Saudis: Inside the Desert Kingdom* (New York: New American Library: 1987).
16. Gibb, 99–113.
17. H. B. Dehqani–Tafti, *The Hard Awakening* (New York: Seabury, 1981).
18. Charles Glass, *Tribes with Flags: A Dangerous Passage Through the Chaos of the Middle East* (New York: Atlantic Monthly Press, 1990), 264.
19. Albert Hourani, *History of the Arab Peoples* (London: Faber and Faber, 1991). See also the definitive book Kenneth Cragg, *The Christian Arab* (Louisville: Westminster/John Knox, 1991).
20. Glass, 3.
21. Pryce–Jones, 13.
22. Gibb, 127.
23. Pryce-Jones, 40.
24. Ibid., 378.

25. Marius Baar, *The Unholy War* (Nashville: Thomas Nelson, 1980), 79.
26. Ibid., 144.
27. *The Invitation*, January 1992. For analysis of Muslims in America, see Yvonne Yazbeck Haddad, ed., *The Muslims of America* (Oxford: Oxford University Press, 1991).
28. Daniel Pipes, "The Muslims are Coming! The Muslims are Coming!" in *National Review*, 19 November 1990, 28–31.
29. Munson, 3.
30. Quoted in Lamin Sanneh, "Reclaiming and Expounding the Islamic Heritage," in *The Christian Century*, 21 August 1991, 778.
31. Samuel Schor, *The Everlasting Nation and Their Coming King* (London: Marshall, Morgan and Scott, n.d.), 76.
32. David Dolan, *Holy War for the Promised Land* (London: Hodder and Stoughton, 1991), 232–233. For a moderate Palestinian perspective, Edward W. Said, *The Politics of Dispossession* (New York: Parthenon, 1994).
33. Wilhelm Dietl, *Holy War* (New York: Macmillan, 1984); Hoag Levins, *Arab Reach: The Secret War Against Israel* (Garden City : Doubleday, 1983); Robin Wright, *Sacred Rage: The Wrath of Militant Tislam* (New York: Simon and Schuster, 1985); Amir Taheri, *Holy Terror: Inside the World of Islamic Terrorism* (Bethesda, Md.: Adler and Adler, 1987).
34. Glass, 267.
35. Edward Rice, *Captain Richard Francis Burton* (New York: Charles Scribner's, 1990), 416. Burton in a real sense prepared the way for British annexation of the Levant.
36. Among my favorite recent travelers: Peter Scholl–Latour, *Adventures in the East: Travels in the Land of Islam* (New York: Bantam, 1988); John Bulloch, *The Persian Gulf Unveiled* (New York: Congdon and Weed, 1984); Elizabeth Warnock Fernea and Robert A. Fernea, *The Arab World: Personal Encounters* (Garden City, N. Y.: Doubleday, 1985).
37. J. Christy Wilson, "Zwemer: Flaming Prophet to Islam," in *World Vision Magazine,* April 1964, 10ff.
38. Abdiyah Akbar Abdul–Haqq, *Sharing Your Faith with a Muslim* (Minneapolis: Bethany, 1980); Anis A. Shorrosh, *Islam Revealed: A Christian Arab's View of Islam* (Nashville: Thomas Nelson, 1988).
39. Wilbur M. Smith, *Egypt in Biblical Prophecy* (Boston: W. A. Wilde, 1957).
40. Anis A. Shorroah, *Jesus, Prophecy and the Middle East (*Nashville: Thomas Nelson, n.d.), 70–71.
41. Charles Malik, quoted in John Wesley White, *World War III* (Grand Rapids: Zondervan, 1977), 154.
42. Henry Grunwald, "The Year 2000: Is it the end—or just the beginning?" in *Time*, 30 March 1992, 73ff.

43. Carl F. H. Henry in *National and International Religion Report*, 23 March 1992, 1.

CHAPTER 10

1. Lane Lambert, *Israel: The Unique Land, The Unique People* (Wheaton, Ill.: Living Books, 1981), 13ff.

2. Linda Osband, *Famous Travelers to the Holy Land* (London: Prion, 1991).

3. T. Dewitt Talmage, *The Holy Land* (Chicago: Rhodes and McClure, 1896).

4. N. John Hall, *Trollope: A Biography* (Oxford: Clarendon Press, 1910), 419–420. Trollope, an astute observer, was not impressed with much that he saw except the tranquil perspective of the Mount of Olives.

5. Joachim Remak, *Sarajevo: The Story of a Political Murder* (New York: Criterion Books, 1959).

6. Leon Wolf, *In Flanders Fields: the 1917 Campaign* (New York: Viking Press, 1958).

7. Mark Helprin, *A Soldier from the Great War* (New York: Harcourt Brace Jovanovich, 1991).

8. Barbara Tuchman, *The Proud Tower: A Portrait of the World Before the War 1890–1914* (New York: Macmillan, 1962), 249.

9. Neville J. Mandell, *The Arabs and Zionism Before World War I* (Berkeley: University of California, 1976), 165.

10. Philip Warner, *Kitchener: The Man Behind the Legend* (New York: Atheneum, 1986), 27.

11. David Fromkin, *A Peace to End All Peace: Creating the Modern Middle East 1914–1922* (New York: Henry Holt, 1989).

12. Jeremy Wilson, *Lawrence: The Authorized Biography* (New York: Atheneum, 1990).

13. Doreen Ingrams, "Palestine Papers, 1917–1918," in *The Zionist Movement in Palestine and World Politics 1880–1918,* N. Gordon Levin, Jr., ed. (Lexington, Mass.: D. C. Heath, 1974), 134.

14. Wilson, 275.

15. Ingrams, 135.

16. Brian Gardner, *Allenby of Arabia* (New York: Coward–McCann, 1965), 110.

17. Paul Johnson, *A History of the Jews* (New York: Harper and Row, 1987), 428.

18. Blanche E. C. Dugdale, *Arthur James Balfour,* II (New York: G. Putnam, 1937), 163ff.

19. Barbara Tuchman, *Bible and Sword: England and Palestine from the Bronze Age to Balfour* (New York: Ballentine Books, 1956), 311.

20. Ingrams, 139.

21. Selig Adler, "The Palestine Question," from Conference on Jewish Relations, 1948, found in *Jewish Social Studies*, X, 4, 303ff.
22. Ibid., 334.
23. Johnson, 430ff.
24. Quoted from John Phillips, *Exploring the World of the Jew* (Chicago: Moody, 1981), 137.
25. Dugdale, 171.
26. Walter Laqueur, *A History of Zionism* (New York: Holt, Rinehart, Winston, 1972), 236ff.
27. Ibid., 204.
28. Johnson, 431.
29. Tuchman, *Bible and Sword*, 341.
30. Ibid., 340.
31. Bernard Wasserstein, *Herbert Samuel: A Political Life* (Oxford: Oxford University Press, 1991).
32. Laqueur, 215.
33. Ibid., 227.
34. Johnson, 439.

CHAPTER 11

1. Robert Slater, *The Life of Moshe Dayan* (New York: St. Martin's Press, 1991.
2. Werner E. Lemke, "Life in the Present and Hope for the Future" in *Interpretation*, "The Book of Ezekiel," April 1984, 176.
3. H. L. Ellison, *Ezekiel: The Man and His Message* (Grand Rapids: Eerdmans 1956) , 131.
4. Ibid., 129.
5. Ibid., 130.
6. Ralph H. Alexander, "Ezekiel" in *Expositor's Bible Commentary*, vol. 6 (Grand Rapids: Zondervan, 1986), 923–928; H. A. Ironside, *Ezekiel the Prophet* (New York: Loizeaux, 1949), 49.
7. Dan Kurzman, *Ben–Gurion: Prophet of Fire* (New York: Simon and Schuster, 1983), 26.
8. Ibid., 27.
9. Ibid., 139.
10. David A. Rausch, *A Legacy of Hatred: Why Christians Must Not Forget the Holocaust* (Grand Rapids: Baker, 1984, 1990), 181.
11. Leonard Mosley, *Gideon Goes to War: The Story of Major–General Orde Wingate* (New York: Charles Scribner's Sons, 1955); Christopher Sykes, *Orde Wingate* (London: Collins, 1959).
12. Kurzman, 218.
13. George T. B. Davis, *Rebuilding Palestine According to Promise* (Philadelphia: The Million Testaments Campaign, 1935).
14. Kurzman, 218.

15. Maurice Samuel, *Light on Israel* (New York: Alfred A. Knopf, 1968), quoted in Jack Van Impe, *Israel's Final Holocaust* (Nashville: Thomas Nelson, 1979), 73.

16. Etty Hillesum, *An Interrupted Life* (New York: Washington Square Press, 1985).

17. Charles Spurgeon, *Sermons,* vol. 1 (New York: Funk and Wagnalls, n.d.), 136.

18. R. B. Girdlestone, *The Grammar Of Prophecy* (Grand Rapids: Kregel, 1955), 138.

19. Mendell Lewittes, *Religious Foundations of the Jewish State: The Concept and Practice of Jewish Statehood from Biblical Times to the Modern State of Israel* (New York: Ktav, 1977), 193.

20. Paul Johnson, *A History of the Jews* (New York: Harper and Row, 1987), 419.

21. Walter Laqueur, *A History of Zionism* (New York: Holt, Rinehart, and Winston, 1972), 535.

22. Chaim Weizmann, *Trial and Error: An Autobiography* (New York: Harper, 1959), 430ff.

23. Laqueur, 534ff.

24. Weizmann, 436.

25. Johnson, 524.

26. Weizmann, 439ff.

27. Erick Silver, *Begin: The Haunted Prophet* (New York: Random House, 1984), 108

28. Johnson, 526.

29. Kurzman, 272.

30. Weizmann, 459.

31. Abba Eban, *An Autobiography* (New York: Random House, 1977), 78.

32. Peter von der Oster–Sacken in *The Holocaust Forty Years After,* Marcia Littell, ed. (Lewiston, N.Y.: Edwin Mellon Press, 1989), 103.

33. Eliezer and Dov Berkovits, "Morally bankrupt still," in *Jerusalem Post*, 9 May 1992.

34. Eban, 999.

35. Johnson, 526.

36. Samuel Katz, *Battleground: Fact and Fantasy in Palestine* (New York: Bantam Books, 1973), 12ff.

37. Avi Shlaim, *Collusion Across the Jordan: King Abdullah, the Zionist Movement and the Partition of Palestine* (New York: Columbia University Press, 1988).

38. Benny Morris, *The Birth of the Palestinian Refugee Problem, 1947–1949* (New York: Cambridge University Press, 1988).

39. Chaim Herzog, *The Arab–Israeli Wars: War and Peace in the Middle East from the War of Independence Through Lebanon* (New York: Random House, 1982). For superb, well-researched novels, nothing sur-

passes Herman Wouk's *The Hope* (New York: Little, Brown, 1993) and *The Glory* (1984).

40. Tad Szulc, *The Secret Alliance: The Extraordinary Story of the Rescue of the Jews Since World War II* (New York: Farrar, Strauss, and Giroux, 1990).

CHAPTER 12

1. Lawrence Meyer, *Israel Now: Portrait of a Troubled Land* (New York: Delacorte Press, 1982), 291.
2. Ibid.
3. Moshe Leshem, *Balaam's Curse: How Israel Lost its Way and How it Can Find it Again* (New York: Simon and Schuster, 1989).
4. Abram L. Sachar, *The Redemption of the Unwanted: From the Liberation of the Death Camps to the Founding of Israel:* (New York: St. Martin's Press, 1983). This careful treatment has one of the best step–by–step analyses of the United Nations' action on the partition of Palestine.
5. Meron Benvenisti, in "Prophets of the Holy Land," in *Harper's Forum,* December 1984, 48.
6. Thomas L. Friedman, "Teddy Kollek's Jerusalem" in the *New York Times Magazine,* 4 August 1985, 16ff.
7. Naomi Shepherd, *Teddy Kollek: Mayor of Jerusalem* (New York: Harper and Row, 1988).
8. In the *Chicago Tribune,* 14 December 1991, 12.
9. Several significant articles from *National Geographic:* "Israel: Search for the Center," July 1985; "Journey into the Great Rift," August 1965; "In Search of Moses," January 1976; "The Land of Galilee," December 1965; "Reunited Jerusalem Faces Its Problems;" December 1968. Helpful pictorial treatments include: Hans Bouma, *An Eye on Israel* (Grand Rapids: Eerdmans, 1978); Shlomo S. Gafni and A. van der Heyden, *The Glory of Jerusalem* (Jerusalem: Excalibur Books, 1978); *Jerusalem, Most Fair of Cities* (Jerusalem: Armon, 1978); H. V. Morton, *In Search of the Land* (New York: Dodd, Mead and Co., 1978).
10. Amos Elon, *Jerusalem: City of Mirrors* (Boston: Little, Brown,1989).
11. Samuel Heilman, *A Walker in Jerusalem* (New York: Summit Books, 1986).
12. Abraham Rabinovich, *Jerusalem: On Earth: People, Passions and Politics in the Holy City* (New York: Free Press, 1988).
13. Stephen Brook, *Winner Takes All: A Season in Israel* (London: Hamish Hamilton, 1990); Ze'ev Chafets, *Heroes and Hustlers, Hard Hats and Holy Men: Inside the New Israel* (New York: William Morrow, 1986).
14. Amos Oz, *In the Land of Israel* (New York: Harcourt, Brace, Jovanovich, 1983).
15. Alan Hart, *Arafat: Terrorist or Peacemaker?* (London: Sidgewick and Jackson, 1984), 75.

16. Hoag Levins, *Arab Reach: The Secret War Against Israel* (Garden City, N. Y.: Doubleday, 1983).

17. Patrick Seale, *Asad: The Struggle for the Middle East* (Berkeley: University of California Press, 1988). This volume shares a fascinating analysis of the Alawite group of Muslim schismatics from which Asad comes.

18. Patrick Seale, *Abu Nidal: A Gun for Hire* (New York: Random House, 1992).

19. Anwar el–Sada, *In Search of Identity* (New York: Harper and Row, 1977).

20. Robert Slater, *The Life of Moshe Dayan* (New York: St. Martin's Press, 1991), 314.

21. Muhammad Heikal, *Autumn of Fury: The Assassination of Sadat* (New York: Random House, 1983).

22. Itamar Rabinovich, *The War for Lebanon 1970–1983* (Ithaca, N. Y.: Cornell University Press, 1984).

23. Jonathan C. Randal, *Going all the Way: Christian Warlords, Israel Adventurers and the War in Lebanon* (New York: Viking Press, 1983); Dan Bavly and Eliahu Salpeter, *Fire in Beirut: Israel's War in Lebanon with the PLO* (New York: Stein and Ay, 1984).

24. Jacobo Timerman, *The Longest War Israel in Lebanon* (New York: Alfred Knopf, 1982); the early volume by Timerman, *Prisoner Without a Name: Cell Without a Number* (New York: Vintage, 1981).

25. Sis Levin, *Beirut Diary* (Downers Grove, Ill.: InterVarsity, 1989).

26. Amos Oz, "Has Israel Altered Its Visions?" in the *New York Times Magazine*, 11 July 1982, 26ff. Two very important treatises by veteran Israel military leaders are essential reading: Major–General Avraham Tamir, *A Soldier in Search of Peace* (New York: Harper and Row, 1988) and General Raful Eitan, *A Soldier's Story* (New York: Shapolsky Publishers, 1991).

27. Daniel Gavron, *Israel After Begin* (Boston: Houghton Mifflin, 1984); Aaron S. Klieman, *Israel and the World After Forty Years* (New York: Pergamon–Brassey 1990); Meron Benvenisti, *Conflicts and Contradictions* (New York: Villard Books, 1986); Benvenisti was the Deputy Mayor of Jerusalem under Teddy Kollek.

28. F. Robert Hunter, *The Palestine Uprising: A War by Other Means* (Berkeley: University of California Press, 1991).

29. Ze'ev Schiff and Ehud Ya'ari, *Intifada: The Palestinian Uprising–Israel's Third Front* (New York: Simon and Schuster, 1989). For a very recent analysis, see Glenn Frankel, *Beyond the Promised Land: Jews and Arabs on a Hard Road to a New Israel* (New York: Simon and Schuster, 1994).

30. Rabbi Meir Kahane, *Uncomfortable Questions for Comfortable Jews* (Secaucus, N.J.: Lyle Stuart, 1987).

31. Seymour M. Hersh, *The Samson Option: Israel's Nuclear Arsenal and American Foreign Policy* (New York: Random House, 1991).

32. James Adams, *The Unnatural Alliance: Israel and South Africa* (London: Quartet Books, 1984).

33. Andrew and Leslie Cockburn, *Dangerous Liaisons: The Inside Story of the U.S.—Israeli Covert Relationship* (New York: HarperCollins, 1991); Stephen Green, *Taking Sides: America's Secret Relations with a Militant Israel* (New York: William Morrow, 1984). This last book is anti-Israeli but a significant study.

34. Judie Oron, "The Gentle strength of a 'fighting Jew'" in *Jerusalem Post,* 30 March 1991, 10ff.

35. Martin Buber, *The Origin and Meaning of Hasidism* (New York: Horizon, 1955); Tom Dunkel, "Hasidic Superstar Rocks All Ages," in *Insight,* 15 April 1991, 54ff.; and for a penetrating analysis of Hasidic spirituality, Ted A. Campbell, *The Religion of the Heart: A Study of European Religious Life in the Seventeenth and Eighteenth Centuries* (Columbia, S.C.; University of South Carolina Press, 1991), 144–151.

36. Belden Menkus, ed., *Meet the American Jew* (Nashville: Broadman, 1963); James Linburg *Judaism; An Introduction for Christians* (Minneapolis: Augsberg, 1987); A. James Rudin, *Israel for Christians: Understanding Modern Israel* (Philadelphia: Fortress, 1983).

37. *National and International Religion Report,* 17 June 1991, 7.

38. Evan Gahr, "Orthodox Jews Get Political," in *Insight,* 27 January 1992, 14ff.; Lynn Davidman *Tradition in a Rootless World: Women Turn to Orthodox Judaism* (Berkeley: University of California Press, 1991).

39. Michael Specter, "Rabbi Menachem Schneerson, The Oracle of Crown Heights," in the *New York Times Magazine,* 15 March 1992, 34ff.

40. Donald A. Hagner, *The Jewish Reclamation of Jesus* (Grand Rapids: Zondervan, 1984); James H. Charlesworth, *Jesus Within Judaism* (New York: Doubleday, 1988).

41. Pinchas Lapide, *The Resurrection of Jesus: A Jewish Perspective* (Minneapolis: Augsburg, 1983).

42. Anthony Powell, *Miscellaneous Verdicts* (Chicago: University of Chicago Press, 1990), 57.

43. Peter Grose, *A Changing Israel* (New York: Vintage, 1985); Lesley Hazleton, *Jerusalem, Jerusalem: A Memoir of War and Peace, Passion and Politics* (New York: Penguin, 1986), 192.

44. In the *Jerusalem Post,* 15 February 1992, endpage.

45. "The Wide Spectrum of Being Jewish," in *American Messianic Fellowship Connection,* January–March 1992, 5.

46. David M. Levy, "The American Jew: Stranger in our Midst," in *Israel My Glory,* October–November 1991, 11ff.

47. Howard M. Sachar, *A History of the Jews in America* (New York: Alfred Knopf, 1992), 748ff. Sachar's earlier definitive volume has already been mentioned but is an invaluable guidebook at this point; cf. Howard M. Sachar, *Diaspora: An Inquiry into the Contemporary Jewish World* (New York: Harper and Row, 1986).

48. Ibid., 761.

49. Barbara Meyerhoff, *Number Our Days: A Triumph of Continuity and Culture among Jewish Old People in an Urban Ghetto* (New York: Simon and Schuster, 1978); Ze'ev Chafets, *Members of the Tribe: On the Road in Jewish America* (New York: Bantam Books, 1988).

50. Wolf Blitzer, *Between Washington and Jerusalem: A Reporter's Notebook* (New York: Oxford University Press, 1985).

51. Michael Greenstein, *The American Jew: A Contradiction in Terms* (Jerusalem: Gefen, 1991); Eliezer Don–Yehiya, ed., *Comparative Jewish Politics: Israel and Diaspora Jewry* (Jerusalem: Bar–Illan University Press, 1991).

52. Sachar, 722.

53. Shlomo Riskin, "It's time to remove the Diaspora masks," in the *Jerusalem Post*, 14 March 1992, next to the end page.

54. Sachar, 902.

55. Ibid., 936.

CHAPTER 13

1. H. Roy Elseth, *Did God Know? A Study of the Nature of God* (St. Paul: Calvary United Church, 1977). This is an example of making virtually all prophecy contingent (and some certainly is) in an effort to sidestep the omniscience of God. Charles G. Finney is better on this point, cf. *Systematic Theology* (Grand Rapids: Eerdmans, 1878), 542ff.

2. Gleason L. Archer, Jr., *A Survey of Old Testament Introduction* (Chicago: Moody Press, 1964), 283.

3. R. B. Girdlestone, *The Grammar of Prophecy* (Grand Rapids: Kregel, 1955), 89 ff.

4. For thorough analysis of the apologetical and evidentiary value of fulfilled biblical prophecy: Batsell Barrett Baxter, *I Believe Because: A Study of the Evidence Supporting Christian Faith* (Grand Rapids: Baker, 1971), 186ff.; John H. Gerstner, *Reasons for Faith* (Grand Rapids: Baker, 1967), 106ff., especially good on comparing secular prophecy with supernatural predictive prophecy; Vernon C. Grounds, *The Reason for Our Hope* (Chicago: Moody, 1945), 52ff.; Josh McDowell, *Evidence That Demands a Verdict* (San Bernardino: Chicago: Great Books, 1952), 277ff.; Blaise Pascal, *Pensees* (Chicago: Great Books, 1952), 33: section XI, "The Prophecies," 301ff.; Bernard Ramm, *Protestant Christian Evidences* (Chicago: Moody, 1953), 81ff.

5. J. Barton Payne, *Encyclopedia of Biblical Prophecy* (Grand Rapids: Baker, 1973), 8. Also very helpful on the prophets is the treatment in Erich Sauer, *The Dawn of World Redemption* (London: Patermoster, 1951), 141 ff.

6. John Peter Lange, *The Revelation of John: A Commentary on Holy Scripture* (New York: Charles Scribner, 1871), 98.

7. H. Bietenhard in *Theological Dictionary of the New Testament* as cited by Robert Saucy in John Feinberg, ed., *Continuity and Discontinuity: Perspectives on the Relationship Between the Old and New Testaments* (Wheaton: Crossway, 1988), 24.

8. J. Christian Beker in *Paul the Apostle* as cited in Feinberg, 248.

9. Insightful and suggestive treatment of the prophetic and typical foreshadowing of God's plan in which the interval in the calendar is followed by the Feast of Trumpets, Israel's Day of Atonement and the Feast of Tabernacles which is plainly millennial in import: A. J. Holiday, *The Feasts of the Lord* (London: Pickering and Inglis, n.d.) and August Van Ryn, *His Appointments: Lectures on the Feasts of the Lord* (New York: Loizeaux, 1944).

10. Ford C. Ottman, *God's Oath* (New York: Our Hope, 1911), 4.

11. Arthur W. Pink, *The Prophetic Parables of Matthew 13* (Covington, Ky.: Calvary Book Room, n.d.).

12. Many students of Scripture before and after the Reformation taught that in addition to accurately representing actual historic churches in the first century, Revelation 2–3 prefigures the entire Christian era. Among those who have held to this viewpoint are Brightman, Forbes, Mede, More, Gill, Sir Isaac Newton, Thomas Beverley, Vitringa, Lampe, and Henry Blount (1838), who wrote: "They not only portray as types but predict as prophecies, the whole church period" as cited in T. Ernest Wilson, *Mystery Doctrines of the New Testament* (Neptune, N.J.: Loizeaux, 1975), 43.

13. Bishop Hans Lilje in *The Last Book in the Bible* as cited by George Ladd, *A Commentary on the Book of Revelation* (Grand Rapids: Eerdmans, 1972), 253.

14. For a probing analysis of Homeric eschatology, see Ralph Stob, *Christianity a Classical Civilization* (Grand Rapids: Eerdmans, 1950), 124ff.

15. Milton C. Fisher, "The Canon of the Old Testament" in *The Expositor's Bible Commentary*, 1:388, as cited by Ramesh Richard in "Application Theory in Relation to the Old Testament" in *Bibliotheca Sacra*, October–December 1986, 304.

16. Ramesh P. Richard in "Application Theory," 304.

17. Sauer, 165.

18. A. C. Gaebelein, *The Prophet Joel* (New York: Our Hope, 1909), 116. Another fine study of Joel and other prophets is H. L. Ellison, *Men Spake from God* (London: Patermoster 1952), 20ff.

19. John D. W. Watts, *Vision and Prophecy in Amos* (Grand Rapids: Eerdmans, 1958).

20. Richard, 305.

21. J. Dwight Pentecost, *Things to Come: A Study in Biblical Eschatology* (Findlay, Ohio: Dunham, 1958), 229ff.

22. An informative survey of diverse views is Gleason Archer, Jr., Paul D. Feinberg, Douglas J. Moo, Richard R. Reiter, *The Rapture: Pre, Mid or Post Tribulational* (Grand Rapids: Zondervan, 1984). For a thorough exploration of imminency, cf. John Walvoord, *The Rapture Question* (Findlay, Ohio: Dunham 1957) 75–82, 149–152.

23. Henry C. Thiessen *Will the Church Pass Through the Tribulation?* (New York: Loizeaux, n.d.). This long–time Wheaton professor makes an appealing case, as does Leon J. Wood, *Is the Rapture Next?* (Grand Rapids: Zondervan, 1956). The classic fictional work which has been widely read through the years is Sydney Watson, *In the Twinkling of an Eye* (Old Tappan, N. J.: Fleming H. Revell, 1921).

24. Merrill C. Tenney, *Interpreting Revelation* (Grand Rapids: Eerdmans, 1957), 190; also the early Wheaton president, Charles A. Blanchard, *Light on the Last Days* (Chicago: Moody Colportage, 1913), 46.

25. Gordon R. Lewis, "Biblical Evidence for Pretribulationism" in *Bibliotheca Sacra,* July 1968, 216–226.

26. William Barclay, *The Mind of Paul* (New York: Harper, 1958), 229–230.

27. Robert Gundry in *The Church and the Tribulation* (Grand Rapids: Zondervan, 1973) argues that the Greek verb *katabaino*, "to descend," implies that Christ will meet His Church in the air and then come down to earth. This is ably refuted by John Walvoord, "Post Tribulationism Today: The Comforting Hope of 1 Thessalonians 4" in *Bibliotheca Sacra*, October–December 1976, 304–305, in which he shows that the descent to the meeting in the air "does not necessarily indicate continued movement in the same direction. Thorough expositions of the Thessalonian passage do not support Gundry, cf. D. Edmond Hiebert, *The Thessalonian Epistles* (Chicago: Moody, 1971); George Milligan, *St. Paul's Epistles to the Thessalonians* (Grand Rapids: Zondervan, 1960); F. F. Bruce, *Word Biblical Commentary: 1 and 2 Thessalonians* (Waco, Tex.: Word, 1982).

28. Wilbur M. Smith, "The Church, the Tribulation and the Rapture" in *Moody Monthly*, March 1957, 26ff.

29. Robert H. Lightner, *The Last Days Handbook* (Nashville: Thomas Nelson, 1990). This thoughtful volume traces competitive options with an irenic spirit.

30. A very careful review of Rosenthal's approach is written by Gerald B. Stanton, "A Review of *The Pre–wrath Rapture of the Church*" In *Bibliotheca Sacra*, January–March 1991, 90–111.

31. Alexander Reese, *The Approaching Advent of Christ* (Grand Rapids: International Publications, 1937).

32. J. Barton Payne, *The Imminent Appearing of Christ* (Grand Rapids: Eerdmans, 1962); and more recently cf. Allen Beechick, *The Pre-Tribulation Rapture* (Denver: Accent Books 1980).

33. A beautiful exposition of "The Marriage and Marriage Supper of the Lamb" with superb researching of ancient marriage customs in Israel is by Renald E. Showers in *Israel My Glory*, June–July 1991, 9–12.

34. J. N. D. Kelly, *Early Christian Doctrines* (New York: Harper, 1978), 462.

35. Robert Jewett, *Jesus Against the Rapture* (Philadelphia: Westminster, 1979).

36. Dave MacPherson, *The Incredible Cover Up* (Plainfield, N. J.: Logo, 1975); Duncan J. McDougall, *The Rapture of the Saints* (Blackwood, N.J.: O. F. M. Publishers, 1970). The essential thesis of MacPherson is faced head–on in a very competent and Christian spirit by Thomas D. Ice, "Why the Doctrine of the Pretribulational Rapture Did Not Begin with Margaret MacDonald" in *Bibliotheca Sacra*, April–June, 1990, 155–168. Canfield's vicious attack on C. I. Scofield is rebutted by John D. Hannah in "A Review of *The Incredible Scofield and his Book*," in *Bibliotheca Sacra*, July–September 1990, 351–364.

37. Not only do we sense the imminency of Christ's coming in the apostle Paul but in Hebrews 10:25, 37–38; James 5:7–9; 1 Peter 4:7; 1 John 2:18, etc.

38. John Walvoord, *The Rapture Question*, cf. 150ff.

39. Louis Goldberg, *Turbulence over the Middle East* (Neptune, N.J.: Loizeaux, 1982), 31.

40. Tenney, 68.

41. A superlative series of articles entitled "A Study of History's 'Signs of the Times'" by Wilbur M. Smith appeared in *Moody Monthly* beginning in October of 1965. The third article was picked up in July–August 1966.

42. A. W. Tozer, "The Decline of Apocalyptic Expectation" in *Alliance Witness*, 28 November 1952, 3.

CHAPTER 14

1. "Has History Come to an End?" in *Time*, 4 September 1989, 57.

2. "Stumbling Toward Armageddon?" in *Time*, 16 April 1990, 30ff.

3. "Apocalypse Now?" in *Time*, 11 February 1991, 88.

4. Thomas Chalmers quoted in Arno C. Gaebelein, *The Harmony of the Prophetic Word* (New York: Our Hope, n.d.), 186.

5. Rene Pache, *The Return of Jesus Christ* (Chicago: Moody, 1955), 251.

6. Thomas Rawson Birks, *Thoughts on the Times and Seasons of Sacred Prophecy* (1880), as cited in Wilbur M. Smith, *World Crises and the Prophetic Scriptures* (Chicago: Moody, 1952), 28ff.

7. J. Dwight Pentecost, *Things to Come: A Study in Biblical Eschatology* (Findley, Ohio: Dunham, 1958), 320ff.; also David L. Cooper, "Will the Old Roman Empire Be Revived?" in *Biblical Research Monthly*, May 1972, 3ff. (contra the idea of a revived Roman Empire expounded by Hal Lindsey, et al.). Walter K. Price in his fine study, *The Coming Anti–Christ* (Chicago: Moody, 1974), 172, quotes the historian Robert Payne to good effect on this point—"The roman Empire perished and went on living . . . its civilization held sway in the West. The legacy of this most worldly of empires was to lie largely in the realm of ideas—in law, language, literature, government, attitudes and styles. In innumerable ways as century followed century, men's minds were to respond to a presence that was shorn of all the panoply of power while gradually becoming transfigured into a dominion of the spirit and of thought."

8. Joseph A. Seiss, *Voices From Babylon* (Philadelphia: Castle Press, 1879), 239.

9. Franz Delitzsch quoted in Robert D. Culver, 134.

10. Robert D. Culver, *Daniel and the Latter Days: A Study in Millennialism* (Westwood, N.J.: Fleming H. Revell, 1954), 141.

11. Delitzsch, 157ff.

12. Sir Robert Anderson, *The Coming Prince* (Grand Rapids: Kregel, 1957); Alva J. McClain, *Daniel's Prophecy of the Seventy Weeks* (Grand Rapids: Zondervan, 1940); Robert D. Culver, 125–160; H. A. Ironside, *The Great Parenthesis: Timely Messages on the Interval Between the 69th and 70th Weeks of Daniel's Prophecy* (Grand Rapids: Zondervan, 1943).

13. Culver, 141.

14. Developed in Sir Robert Anderson, 76–87.

15. Hippolytus, *Fragments on Daniel* in *Anti–Nicene Fathers,* vol. V (Grand Rapids: Eerdmans, 1956), 180–184.

16. Seiss, 252.

17. Nathaniel West, *The Thousand Years in Both Testaments* (New York: Fleming H. Revell, 1880), 197.

18. The most helpful overall study of Satan's treachery is Donald Grey Barnhouse, *The Invisible War* (Grand Rapids: Zondervan, 1965); cf. also Lewis Sperry Chafer, *Satan* (Findley, Ohio: Dunham, 1919); Frederick A. Tatford, *Satan: The Prince of Darkness* (Grand Rapids: Kregel, n.d.); Herbert Lockyer, *Satan: His Person and Power* (Waco, Tex.: Word, 1980); Hal Lindsey, *Satan is Alive and Well on Planet Earth* (Grand Rapids: Zondervan, 1972).

19. Samuel J. Andrews, *Christianity and Anti–Christianity* (Chicago: Moody Bible Institute Colportage Association, 1898), 3ff.

20. George Eldon Ladd, *The Last Things* (Grand Rapids: Eerdmans, 1978), 59.
21. George Eldon Ladd, *A Commentary on the Revelation of John* (Grand Rapids: Eerdmans, 1972), 183.
22. Ibid, 70.
23. Edmond Hiebert, *The Thessalonian Epistles: A Call to Readiness* (Chicago: Moody, 1971); F. F. Bruce, *Word Biblical Commentary: I and II Thessalonians* (Waco, Tex.: Word, 1982); Leon Morris, *The First and Second Epistles to the Thessalonians,* NICNT (Grand Rapids: Eerdmans, 1959); John Walvoord, *The Thessalonian Epistles* (Findley, Ohio: Dunham, 1955).
24. Arthur W. Pink, *The Anti–Christ* (Minneapolis: Klock and Klock, 1979 reprint).
25. Price, 162.
26. For the classical fictional exploration of this motif, see Sydney Watson, *The Mark of the Beast* (Los Angeles: Biola Book Room, 1918).
27. Alexandre Kojeve, in "Has History Come to an End?" 57.
28. Smith, 75ff.
29. George Otis, Jr., *The Last of the Giants* (Tarrytown, N.Y.: Chosen, 1991). The "King of the South" (Daniel 11:4). The other part of this pincer movement against Israel would represent the League working from Egypt. The strong Russian vote-getter, the vicious anti-Semitic, Vladimir Zhirinovsky's book, *The Last Drive to the South* (Moscow: Pisatel, 1993) calls for a Russian military move to the Mediterranean and the Indian Ocean.
30. Philip E. Johnson, *Darwin on Trial* (Downers Grove: InterVarsity, 1991).
31. Alexander Hislop, *The Two Babylons* (New York: Loizeaux, 1916).
32. G. H. Lang, *The Histories and Prophecies of Daniel* (Grand Rapids: Kregel, 1973), 44.
33. For a strong case against the restoration of historic Babylon, see Charles Lee Feinberg, *Jeremiah* in *Expositor's Bible Commentary* (Grand Rapids: Zondervan, 1986), 685ff.
34. W. Graham Scroggie, *The Great Unveiling: An Analytical Study of Revelation* (Grand Rapids: Zondervan, 1979), 50.
35. Ladd, 154.
36. In the wake of Operation Desert Storm there arose new interest in the restoration of historic Babylon. Cf. Charles H. Dyer, *The Rise of Babylon: Sign of the End Times* (Wheaton: Tyndale, 1991); C. I. Scofield's note "The notion of a literal Babylon to be rebuilt on the site of ancient Babylon is in conflict with Isaiah 13:19–22. In all of Scripture we see the Babylon vs. Israel alignment very prominently.
37. As quoted in Joseph A. Seiss, 220.
38. Ibid., 221.

39. Merrill F. Unger, *Commentary on Zechariah* (Grand Rapids: Zondervan, 1963).

40. Arno C. Gaebelein, *The Olivet Discourse* (Grand Rapids: Baker, 1969 reprint), 3ff.

CHAPTER 15

1. David L. Cooper, founder of the Biblical Research Society, highly respected and able editor and author of the seven volume "Messianic Series." I recall the very high tribute Dr. Wilbur M. Smith paid to Cooper.

2. Douglas Stuart, *Word Biblical Commentary: Hosea–Jonah,* vol. xxiii (Waco, Tex.: Word Books, 1987), 7.

3. Ibid., 271.

4. Ibid., 399.

5. Ibid., 218.

6. Ibid., 400. A similar position with regard to the book of Revelation is to be found in Michael Wilcock, *I Saw Heaven Opened: The Message of Revelation* (Downers Grove, Ill.: InterVarsity, 1975).

7. C. I. Scofield, *Rightly Dividing the Word of Truth* (Oakland, Calif.: Western Book and Tract, n.d.), 14ff.

8. S. J. Whitmee, "Tusitala" in *The Atlantic Monthly,* 131: 344–353, quoted in Frank E. Gaebelein, *The Servant and the Dove: Obadiah and Jonah* (New York: Our Hope, 1946), 33ff.

9. "Zion" in *International Standard Bible Encyclopedia, IV, 3150–3152.*

10. A. Edersheim, *The Temple: Its Ministry and Services as They Were at the Time of Jesus Christ* (London: The Religious Tract Society, 1908). A veritable goldmine.

11. A. Skevington Wood, "The Golden Gate" in *Your Tomorrow,* January 1991, 18ff. (This is the new name for the old *Prophetic Witness and Testimony* periodical.)

12. Edward Gibbon, *The Decline and Fall of the Roman Empire,* 40, book one (Chicago: Great Books, 1952) , 354.

13. Murray Stein, "How Herod Moved Gigantic Blocks to Construct Temple Mount," in *Biblical Archaeological Review,* May/June 1981, 42ff.

14. Nahum L. Rabinovitch, "The beckoning promise of our future," in *A City and A People United: Jerusalem 1967–1992* (published by the *Jerusalem Post*), 21ff.

15. Barbara and Michael Ledeen, "The Temple Mount Plot," in the *New Republic,* 18 June 1984, 20.

16. "Should the Temple Be Rebuilt?" in *Time,* 30 June 1967, 56.

17. Moshe Kohn, "Speedily, in our time?" in the *Jerusalem Post,* 30 December 1989, 9ff.

18. Abraham Rabinovich, "Judgment on the Temple Mount," in the *Jerusalem Post,* 6 July 1991, 11.

19. "Israel: The Chosen One," in *Newsweek,* 20 October 1969, 61, as quoted in Thomas S. McCall, "How Soon the Tribulation Temple?" in *Bibliotheca Sacra,* October–December, 1971, 350.
20. Ledeen, 20ff.
21. "Rabbis Want Synagogue Built on Temple Mount" in the *New York Times,* 6 August 1986, 2.
22. Abraham Rabinovitch, "Temple Mount mysteries revealed," in the *Jerusalem Post,* 17 February 1990, 9ff.
23. Asher S. Kaufman, "Where the Ancient Temple of Jerusalem Stood," *Biblical Archaeological Review,* March/April 1983, 40–59; a superb summation of the issues is to be found in Harold A. Sevener, "Solving Jerusalem's 2000 Year Old Puzzle: Where Did the Temple Stand, Where Will It Be Rebuilt?" in *The Chosen People,* January 1987 and February 1987.
24. Rabbi Shlomo Goren, interviewed for *Biblical Research Monthly,* February 1975, 7.
25. Tom Bethell in *National Review,* 16 April 1990, 41.
26. "Time for a New Temple?" in *Time,* 16 October 1989, 64ff.
27. Haim Shapiro, "Treasures of the Temple," in the *Jerusalem Post,* 30 July 1988, 9.
28. Elwood McQuaid, "Temple Fervor," in *Israel My Glory,* June/July 1990, 5.
29. Joel Rebibo, "On the trial of the holy cow," in the *Jerusalem Post,* 19 August 1989, 8b.
30. Dell Grifin, "Seekers of the Lost Ark," in the *Jerusalem Post,* 10 June 1989, 8b.
31. Barbara Sofer interview with Gershom Salomon, "Mission on the Mount," in *Your Tomorrow,* July 1991, 6ff.
32. Ruth F. Brin, "the New Messiah," in *Identity* (Minneapolis: The Jewish Community Center, April 1975), 5.
33. Billy Graham, *Approaching Hoofbeats: The Four Horsemen of the Apocalypse* (Waco, Tex.: Word, 1983), 73ff.
34. Ibid., 80.
35. Quoted in John Wesley White, *Arming for Armageddon* (Milford, Mich.: Mott Media, 1983), 95. Dr. White has an invaluable plethora of volumes brimming with helpful quotations and insights such as are entitled *Future Hope, Re–Entry, World War III,* etc.
36. Thomas S. McCall and Zola Levitt, *Satan in the Sanctuary* (Chicago: Moody, 1973), 95.
37. C. E. B. Cranfield, *The Epistle to the Romans,* ICC (Edinburgh: T. & T. Clark, 1979), 445ff. Cranfield perceptively observes: "These three chapters (Romans 9–11) emphatically forbid us to speak of the Church as having once and for all taken the place of the Jewish people" (448). In deploring C. K. Barret's contrary position he admits, "And I confess with shame to having also myself used in print on

more than one occasion this language of replacement of Israel by the Church" (448). Cranfield represents what I have already pointed to as a growing group of scholars and theologians who are seeing a positive role for the Jews as an identifiable people.

38. Richard Ostling, "Armageddon and the End Times," in *Time*, 5 November 1984, 73. A very thoughtful treatment of the Anti-christ's role in these events is by the Roman Catholic philosopher, Vincent Miceli, *The Anti-Christ: Has He Launched His Final Campaign Against the Savior?* (Harrison, N.Y.: Roman Catholic Books, 1981). Miceli well recommends J. H. Newman's justly famous *Advent Sermons on the Anti-Christ: The Times of Anti-Christ; The Religion of Anti-Christ; The City of Anti-Christ; and the Persecution of Anti-Christ.*

39. *Time*, 21 May 1965 in which the figure 200,000,000 is used for the Red Chinese militia (cf. Revelation 9:16).

CHAPTER 16

1. Jürgen Moltmann, *The Church in the Power of the Spirit* (San Francisco: Harper, 1977), 138.
2. Ibid., 143.
3. Ibid., 144.
4. Arthur C. Custance, *Time and Eternity and Other Biblical Studies* (Grand Rapids: Zondervan, 1977), 72.
5. Philip Marchand, *Marshall McLuhan: The Medium and the Messenger* (Toronto: Ticknor and Fields, 1989).
6. Quoted in H. L. Wilmington, *Signs of the Times: Current Events Point to the Imminent Return of Jesus Christ* (Wheaton, Ill.: Tyndale, 1981), 137.
7. J. Ridderbos, *Deuteronomy* in *The Bible Student's Commentary* (Grand Rapids: Regency-Zondervan, 1984), 268.
8. Charles H. Stevens, *The Wilderness Journey* (Chicago: Moody, 1971), 38.
9. George T. B. Davis, *Fulfilled Prophecies that Prove the Bible* (Philadelphia: The Million Testaments Campaign, 1931), 88–104.
10. T. B. Baines, *The Lord's Coming, Israel and the Church*, series II, volume XI of *The Serious Christian* (Charlotte, N.C.: Books for Christians, n.d.), 159.
11. Helpful expositions of the book of Zechariah are Merrill F. Unger, *Commentary on Zechariah* (Grand Rapids: Zondervan, 1963); Charles L. Feinberg, *God Remembers: A Study of Zechariah* (Wheaton, Ill.: Van Kampen, 1950); David Baron, *The Visions and Prophecies of Zechariah* (Fincastle, Va.: Scripture Truth Book Co., 1918).
12. J. A. Seiss, *The Apocalypse,* Fifth reprint (Grand Rapids: Zondervan, 1964), 161.

13. George E. Ladd, *A Commentary on the Revelation of John* (Grand Rapids: Eerdmans, 1972), 114.
14. Charles Lee Feinberg, *Israel in the Spotlight* (Wheaton, Ill.: Scripture Press, 1956), 71.
15. Typical of this perspective is Leon J. Wood, *The Bible and Future Events* (Grand Rapids: Zondervan, 1973), 128.
16. J. Dwight Pentecost, *Things to Come: A Study in Biblical Eschatology* (Findley, Ohio: Dunham, 1958), 123.
17. Charles Lee Feinberg, ed., *Prophecy and the Seventies* (Chicago: Moody, 1971), 181.
18. Wilbur M. Smith, "Revelation" in *Wycliffe Bible Commentary* (Chicago: Moody, 1962), 1510.
19. Arno C. Gaebelein, *The Revelation* (New York: Loizeauz, 1961), 73.
20. Arnold T. Olson, *Inside Jerusalem: City of Destiny* (Glendale, Calif.: Regal, 1968).
21. Charles Lee Feinberg, ed., *Jesus the King Is Coming* (Chicago: Moody, 1975), 185.
22. J. Ellwood Evans in J. Dwight Pentecost, "The Godly Remnant of the Tribulation Period," *Bibliotheca Sacra*, April, 1960, 131.
23. Joseph Klausner, *The Messianic Idea in Israel* (New York: Macmillan, 1955), 13.
24. Wilbur M. Smith, *A Treasury of Books for Bible Study* (Grand Rapids: Baker, 1960), 144ff.
25. See my chapters "The Theology of Conversion" and "The Psychology of Conversion," David L. Larsen, *The Evangelism Mandate: Recovering the Centrality of Gospel Preaching* (Wheaton: Crossway, 1992).
26. Ladd, 154, 158–159.
27. Arno C. Gaebelein, *Gabriel and Michael the Archangel* (New York: Our Hope, 1945). A most valuable study.
28. Donald Grey Barnhouse, *Revelation: God's Last Word* (Grand Rapids: Zondervan, 1971), 231.
29. Carl Armerding, "Asleep in the Dust," in *Bibliotheca Sacra*, April 1964, 153–158; Arno C. Gaebelein, *The Prophet Daniel* (Grand Rapids: Kregel, 1955), 200; H. A. Ironside, *Lectures on Daniel the Prophet* (Neptune, N.J.: Loizeauz, 1911), 230ff.
30. J. A. Seiss, *Voices from Babylon, Or the Records of Daniel the Prophet* (Philadelphia: Castle Press, 1879), 316.
31. Arnold Toynbee, *A Study of History,* I (London: Oxford University Press, 1957), 194.
32. Will Durant, *Our Oriental Heritage* in the *The Story of Civilization,* I (New York: Simon and Schuster, 1967).
33. David L. Cooper, *Preparing for World–wide Revival* (Los Angeles: Biblical Research Society, 1938); also *An Exposition of the Book of Revelation* (Los Angeles: Biblical Research Society, 1972), 94ff.

CHAPTER 17

1. Erich Sauer, *The Triumph of the Crucified* (London: Paternoster, 1953), 144.

2. Note Robert Van Kampen, *The Sign* (Wheaton, Ill.: Crossway, 1992), a new book representing an incredible amount of work but honey-combed with bizarre interpretations, e.g. that Michael is the "restrainer" of 2 Thessalonians 2, that Germany is the seventh "king"" of Revelation 17:9, and that the Antichrist will probably be Hitler resurrected. Van Kampen does not see Daniel 9:24 as fulfilled within the seventy sevens but finally (the last three events) fulfilled in the days after the seventy sevens, 323ff.

3. Robert Gundry, *The Rapture Position of the Early Church Fathers* (Grand Rapids: Zondervan, 1973), 173.

4. Charles C. Ryrie, *The Basis of Premillennial Faith* (New York: Loizeaux, 1953), 12.

5. Hans Frei, *The Eclipse of Biblical Narrative* (New Haven, Conn.: Yale, 1974) 35, cf. also, 30ff.

6. Edward H. Hall, *Papias and His Contemporaries* (Boston: Houghton, Mifflin Co., 1899), 106, 109.

7. Robert D. Culver, *Daniel and the Latter Days: A Study in Millennialism* (Westwood, N.J.: Revell, 1954), 35.

8. Will Durant, *The Story of Civilization,* quoted in Renald E. Showers, *There Really is a Difference* (Bellmawr, N.J.: Friends of Israel, 1990), 118.

9. For a strong premillennial statement, see James Montgomery Boice, "Will There Really Be a Golden Age?" in *Eternity,* September 1972, 28.

10. G. Campbell Morgan, *God's Methods with Man* (New York: Revell, 1898), 103. Morgan also has a notable chapter on "After the Thousand Years," 131–143.

11. Erich Sauer, *From Eternity to Eternity* (Grand Rapids: Eerdmans, 1954), 141–142.

12. Jack S. Deere, "Premillennialism in Revelation 20:4–6, 11" in *Bibliotheca Sacra,* January–March 1978, 58–73.

13. George E. Ladd, *The Gospel of the Kingdom* (Grand Rapids: Eerdmans, 1959), 107ff.

14. Gordon R. Lewis, "Theological Antecedents of Pretribulationism," in *Bibliotheca Sacra*, April 1968, 137.

15. Fausset, in Lewis, 476.

16. Louis T. Talbott, *God's Plan of the Ages* (Los Angeles: privately published, 1936), 186–187.

17. J. Sidlow Baxter, *The Strategic Grasp of the Bible* (Grand Rapids: Zondervan, 1968), 199.

18. J. Oliver Buswell, *A Systematic Theology of the Christian Religion,* II (Grand Rapids: Zondervan, 1963), 347–48.

19. Lewis, 136.

20. Rene Pache, *The Return of Jesus Christ* (Chicago: Moody, 1955), 418.

21. Frederick L. Godet quoted in Alva L. McClain, *The Greatness of the Kingdom* (Grand Rapids: Zondervan, 1959), 256.

22. Clarence E. Mason, Jr., *Prophetic Problems with Alternate Solutions* (Chicago: Moody, 1973), 245.

23. McClain, 217–254.

24. John F. Walvoord, *The Millennial Kingdom* (Grand Rapids: Zondervan, 1959), 320–321.

25. John F. Walvoord, "The Millennial Kingdom and the Eternal State," in *Bibliotheca Sacra,* October 1966, 293.

26. Herman A. Hoyt, in *The Meaning of the Millennium,* Robert G. Clouse, ed. (Downers Grove, Ill.: InterVarsity, 1977), 83.

27. Roy L. Aldrich, "Divisions of the First Resurrection," in *Bibliotheca Sacra,* April 1971, 117ff.

28. Arno C. Gaebelein, *The Harmony of the Prophetic Word* (New York: Our Hope, n.d.), 169. Note the similar position taken by Clarence E. Mason, Jr., 242–251; J. Dwight Pentecost, "The Relation between Living and Resurrected Saints in the Millennium," in *Bibliotheca Sacra,* October 1960, 331–340.

29. Samuel J. Andrews quoted in Alva L. McClain, 206.

30. Walvoord, *The Millennial Kingdom,* 136.

31. Boice, 28.

32. Buswell, 54.

33. Pache, 381.

34. Goldberg, *Turbulence over the Middle East* (Neptune, N.J.: Loizeaux, 1982), 258.

35. Frederick A. Tatford, *God's Program of the Ages* (Grand Rapids: Kregel, 1967), 128.

36. Goldberg, 258.

37. Ralph H. Alexander, "Ezekiel," in *The Expositor's Bible Commentary,* Frank E. Gaebelein, ed., VI (Grand Rapids: Zondervan, 1986).

38. Sauer, *From Eternity to Eternity,* 182.

39. Alexander, 951.

40. Robert H. Mounce, *The Book of Revelation,* NIC (Grand Rapids: Eerdmans, 1977), 353, quoted in Jeffrey Townsend, 216.

41. Culver, 35.

42. Arthur H. Lewis, *The Dark Side of the Millennium* (Grand Rapids: Baker, 1980), 53. A superlative analysis of and answer to Lewis is found in Jeffrey L. Townsend, "Is the Present Age the Millennium?" in *Bibliotheca Sacra,* July–September 1983, 206–224.

43. Alexander, 945.

CHAPTER 18

1. H. D. Beeby, *Grace Abounding* (Grand Rapids: Eerdmans, 1989), 141.
2. Paul Johnson, *A History of the Jews* (New York: Harper, 1987), 586.
3. Herbert Butterfield, *Christianity and History* (London: Fontana, 1957), 105.
4. Douglas Clyde MacIntosh in John Walvoord, *The Millennial Kingdom* (Grand Rapids: Zondervan, 1959), 15–16.
5. Jonathan Kellerman in *Context*, 15 July 1992, 2–3.
6. "Christians Fear Jewish Takeover of Old City" in *Christianity Today*, 13 January 1992, 50ff. Along the same line is "Israeli Police, Christian clerics battle," in *Chicago Tribune*, 13 April 1990, 3.
7. Yosef Goell, "Israeli Arabs: monumentally neglected," in the *Jerusalem Post*, 22 June 1991, 15.
8. Rafik Halabi, *The West Bank Story: An Israeli Arab's View of Both Sides of a Tangled Conflict* (New York: Harcourt, Brace, Jovanovich, 1981.
9. Walter Reich, *Stranger in My House: Jews and Arabs in the West Bank* (New York: Holt, Rinehart and Winston, 1984).
10. Mark A. Heller and Sari Nusseibeh, *No Trumpets, No Drums: A Two-state Settlement of the Israeli–Palestinian Conflict* (New York: Hill and Wang, 1991).
11. Naim Stifan Ateek, *Justice and Only Justice: A Palestinian Theology of Liberation* (Maryknoll, N.Y.: Orbis, 1989). The author of this book has been Canon of St. George's Cathedral in Jerusalem.
12. David Grossman, *The Yellow Wind* (New York: Farrar, Straus and Giroux, 1988); also treating life in the territories in a very graphic way is Michael Ben Zohar, *Facing a Cruel Mirror: Israel's Moment of Truth* (New York: Charles Scribner's, 1990).
13. Michael Romann and Alex Weingrod, *Living Together Separately: Arabs and Jews in Contemporary Jerusalem* (Princeton, N.J.: Princeton University Press, 1991).
14. Marcia Kunstel and Joseph Albright, *Their Promised Land* (New York: Crown, 1990); Daniel Rubinstein, *The People of Nowhere: The Palestinian Vision of Home* (New York: Times Books, 1990).
15. Michael Gorkin, *Days of Honey, Days of Orion: The Story of a Palestinian Family in Israel* (Boston: Beacon Press, 1990). This is a very deeply moving and most informative treatment. It is imperative for any measured judgment of the situation in the Middle East to read somewhat even-handedly. I try to read both the *Jerusalem Post* and *The Middle East*, an Arab viewpoint published in London.
16. David Baron, *The Visions and Prophecies of Zechariah* (Grand Rapids: Kregel, 1975), 491–493.
17. Robert Nisbet, *History of the Idea of Progress* (New York: Basic Books, 1980), 68. I am indebted to my brother, Dr. Paul Larsen, for calling this reference to my attention.

18. "Christian Zionism: Israel Right or Wrong" in *Christianity Today*, 9 March 1992, 46–50.

19. Peter Costello, *Jules Verne: Inventor of Science Fiction* (New York: Charles Scribner's, 1978).

20. Gerard Willem Van Loon, *The Story of Hendrik Van Loon* (Philadelphia: J, Lippencott, 1972).

21. Mark Aaron and John Loftus, *Unholy Trinity: Vatican, Nazis and Soviet Intelligence* (New York: St. Martin's Press, 1991).

22. Robert W. Ross, *So it Was True: The American Protestant Press and the Nazi Persecution of the Jews* (Minneapolis: University of Minnesota Press, 1980), 174.

23. Daniel S. Levy, "The Cantor and the Klansman," in *Time*, 17 February 1992, 14ff.

24. Howard M. Sachar, *A History of the Jews in America* (New York: Alfred Knopf, 1992), 35.

25. John Meier, "A Marginal Jew: Rethinking the Historical Jesus" in *The Roots of the Problem and the Person* (New York: Doubleday, 1991).

26. Michael Rydelnik, "Did God Really Say That the Gospel Is to the Jew First?" in *The Chosen People*, January 1991, 8–11.

27. Tony Higton, "Carey Says No" in *Your Tomorrow*, June 1992, 6.

28. James G. D. Dunn, *The Parting of the Ways: Between Christianity and Judaism and Their Significance for the Character of Christianity* (London: Trinity Press International, 1992).

29. Mike Saunier, "God is at Work in Israel," in *Alliance Life*, 18 July 1990, 16–18.

30. A. A. Berle, *The World Significance of the Jewish State* (New York: Mitchell Kennerley, 1918), 44.

31. M. Herbert Danziger, *Returning to Tradition: The Contemporary Revival of Orthodox Judaism* (London: Yale University Press, 1991).

32. Sarah Bershtel and Allen Graubard, *Saving Remnant: Feeling Jewish in America* (New York: Free Press, 1992).

33. Yeshayahu Leibowitz, *Judaism, Human Values and the Jewish State* (Cambridge, Mass.: Harvard University Press, 1991).

34. Charles Lee Feinberg, "Is Jewish Evangelism God's Step–child?" in *Israel in the Spotlight* (Chicago: Scripture Press, 1956), 151–155.

35. "In the Enemy's Camp: A Convert's Sadness," in *The Christian Century*, 15 April 1992, 390–391.

36. Louis Meyer, *Eminent Hebrew Christians of the Nineteenth Century*, ed. David A. Rausch (New York: Edwin Muller Press, 1983).

37. Arthur W. Kac, *The Spiritual Dilemma of the Jewish People: Its Cause and Cure* (Grand Rapids: Baker, 1963, 1983), 132.

APPENDIX

1. Johannes Behm in *Theological Dictionary of Old Testament*, ed. Gerhard Kittel (Grand Rapids: Eerdmans, 1964), 109ff.

APPENDIX

2. Jacob Jocz, *The Covenant: A Theology of Human Destiny* (Grand Rapids: Eerdmans 1968), 23.

3. Walter C. Kaiser, Jr., *Toward an Old Testament Theology* (Grand Rapids: Zondervan,1963), 93.

4. Meredith G. Kline, *The Structure of Biblical Authority* (Grand Rapids: Eerdmans, 1972), 132ff.

5. Dennis J. McCarthy, *The Form and History of the Abrahamic Covenant Traditions* (Amsterdam: F. Vandevelder, 1967), 300.

6. Ibid., 55ff.

7. Thomas B. McComiskey, *The Covenants of Promise: A Theology of the Old Testament Covenants* (Grand Rapids: Baker, 1985), 59ff.

8. George E. Mendenhall, "Covenant Forms in Israelite Tradition," in *The Biblical Archaeologist*, September 1954, 62.

9. J. Barton Payne, *The Theology of the Older Testament* (Grand Rapids: Zondervan, 1962), 99.

10. John Arthur Thompson, *The Ancient Near Eastern Treaties and the Old Testament* (London: Tyndale, 1964).

GLOSSARY OF TERMS

ABOMINATION OF DESOLATION: literally, "the abomination that causes desolation," an idolatrous artifact, first mentioned historically in the days of Antiochus, then prophetically in Daniel 9:27; 11:31; 12:11 and by our Lord in the Olivet discourse, Matthew 24:15, Mark 13:14. Probably a representation of the Antichrist set up in the Tribulation Temple which scandalizes the Jews.

ALAWITE: an unorthodox Muslim sect concentrated in Syria from which President Asad and his family come.

ALEXANDRIAN TRADITION: a tendency to allegorical interpretation of Scripture originating in Alexandria, Egypt with Clement and Origen.

ALIGNMENT: the Israeli political factions which comprise the Labor Party.

ALIYAH: making return to the land of Israel.

AMILLENNIAL: denial of the literal 1000 year reign of Christ on earth as part of a system of biblical interpretation that tends to spiritualize the promises of the Old Testament to Israel and apply them to the church.

ANTIOCHENE THEORIA: the approach to biblical interpretation supported in Antioch that emphasized historico-grammatico exegesis.

APOCALYPSE: the unveiling or revealing, the name of the last book in the Bible, the book of Revelation.

APOCALYPTIC: a genre of literature having to do with end-time events, often using rich symbolism, confident of the ultimate victory of God. The last half of the book of Daniel would be an example of apocalyptic.

ARMAGEDDON: the site in the Valley of Megiddo where the climactic military confrontation of the Tribulation period will take place; the battle ended by the glorious and powerful return of Jesus Christ with His saints and angels.

ASHKENAZIC: northern European Jews, its earliest referent being Genesis 10:3.

BETAR: Jewish youth movement in Poland with Zionist interest in which Menachem Begin and other Israeli leaders were involved.

BLACK SEPTEMBER, 1971: the massacre of many in the Palestine Liberation Organization by Jordanian King Hussein, as he and his Beduin felt increasingly dominated by outsiders.

CONVERSOS: Jewish converts to Catholicism in Spain and Portugal; see Marranos.

COVENANTAL THEOLOGIANS: mainly amillennial (with some premillennial supporters) who tend to emphasize the covenantal structures of Scripture as the basic motifs of interpretation, although "covenant of works" referring to God's covenant with our first parents is not language used as such in Scripture.

DAY OF LORD: the eschatological epoch of judgment, often described by the Old Testament prophets, extending through the whole Tribulation period (not a period of 24 hours anymore than the "Day of Grace").

DEISM: the heretical teaching that God created His universe and then basically detached His interest and involvement in what He had made.

DIASPORA: the Jews scattered and dispersed through the world, outside Israel.

DISPENSATIONAL THEOLOGY: the system of interpretation that strongly emphasizes a more literal, natural, and plain reading of the text, the difference between Israel and the church and the sense of progressive and sequential ages and periods in the unfolding plan of God.

EINSATZGRUPPEN: mobile killing units used by Hitler's Nazis in World War II.

ERETZ ISRAEL: the land of Israel.

ESCHATOLOGY: the doctrine and matters relating to the end time, last things.

ESCHATON: the last days, the consummation.

FATAH: a militant branch and expression of the Palestine Liberation Organization.

FUTURIST: the school of prophetic interpretation that sees the Bible prophesying predictively of events at the windup of human history.

GALUT: the Jews in exile (of *Yishuv*).

GEMARA: the Aramaic rendition of the Mishna coming out of the Babylonian dispersion.

GHETTO: first used in Italy to describe the Jewish quarter, the segregation of the Jewish population.

GOY, GOYIM: Gentile, the Gentiles.

HAGANAH: the Jewish defense force that rose to fight Arab incursion and resist British forces in Palestine before and after World War II.

HALACHA: the Jewish system of religious law.

HAMAS: the Muslim Fundamentalist movement in Israel and the occupied territories.

HAREDIM: the ultraorthodox parties in Israel.

HASKALA: Jewish-German enlightenment thinking which moved in the direction of assimilation.

HASSIDIM: Separate or holy ones, the movement of enthusiastic, observant Jews surviving into our own time and usually centered around historic rebbes.

HEJIRA OR HEGIRA: the Prophet Mohammed's flight from Mecca to Medina in A.D. 622 in the face of growing opposition and hostility.

HERMENEUTICS: the principles of biblical interpretation (from Heremes, the messenger of the Greek deities).

HEJAZ OR HIJAZ: Arab territory along the coasts of the Red Sea toward which T. E. Lawrence turned in his desert strategy.

HISTORICO-GRAMMATICO EXEGESIS: the approach to the scriptural text which stresses the most careful attention to the words and grammar as well as the original situation and intent of the writer.

HISTORICIST: the system of prophetic interpretation that sees the full outline of world history in predictive prophecy, such as the siege of Vienna and the Napoleonic Wars. This school has largely fallen out of favor in our time.

IMAM: Muslim holy man and leader.

INTERREGNUM: during the period before the final and ultimate establishment of the Kingdom of God.

IRGUN: the IZL, Zwai Leumi, the national military organization of Begin and the right-wing resistance in Israel.

JIHAD: Muslim holy war.

KABBALISM OR CABBALISM: Jewish mysticism.

KARAITES: reforming sect of the Jews originating in Mesopotamia in the eighth century A.D. and urging a return to the Law without the burden of the Talmud.

KASHRUT: the system of kosher food laws.

KIBBUTZ: the Israeli communes especially popular among early settlers.

KNESSET: the Israeli parliament in Jerusalem.

LIKUD: the right-wing party of Begin, Shamir, Levy, and Sharon.

LOCUS CLASSICUS: the authoritative or most frequently quoted source.

MAHDI: Islamic Messianic figure awaited especially by the Shi'ites.

MARRANOS: secret Jews in medieval Spain and Portugal; outwardly they became Roman Catholics but retained inward and secret Jewish observance.

MEGIDDO: the Valley of Esdraelon guarded by the Vale of Jezreel, where the Battle of Armageddon will be fought.

MIDRASH: exposition of the Old Testament text through allegory and homily.

MILLENNIUM: the one-thousand-year rule of Jesus Christ upon earth.

MISHNA: Greek-influenced interpretation of the Old Testament text further diluting the teaching of the original revelation.

MOSHAV: cooperative farms in Israel, not as structured or communal as the kibbutz.

MUTATIS MUTANDIS: after making the changes that have to be made.

NOSTRA AETATE: the declaration of Vatican II issued in 1965 that opened dialogue between the Roman Catholic Church and Jewish religious leaders.

OLIM: Jews who have come to settle in Israel from many nations.

ONTIC REFERENCE: reference that has to do with real being and actual existence.

OSTJUDEN: the vast Jewish population in Poland and Russia.

THE PALE OF SETTLEMENT: the areas allotted to Jewish population under the czar's control in which there were frequent persecutions.

PALMACH: the crack Israeli fighting force after World War II, played a very critical role in the War of Independence, a part of the Haganah.

PALESTINIAN NATIONAL COVENANT: the agreement among Palestinians that reflects the determination to destroy the Jewish state.

PAROUSIA: the glorious presence and return of Jesus Christ, experienced in two phases, the Rapture and the Revelation.

PETITIO PRINCIPII: begging the question, assuming what has to be proved.

P. L. O.: Palestine Liberation Organization, the Arafat umbrella group of Arab radicals.

POGROM: an anti-Semitic persecution, massacre, and murder.

POSTMILLENNIAL: the view that the church will triumph before Christ's return, it reappears in our time as Dominion or Theonomy theology.

PRAETERIST: the system of prophetic interpretation that sees the book of Revelation as essentially descriptive of first-century Roman persecution.

PREMILLENNIAL: the view that Jesus Christ will return in power and glory to establish His Kingdom and rule for 1000 years.

PROLEPTIC VISION: an anticipatory vision, a glimpse of what is to come.

RAPTURE: when Christ will come to translate His church to heaven before the manifestation of the Antichrist and the beginning of the Tribulation period of seven years.

REALIZED ESCHATOLOGY: the view of C. H. Dodd and others that the great predictions of judgment and the Parousia are already being experienced in time-space history (cf. "Inaugurated Eschatology" that emphasizes that the fulfillment has begun in the overlap period but the fullness and completion are future).

SABRAS: Jews who are born in Israel.

SEPHARDIC: Jews from the Mediterranean area, Iberia, North Africa, Turkey, Greece, speaking Ladino (cf. Ashkenazic Jews who speak Yiddish).

SHARI'A: Islamic penal law, being reinstituted in several Muslim countries.

SHOAH: the Holocaust.

SHTETLS: the ghettos and insulated communities of Jews particularly in Eastern Europe.

SOTERIOLOGY, SOTERIOLOGICAL: having to do with God's salvation.

SPIRITUALISTIC SCHOOL: the system of prophetic interpretation that sees prophecy as sharing timeless spiritual principles without specific historic reference or prediction.

STERN GANG: the most violent Jewish resistance movement named for its founder, a break-off from the Irgun; it included Yitzchak Shamir, thought to be responsible for the murder of U. N. Mediator, Count Folke Bernadotte of Sweden.

SUFIS: mystical Muslims, the whirling dervishes.

SYNCHRONICAL: having to do with present events.

TALMUD: the compendious written version of the oral law, the Gemera and the Mishna.

THEODICY: the justification and vindication of God.

TORAH: the Law of God, the first five books of the Old Testament.

TRIBULATION: the seven-year period of the work and evil machinations of the Antichrist and his cohorts, the last three-and-a-half years of which are known as "the great tribulation" and "the time of Jacob's trouble."

WAR OF ATTRITION: the standoff between Israel and Egypt in 1972–73 that led finally to the Yom Kippur War of 1973.

YESHIVA, YESHIVOTS: centers for the study of the Torah and all holy writings, where Rabbis are trained.

YISHUV: Jews living in *eretz* Israel.

PERSON AND TITLE INDEX

(Ancient and Modern Names)

SUBJECT INDEX

SCRIPTURE INDEX

Note to the Reader

The publisher invites you to share your response to the message of this book by writing Discovery House Publishers, P. O. Box 3566, Grand Rapids, MI 49501, U. S. A. For information about other Discovery House books and music, contact us at the same address or call 1-800-653-8333